SELECTED PLAYS
OF
HUGH LEONARD

Irish Drama Selections

General Editors
Joseph Ronsley
Anne Saddlemyer

IRISH DRAMA SELECTIONS

ISSN 0260–7962

Each volume contains a representative selection of plays by the playwrights, together with a critical introduction and a checklist of works. Available in hardcover and paperback.

1. SELECTED PLAYS OF LENNOX ROBINSON
   Chosen and introduced by Christopher Murray

2. SELECTED PLAYS OF DENIS JOHNSTON
   Chosen and introduced by Joseph Ronsley

3. SELECTED PLAYS OF LADY GREGORY
   Foreword by Sean O'Casey
   Chosen and introduced by Mary Fitzgerald

4. SELECTED PLAYS OF DION BOUCICAULT
   Chosen and introduced by John Cronin

5. SELECTED PLAYS OF ST. JOHN ERVINE
   Chosen and introduced by John Cronin

6. SELECTED PLAYS OF BRIAN FRIEL
   Chosen and introduced by Seamus Deane
   Our edition of this title is only for sale in North America

7. SELECTED PLAYS OF DOUGLAS HYDE
   Chosen and introduced by Janet Egleson Dunleavy
   and Gareth Dunleavy

8. SELECTED PLAYS OF GEORGE MOORE
   AND EDWARD MARTYN
   Chosen and introduced by David B. Eakin and Michael Case

9. SELECTED PLAYS OF HUGH LEONARD
   Chosen and introduced by S. F. Gallagher

10. SELECTED PLAYS OF T. C. MURRAY
    Chosen and introduced by Richard Allen Cave

11. SELECTED PLAYS OF MICHEÁL MacLIAMMÓIR
    Chosen and introduced by John Barrett

All titles contain a Bibliographical Checklist. For details of plays, see the advertisement at the back of this book.

SELECTED PLAYS
OF
HUGH LEONARD

chosen and with an introduction by

S. F. Gallagher

Irish Drama Selections 9

1992
COLIN SMYTHE
Gerrards Cross, Bucks.

THE CATHOLIC UNIVERSITY
OF AMERICA PRESS
Washington, D.C.

The Patrick Pearse Motel copyright © 1971 by Hugh Leonard
The Au Pair Man copyright © 1968, 1974 by Hugh Leonard
Da copyright © 1973 by Hugh Leonard
Summer copyright © 1979 by Hugh Leonard
A Life copyright © 1980 by Hugh Leonard
Kill copyright © 1982 by Hugh Leonard
Introduction copyright © 1992 by S. F. Gallagher

All performing rights in these plays are fully protected and permission
must be obtained in advance from Lemon Unna & Durbridge Ltd.,
24 Pottery Lane, Holland Park, London W11 4LZ

All rights reserved

This collection first published in 1992 by Colin Smythe Limited,
Gerrards Cross, Buckinghamshire

British Library Cataloguing in Publication Data

Leonard, Hugh *1926–*
    Selected plays. – (Irish drama selections)
    I. Title   II. Series
    822.914

    ISBN 0–86140–140–9
    ISBN 0–86140–141–7 pbk.

First published in North America in 1992 by
The Catholic University of America Press, Washington, D.C.

Library of Congress Cataloging-in-Publication Data

Leonard, Hugh
    [Selections. 1992]
    Selected plays of Hugh Leonard / edited by S. F. Gallagher.
    p.   cm. – (Irish drama selections: 9)
    Contents: The au pair man – The Patrick Pearse Motel –
    Da – Summer – A life – Kill.
    I. Gallagher, S. F. (Sean Finbarr)   II. Title.   III. Series.
    PR6062.E7A6   1992   822'.914–dc20
    91–25924   CIP

    ISBN 0–8132–0759–2
    ISBN 0–8132–0760–6 (pbk.)

Produced in Great Britain

Contents

Introduction   1

The Au Pair Man   13
The Patrick Pearse Motel   87
Da   165
Summer   233
A Life   303
Kill   379
Bibliographical Checklist   458
Irish Drama Selections Series   463

Introduction

Dalkey, a modest coastal town on the southern outskirts of Dublin, has exerted a remarkable attraction on Irish writers and performers. George Bernard Shaw recalled as the happiest moment of his life his mother's announcement that they were going to live on Dalkey hill, and in his nineties proclaimed himself 'a product of Dalkey's outlook'. More recent denizens of Dalkey have included the actors Cyril Cusack, Vincent Dowling, Dan O'Herlihy, Milo O'Shea, Liam Redmond, Norman Rodway and Maureen Toal; the writers Maeve Binchy, Constantine Fitzgibbon, Sean O'Faolain, Denis Johnston, Lennox Robinson, Mervyn Wall and Hugh Leonard.

'Hugh Leonard' is the pen-name of John Keyes Byrne, adoptive son of a Dalkey couple, Nicholas and Margaret Keyes. Leonard was born in Dublin, 9 November 1926, and grew up in Dalkey, first at 3 Kalafat Lane, off Sorrento Road, and later at 19 St. Begnet's Villas; neither abode likely to have been listed among the most fashionable of Dalkey addresses. Nicholas Keyes worked as factotum to the affluent Jacob family at 'Enderley', one of the 'big houses' on the hill. His initial wage, at the age of fourteen, was ten shillings a week; coincidentally, the same amount as his pension when he retired fifty-four years later.

If childhood is, as Seamus Heaney suggests, 'the great forcing house of artistic talent', serious students of Leonard will find invaluable his autobiographical *Home Before Night* (Deutsch, 1979; Penguin, 1981) and *Out After Dark* (Deutsch, 1989; Penguin, 1990), works fully worthy of the superlatives heaped upon them by enthusiastic reviewers, and written with such verve as to make all the more incomprehensible Leonard's earlier expressed diffidence: 'I don't think I'm very good at writing stories. I tie myself in knots with prose.' (*A Paler Shade of Green*, 1972, p. 199).

Leonard first went to school locally, to 'the Nuns' at Loreto Convent and then to Harolds Boys' where he proved bright enough to earn a scholarship to secondary school at Presentation College in nearby Glasthule. Initially enthusiastic — he had avidly

1

devoured in English comics fictitious accounts of public-school life – he was soon disillusioned, in part by the philistinism of some of his teachers but even more by the petty snobbery of his schoolfellows. The academic promise implicit in his scholarship status was stillborn, and increasing apathy towards his studies resulted in his deliberately languishing three years in the same grade. Later he would reflect that at Presentation College he had learned 'next to nothing' and 'made not one lasting friendship'. Inept at physical combat, he developed instead a skill at deadly insult: 'My success at excoriation was such that I became a crowd-pleaser, incapable of suppressing a well turned jibe, no matter how dire the retribution.' (*Home Before Night*, 98–99). The politicians and celebrities who later became the target of 'Leonardisms' in his *Hibernia* or *Sunday Independent* columns must rue the day he set foot in Presentation College.

In 1945, yielding to family pressure, Leonard entered the Irish civil service and found himself writing Receivable Orders for the Land Commission Branch. Though he still reproaches himself for the fourteen years he spent in the civil service he does not regard them as a complete waste. He did make a few friends, joined the amateur dramatic society 'Lancos' (from 'Land Commission') and began to write plays. Except for a performance of Boucicault's *Colleen Bawn* in Dalkey town-hall, Leonard had never seen a play until during his first year in the civil service a colleague derided his ignorance of theatre and goaded him into attending an Abbey Theatre production of Sean O'Casey's *Plough and the Stars*, whose talented cast included F. J. McCormick and Cyril Cusack:

But it was more than the acting that made Jack [Leonard] stand outside the theatre afterwards, looking towards the roof tops for the red glow of Dublin burning that he had seen through the window of Betty Burgess' attic room. The life that roared through the play itself had spilled over from the stage, sweeping him with it so that he would never again be content just to sit and watch and applaud with the rest of them. The thought burned him like fever.

(*Home Before Night*, p. 159)

On the train home to Dalkey that night, 'his breath in the unheated compartment threw a mist upon the glass, but even then he could see, as if it were out there by the tracks, the door he would escape through' (*ibid.*). Hugh Leonard, Playwright, if yet to be born had at least been conceived.

His embryonic efforts were a few plays for amateur production: 'Nightingale in the Branches'; its sequel, 'Another Summer'; a one-act play about Parnell, 'The Man on Platform Two'; then, 'The Italian Road' (1954), entered for an Abbey Theatre competition but rejected along with all the other entries: the level that year was considered too low for any awards to be made. Leonard next sent to the Abbey his 'Nightingale in the Branches', changing its title to 'The Big Birthday' and adopting the pseudonym Hugh Leonard; 'Hughie Leonard' having been the name of a character in the play rejected by the Abbey. The Abbey accepted 'The Big Birthday', leaving Leonard lumbered with a name he did not really want.

Within a few years, mainly by writing serials for sponsored radio, Leonard had become a full-time professional. In 1959 he resigned from the Land Commission. He had by then acquired a wife, Paula, and a daughter, Danielle, and, after a hectic period of churning out material for five sponsored programmes a week and trying to write for the annual Dublin Theatre Festival, he accepted an offer from the British Television company Granada which, for a year, necessitated his commuting weekly between Dublin and Manchester. When he signed for a second year with Granada, he was persuaded by his wife to move the family to Manchester. By the end of his two-year session at Granada, which he spent almost entirely editing or adapting the works of others but yearning to write his own plays, he moved to Barnes in London. Throughout the rest of the 1960s he wrote almost incessantly for television, film and the stage; the first two providing him financial independence but never altering his clear preference: 'First and last I flatter myself as being a writer for the stage. I don't think there's anything as good as writing for the theatre. . . . there is nothing to equal the excitement of a first night, particularly a first night in Dublin' (*A Paler Shade of Green*, pp. 196, 200).

In the spring of 1970, Leonard returned to Ireland, where he has since lived — with frequent excursions abroad — in the Dalkey-Killiney area. He served about a year (1976–77) as Literary Editor for the Abbey Theatre, and in 1978 became Programme Director for the Dublin Theatre Festival, to which he has contributed no less than eighteen plays. His astounding output of plays, journalism, theatre criticism and book reviews has hardly diminished, and he published his first novel, *Parnell and the Englishwoman* (Deutsch; Penguin, 1991).

*

Christopher Fitz-Simon has described Hugh Leonard as 'the

3

most prolific and the most technically assured of modern Irish playwrights' (*The Irish Theatre*, 1983, p. 191). He may also be the least pretentious. During the 1985 rehearsals of *The Mask of Moriarty*, based on characters culled from stories by A. Conan Doyle, Leonard, asked by a journalist why he had not written 'a Festival play that Says Something', replied:

I *am* saying something, if with a small 's', and it is this. If you care to come in out of the rain for a couple of hours, I shall attempt to entertain you and send you out again feeling as if you have had a good meal. Mind, I may not be successful in this intention, for I am not using the crutches of either the missionary or the Artist (capital 'A'), which, if they do not keep the play upright, at least excite our pity and indulgence.

(Introduction, *The Mask of Moriarity*, 1987, p. 16)

As the journalist leaves, Leonard overhears him wail to a companion, 'Oh God, why couldn't Jack at least have written an Irish play?' (*ibid.*).

The episode encapsulates two − perhaps they are really one? − fairly common charges against Leonard as dramatist: that his plays are lightweight or insubstantial, and that they fail to address current Irish problems. Christopher Murray, in the *Irish University Review* (Spring, 1988), readily recognizes Leonard as 'a craftsman of the highest order, inventive, witty and humorous', but avers, 'The problem is that these qualities, divorced from a social or political impulse, seem to be no longer entirely in favour. A writer such as Tom Stoppard, for example, who shares with Leonard the qualities just mentioned, has had to take account in his work of the increasing interest in dilemmas that have a political as well as a moral implication...' (p. 136). Leonard is hardly impervious to such comments; he seems, indeed, to have anticipated something of the sort. As early as 1973, he had observed: 'I am conscious that my main faults are the cleverness (in the structural sense) . . . and at times an irresponsible sense of comedy which is not so much out of place as inclined to give my work an unintended lightness' (*Contemporary Dramatists*, 4th edn., 1988, p. 321). A less modest writer might have cited, as corroboration, O'Casey's lively defence of Shaw against similar misconceptions:

By many, too, Shaw was thought to be 'an irresponsible joker'; but his kind of joking is a characteristic of the Irish; and Shaw in his temperament is Irish of the Irish. We Irish, when we think, and we often do this, are just as serious and sober as the Englishman; but we never hesitate to give a serious thought the benefit and halo of a laugh. That is why we are so often thought to be irresponsible, whereas, in point of fact, we are critical realists, while Englishmen often mistake sentimental mutterings for everlasting truths.

(*The Green Crow*, New York, 1956, p. 204)

The unidentified journalist's Parthian shot − 'Oh God, why couldn't Jack at least have written an Irish play?' − not only seems incredibly oblivious of the predominantly Irish content in Leonard's plays but may also symptomize an insularity that Leonard perceives as bedevilling too much of Irish drama in recent decades, an insularity that in his own work he strives to avoid: 'Being an Irish writer both hampers and helps me: hampers, because one is fighting the preconceptions of audiences who have been conditioned to expect feyness and parochial subject matter . . . Ireland is my subject matter, but only to the degree in which I can use it as a microcosm . . .' (*Contemporary Dramatists*, p. 321). When in 1986 he was lured to a conference in Monaco on 'Irishness in a Changing Society', the provocative title of his address was 'The Unimportance of Being Irish' and he told the select assembly of scholars, writers, journalists, librarians, publishers and policy-makers:

My belief is that our attitude towards Irish writing is as parochial as the communal water-tap and the horse-trough at the end of the village street. Poets, novelists, and playwrights − unless the names happen to be Yeats or Joyce or Beckett − write about Irishmen first, as a separate species that is, and mankind a very distant and unimportant second. And, yes, I have read Blake on the virtue of seeing the world in a grain of sand and heaven in the wild flower. Indeed, why else, one might say, does the commonplace exist in art if not to contain the universal? Pardon me if I say that I find little that is universal in the contemplation of the navel that passes for our literature.

(*Irishness in a Changing Society*, 1988, pp. 19–20)

Leonard's cosmopolitanism is evinced by the range of his adaptations for stage and television. 'The Passion of Peter Ginty' (1961), from Ibsen's *Peer Gynt*, was followed by two adaptations of Joyce: *Stephen D* (1962) from *A Portrait of the Artist as a Young Man* and *Stephen Hero*; 'Dublin One' (1963) from *Dubliners*. Other adaptations for the stage were 'The Family Way' (1964) and 'Some of my Best Friends Are Husbands' (1976) from plays by Eugene Labiche; 'Liam Liar' (1976) from the play *Billy Liar* by Waterhouse and Hall; 'The Saints Go Cycling In' (1965) from Flann O'Brien's novel *The Dalkey Archive*; 'The Barracks' (1969) from John McGahern's novel. His numerous adaptations for television have drawn not only on the works of Irish writers

Frank O'Connor, Sean O'Faolain, Jennifer Johnston, Molly Keane, James Plunkett, but also on those of H. E. Bates, Emily Bronte, G. K. Chesterton, Wilkie Collins, Norman Collins, Dickens, Dostoevsky, Flaubert, Giovanni Guarchi, Somerset Maugham and Georges Simenon.

*

The Au Pair Man (1968) has a Pygmalion-like plot. An older woman, Mrs. Elizabeth Rogers, who lives in a cluttered London town-house that resembles a museum for a British Empire on which the sun has long set – the doorbell plays the National Anthem and the clock chimes out 'Land of Hope and Glory' – induces an uncouth but ambitious young Irishman, Eugene Hartigan, to abandon his 'initiative test' as a bill-collector and become her live-in 'secretary', ultimately to the point of sexual exhaustion, in return for which she undertakes to teach him how to be a gentleman.

Mrs. Rogers' husband, a philatelist, is 'out there somewhere, selling his colonials'. At one time he had an enormous collection and was forever adding to it, but 'after all those years of blood, toil, tears and perspiration', decided that in an 'age of specialization' it would be better 'to concentrate on one's British collection and ignore the rest'. She, herself, is 'hopelessly housebound', not daring to venture on streets that now 'teem with incivility, infested with foreign persons' pretending 'that everyone is as good as everyone else'. It is all quite unlike the old days when people knew how to behave themselves; when even some natives of India that Daddy was 'obliged to crucify' – they had 'behaved rather badly' – were touched by the 'austere little speech' he made while the nails were being hammered in, 'all the time with a twinkle in his eye and the occasional chuckle'. 'That kind of gentleness', she sighs, 'isn't to be found any more'.

Eugene's eyes, however, are fixed on the future. He endures his indentures only in order to realize what he frankly calls his 'ignoble ambitions' of materialistic success. He does suffer the odd bout of nostalgia: 'When I'm jarred, I go back home . . . that's all. It's like standing on a hill and seeing the two bays . . . next to one another like a pair of spectacles cut across the middle. . . . I miss them'. Whatever the sexual commerce between Eugene and Mrs. Rogers, neither expects any emotional involvement. As she puts it, 'We are separate islands. I am lush and crammed with amenities, a green and pleasant land; you have good fishing . . . but are

6

sadly under-developed. We aren't even in the same archipelago.'

There are enough of such exchanges to prompt some commen-
tators – the kind of critic, Leonard chides, 'whose byword is
serendipity' – to read the play as an allegory of the age-old conflict
between England and Ireland. Irving Wardle, who acknowledges
that the cleverness of *The Au Pair Man* may tempt one to read too
much into it, still praises 'its precision as a comedy of Anglo-Irish
manners, and an object lesson (very pertinent to the 1960s) in how
the establishment disarms plebeian rebels'. He notes Mrs. Rogers'
initials (E.R.) and that when her territory is threatened she reverts
to 'the full-blooded utterance of Elizabeth I'. The debt Eugene was
assigned to collect is for a wall-unit now being used as a room-
divider. And Rose, whom Eugene is surreptitiously courting but
apparently doomed to lose – he discovers that Mrs. Rogers is
Rose's favourite rich relative; 'We're having such trouble getting
that girl settled', Mrs. Rogers admits – might well stand for Northern Ireland. Leonard, however, who has confessed his fascination with the class structure in Britain – 'Class is about the only
facet of English life which excites me or about which I care intense-
ly' – says '*The Au Pair Man* is about an outsider despising this
structure whilst using it for his own material good' (*A Paler Shade
of Green*, p. 198).

Leonard doubts that he could have written *The Au Pair Man* had
he remained in Ireland, but even before he returned to Dalkey in
1970 he had developed an acute interest in what he saw emerging
in Ireland as a new aristocracy – more a plutocracy, perhaps –
situated primarily in the affluent south-Dublin suburb, Foxrock:
'It has sprung up full of new business executives, all of whom seem
to be called Brendan. It's a classless aristocracy' (*ibid.*). 'The
folks', he has elsewhere dubbed them, 'that live on the Pill'.

The Patrick Pearse Motel (1971), Leonard's first major attempt
at portraying the mores of Foxrock and similar communities, is in
the manner of Feydeau bedroom-farce. The first act is set in a Foxrock living-room; the second, in the eponymous motel. Most of the
characters are incongruously endowed with legendary Irish names;
even the night-watchman at the new hotel, a veteran of the 1916
Rising, bears the appellation Houlihan. The eighty-four motel
rooms are dedicated to Irish patriots: the Manchester Martyrs
room is appropriately furnished with three single beds, and the
would-be-adulterous escapades are set in the Nineteenth Century
wing, specifically in the matching Parnell and Robert Emmet
rooms, both double-bedded.

7

Ostensibly farcical, *The Patrick Pearse Motel* has its hints of satirical intent; Irving Wardle, indeed, regards it as 'single-mindedly aimed at the new prosperity, and picking up threads from Shaw's *John Bull's Other Island* to show the Irish as fully capable of Americanizing their holy places without any help from outside'. The sexual maladroitness of the characters may suggest more sinister social shortcomings in modern Ireland. By the same token, while the play mocks excesses of patriotism, it also castigates the commercial exploitation of nationalist sentiment and, occasionally, strikes a note curiously resonant of the reproachful strain of Yeats's 'September 1913' ('Was it for this . . .?'). Just as one senses in *The Au Pair Man* some authorial empathy with Mrs. Rogers' nostalgia, here, too, Leonard intermittently surfaces as a *laudator temporis acti*.

The Au Pair Man and *The Patrick Pearse Motel* may be accommodated under the capacious umbrella of contemporary comedy of manners. *Da* (1973), however, defies categorization. It is as blatantly autobiographical as *Home Before Night*, and both appear to have been prompted by Ibsen's observation that to be a writer is to sit in judgment on oneself.

When *Da* begins, it is May 1968, the evening of Da's funeral, and his playwright son Charlie, home from England for the funeral, is sorting letters, family papers, old photos, etc. From then on, the play mingles memories of Charlie's childhood, youth, and later moments, with a couple of episodes in the present, two visits prompted by Da's demise. During the earlier visit, as Charlie chats with his boyhood friend Oliver, the 'ghost' of Da makes his initial intrusion into Charlie's consciousness, and thenceforth obstinately resists all Charlie's efforts to expel him.

Most of the action occurs in the kitchen, 'the womb of the play', but other stage-areas defined largely by lighting create the locales for most of Charlie's memories: the seafront, the garden where Da worked for 54 years, the civil-service office where Charlie had his first job. A series of connecting steps and ramps, climbing up and behind the kitchen, represents a hill (Dalkey Hill, in fact, and recognizably the hill evoked by Eugene's nostalgia in *The Au Pair Man*). Leonard's cinematic technique facilitates a fluent succession of entrancing vignettes; past and present become the warp and woof of a virtually flawless fabric.

Da is a cornucopia of comedy, and Leonard's ability to turn a show-stopping line – an ability that has tempted some to suspect him of constructing his plays around such memorable lines –

is here securely anchored in character and situation; so much so, indeed, that citing lines from *Da* out of context radically reduces their original cogency. No less impressive is the controlled pathos of several scenes; *Da* is exquisitely moving but it is never mawkish.

The characters in *Da* are a cross-section of the local community: Charlie's working-class parents and Mary Tate (alias The Yellow Peril) of 'the Dwellin's'; the upwardly-immobile Oliver; Drumm, chief clerk in and scourge of the civil service; Mrs Prynn, Quaker lady and relic of 'the Quality'; Charlie, local lad who has made good abroad as playwright ('CHARLIE. At the funeral this morning I heard one of your old cronies muttering what a great character you were and how I'll never be the man me da was. DA. Don't belittle yourself: yes, you will.'). Each character is invested with appropriate attitude and authentic idiom. Yet the meticulous local colouring in no way impairs the universal appeal of *Da*; Leonard treasures a letter he received from one Sam Silverman, of the United States, congratulating the author 'on a great Jewish play'.

Summer (1974, revised 1988) evolved from Leonard's sudden realization in his mid-forties that he was going to die. In his illuminating Introduction to the 1988 revision, he says he set himself to discover how others of his age were coping with their own intimations of mortality.

From the beginning, Leonard envisaged the play as 'virtually plotless: so low-key as to be designed less for an audience than eavesdroppers' (*Summer*, 1988, p. 6). He devised two picnics, six years apart, 1968 and 1974, set on 'a hillside overlooking Dublin' – the ubiquitous Dalkey Hill of Leonard's plays or possibly its neighbour, Killiney Hill – attended by three married couples in early middle-age and two young people (the daughter of one couple, the son of another). In Act One the older people are still consciously in the prime of their lives, basking in the high-summer sunshine, almost entirely oblivious to the winged chariot. In Act Two it is late summer; the sunlight harsh, the air chilled, the picnic-area threatened by the encroachment of nearby housing developments. We overhear from the older characters to what extent if at all each has been coping with what one calls 'the clock in the room'; another, 'vultures in the front garden'. The young couple 'serve, at first, as sounding boards, later as counterpoint' (*ibid.*).

Leonard long regarded *Summer* as his best, though not his favourite, play, and appears to have developed a peculiar protectiveness towards it: '. . . if it is not perfectly cast and played at the correct level, then it may as well not be done at all' (*ibid.*, p. 7). Written for the Olney Theatre, Maryland, and given 'a hauntingly elegiac' production there, it later played in Chicago and even with the Olney cast and director proved 'a disaster': instead of what he had designed as two acts, each almost self-contained, of 'observed life', it had 'fatally and almost surreptitiously become drama. . . . now characters were touching each other, if not physically, then in an emotional sense. The play's temperature went up, and it shrivelled and died'. The first Dublin production, in 1974, was a hit, if perhaps for the wrong reasons. Because the characters had been made natives of Dalkey and Killiney, 'there were those who quite wrongly took the play to be a *roman a clef*, an expose of a suburban *dolce vita*. It was and is nothing of the sort' (ibid., 6).

A *Life* (1979) continues and intensifies the theme of mortality. Its core character is the civil servant Drumm, a mere cameo in *Da*. As prickly as ever, he has just been informed by his doctor that he has less than six months to live, and has embarked on a voyage of self-assessment. 'I need to know what I amount to', he tells Mary, the woman he lost years earlier to his friend Kearns and the only one to whom he confides the doctor's verdict, 'Debit and credit, that much I am owed. If the account is to be closed, so be it. I demand an audit. Or show me the figures: I can add and subtract: I'll do my own books'. Close to retirement, he has been promoted to Keeper of Records: 'I seem', he complains, 'to have access to everyone's file but my own'.

The atmosphere of *A Life*, in contrast to that of *Da*, is predominantly sombre. Drumm's opening address, delivered to an unseen audience of walkers at the end of their conducted tour, is punctuated by 'terminal' images and is itself an ironical metaphor. Another index to the contrasting moods is that whereas in *Da* Drumm gleefully misleads acquaintances into thinking his 'tummy trouble' is cancer, in *A Life* he steadfastly pretends, except to Mary, that his malignancy is merely 'a duodenal ulcer . . . tummy trouble'.

Besides the character of Drumm the two plays have much in common. Again in *A Life* Leonard creates distinct playing-areas: on one side of the stage is the modern living-room of Mary's small red-bricked Edwardian house; on the other side, its kitchen of forty years ago; centre-stage and elevated, a broken-down bandstand in a small park on a hillside identified by Drumm as 'all that remains of what was called the commons of Dalkey'. As in *Da* so in *A Life* times past and present intersect; Drumm, his wife Dolly, Mary and her husband Kearns share the stage with their adolescent selves, Desmond, Dorothy, Mibs and Lar, respectively. A striking simultaneity between the two plays is established by Kearns's allusion to 'poor oul' Nick Tynan (Da) who was brought to the chapel yesterday', and Kearns himself is remarkably akin to Da: both characters are incorrigibly optimistic, endearingly impervious to insult and, to Drumm, equally exasperating.

A Life advances the trend perceptible in *Summer* towards more overtly serious drama. Its theme of impending death is sustained by apt imagery and its irony is more profound. If, despite its merits, the play proves vaguely disappointing, it may be so mainly because it arouses expectations of some growth in Drumm's self-knowledge but fails to satisfy them. Drumm has few illusions about himself. He knows all along that his job in the civil service has been doing work of doubtful value for a government of doubtful morality: 'Cogito ergo sum. I am a cog, therefore I am.' He knows too that the chief mourners at his funeral are likely to be 'a small weeping group of unsplit infinitives'. Towards the end of the play, when Drumm admits to Dolly that he has 'achieved nothing', and elaborates, 'What I called principles was vanity. What I called friendship was malice', his speech (at least in print, perhaps not in performance?) rings less of revelation than reprise.

Kill, performed at the 1982 Dublin Theatre Festival, is, in contrast to *The Au Pair Man*, blatantly a political allegory. Set in a deconsecrated and run-down church — 'kill' is an anglicized form of 'cill', Irish for 'church' — that suggests a recently laicized Republic of Ireland, with a besieged and much disputed alms house (Northern Ireland) attached, the play is peopled with representatives of institutionalized power: the law (an indecisive Judge Lawless), the church (Father Bishop, a cleric whose speech is enriched by bad language because he believes that the church, to be truly ecumenical, should speak with the voice of the people: 'It's a shagging nuisance, but I do it'), the arts (Iseult Mullarkey, self-effacing genius on the musical saw), business (the provincial upstart, Tony Sleehaun), and, in the mendacious prime minister Wade, government. Wade's out-of-touch wife (vaguely reminiscent of Mrs Rogers in *The Au Pair Man*) seems to be a relic of the Anglo-Irish ascendancy, and in the sinister if bumbling Mort Mongan Leonard lampoons the Provisional I.R.A. The formidable Madge Lawless, wife to the judge, is Wade's only outspoken, but ultimately out-manoeuvred, antagonist. Though Leonard calls it 'a comedy, not a tract',

Kill is clearly a satirical shotgun aimed at several of his regular journalistic targets, primarily at what he considers the hypocrisy of official attitudes towards Northern Ireland: 'the vocal outrage counterpointed with the unspoken indifference or partisanship on the side of the terrorists'. Ironically, if perhaps predictably, some of those who deplore Leonard's apparent lack of social or political commitment have found *Kill* unpalatable.

Hugh Leonard's initial impulse to write plays derived from his attending O'Casey's *Plough and the Stars*. O'Casey's early plays drew on his familiarity with inner-city life in Dublin. Leonard likewise tends to focus on what he knows best, life in the southern suburbs of Dublin. More plausibly than Shaw he is 'a product of Dalkey's outlook'; witness the allusions to, even the physical presence of, Dalkey hill in the plays that follow. If in his work one detects the odd affinity to Albee, Coward, Miller, Pinter, Ayckbourn or others, Hugh Leonard remains quintessentially, but with no connotation of parochialism, the Dalkey Archivist.

*

The plays selected for this volume have been variously dedicated. This Introduction I affectionately dedicate to another indomitable Da of Dalkey: my father, now in his ninety-seventh year, Daniel J. Gallagher, who, though a native of Dunmanway, County Cork, spent three decades of his retirement in Dalkey, living for some of that time almost literally within a stone's throw of Hugh Leonard's Da.

June, 1991   S. F. Gallagher

THE
AU PAIR MAN

This play was produced by Joseph Papp at the Vivian Beaumont Theatre, New York City, on 27 December 1973, with the following cast:

CHARACTERS

MRS. ROGERS
EUGENE HARTIGAN

MRS. ROGERS   Julie Harris
EUGENE HARTIGAN   Charles Durning

Producer: Joseph Papp   Director: Gerald Freedman
Settings: John Conklin   Costumes: Theoni V. Aldredge

The home of Mrs. Elizabeth Rogers, London, England.

ACT I

Sometime in the not-too-distant present.

ACT II

Scene 1: A few months later.
Scene 2: Several months later.

ACT III

Sometime later.

(Note: the stage directions, as given, are from the New York production and are not part of the author's original text.)

14

THE AU PAIR MAN

ACT ONE

EUGENE *appears outside. He rings the doorbell; chimes are heard. They play the first six notes of the National Anthem. Pause. MRS. ROGERS appears. She wears a day dress. She waits expectantly. The next six notes of the National Anthem are heard. She smiles; she is a music lover. Pause. Mild anxiety. The final notes ring out.*

MRS. ROGERS. What do you want of me?

EUGENE. Mrs. Rogers?

MRS. ROGERS. Well, that depends.

EUGENE. My name is Eugene Hartigan. Can I come in?

MRS. ROGERS. I'm sure you can. (MRS. ROGERS *steps behind door.* EUGENE *comes in and trips over the Victoria bust.* MRS. ROGERS *steps out from behind the door and closes it.*) That wasn't quite what I meant.

EUGENE. (*Turning up to wall unit and moving to Stage Right of room behind large table.*) I see you still have it.

MRS. ROGERS. Have I?

EUGENE. (*Looking around room.*) The wall unit.

MRS. ROGERS. Oh, that. How could one possibly have lost it?

EUGENE. (*Crossing Up Right of sofa.*) I'm from Weatherby and Fitch.

MRS. ROGERS. . . . and Fitch?

EUGENE. You bought it from us.

MRS. ROGERS. The . . .?

EUGENE. . . . wall unit. Although I can see you're using it as a room divider.

MRS. ROGERS. Am I?

EUGENE. What I mean is, it really ought to be put up against a wall.

MRS. ROGERS. That's a very forward thing to say.

EUGENE. It's entirely your own business, but with all those books and the clock and the radio it must look odd from the other side.

15

MRS. ROGERS. I don't look at it from the other side.

EUGENE. No?

MRS. ROGERS. Mr . . .?

EUGENE. Hartigan.

MRS. ROGERS. Mr. Haritgan, I see no reason why I should explain the raison d'etre of my furniture to an utter stranger . . .

EUGENE. Of course not.

MRS. ROGERS. But I don't want you to go away from here telling everyone that not only do I use my wall unit as a room divider, but that I make a fetish of not looking at it from the other side.

EUGENE. I wouldn't do that.

MRS. ROGERS. Originally there was a wall directly behind it, but it fell down.

EUGENE. The wall did?

MRS. ROGERS. One terrible evening. And the ceiling of that room collapsed shortly afterwards. Which is why I never go in there.

EUGENE. I don't blame you.

MRS. ROGERS. As a matter of grim fact, I don't think this flat is going to last for much longer. The . . . (*A gesture.*)

EUGENE. Wall unit?

MRS. ROGERS. Thank you; you are helpful. It keeps those two walls apart . . . that one and that one.

EUGENE. We use only the sturdiest timber. Hearts of oak.

MRS. ROGERS. How comforting. You say you want to buy it from me.

EUGENE. *Buy* it? No, missis; you bought it from us.

MRS. ROGERS. I did?

EUGENE. Three years ago.

MRS. ROGERS. You seem a very sweet young man, but you have been cruelly hoaxed. I did not buy it. Someone has been lying to you. I don't even like it particularly; it makes the room look like what the Germans call ein Beidermeier zimmer. Do you know what that means?

EUGENE. No, missis. Tell me.

MRS. ROGERS. I don't mean to be patronizing, but if you have to ask, you can't possibly afford to know. That article was not bought by me (*Moves to Up Right of curved area.*) It came here as a gift, as an intimate keepsake.

EUGENE. It hasn't been paid for. (*Moves slowly to front of sofa.*)

MRS. ROGERS. Are you sure?

EUGENE. There's a total of . . .

MRS. ROGERS. Are you a debt collector?

EUGENE. Weatherby and Fitch, you see, I work for them, they have this initiative test . . . test of initiative. They send out the most . . . (*Reaches front of sofa*.) . . . junior employee from the accounts department and he's supposed to . . .

MRS. ROGERS. Yes.

EUGENE. It's a rotten old job.

MRS. ROGERS. And you are the youngest employee.

EUGENE. No, the newest.

MRS. ROGERS. (*Moves to front of green chair*.) When I was a Girl Guide, which was some little time ago, ha! ha! they sent our troop out into the country for twenty-four hours on an initiative test. (*Moves to* EUGENE.) And it's true, you know, what they say: one *can* make a fire by rubbing two Boy Scouts together. (*She smiles suddenly*.)

EUGENE. Ha-ha. I wouldn't do this job regularly.

MRS. ROGERS. Collecting debts.

EUGENE. Oh, no.

MRS. ROGERS. Let me take your coat, Mr. Hartigan. (EUGENE *puts briefcase between his legs, then gives coat to* MRS. ROGERS. *She puts coat on side chair.* EUGENE *follows her to left*.) And do sit down or walk around or whatever. May I offer you a drink?

EUGENE. I don't want to put you to any . . .

MRS. ROGERS. (*At side chair*.) . . . trouble. You're an apologetic young man. Whiskey, perhaps?

EUGENE. (*At left of green chair*.) A drop of Irish, if you have it.

MRS. ROGERS. (*Crossing to bar*.) Do you like my flat?

EUGENE. It's lovely. (*Starts pacing straight up towards Victoria. He walks about, hands clasped behind his back, head inclined forward*.)

MRS. ROGERS. (*From bar*.) Would you mind not doing that?

EUGENE. Doing what?

MRS. ROGERS. You look exactly like the poor Duke of Edinburgh.

EUGENE. Well, I wasn't. (*Crosses to table of music boxes*.)

MRS. ROGERS. I should hope not. (*A smile*) You're forgiven. But there's only scotch, as a punishment.

EUGENE. Thanks very much.

MRS. ROGERS. Water? (EUGENE *blows nose with his handkerchief and puts it back in his sleeve*.

EUGENE. Right up.

MRS. ROGERS. Oh, yes? (*She fills his glass.* EUGENE *picks up china bell, hears it is a music box and puts it right down*.

17

MRS. ROGERS *crosses to* EUGENE. *They have music box table between them.*)

EUGENE. Ta.

MRS. ROGERS. What an attractive fountain pen. May I? (*She takes it.*)

EUGENE. It's . . .

MRS. ROGERS. I just want to look at it. Nice. Was it a gift?

EUGENE. No, I've had it for years.

MRS. ROGERS. It's large, isn't it? Burly, that's the word for it, burly and, I'm sure, serviceable. (MRS. ROGERS *crosses to her chair with pen.* EUGENE *follows but goes to the sofa.*) I dislike ballpoints, such inadequate imitations, a fountain pen always looks as if it means business. Does it leak? (MRS. ROGERS *sits.*)

EUGENE. Not so far. (EUGENE *sits.*)

MRS. ROGERS. But you ought to keep it inside, out of sight. You don't want everyone to know what you're about, do you? (MRS. ROGERS *gets up to put pen in* EUGENE'S *pocket. She then goes behind her chair.*) Zoom . . . here it goes, right in, and . . . clip! There's no place like home, is there?

EUGENE. Good health. (*He drinks. He then puts glass on seat of* MRS. ROGERS' *chair.*)

MRS. ROGERS. Bless you. (*Standing behind her chair,* MRS. ROGERS *picks up the glass.*)

EUGENE. (*Picks up his briefcase but has much trouble from slipping off the sofa.*) According to the original invoice for the wall unit . . .

MRS. ROGERS. And bless you again, you're embarrassed. You're in a hurry to have the unpleasantness over with and enjoy your drink. I'm so very much in sympathy; embarrassment in other people always turns my own cheeks to fire. But debt collecting should really be a woman's profession. (MRS. ROGERS, *crossing to left behind the sofa, puts glass on metal table.* EUGENE *gets off sofa and moves to green chair and sits.*) Women are merciless by nature, they don't mind being querulous and asking for money on various pretexts. Men do. You go into Harrods or Fortnum and Mason's and the only men you'll ever see at the complaints counter are homosexuals looking for someone to talk to. (MRS. ROGERS *stands behind green chair.*)

EUGENE. It was bought in your name, you see.

MRS. ROGERS. But I accepted it as a gift. Was I duped?

EUGENE. Two hundred and thirty-eight pounds, nineteen . . .

MRS. ROGERS. Although they say it's the thought that counts. (*Sits*

18

on sofa.) Would you be terribly upset if I refused to pay for it?

EUGENE. Me?

MRS. ROGERS. Would you?

EUGENE. I wouldn't give a continental.

MRS. ROGERS. How nice you are. But if you went back to Messrs. Weatherby and . . .

EUGENE. Fitch.

MRS. ROGERS. . . . and told them you had failed your initiative test, that Mrs. Rogers had refused to pay for the wall unit on a point of principle . . . what then?

EUGENE. Ah, well!

MRS. ROGERS. You would be discharged.

EUGENE. I wouldn't mind.

MRS. ROGERS. No?

EUGENE. There are plenty of other jobs.

MRS. ROGERS. Is.

EUGENE. What?

MRS. ROGERS. There is plenty of other jobs.

EUGENE. Are there?

MRS. ROGERS. Hundreds. In fact . . .

EUGENE. Yes?

MRS. ROGERS. When you came to the door just now, I thought for a moment it was in answer to the advertisement.

EUGENE. No.

MRS. ROGERS. No.

EUGENE. No, I came about the . . .

MRS. ROGERS. Yes (*Pause*.)

EUGENE. What advertisement was that?

MRS. ROGERS. Do you take 'The Times'?

EUGENE. I've heard of it.

MRS. ROGERS. I advertised for an au pair man. (*Moves to Down stage side of desk and picks up paper.*)

EUGENE. For a what? (EUGENE *follows, stays to her left.*)

MRS. ROGERS. An au pair man.

EUGENE. A kind of . . .?

MRS. ROGERS. Mother's help. No, I'm being naughty. Father's help, really . . . clerical, not culinary. You see, my husband is . . .

EUGENE. Oh, yes?

MRS. ROGERS. . . . is frequently absent. I miss him.

EUGENE. I'm sure.

MRS. ROGERS. It's a man's world, Mr. Hartigan. While I remain

19

hopelessly housebound, my husband is out there somewhere, selling his colonials. He is a philatelist.

EUGENE. Stamps. (MRS. ROGERS *takes box of stamps off the albums, puts down paper and picks up stamp book*.)

MRS. ROGERS. There was a time when we had an enormous collection. He was forever abroad, adding to it, acquiring new rarities. All one had to do was mention the word 'Unperforated' and he was off like a rabid bulldog. Timbromania.

EUGENE. What?

MRS. ROGERS. He suffered from it. When not cavorting around Mauritius or the Aden Protectorate, he was off being exotic in British Guiana, scouring the equitorial forests for a Penny Magenta. Then, having taken ages to build up his colonials, after all those years of blood, toil, tears and perspiration . . . (EUGENE *pulls hand off stamp album, puts stamp book down and sits at desk chair, picks up box of stamps*.) . . . he proceeded to get rid of them. Said it was the age of specialization, better to concentrate on one's British collection and ignore the rest. If you ask me he was just being peevish because he never managed to get a full set of anything. (*Looking at one particular stamp*.)

EUGENE. Where does the au pair come in?

MRS. ROGERS. You're tenacious, aren't you?

EUGENE. Pardon?

MRS. ROGERS. You hold on grimly. Would you like another drink?

EUGENE. I don't mind. (*Both jump and run to front of sofa. *EUGENE *gets glass off of metal table and drains it*.) A helicopter never flew on one wing. (*Pause*.) That's an expression of mine.

MRS. ROGERS. Is it? (*Crosses to bar. *EUGENE *follows to music box table*.)

EUGENE. It's one of those, what they call a non-sequitur. Because a helicopter hasn't got . . .

MRS. ROGERS. I always thought the word was 'auto gyro.' (*Adding water to his drink*.) Right up?

EUGENE. Lovely. (EUGENE *lifts lid of gold music box as she pours*.) Urgle-urgle-urgle.

MRS. ROGERS. Yes, indeed. Cheers. (*Starts to *EUGENE, *remembers bottle and goes back to the bar and gets bottle. *MRS. ROGERS *and *EUGENE *face each other over music box table*.)

EUGENE. The best of luck.

MRS. ROGERS. Don't you ever drink to the Royal Family?

EUGENE. Who?

MRS. ROGERS. You should, you know. It costs so little and it means so much.

EUGENE. I think I've left it a bit late.

MRS. ROGERS. Late?

EUGENE. This is my second.

MRS. ROGERS. Well?

EUGENE. I mean, it wouldn't be manners. (*Both sit;* MRS. ROGERS *on her chair.* EUGENE *on sofa.*) If you don't do it before your first mouthful you may as well throw your hat at it.

MRS. ROGERS. Nothing of the sort.

EUGENE. I always thought . . .

MRS. ROGERS. You mustn't be so fuddy-duddy, Mr. Hartigan. Toasting the Royal Family is like praying: it's efficacious no matter when you do it.

EUGENE. (*Looking into his glass.*) I wish I'd known.

MRS. ROGERS. (*Kindly.*) Perhaps next time.

EUGENE. Oh, sure. Next time for certain.

MRS. ROGERS. (*Tantalus poised.*) Ready?

EUGENE. Won't be a tick.

MRS. ROGERS. Do forgive my enthusiasm. I always get carried away when I think of how the old barriers are being broken down . . . (EUGENE *offers empty glass.*) with protocol thrown to the four winds, so that now we can toast the Royal Family . . . (MRS. ROGERS *pours drink.*) . . . whenever we like – after the hors d'oeuvres, if we want to. (EUGENE *leans way back on couch.*)

EUGENE. Or the main course, even.

MRS. ROGERS. Why not!

EUGENE. Not to mention the sweet.

MRS. ROGERS. Yes!

EUGENE. Or the cheese and biscuits.

MRS. ROGERS. The what? (EUGENE *sits up nervously.*)

EUGENE. The camembert and biscuits.

MRS. ROGERS. We mustn't get too fanciful.

EUGENE. It'll come.

MRS. ROGERS. Not in our lifetime.

EUGENE. Oh, I don't know.

MRS. ROGERS. I am all for progress; in fact, at times I verge upon the radical. But I could never happily toast the Royal Family in port.

EUGENE. Port wine?

MRS. ROGERS. With cheese and biscuits.

EUGENE. I forgot about that.

MRS. ROGERS. Evidently. (*With the tantalus.*) Finished?

EUGENE. Any second now.

MRS. ROGERS. Please don't hurry. (*Pause.*)

EUGENE. So where does the au pair come in?

MRS. ROGERS. Oh, dear.

EUGENE. I just wondered.

MRS. ROGERS. No wonder your national symbol is the harp.

EUGENE. Ha-ha. (EUGENE *nervously changes position on the couch to face her.*)

MRS. ROGERS. My husband, who is incurably and inescapably absent from home, needs someone to keep the poor remnants of his collection in order, someone who will write letters and pay the accounts . . . Those accounts which are just and reasonable.

EUGENE. A secretary.

MRS. ROGERS. No. A secretary is a paid employee, whereas au pair – from the French – means giving a mutual service, without payment (EUGENE *changes position on couch, picks up briefcase.*) on either side. I find that when there is no question of payment one always attracts a better sort of person.

EUGENE. Ah. (EUGENE *sets glass on couch to his left.*)

MRS. ROGERS. (*Gets up, holding bottle.*) But I'm afraid you wouldn't be in the least bit suitable.

EUGENE. Me?

MRS. ROGERS. (*She crosses to left behind sofa.*) Not at all your cup of tea.

EUGENE. I wasn't hinting.

MRS. ROGERS. Weren't you? Oh, good.

EUGENE. As you say, it's not my cuppa.

MRS. ROGERS. No.

EUGENE. The kind of job I like, I like the kind of job with prospects. (MRS. ROGERS *picks up glass and puts it on metal table with bottle.*)

MRS. ROGERS. Naturally. (*Crossing Upstage to red chair.*)

EUGENE. And I can't see this one having a pension scheme.

MRS. ROGERS. Ha-ha.

EUGENE. Or lunch vouchers.

MRS. ROGERS. (*Behind red chair.*) Meals are included.

EUGENE. Well, you know what I mean.

MRS. ROGERS. Quite. (*Pause.*) You . . .

EUGENE. *Why* wouldn't I be suitable?

MRS. ROGERS. What? (*Looking at self in mirror.*)

EUGENE. I mean it's not because you're trying to attract a better sort of person, and I'm not?

MRS. ROGERS. Aren't you? (*Crossing right to her chair.*)

EUGENE. Is it?

MRS. ROGERS. Well, yes.

EUGENE. Yes? Well, I don't want it.

MRS. ROGERS. I'm so glad. (*Standing Upstage Right from her chair.*)

EUGENE. But I'm not going to be turned down for it on the grounds of class distinction.

MRS. ROGERS. Aren't you?

EUGENE. You said you wanted a better sort of person.

MRS. ROGERS. Well?

EUGENE. Better than who?

MRS. ROGERS. (*Stressing the missing 'm.'*) Who-meh.

EUGENE. Who-meh. You said I wasn't suitable.

MRS. ROGERS. Neither are you.

EUGENE. Why? Give me a reason.

MRS. ROGERS. A dozen reasons.

EUGENE. Trot them out.

MRS. ROGERS. All twelve?

EUGENE. Yeah.

MRS. ROGERS. (*Crossing left behind to sofa to just Upstage of green chair.*) I'd rather not. Some of them you may regard as verging upon the personal.

EUGENE. I don't care what reasons you give, so long as I'm not being differentiated against.

MRS. ROGERS. You'll be offended.

EUGENE. Me? I've a skin like an armadillo. (*Still on sofa with both arms stretched out on back of it.*)

MRS. ROGERS. Your fingernails are unclean.

EUGENE. What?

MRS. ROGERS. I've started: that was Number One. You walk with a defeated stoop. Instead of sitting properly, you subside like a dispirited midwife. Your hair could do with a medicated shampoo. I can see dirt in the turns-ups of your trousers, your fingers are stained (*Moves to left of desk.*) with nicotine, and one can detect a slight but pungent body odour. You speak ungrammatically. In manner you veer from the apologetic to the impolite. You appear not to be of independent means . . . the position, as I have already mentioned, is unsalaried. And all I know of you from a professional standpoint is that as a debt

23

collector (*Leaning on Downstage side of her chair.*) you leave much to be desired. That makes twelve, I think, but if you want a baker's dozen I would say that when I answered the door a few minutes ago you stomped in here with all the presumptuous arrogance of an American Latter-Day Saint.

EUGENE. That the lot?

MRS. ROGERS. Yes.

EUGENE. I knew it. Sheer bloody class distinction.

MRS. ROGERS. Oh, really . . . !

EUGENE. Nothing else but.

MRS. ROGERS. A skin like an armadillo! (*Crossing Downstage Right of green chair.*)

EUGENE. (*Upstage of sofa, takes two steps to* MRS. ROGERS.) I'll tell you something. Just because I wear my fountain pen on the outside is no grounds for discrimination. I don't want to give offence or to rise up above me station . . . but I'm as good as you are! (*Pause. The Annigoni falls to the floor. Both* EUGENE *and* MRS. ROGERS *jump.*) MRS. ROGERS *hurries up to picture.*)

MRS. ROGERS. People who say they're better than other people never are. (*She looks coldly at* EUGENE *and hangs the Annigoni back in its place.*)

EUGENE. I see red whenever I'm differentiated against. Anyone would think I was only a black or something.

MRS. ROGERS. (*To the painting.*) There, now. Did that nasty man frighten ums?

EUGENE. (*Crossing Upstage to red chair.*) The class system in this place is nothing short of fascistic.

MRS. ROGERS. I shouldn't sneer at fascism if I were you; it's coming back.

EUGENE. I'm Irish and I'm proud of it. (*Behind red chair.*)

MRS. ROGERS. Perverse boy.

EUGENE. My da walked on a hunger strike from Dublin to Belfast, in the hard November of 1936.

MRS. ROGERS. (*Moving to Right of large table.*) It's the best time of year to see Belfast.

EUGENE. (*Moves down to sofa.*) And for what? For his son's origins to be sneered at, just because I never went to a pubic school.

MRS. ROGERS. A what? (*Moving to her chair.*)

EUGENE. What?

MRS. ROGERS. (*At her chair getting stuff.*) You said, to a . . .

EUGENE. No. No, I didn't mean that, it was a lapsus lingae,

24

it slipped out. Now I'm going crimson; it's a word I use for a joke. I mean public school.

MRS. ROGERS. Oh, good.

EUGENE. (*Abashed.*) You must take me for a right eejit.

MRS. ROGERS. Nonsense. It's been lovely having you.
(*Crossing Left to* EUGENE *in front of sofa.*)

EUGENE. I see.

MRS. ROGERS. May I take your glass?

EUGENE. I didn't toast the Royal Family yet.

MRS. ROGERS. (*Crossing to bar with his glass.*) Perhaps some other time.

EUGENE. I want to, I'm dead keen.

MRS. ROGERS. How nice. (*She takes his glass at bar.*) I put your coat somewhere: ah, yes. (*Crossing Left to chair with* EUGENE'S *coat, above sofa.*)

EUGENE. I dirtied my bib, didn't I!

MRS. ROGERS. May I help you? (*She holds his coat.*)

EUGENE. You think I'm a vulgarian.

MRS. ROGERS. No!

EUGENE. Yes, you do.

MRS. ROGERS. I enjoyed your little visit.

EUGENE. I try too hard, that's my trouble. Put me in the presence of a gold-embossed accent (*Putting on coat.*) and in a room with a bit of decor in it, and I go to pieces. I try to be witty and pithy and grammatic at the same time, and for a fellow like me that takes coordination.

MRS. ROGERS. Not at all easy (*Both moving to door.* MRS. ROGERS *turns to get briefcase.*)

EUGENE. Whenever I try to be fluent I get as awkward as a new whore. (*Bending to get briefcase.*) There! . . . do you see?

MRS. ROGERS. (*Moving up to edge of hall platform.*) It's a charming simile. Now I mustn't keep you. I'm sure you're dying to rush home, have a bath and change for dinner.

EUGENE. Ha-ha.

MRS. ROGERS. It's been so nice.

EUGENE. I don't get the job, then?

MRS. ROGERS. The . . .?

EUGENE. . . . position.

MRS. ROGERS. But you don't want it.

EUGENE. I do.

MRS. ROGERS. You're a wag, aren't you?

EUGENE. I wouldn't ask, only I'm due for the high jump on account of your wall unit.

MRS. ROGERS. Employers can be beastly.

EUGENE. Weatherby and Fitch have a terrible name.

MRS. ROGERS. Especially Fitch.

EUGENE. No fear of that lot giving you a golden handshake.

MRS. ROGERS. Well, you can have one from me. (*She offers him her hand.* EUGENE *does not let it go.*) Goodbye, dear Mr. Hartigan. I'm sure you'll be far better off without them.

EUGENE. Yes. Well, goodbye, so.

MRS. ROGERS. And do forgive my mentioning it, but you won't forget about the shampoo, will you? It can make such a difference.

EUGENE. Medicated.

MRS. ROGERS. Sebbix for preference.

EUGENE. Right. (*Pause. She waits for him to leave.*) Well, thanks very much for the two drinks, and I hope I haven't given umbrage.

MRS. ROGERS. It's been lovely.

EUGENE. You've been very patient with me, giving me the twelve reasons and so forth, and all I want to say is, in connection with this job you're offering . . .

MRS. ROGERS. Yes, dear? (*She smiles unseeingly.*)

EUGENE. You needn't bother your arse about it. (*He goes out.* MRS. ROGERS *stands quite still. The clock chimes the hour. The chimes play the first few bars of 'Land of Hope and Glory.'* MRS. ROGERS *takes bottle off of metal table, takes it to the bar and then exits into bedroom humming.*)

MRS. ROGERS. (*Singing.*) 'Mother of the free . . .!' (*She goes into the bedroom, humming.* EUGENE *returns. The door chimes are heard.* MRS. ROGERS *returns at once and looks uncertainly at the clock. The door chimes are heard again, playing the next few notes of the National Anthem.* MRS. ROGERS *smiles, relieved, and waits. Silence. She becomes annoyed and goes to the door. The caller is* EUGENE.)

EUGENE. I'm sorry for . . .

MRS. ROGERS. (*Hissing.*) You might have finished it. (*She leans out past him and rings the doorbell. The final notes of the anthem ring out.* EUGENE *comes into the room.* EUGENE *trips over Queen Victoria on way in.* MRS. ROGERS *is to Left of glass table.* EUGENE *is exactly opposite her.*) It's the short version one hears in cinemas and billiard halls. Dreadful, I know; I wanted to have it complete and unexpurgated, the doorbell people said it would take an electronic miracle.

EUGENE. Go on!

MRS. ROGERS. And, besides, callers would never stay at the door that long.

EUGENE. Not unless they were patriots.

MRS. ROGERS. Quite. (*Pause.*) Was there something?

EUGENE. What?

MRS. ROGERS. You bade me an Anglo-Saxon goodbye.

EUGENE. You don't forget much, do you?

MRS. ROGERS. What do you want of me?

EUGENE. I was on the stairs. Hartigan descending, as you might say, and I said to myself: now that was an uncalled-for remark to make. A nice woman like MRS. ROGERS, she'll think you're a barbarian or scabrous or something. Go on back in and make it up to her.

MRS. ROGERS. That won't be necessary.

EUGENE. I *want* to.

MRS. ROGERS. (*Playing with her pearls.*) Mr. Hartigan, it's past six o'clock. I was just about to change for the evening. (*Long pause.*)

EUGENE. You mean, into something nocturnal?

MRS. ROGERS. If you like. So . . . (MRS. ROGERS *crosses to Right of pedestal table.* EUGENE *follows and stands opposite her at Right.*)

EUGENE. Oh, sure. Anyway, I thought you might like to know how they found out your address.

MRS. ROGERS. Found out?

EUGENE. How Weatherby and Fitch got to know about it. How they got on to you.

MRS. ROGERS. Got on to me?

EUGENE. You must have wondered.

MRS. ROGERS. The wall unit was delivered here, to this address. Surely your employers keep records of such events?

EUGENE. Ah well . . .

MRS. ROGERS. Therefore they knew where I was living. So why do you imply that my address had to be *found out?*

EUGENE. Our records, you see, they . . .

MRS. ROGERS. They were destroyed! Burned, perhaps?

EUGENE. They were whipped.

MRS. ROGERS. Whipped? (*Eyes brightening.*) Are we talking about flagellation?

EUGENE. They were stolen.

MRS. ROGERS. Ah.

27

EUGENE. Very interesting anecdote. There was this fellow name of Matthew Wilson . . .

MRS. ROGERS. Oh?

EUGENE. Do you know him?

MRS. ROGERS. (*Starting moving to front of sofa.*) It just so happens that I abominate Matthew as a Christian name. I looked it up once. It's from the Hebrew; it means 'Gift of Yah.'

EUGENE. My name is Eugene.

MRS. ROGERS. Oh, yes?

EUGENE. It means 'well-born.'

MRS. ROGERS. How apt.

EUGENE. Better than the gift of Yah.

MRS. ROGERS. Tell me about this Mr. Wilson. (*Moves to* EUGENE, *sits on sofa.* EUGENE *sits on green chair.*)

EUGENE. He was with Weatherby and Fitch. Junior, like me, only before my time. Time was about a year ago.

MRS. ROGERS. Then you never knew him . . .?

EUGENE. Not in those days. They sent him out on an initiative test. He was supposed to collect the money for your wall unit.

MRS. ROGERS. Just like you.

EUGENE. It's a legend in the accounts department. Because he vanished.

MRS. ROGERS. *Did* he?

EUGENE. The way they tell it, he went galloping off into a soft drizzle and was never heard of again.

MRS. ROGERS. How extraordinary.

EUGENE. And what's interesting is, he took everything that had your address on it; carbon copies, IBM cards, the lot; so what do you make of that?

MRS. ROGERS. Yet you seem to have recovered the documents. Might one ask how?

EUGENE. Ah. Ah, well, he came back.

MRS. ROGERS. Came back?

EUGENE. Yesterday. Pitiful.

MRS. ROGERS. What was?

EUGENE. Middle of coffee break, he came in in this emaciated condition. Eyes sunk back in his forehead, fingers as thin as pencils.

MRS. ROGERS. Did he say where he had been?

EUGENE. Not to me. Some place where he'd been malnutreated, I suppose. They say he used to be a plump, jocular fellow with a ruddy complexion.

28

MRS. ROGERS. Sic transit.

EUGENE. I heard the reason he turned up again was to strike a bargain.

MRS. ROGERS. Oh?

EUGENE. He offered to give them your address in return for his job back.

EUGENE. I don't believe you.

EUGENE. Not that it did him much good. They . . .

MRS. ROGERS. (*Stands, moves to desk.*) Are you saying that to regain his paltry livelihood as a junior clerk, Matthew Wilson not only betrayed my whereabouts but jeopardized my most cherished possession? No.

EUGENE. (*Stands and takes two steps.*) I'm sure there was nothing personal. As far as he was concerned you were only a couple of holes in a IBM card.

MRS. ROGERS. Thank you.

EUGENE. Anyhow, if it's proof you want . . . (MRS. ROGERS *crosses to* EUGENE, *takes papers and moves back to desk.*)

MRS. ROGERS. Proof.

EUGENE. Here's a briefcaseful. (*Crosses to Upstage Left of desk.*)

MRS. ROGERS. Show me. (*She takes the briefcase.*)

EUGENE. Give you a laugh . . .

MRS. ROGERS. (*Taking out some documents.*) Oh, my God.

EUGENE. This is a riot. (MRS. ROGERS *sits at desk.*) He thought he'd get on their soft side, ingratiate himself – is that a word? – so he offered to hand all this stuff back as a token of good faith and sincerity. (MRS. ROGERS *looks at the documents in dismay.*) And no sooner did he hand over the loot when they turfed him out on his ear. The eejit.

MRS. ROGERS. Have I somehow deserved this?

EUGENE. It would have been funny if he hadn't looked so emaciated.

MRS. ROGERS. Funny?

EUGENE. Look, you're taking this too much to heart. I mean, it isn't as if he was a friend of yours.

MRS. ROGERS. A friend? (MRS. ROGERS *throws papers and handkerchief on desk.*) He was more than a friend. He was our au pair man.

EUGENE. Him?

MRS. ROGERS. My husband's and mine.

EUGENE. Was he?

MRS. ROGERS. (*Picks up papers.*) And I must apologize for lying to you.

EUGENE. Holy God.

MRS. ROGERS. (*Starts folding papers.*) A year ago I engaged him in my husband's absence and against my better judgment. One should always heed one's instincts in these matters: he proved to be most unsatisfactory. Furtive, and with revolting personal habits. (*Rises and crosses to Upstage Left of chaise.*)

EUGENE. That'd be him.

MRS. ROGERS. There was nothing upright about him. Nothing.

EUGENE. The gift of Yah.

MRS. ROGERS. Exactly.

EUGENE. Where I come from we'd call him a sleeveen.

MRS. ROGERS. Oh?

EUGENE. It means a little mountainy man.

MRS. ROGERS. What facility you have for le mot juste, Mr. Hartigan. Sleeveen.

EUGENE. (*Crossing three steps to left.*) It's a sort of gift I've got for the right expression.

MRS. ROGERS. I'm sure. (*Crossing to Upstage Right of curved area.*)

EUGENE. A great man for the precise . . . (*Pause.*)

MRS. ROGERS. Word.

EUGENE. Yeah.

MRS. ROGERS. Lazy, slovenly and inept.

EUGENE. Who?

MRS. ROGERS. He came here, played 'God Save the Queen' on my door chimes and said that he was on an initiative test. The wall unit.

EUGENE. Ah.

MRS. ROGERS. I was unwise enough to mention that I required an au pair man. At once he was seized by an obsession: the position I offered was exactly his cup of tea; he must have it at all costs.

EUGENE. That rings a bell.

MRS. ROGERS. Doesn't it. (*Moves to Upstage of green chair, then moves to Upstage of chaise and pats tiger on head.*) He seemed so boyish, so ingenuously eager to be . . . up and at it that I capitulated. I bade him welcome, lavished all my resources on him. (*Sits on chaise, on Downstage side.*) Oh, the things I did for that man . . . (*Reclining on chaise, folding papers into cone.*) virginal white sheets on his bed, not to mention a Paisley quilt and in winter a hot water jar from Smethick in Staffordshire. I fed him on prime Scotch beef and double Devon cream.

EUGENE. You were too good to him. (*Moves to Upstage side of chaise.*)

MRS. ROGERS. And oysters.

EUGENE. Get away!

MRS. ROGERS. That was towards the later stage of his employment. As a last resort. Raw oysters from the Channel Islands.

EUGENE. Brain food.

MRS. ROGERS. You do penetrate my motives, don't you?

EUGENE. Ha-ha.

MRS. ROGERS. Yes. (*Sits up facing Offstage.*) I tried to arouse him from his lethargy. But I'm afraid Mr. Wilson's brain was beyond nourishing. He seemed incapable of effort. Always excuses, excuses, to avoid work. His fountain pen had no ink in it or the nib was bent or the plunger defective.

EUGENE. (*Taking out his pen.*) Mine is top-top.

MRS. ROGERS. So you said. (*Reclining again.*) Are you about to use it?

EUGENE. No.

MRS. ROGERS. Then put it away . . . (*Sits up.*) . . . there's a dear. I should have discharged him months ago.

EUGENE. Too soft-hearted. (EUGENE *reaches over and takes papers back.*)

MRS. ROGERS. The day before yesterday, in the small hours, he took the bit between his teeth, as it were, and absconded. No goodbyes, nothing of that nature, he just slunk or slank – whichever it is – out.

EUGENE. He never said thanks?

MRS. ROGERS. Not so much as a scribbled note. (*Up from Downstage side moves to green chair.*) I daresay his fountain pen was out of order. But what hurts most, what rankles, what cuts deep, is that he swore to me he had torn up those papers you have in your briefcase.

EUGENE. He never. (*Moves Upstage to front of sofa.*)

MRS. ROGERS. An oath.

EUGENE. Hunh.

MRS. ROGERS. Swore to me. (*Sits in green chair.*)

EUGENE. Hm. (*Pause.*)

MRS. ROGERS. Hm?

EUGENE. I know, I know.

MRS. ROGERS. So what do you think of that?

EUGENE. It's the sort of thing will sicken me for days to come. (*Sits on sofa.*)

MRS. ROGERS. And me.

EUGENE. Yeccch!

MRS. ROGERS. Not that I ever asked him to tear up those ridiculous papers. Why should I? The wrath of Weatherby and Fitch is something I hope I can bear with serenity.

EUGENE. Amen. Tell you something.

MRS. ROGERS. Yes?

EUGENE. If I wanted a job as your au pair man – I mean, just supposing, say I was in Wilson's boots – I wouldn't tell you I'd torn up what's in here.

MRS. ROGERS. No? (*Leaning back in chair.*)

EUGENE. No, I'd do this. (*He takes a paper from his briefcase and tears it in two.*)

MRS. ROGERS. (*Sitting up in chair.*) Oh, my goodness.

EUGENE. In front of your face. (*He tears it into smaller pieces.*)

MRS. ROGERS. But was that important?

EUGENE. This? No.

MRS. ROGERS. (*Piqued.*) I'm so glad.

EUGENE. But this one is. (*He takes another paper and tears it up.*)

MRS. ROGERS. Good heavens.

EUGENE. So is this lot. (*He tears up a batch of papers stapled together.*) It's a pity you haven't a fire going.

MRS. ROGERS. Mr. Hartigan, you mustn't.

EUGENE. A roaring big fire, that'd be the dodge. 'Depart from me, ye accursed, into everlasting flames.'

MRS. ROGERS. Biblical?

EUGENE. We have Catholic connections. Nothing left now but the IBM card. Do you know, your whole life story is on this thing, in terms of apertures.

MRS. ROGERS. Oh, please don't. (*Looks away modestly; he tears card 3 times. Each time* MRS. ROGERS *lets out little groan. He tries a fourth time but can't and throws pieces on sofa. The IBM card, too, is torn up.* EUGENE *smiles at her. A pause.*) Is that all? (EUGENE *holds the briefcase upside down to show that it is empty. He smiles at her expectantly.*) You believe in burning your bridges, don't you?

EUGENE. What?

MRS. ROGERS. I mean, you throw caution to the winds.

EUGENE. Well, you know me: my favourite film has always been 'Beau Jest.'

MRS. ROGERS. (*Acidly.*) You mean 'Geste.'

EUGENE. The one with all the Arabs.

32

MRS. ROGERS. (*Stands and crosses Downstage and curves to right next to desk*.) Why did you tear up those papers?

EUGENE. Why?

MRS. ROGERS. (*At desk, picks up her handkerchief*.) Was it to coerce me into giving you employment?

EUGENE. There's a thing to . . .

MRS. ROGERS. Because now we both know, don't we, that you can never return to your position in the accounts department.

EUGENE. I've no intention of . . .

MRS. ROGERS. If I'm being cynical it isn't without some justification. Weatherby and Fitch have brought much suffering into my life.

EUGENE. We're not all like Wilson, you know.

MRS. ROGERS. Aren't you? (*Moves to Downstage side of her chair and leans on it*.)

EUGENE. Give us a chance.

MRS. ROGERS. For no apparent reason, you . . .

EUGENE. It was on the spur of the moment. Thought I'd try and gratify you in some way, make up to you for all that fellow's lies and deceit and dup . . .

MRS. ROGERS. Duplicity.

EUGENE. (*Annoyed*.) Yes, yes! . . . icity!

MRS. ROGERS. What you mean is, you were being quixotic. (*A pause. He eyes her narrowly. He would like to know what 'Quixotic' means*.) Is that it? Is it?

EUGENE. (*Inscrutably*.) Que sera, sera.

MRS. ROGERS. (*Moves to desk*.) In any event, Mr. Hartigan, you should have known better than to throw yourself upon the mercy of a woman. We have no sense of fair play. (*Moves in circle Downstage of puff and Upstage past green chair*.)

EUGENE. What does that mean?

MRS. ROGERS. We're such ungrateful creatures; we never return favour for favour.

EUGENE. (*Darkly*.) Oh? (*Stands*.)

MRS. ROGERS. And now I really must go and change.

EUGENE. Do you know I could be prosecuted?

MRS. ROGERS. You will excuse me?

EUGENE. (*Angrily*.) Right! (*He starts towards the door*.)

MRS. ROGERS. But don't go. Talk to me. (*Behind sofa*.)

EUGENE. Stay?

MRS. ROGERS. If you want to. (*She crosses to the bedroom door*.)

EUGENE. Look, am I being offered the . . . (MRS. ROGERS *goes*

33

into the bedroom, closing the door firmly. A pause. Then EUGENE *goes to the door and taps on it very softly.*) Hello? Mrs. Rogers? Madam? Can you hear me? (*At door. Silence.*) Well, the rotten old rip. Then he notices the torn documents. *He becomes apprehensive, regretting his action. He kneels, finds some of the pieces of the Hollerith card, and attempts to reassemble them. A piece is missing; he searches for it with mounting concern. The section of wall to which the Kitchener poster is affixed swings outwards, revealing a hatch through which* MRS. ROGERS *can be seen looking into the room.*)

MRS. ROGERS. Big sister is watching you.

EUGENE. (*Guiltily.*) Ha-ha.

MRS. ROGERS. What are you doing?

EUGENE. Nothing.

MRS. ROGERS. Oh?

EUGENE. I was just . . . being quixotic. (*At pouffe, on knees, head covered. He throws away the pieces of the Hollerith card.* MRS. ROGERS *laughs carnivorously.*)

MRS. ROGERS. Who are you, Eugene Hartigan.

EUGENE. Pardon me?

MRS. ROGERS. I said, who are you? Don't be self-conscious. Pretend I can't hear. (*She goes out of sight. Pause. Off:*) Have I asked the unanswerable question?

EUGENE. No, no, I wouldn't say that. Most people couldn't answer you, not in a fit, (*Stands.*) but I can. I could tell (*Up to door one-and-a-half steps.*) you straight off who I am, because . . . Can you hear me? (*On steps.*)

MRS. ROGERS. (*Off.*) No.

EUGENE. Ha-ha. (*Shouting.*) Because I'm in the middle of what you might call a bit of personal retrenchment. (*Moves to Upright of sofa, on same level as pedestal table.* MRS. ROGERS *off, begins humming a waltz tune.*) Who are you Eugene Hartigan? – I can tell you succinctly. Went into the pictures one evening, pitch dark, middle of the program, 'Gunga Din' and 'Captains Courageous.' It was Rudyard Kipling week. The usherettes were all drunk or dying or something, so I felt my way into this row, kept going till I got to an empty seat. Right. I was just taking my coat off when this girl, girl next to me, utter stranger, started interfering with me. True as God. No preliminaries, not even an exploratory nudge. Frontal attack, full throttle, hand up me cardigan. And panting. (MRS. ROGERS *appears at the hatch and directs his attention towards the drinks table.*)

MRS. ROGERS. Do please help yourself.

EUGENE. Ta. *Panting and gnawing at me like Dracula's daughter.*
Well, (*Crosses to bar.*) I'm not one for censuring others. You
won't see me sending for the manager. (*At bar.*) No, if she was
lonely and needed a bit of affection, then she'd come to the
right shop. (*Leaning on railing at window.*) I know how it is.
(*Louder.*) I say I participated. (MRS. ROGERS *is heard humming again.*) And it was great: me dug in there, coorting away
goodo, getting the face bitten off of me, and Spencer Tracy up
on the screen in his fisherman's cap, singing 'Don't Cry, Leetle
Feesh, Don't Cry, Don't Cry.' Great. (*Crosses to metal table
and places drink on table.*) And I wasn't going to ditch her after
the show either; as far as I was concerned, this was only the first
of many such happy evenings. You wait a long time to meet someone who's . . . honest. (*Moves to Downstage Left of pouffe*.)
Then the picture was over and the lights came on and she started
tidying her hair. She looked at me, and do you know what she
said? The flamin' rip, she didn't even say it, either; she roared
at me, top of her voice, she said to me: 'You're not Charlie.'
(*Looks Downstage Left. He rises and goes to pour himself a
drink.*) Stood up in her seat and told me I wasn't Charlie.
Needless to say, what with her screaming and imprecating, I
had to get out of there. Lucky I wasn't arrested. And don't ask
me what happened to Charlie, whoever he was, that's one of the
great unsolved mysteries; he must have gone to the lavatory and
fell in or something, I don't know what happened to him.
(MRS. ROGERS *comes in. She is now wearing a resplendent and
extravagant negligee. She carries a metal wastepaper bin.*) 'Who
are you, Eugene Hartigan?' Well, there's your answer: I'm not
Charlie. (*Pause.*) That's a nice dress you have on.

MRS. ROGERS. Thank you, Eugene! (*Poses on landing in light,
then moves to papers.*)

EUGENE. And your hair! Lovely piece of material. (*Helping pick
up paper. He pinches the fabric, then takes his hand away dif-
fidently. Dolefully*) And I never will be Charlie, either. (MRS.
ROGERS *smiles at him, then kneels and sets about picking up
the torn documents, which she puts into the wastepaper bin.*)
Can I give you a hand?

MRS. ROGERS. (*Sitting on the sofa.*) No, no, it's woman's work.
Women must work and men must weep, that's the new order
of things, wouldn't you say?

EUGENE. (*Picking up papers.*) *I* don't weep.

35

MRS. ROGERS. No, dear.

EUGENE. I mean, don't think I'm feeling sorry for myself on account of that story I told you.

MRS. ROGERS. Story? I'm afraid I was out of earshot.

EUGENE. I shouted it at you.

MRS. ROGERS. Anyway, if the truth were known, this Charlie, as you call him, was probably a very tiresome person: not at all worth envying. (*Rising.*) And, who knows: you may very well have been a refreshing and memorable landmark in the life of that young woman. I'm sure she has never ceased to regret her foolhardiness in crying out as she did.

EUGENE. (*Pleased.*) Now you're coming the hound. (MRS. ROGERS' *hand touches the side of his head.*)

MRS. ROGERS. (*Leaning to him and fondling his hair.*) What a goose you are. Is that the very pinnacle of your ambition: to be owned by some flaccid shopgirl, to become just one more addition to a world of . . . Charlies? (*A pause.* EUGENE *begins to look at her rapaciously. Then he winces as she pulls a hair from his head.*) I found a grey hair.

EUGENE. Well . . . that's better out than in.

MRS. ROGERS. Now go and pour me a drink and no more nonsense, there's a dear. I think I should like a sherry. (EUGENE *goes to the drinks table.* MRS. ROGERS *stands, moves waste bin to Right of pouffe, moves Upstage Right of chaise and then to Downstage side of it.*) Why I said just now that men must weep is because in my youth – which isn't as far off as you might imagine – (EUGENE *arrives with drink.*) men were all such silent, imperturbable creatures. Nowadays they seem to be noisy and lachrymose. The man Wilson was a case in point. (*At Downstage side of chaise.*) He wept incessantly. (*Sitting.*)

EUGENE. (*Upstage side of chaise standing.*) Why was that?

MRS. ROGERS. I'm blest if I know. One wouldn't say boo to him, but he burst into tears. A waste of raw oysters.

EUGENE. (*Slowly takes long look at her legs. She is playing with her toes.*) How did he get so emaciated? (*He brings her a glass of sherry.*)

MRS. ROGERS. Well, it wasn't from physical exertion, I can tell you that much . . . (*He offers glass.*) No, dear; sherry goes in one of the narrow glasses; that one is for whisky.

EUGENE. Is it? (*Without enthusiasm, he offers glass again.*)

MRS. ROGERS. Would you . . .? (*He obediently takes the glass back to the drinks table.*) Possibly he suffered from a kind of glandular deficiency or was small-boned or something. But I should say *you're* a vastly different kettle of fish.

EUGENE. Am I? (*Crosses back to* MRS. ROGERS.)

MRS. ROGERS. Oh, yes. (EUGENE *transfers the contents of the whiskey tumbler to a sherry glass and returns with it to* MRS. ROGERS.)

EUGENE. (*Moving to chaise.*) Do you know, when I came in here I was down in the dumps. Didn't know where me next optimistic (*At chaise.*) thought was coming from.

MRS. ROGERS. But you feel better now?

EUGENE. Massive! You cheered me up.

MRS. ROGERS. I do have that effect on people: upon men, particularly. I'm afraid it's deliberate.

EUGENE. Oh, ah?

MRS. ROGERS. You see . . . (*Carefully.*) just as a gentleman is one who dabbles neither in trade nor in commerce – gentility being in itself a full-time and onerous occupation – so I devote myself passionately to the intricate art of being feminine. (EUGENE *sits on floor at foot of chaise.*) Foolish young girls believe that beauty is all-sufficient, that, possessing it, one can do without such minor attributes as charm, wit, intellect, cunning, elegance and . . . sensuousness, if I might use that word in the nicest possible connotation.

EUGENE. Oh, sure.

MRS. ROGERS. But *I* was born cautious. (*Sits up on Downstage side of chaise.*) I looked in my glass one day and said to myself: 'Lilith, my girl . . .' Lilith was one of my two pet names as a child, Lilith and Lilibeth, for Elizabeth, pet names – 'Lilith, my girl, the time comes when the bloom goes off the tenderest peach; (MRS. ROGERS *rises and moves Upstage around green chair and behind sofa.*) when flesh begins to spread outwards and down, like a house settling comfortably into its foundations; when the first lines appear, as though one had blundered into a cobweb.' It happens. Not to me, thank God: not yet, at any rate; not to me. But it does, I believe, happen. And I resolved, as I looked at my young, quite perfect self in that glass, that I would turn time into an object of ridicule. I would become so accomplished, so magnificently feminine, (MRS. ROGERS *picks up picture of little girl from pedestal table and moves Downstage Right of pouffe. She puts picture on pouffe.*) as to make beauty seem dull and unnecessary by comparison: a toy for children. The problem, as I discovered, lay in teaching oneself the finer distinctions: how, for example, to acquire the virtues of a woman, but not the virtuousness; how to possess (MRS. ROGERS *takes 2 steps to Stage Right*.) the feminine vices, as opposed to female viciousness. It was hard work, (MRS. ROGERS *crosses to Upstage of chaise and moves to Downstage side*.) but I succeeded brilliantly. I learned to become an emotional quick-change artist: (MRS. ROGERS *sits again, pats chaise and has* EUGENE *sit next to her*.) to be maternal and feline almost in the same breath; to calm the boisterous, cheer up the dejected, and become femme fatale or tender comrade at the drop of a hint. I am prepared to join in a bacchanalia or fall into a corpse-like silence, whichever you prefer; to be meek or imperious, wilful or winsome; an infinity of different women in the course of an evening, and each one a compendium of perfection. I have, to be sure, many other (*Rubbing her glass up and down; she stops rubbing*.) accomplishments, which our brief acquaintance precludes me from mentioning; but I am never, never petulant, jealous, ill-tempered or possessive. You see: I aim to please. (*A pause*.) Well?

EUGENE. I wish there was more like you.

MRS. ROGERS. (*Modestly*) It's my life's work. Do you have a match?

EUGENE. Mm. (MRS. ROGERS *gets up, moves to metal table, puts drink on it and gets waste bin. He produces a box of matches.* MRS. ROGERS *takes a piece of paper from the metal bin and holds it out to be lit.* EUGENE *pulls match away from paper*.) What's that for?

MRS. ROGERS. You said what a pity it was I didn't have a fire going.

EUGENE. When?

MRS. ROGERS. Just now, when you tore up those documents. A big, roaring fire, you said. Don't you *want* to burn them?

EUGENE. (*Weakly*.) Yes.

MRS. ROGERS. Well, then! (*As he hesitates*.) After much thought, I have decided to engage you as our au pair man on a probationary basis. Does that suit you?

EUGENE. Lovely!

MRS. ROGERS. Good. We'll see how we get on, shall we?

EUGENE. Ha-ha. (*He strikes a match and sets the piece of paper alight.* MRS. ROGERS *drops it into the metal bin. A blaze starts.* MRS. ROGERS *moves 3 steps Upstage with waste bin and puts it on floor*.)

MRS. ROGERS. And now, if you like you can toast the Royal Family.

EUGENE. (*Jumps and gets drinks off metal table.*) Yes. Yes, I don't mind. Right, then. We're off. (*He lifts his glass.*) Here's to me.

MRS. ROGERS. To you?

EUGENE. Since I'm going to be here for a while, I thought I'd start at the bottom, like, and work my way up.

MRS. ROGERS. What a good idea. Dear Eugene . . . cheers! (MRS. ROGERS *walks to door of bedroom, gives* EUGENE *a look and goes into bedroom.* EUGENE *runs up bedroom steps.*)

CURTAIN

ACT TWO

Scene 1

EUGENE *is alone and reads aloud from a book. His diction is much improved, although he makes the occasional mistake in pronunciation. His clothes are new and expensive.*

EUGENE. (*Reclining on chaise.*) 'If you will not take my advice and persist in thinking a commerce with sex inevitable, then I repeat my former advice (*Up and moves Upstage of red chair.*) that in all your amours you should prefer old women to young ones. You call this a paradox and demand my reasons. They are these . . .' (MRS. ROGERS *comes in from bedroom and sits at a table which has been set for tea.*)

MRS. ROGERS. One.

EUGENE. (*From behind couch.*) 'Because since they have more knowledge of the world and their minds are stored with observations, the conversation of old women is more improving and more lastingly agreeable.'

MRS. ROGERS. Two. (*She begins to pour tea.*)

EUGENE. 'Because when women cease to be handsome they study to be good. To maintain their influence over men they supplant the diminution of beauty by an augmentation of utility. They learn to do a thousand services, small and great, and are the most tender and useful of friends when you are sick.' (MRS. ROGERS *sits at tea table. As she sips tea, holds up three fingers.* EUGENE *moves to Upstage Left of green chair.*) 'Three. Because there is no hazard of children, which, irregularly produced, may be attended with much inconvenience.'

MRS. ROGERS. Four.

EUGENE. (*As* MRS. ROGERS *moves to* EUGENE *with tea.*) 'Because in every animal that walks upright the deficiency of fluids that fill the muscles appears first in the highest part. The face first grows lank and wrinkled, then the neck, then the breast and arms; the lower parts continuing to the last as plump as ever; (*Gets tea from* MRS. ROGERS.) so, covering all above with a

40

basket, it is impossible of two women to tell an old one from a young one. And, as in the dark all cats are grey, the pleasure of corporal enjoyment with an old woman is at least equal and frequently superior, every knack being, by practice, capable of improvement.' (MRS. ROGERS *brings him a cup of tea and smiles encouraging.*)

MRS. ROGERS. (*Moving back to tea table.*) Five.

EUGENE. 'Because the sin is less. The debauching of a virgin may be her ruin and make her life unhappy.'

MRS. ROGERS. (*Musically.*) And six!

EUGENE. 'Because the compunction is less. The having made a young girl miserable may give you frequently bitter reflection: none of which can attend the making of an old woman happy. Seventh, and lastly . . .'

MRS. ROGERS. '. . . an old woman is so grateful.' That passage never fails to move me, somehow.

EUGENE. Was I all right? (*Puts book on metal table.*)

MRS. ROGERS. You read it beautifully. But what a nice man that Benjamin Franklin must have been. I mean, for a colonist. (EUGENE *sits and proffers a plate to* MRS. ROGERS.) So wise and compassionate.

EUGENE. Would you like a crumpet?

MRS. ROGERS. Oh rare Ben Franklin! But then of course his father was English. That's a muffin, dear: crumpets are what we had yesterday. Came from Banbury. (*Sits in her chair.*)

EUGENE. The crumpets?

MRS. ROGERS. No, darling: you're thinking of Banbury cakes, which have currants in them. Crumpets don't come from anywhere in particular. They are what is known as ubiquitous.

EUGENE. How about muffins?

MRS. ROGERS. The same.

EUGENE. (*Darkly.*) Then what came from Banbury?

MRS. ROGERS. Benjamin Franklin's father. I told you, but you weren't paying attention. His name was Josiah and he hailed from Banbury.

EUGENE. (*Surly.*) Do you want a muffin? (*Standing over her Upstage Left of chair with muffin plate, he shoves it at her.*)

MRS. ROGERS. How nice. So if anyone ever asks you what Banbury is famous for, you can tell them currant cakes and Josiah Franklin.

EUGENE. Not to mention cock horses. (*Sits on sofa.*)

MRS. ROGERS. Oh?

41

EUGENE. I suppose it's an obsolete word for stallions. There's this poem, you see –

MRS. ROGERS. Ah, the nursery rhyme!

EUGENE. First poem I ever learned. 'Ride a cock horse to Banbury Cross, to see a fine lady upon a –'

MRS. ROGERS. This will interest you. Did you know, are you aware, that the fine lady really existed? . . . that she was, in fact, none other than the first Elizabeth?

EUGENE. I never knew that.

MRS. ROGERS. The Virgin Queen.

EUGENE. To coin a phrase.

MRS. ROGERS. She passed through Banbury one day on a white charger, and people flocked to see her. They came from farm and hamlet, by oxcart and in coaches, on foot and on –

EUGENE. . . . cock horses.

MRS. ROGERS. Yes. And to commemorate the occasion they took an old nursery rhyme and put new words to it.

EUGENE. Get away.

MRS. ROGERS. 'Rings on her fingers and bells on her toes . . .'
(*Clock plays 'Land of Hope and Glory' chiming the ¼ hour.*)

EUGENE. 'And she shall have music where –'

MRS. ROGERS. (*Smiling; softly.*) Quite. (*Stands.*) Just so. More tea? (*Moves to tea table.*)

EUGENE. Ta. (*Amending.*) Thank you.

MRS. ROGERS. The original rhyme was quite pretty too. (*At tea table, quoting.*)
'Ride a cock horse to Banbury Cross,
To buy little Johnny a galloping horse;
It trots behind and it ambles before,
And Johnny shall ride till he can ride . . . no more.'
(*A pause.*)

EUGENE. (*Nervously.*) How do they think them up?

MRS. ROGERS. Don't you find it all fascinating?

EUGENE. Oh, sure. Except . . .

MRS. ROGERS. Except what? (*Crosses to Upstage of tea tray,* EUGENE *still sitting on couch.*)

EUGENE. Well, nursery rhymes and obscure cakes, they're not what you might call indispensable information. I mean, it's not as if they'll come in handy.

MRS. ROGERS. Handy?

EUGENE. Of practical use.

MRS. ROGERS. I wasn't aware that you had leanings towards

technical education. Shall we talk about fretwork instead?

EUGENE. There's no need to get rattled.

MRS. ROGERS. Or cobbling, perhaps.

EUGENE. Look . . .

MRS. ROGERS. Or fellmongering.

EUGENE. There's no reason for a frenzy. (*Stands.*) All that stuff about buns and Banbury, it held me riveted. I had to ask meself: can such things be?

MRS. ROGERS. Now you're being insincere. (*Moves Upstage Right to glass table.*)

EUGENE. I'm not: I was transfixed. I've got years of ignorance to make up for. I've got to learn things in a hurry.

MRS. ROGERS. What sort of things?

EUGENE. Well . . . (*Standing in front of couch.*)

MRS. ROGERS. For example?

EUGENE. Aids to conversation.

MRS. ROGERS. Such as?

EUGENE. Famous sayings.

MRS. ROGERS. Ah.

EUGENE. Thoughts of great thinkers. Funny definitions out of digests. Pithy precepts. The sort of stuff that puts you in the social swim.

MRS. ROGERS. You could remain silent.

EUGENE. Say nothing?

MRS. ROGERS. Cultivate a taciturn facade.

EUGENE. I'd be branded as a thick.

MRS ROGERS No. Nowadays conversation is the triumph of one interruption over another. (*Cross to Stage Left behind sofa.*) Better to stay silent, Eugene, and forget about pithy precepts.

EUGENE. What if I'm asked something?

MRS. ROGERS. (*Stage Right of sofa.*) In that case, barely open your mouth and allow polite but unintelligible sounds emerge: sounds which will necessarily differ in timbre according to disposition, diet and the time of day. (*Moving to tea tray.*) Just now I have been endeavouring to teach you how to make tea-time noises . . .

EUGENE. I see.

MRS. ROGERS. . . . not, I fear, with success. (*Removes tea tray to Crystal Palace.*)

EUGENE. I thought I kept my end up.

MRS. ROGERS. Tea-time noises . . . clear and tiny like Swiss cowbells. Kept your what up?

EUGENE. My end, conversationally.

MRS. ROGERS. You expressed dissatisfaction . . .

EUGENE. Don't get huffy.

MRS. ROGERS. Said you preferred more functional topics.

EUGENE. It's all right for you: you have it made; you can sit here in polite grandeur eating (MRS. ROGERS *moves to her chair and sits*.) muffins til the cows come home. But I've got to equip myself for the world outside.

MRS. ROGERS. (*Alarmed*.) Out there?

EUGENE. Because –

MRS. ROGERS. (*The tiniest hint of terror*.) That place?

EUGENE. Because I've got to look to the future. This job won't last forever.

MRS. ROGERS. This position.

EUGENE. (*Crosses Upstage Left towards door*.) Position. Once your husband's stamps are sorted –

MRS. ROGERS. Won't last? Why shouldn't it last, if you go on being satisfactory, if you are honest, industrious, energetic? (*Stands*.) You don't want to go out there. Why, only this morning I wrote a glowing account of you to my husband. (*Moves over to him, next to glass table*.)

EUGENE. Did you?

MRS. ROGERS. Don't you remember: I borrowed your fountain pen. (EUGENE *nods, yawning hugely*.) I told him how tireless you are, and how pleased I have been.

EUGENE. It's a question of prospects . . .

MRS. ROGERS. The prospects are infinite.

EUGENE. Here?

MRS. ROGERS. (*Moving Stage Right behind big table*.) Limitless. Don't you enjoy your work? Aren't you well looked after?

EUGENE. Sure. I –

MRS. ROGERS. Aylesbury duckling, Dover sole, potatoes from Norfolk, Scotch steaks . . .

EUGENE. I'm spoiled rotten.

MRS. ROGERS. Not to mention Welsh rarebits in the wee small hours.

EUGENE. It's all lovely . . . (MRS. ROGERS *Stage Left of pedestal table,* EUGENE *next to her*.)

MRS. ROGERS. And isn't your room comfortable? (*She indicates the dark area behind the wall unit*.) . . . with that chic little canopy over your bed to catch any falling plaster. Not a pretty room, but snug.

EUGENE. Very homey . . .

MRS. ROGERS. And what's a collapsed ceiling between friends?

EUGENE. Eyes down for a full house.

MRS. ROGERS. (*Crossing to her chair.*) So we'll have no more talk about leaving. After all, what's out there for anyone?

EUGENE. You can't stay indoors all your life.

MRS. ROGERS. (*Coldly.*) No?

EUGENE. (*Moves Downstage Centre of big table.*) I mean –

MRS. ROGERS. Have you been in the High Street lately? Have you seen them . . . the people who now live in, who infest, this Royal Borough? Foreign persons; (*Sits.*) dusky gentlemen; Americans whose cameras hang in front of them like twentieth-century cod-pieces . . . somehow it always seems to me that telephoto lenses must be the quintessence of boastfulness. And the people who were once one's friends: (EUGENE *lifts lid of music box.*) nowadays they eat paté maison and drink Portuguese rosé and go to parties where to have congress with someone of the opposite sex – or, indeed, of one's own sex – is as obligatory as arriving properly dressed once used to be. They wear ragged clothes on Sunday; (EUGENE *sits in side chair.*) they are compassionate towards criminals, perverts and foreigners, but not towards each other; and they blame themselves shrilly and with relish for what happened in Buchenwald and other such tiresome places abroad. Why this should be, I'm sure I don't know. And they play a strange game; they pretend that everyone is as good as everyone else, each unto the other; and so there are no special people any more, no one is out of the ordinary or above the herd. (EUGENE *sits on chaise.*) This is what they pretend to believe, and they frown as they make love, and are self-effacing to the point (EUGENE *crosses to desk and sits.*) of facelessness. Is that the place you want to live in?

EUGENE. Where else is there?

MRS. ROGERS. Here. (*A pause. A creaking noise is heard from the wall unit, and a few flakes of plaster flutter down.* EUGENE *looks up towards the ceiling.*)

EUGENE. (*Nodding appreciatively.*) Snug.

MRS. ROGERS. (*Puts on hat she has been holding.*) Nowadays one daren't go out on the streets alone. They teem with incivility. It was once so different. Nice, friendly, respectful people. They came out on bank holidays, and what a happy time they had, bless them, in the parks and on pleasure steamers. In those days the younger generation had little or no money (MRS. ROGERS

45

moves to Upstage of desk where albums are, shows him pictures.) to spend, so the people one saw out and about were all middle-aged and knew how to behave themselves. My family, you know, has always had a great affection for the ordinary people, Daddy . . . my father, to the day of his death remembered how once during the Great War he saw a number of Tommies bathing together and how pleasantly surprised he was to see the whiteness of their skins. It warmed, so he said, the cockles of his heart. And later in India when he was obliged to crucify some natives who had behaved rather badly, he never once lost the common touch. As the nails were being hammered in, he walked down the line of crosses and made an austere little speech; but all the time with a twinkle in his eye and the occasional chuckle, his middle finger entwined in his moustache . . . so. They all adored him. That kind of gentleness isn't to be found any more. (*A pause. She looks at* EUGENE, *then at the room.*) Yes, it is, as you say, snug. A world is none the worse for being a small one.

EUGENE. I thought . . . (*He falters.*)

MRS. ROGERS. What?

EUGENE. All the lessons you've been giving me . . .

MRS. ROGERS. Not lessons: hints, pointers. (*Turns Upstage, puts hat on stool.*)

EUGENE. The suit of clothes and the nail file and the bottle of Sebbix.

MRS. ROGERS. What about them?

EUGENE. I thought it was to help me do well for myself.

MRS. ROGERS. To do well? (*Crossing to Centre just Down Stage Right of pouffe.*)

EUGENE. Out there.

MRS. ROGERS. Good God, no.

EUGENE. (*A quaver.*) No?

MRS. ROGERS. What an insensate idea.

EUGENE. Is it?

MRS. ROGERS. Out there?

EUGENE. I thought –

MRS. ROGERS. Do you take me for a technical educationalist? Art . . . true art has no purpose except to please the senses. If I help you in small ways it is because I have, always have had, a passion for . . . silk purses. (*She touches his ear with the tips of two fingers.*)

EUGENE. Aha?

46

MRS. ROGERS. Soft, silky purses.

EUGENE. Yah. (*He moves away from her, disturbed. Her fingers remain outstretched to where his ear was a moment ago.*) I'm a bit disappointed. If I'd known that at the outset I'd –

MRS. ROGERS. (*Wincing.*) Oooh.

EUGENE. What's up?

MRS. ROGERS. A twinge of some sort. I think I must have a pustule.

EUGENE. On your finger? (*She regards her outstretched finger, then turns it inwards so that it touches her breast.*)

MRS. ROGERS. Here.

EUGENE. That's a . . . sore spot.

MRS. ROGERS. I don't mind the discomfort, but it could affect what I was planning to wear for the evening. In a woman, unsightliness is next to ungodliness. Does it show?

EUGENE. No.

MRS. ROGERS. You haven't looked.

EUGENE. Never mind your pustule for a minute. If I'd known from the beginning –

MRS. ROGERS. I asked you does it show?

EUGENE. Not from here.

MRS. ROGERS. You still aren't looking.

EUGENE. I'm staring right at you.

MRS. ROGERS. Will it show later? (*Sits on foot of chaise. A pause.* EUGENE *glares. He moves to her.*)

EUGENE. 'Scuse me. (*He hooks a finger in the front of her dress and poors down it.*)

MRS. ROGERS. Well? Watchman, what of the night?

EUGENE. I can't see a jot.

MRS. ROGERS. It stings . . . here.

EUGENE. I'm in me own light, I could do with a flashlamp. Move a bit.

MRS. ROGERS. They say there's a new kind of fountain pen with a flashlight incorporated. One can see what one is –

EUGENE. Breathe in. Ah, now I can – (*He straightens up abruptly.*)

MRS. ROGERS. Yes?

EUGENE. All clear. (*Crosses to desk.*)

MRS. ROGERS. Nothing at all?

EUGENE. You're grand. Swinging.

MRS. ROGERS. Then it must be growing pains. Thank you, Eugene: you're a treasure. (*He scowls.*) Don't look so glum.

EUGENE. It's a hell of a let-down. I thought you were training me so as I could leave here and get a job and be a credit to you.

MRS. ROGERS. Bless your heart.

EUGENE. But no such thing. I'm being cultivated for . . . for –

MRS. ROGERS. Domestic consumption, dear, and to hell with exports.

EUGENE. I feel like the prisoner of the Vatican.

MRS. ROGERS. A prisoner?

EUGENE. What else?

MRS. ROGERS. Your Papist imagination is running rampant. A prisoner? Is that door ever locked. Don't you go out every day on errands and to the cinema on Thursdays? Running like a demented stag towards Swedish subtitles and frontal nudity. All the silicone a young man. (*Stands.*) could ask for. Is that what you call imprisonment?

EUGENE. I don't go to the pictures . . . I'm *let* go to the pictures.

MRS. ROGERS. Now you're talking like a child or a husband. (*Moves in curve Downstage and up around chaise.*)

EUGENE. You want me to stay here forever.

MRS. ROGERS. Do I?

EUGENE. Yes, you said so. You said –

MRS. ROGERS. No, no, no, no . . . not forever: no such thing. Indefinitely. I said indefinitely. There *is* a difference. (*Down Left of green chair.*)

EUGENE. Is there?

MRS. ROGERS. But of course you must leave whenever it suits you. Go this instant if you have a mind to. Run! Fly! Don't wait to change back into the clothes you came in: the ogress might gobble you up, cook you in an Anglo-Irish stew.

EUGENE. I can't change into the clothes I came in. You gave them to the ragman.

MRS. ROGERS. Did I? So I did. (EUGENE *sits at desk.*) Naturally, I should be sorry to see you scatter my poor pearls before the swine you seem determined to consort with . . . and even sorrier (MRS. ROGERS *moves to Stage Right to pedestal table.*) if you were to leave here . . . without the final all-important veneer. I am a craftswoman (*Picks up letter tray.*) in my way: I take a stupid pride in my little achievements, (EUGENE *stands.*)

EUGENE. I didn't intend to rush off.

MRS. ROGERS. Weren't you? Oh, good.

EUGENE. All I'm saying is that sooner or later –

MRS. ROGERS. As you wish.

EUGENE. So long as it's understood . . .? (MRS. ROGERS *does not reply. She moves to desk, sits.* EUGENE *moves to couch, sits.*) I have ignoble ambitions, that's my trouble, and you're right to be narked. Know what I want? You'll laugh. I want to take out tawny women in an E-type, true as God, screeching to an impudent standstill . . . throw an oblong chip to the croupier and ask a waiter: 'How are the aubergines today, and I shall know if you're lying.' Did you ever see those advertisements for hair cream? That's the life. (EUGENE *stands and crosses Down Right of pouffe.*) Me left hand paralyzed with the weight of a wrist watch that does everything except sing 'Ave Maria.' God, just once to arrive at a hooly crisp as lettuce and taxi-fresh, instead of limping up the front steps with me breath in me fist.

MRS. ROGERS. My breath in my fist.

EUGENE. Sure. Walk in very suave-like. (*Moves two steps to Right.*) 'Don't be an ass, Michael: glad I could make it.' Halfway through the first vodka, over she comes, this panther of woman in depraved black . . . what's the word? . . . undulating (*Moves to chaise, sits.*) towards me. The flash of bosom at me elbow. Give her a careless nod: she'll keep, the job is right, there when wanted, carry on with the repartee. 'You say David is still living with his mother? Dear me, I thought that was all off.' (*He laughs.*) Sharp as a tack. (*Stands and moves to* MRS. ROGERS *at desk.*) Make me maximum impact, then a kind word to the bosom: 'Let's go, darling; your place or mine?' Then, back at the pad, the clash of intellects. 'Sorry, darling. (*Circling desk.*) I don't have a bidet, it's against my religion. You'll just have to do handsprings under the shower.' (*He cackles to himself, then looks at* MRS. ROGERS *and reddens. Crosses to front of pouffe.*) I suppose you think I'm awful.

MRS. ROGERS. I do, rather.

EUGENE. A bit frivolous.

MRS. ROGERS. A bit.

EUGENE. Don't be too sure. It's not all fun and frolics. Tell you: I have one serious ambition.

MRS. ROGERS. Oh?

EUGENE. A little dream. No doubt it'll amuse you, put you in kinks; but still. I want to go home one day. Step off the mailboat in a decent suit, clean shirt, me shoes polished, a few quid in me pocket . . . my own man, quiet self-assurance. Catch the 45A up to our house, let myself in with this key. My mom will be there, just back from early Mass, (*Standing Stage left of* MRS. ROGERS.) cups on the table. She won't know me for a minute, think I'm a robber. Then it'll come to her . . . and the old bitch will drop down dead from rage. (*A pause.*)

MRS. ROGERS. I never knew you had such a serious side.

EUGENE. Well, you do now.

MRS. ROGERS. I'm touched. And you must leave here whenever you like. Possessiveness is not in my nature.

EUGENE. I know that.

MRS. ROGERS. And you shall go home some day: I promise.

EUGENE. I'm a terrible pup.

MRS. ROGERS. No, you aren't.

EUGENE. But I try. I work hard. You want to hear something nice?

MRS. ROGERS. Tell.

EUGENE. Yesterday a bus conductress called me 'sir.'

MRS. ROGERS. Well, now!

EUGENE. I jumped on, rang the old bell, and she said, 'Passengers aren't allowed to give the starting signal, sir.'

MRS. ROGERS. Sir!

EUGENE. Yep.

MRS. ROGERS. Was she coloured?

EUGENE. Oh, no: that wouldn't count. Welsh.

MRS. ROGERS. But how splendid. My, we are making progress, leaps and bounds. (*A pause.*) What were you doing on a bus?

EUGENE. Who, me? (*Retreats to Stage Right of green chair.*)

MRS. ROGERS. Where were you going?

EUGENE. Me?

MRS. ROGERS. You're a close one, aren't you? Bus rides.

EUGENE. (*Expansively.*) We-ll . . .

MRS. ROGERS. Surreptitious bus rides. Where to?

EUGENE. Why?

MRS. ROGERS. You were supposed to post my letters.

EUGENE. (*Moves 2 steps to Centre.*) I did. I sent them from Putney. Then I –

MRS. ROGERS. My God, oh my God, a Putney postmark on my correspondence. Oh you wretch, wait until my husband sees that, he'll think I've moved there! But go on. And then you . . .? And then you did what (*Stands.*) in Putney after your carnal interlude with that Welsh trollop?

EUGENE. Eh?

MRS. ROGERS. That whore from Swansea. She didn't call you 'sir' for nothing.

EUGENE. She's not a whore.

50

MRS. ROGERS. (*Marching to* EUGENE; EUGENE *backing away*.) And don't lie to me. I wasn't born yesterday.

EUGENE. I know you weren't.

MRS. ROGERS. (*Pulls paper opener on him, backs him to curved area*.) I shall remember that, Eugene. What did you do in Putney?

EUGENE. Nothing.

MRS. ROGERS. I'm sure!

EUGENE. I looked at the swans.

MRS. ROGERS. The swans?

EUGENE. Yes! (*A pause*.) I leaned on the bridge at Putney and I –

MRS. ROGERS. Pervert! (*A pause*.)

EUGENE. I'd better do a bit of work. (*Moves to desk, pulls back chair and*:)

MRS. ROGERS. (MRS. ROGERS *ignores him, falling into*:) Cygnet-watcher! An Aberystwyth putain would be more than enough for most people, thank you very much, but not you. Royal swans, no less. (*Moves to Upstage end of desk as*:) If I were a possessive woman, you'd get what-for, my lad: I hope you know that. Work, then: go and work. (*She tosses letter opener onto desk, then circles Upstage behind her chair and then behind pedestal table to the magazine on Stage Right side of table and looks at one. The clock chimes the half hour. Airily*.) Three hours to dinner. I think I shall write a chatty letter to my husband, all about shoes and ships and Putney Bridge, (MRS. ROGERS *moves to Stage Right side of* EUGENE *who is now writing away like mad with his pen*.) and cabbages and swans. Hm? Shall I? (*A pause*. EUGENE *does not reply*.) I shall need a pen. I say, I shall need something to write with. Will you lend me yours, Eugene? (*He looks at her*.) Your fountain pen.

EUGENE. Again?

MRS. ROGERS. Yes.

EUGENE. You had it this morning.

MRS. ROGERS. And I want it now. Give it to me.

EUGENE. No.

MRS. ROGERS. No?

EUGENE. You'll break the nib. Why don't you buy your own pen?

MRS. ROGERS. Don't be absurd.

EUGENE. People shouldn't borrow other people's pens. That's how they get ruined. You've had it so often I can't write with it anymore. (MRS. ROGERS *tries* EUGENE *from the Upstage side*.)

MRS. ROGERS. Probably you've forgotten to fill it. Give me the pen, Eugene. Don't be miserly.

EUGENE. No.

MRS. ROGERS. (*Tries Downstage side of* EUGENE.) You know I write to my husband every day.

EUGENE. Why don't you wire him?

MRS. ROGERS. (*Embarrassing* EUGENE.) Be nice. Be a good boy. How would you like an increase in pocket-money?

EUGENE. It's the only pen I've got.

MRS. ROGERS. You'll get it back. Please?

EUGENE. No.

MRS. ROGERS. Pretty please?

EUGENE. No.

MRS. ROGERS. Aren't you disobliging! (*She pats him on the back.*) Very well, then. Keep it . . . if you can! (*She bites his ear, takes pen and runs straight Upstage to table next to book case, puts pen in box, locks box and runs up 3 steps.*)

EUGENE. Give it back. You break that nib, and – (*Following* MRS. ROGERS. *Upstage.*) Me pen. Me good pen.

MRS. ROGERS. If you want the key, Eugene – (*Drops key down her decolletage.*)

EUGENE. I don't want it that bad – (*He grabs the box, runs Downstage to desk and tries forcing lid with letter opener on desk.*)

MRS. ROGERS. (*Follows.*) Don't you dare force that lid. Leave it alone. If you break that – (*An avalanche of fountain pens pour out as the lock breaks. As* EUGENE *looks at* MRS. ROGERS:)

CURTAIN

ACT TWO

Scene 2

The room is dark. EUGENE *opens the front door and enters stealthily and drunkenly.*

EUGENE. Hey-up. First things first. Where's the room? (*He strikes a match, sees the room and is gladdened by the discovery.*) Goodo. (*The clock chimes the half-hour with the first two lines of 'Land of Hope and Glory.'*) Go to bed. Done enough damage for one night. Down the M.1 to Bedfordshire. Zoom. Zoom. Hand-brake off and . . . (*He hurtles himself across the room. The match goes out. He trips over a chair.*) Eugene. Speak to me, are you hurt? Don't know: the sun is warm on my hands, but the room is dark. And I can't feel my legs. Doctor: my legs, what about my legs? (*Doctor's voice.*) Your legs? I think they're lovely. (*He crawls on all fours to a table and switches on a lamp.*) No, you're a good lad. Oh, dear God, I'm so drunk. Oh, lovely girl in the pictures, please help me, please have pity. I'm sorry to wake you up at this hour, with Charlie there asleep next to you, great big warm stupid lump. But I've got to have someone to talk to, and there's only you. Oh, God, you're up there all right, you old divil, you exist. This loneliness couldn't happen by accident. It's hand-made. Lovely girl in the pictures, sit here. (EUGENE *sets puff right and sits on floor next to it.*) I won't make a pass . . . just want someone to . . . Please? (*He pats the floor beside him. He takes out a coin and elaborately prepares to palm it. The coin flips out of his fingers and rolls away. He looks futilely for the coin, then his shoulders convulse in a great shuddering sob.*) I love . . . (*But there is no object for the verb.*) Oh, God. I . . . love . . . (*Pause. From her bedroom,* MRS. ROGERS *cries out, paralyzing* EUGENE *with terror.*)

MRS. ROGERS. (*Off.*) My lord Cecil!

EUGENE. Jesus, she's up.

MRS. ROGERS. (*Off.*) My lord Burleigh, my lord Essex!

EUGENE. Don't let her be up, don't let her be up.

MRS. ROGERS. (*Off.*) All my possessions for a moment of time!

EUGENE Nightmares. Thank you, God . . . good old God.

MRS. ROGERS. (*Off.*) How is the empire?

EUGENE. It's swinging. Now shaddup. (*He frenziedly pulls off his shoes, then – through the following – removes his jacket and throws it on the floor, loosens his tie, pulls out his shirt-tails and unfastens one or two trouser buttons.*) Go to bed, go to bed, or you're destroyed. (*Moving Upstage to bookshelf table. To his invisible companion.*) Sorry about this. Tell you something. That room in there, my room . . . well, theorect . . theoretic'ly – good man! – it can only be reached by going thataway . . . (*He indicates the door to* MRS. ROGERS' *room.*) through the Chilicoot Pass, Gestapo headquarters, the Twilight Zone . . . the gap of danger. (EUGENE *turns out light.*) Beyond that point, there be dragons. But the Sundance Kid has blazed a new trail. This'll kill you. (*Bumps into bookcase. He winks, brings over a table to the wall unit, stands on it and removes one of the shelves.*) Take down two little shelves and there's room for any army. (*Chuckling.*) I'm cute as a hawk. A terrible hook and a foxy fella. (*Pleased with himself, he embarks on a pas seul on the table top.*)

    'My Rio
      Rio by the sea-o,
      Flying down to Rio
      Where there's rhythm and rhyme.
      Hey, feller,
      Twirl that old propeller,
      Got to get to Rio
      And we've got to make time.'

Great old picture, that All them girls up on the aeroplane.

    'You'll love it,
      Soaring high above it,
      Looking down on Rio
      From a heaven of blue.
      Hey, Rio –'

As EUGENE *dances, holding the shelf over his head with both hands and swinging it in an arc from side to side, his trousers slowly descend. The Kitchener poster shoots up and* MRS. ROGERS *looks into the room.*)

MRS. ROGERS. Who's there?

EUGENE. Oh, God, God. (MRS. ROGERS *disappears from the hatch.* EUGENE *tries to dive headfirst through the wall unit, but as only one shelf has been removed he sticks halfway through, his trousers around his ankles.* MRS. ROGERS *comes in and switches on the lights.*)

MRS. ROGERS. What aberration is this? Are you Eugene?

EUGENE. (*Struggling.*) Who – me?

MRS. ROGERS. Have the kindness to get out of my wall unit at once.

EUGENE. Yes, yes. I'm coming. (*He endeavours to squeeze back into the living room. Trips shelf with vase, boxes over* EUGENE'S *head.*)

MRS. ROGERS. Gently, gently. Do you want to pull the house down about my ears? Oh, you fool, don't thresh about so. Are you out?

EUGENE. (*Slithering to the floor.*) Yes. Out.

MRS. ROGERS. Stand up. Adjust your dress. (*Coming down steps.*)

EUGENE. Pardon? (*Stands Stage Right of red chair.*)

MRS. ROGERS. Your nether garments.

EUGENE. (*Realizing and pulling up his trousers.*) Oh, God: it's terrible. (*Coming Downstage Left of pouffe.*)

MRS. ROGERS. (*Pointing.*) Is that yours? (*Moving Downstage to between her chair and couch.* EUGENE *sees that his fountain pen has fallen on the floor. He retrieves it hastily.*)

EUGENE. Terrible, terrible. Oh, je suis mortifé. (EUGENE *picks up pen and gets it caught in his zipper.*)

MRS. ROGERS. Stand up straight. Fasten your front. Put away that fountain pen. Now what were you doing in my wall unit? (MRS. ROGERS *moves three feet more Downstage.*)

EUGENE. Nothing.

MRS. ROGERS. Don't lie. You're drunk. You were trying to destroy it in a drunken frenzy.

EUGENE. No such thing.

MRS. ROGERS. What, then?

EUGENE. What what?

MRS. ROGERS. Why were you tampering with it?

EUGENE. I was trying to get to me bed.

MRS. ROGERS. *My* bed.

EUGENE. No, mine. Just taking a shortcut.

MRS. ROGERS. Through there?

EUGENE. Didn't want to wake you.

MRS. ROGERS. I doubt if I can make much impression on you in your deplorable condition, but I shall try. You must never do that again.

EUGENE. Hokay. (*Both are Upstage of red chair,* MRS. ROGERS *to Right,* EUGENE *the left.*)

MRS. ROGERS. I have told you that the wall which was once there collapsed and fell. Only my poor wall unit now saves us from obliteration. If it should once give way, we – Look! (EUGENE *looks towards the ceiling. A few flakes of plaster flutter down, very fast, one after the other.*)

EUGENE. Jingle bells.

MRS. ROGERS. You see what you've done?

EUGENE. Very sorry.

MRS. ROGERS. (*Moving to Left and picking up some of the garbage.*) A house must have walls; without them, we should all live in one vast communal enclosure: an impossible arrangement, insanitary andunsavoury. One of the reasons I am fond of God is because in His Father's house there are so many mansions. He knows the necessity for segregation, and I consider it very proper of Him.

EUGENE. I'd love a drink.

MRS. ROGERS. People like you have no regard for the sanctity of walls.

EUGENE. I have, I have.

MRS. ROGERS. Then come through my room in future. Don't be afraid of waking me up. I shan't mind. (*Crossing Stage Left to* EUGENE *who is just Downstage of red chair.*)

EUGENE. Sure?

MRS. ROGERS. (*Fondly.*) Silly boy. Just keep away from my wall unit, you vandal, you visigoth. No more shortcuts . . . (*Pointing.*) that's the way. (MRS. ROGERS *moves to bar.* EUGENE *Up two steps to bedroom.*)

EUGENE. Goo'night, so. (*He starts towards the door.*)

MRS. ROGERS. Did you say you would like a drink? (*At bar.*)

EUGENE. (*Halting.*) Maybe it's a bit late.

MRS. ROGERS. Let me get it for you.

EUGENE. (*Aware of danger.*) No, I'm up to the gills.

MRS. ROGERS. Yes, I noticed . . . your colonial accent is back, as awful as ever. But one more drink won't harm you, especially as you're becoming more sober by the moment. (EUGENE *crosses from steps to music box table.*) Scientific friends of mine tell me that it seems that terror causes the glands to secrete adrenalin into the system, which quite oxidizes the alcohol. Don't look so serious, dear . . . I'm chaffing. (*She brings him his drink.*)

EUGENE. Ta. Nothing for me to be afraid of.

MRS. ROGERS. No. (MRS. ROGERS *crosses to Stage Right of music box table so they have table between them.*) Did you enjoy yourself?

EUGENE. Went to the pictures.

MRS. ROGERS. Good.

EUGENE. (*Dancing Downstage over and on stool.*) It was a musical. Very old film. Fred Astaire.

MRS. ROGERS. (*Crossing to sofa and sits.*) Was it one of those midnight matinees?

EUGENE. No. (EUGENE *sits to* MRS. ROGERS' *Right.*)

MRS. ROGERS. Oh. A long programme, perhaps.

EUGENE. Uh . . . no.

MRS. ROGERS. Then my clock must be fast.

EUGENE. I went for a drink.

MRS. ROGERS. Of course you did, that explains it. Do (*Stands and crosses to desk.*) the public houses still close at certain hours, or has all that been done way with?

EUGENE. I went to a club.

MRS. ROGERS. (*Leaning on her chair.*) That wasn't what I asked. You must know by now that I never pry. A club.

EUGENE. The . . . um, the Incest-a-Gogo.

MRS. ROGERS. It sounds very jolly. Was it? (*Sits in her chair.*)

EUGENE. Not bad.

MRS. ROGERS. Were there females present?

EUGENE. Well, it isn't a monastery.

MRS. ROGERS. Nor a nunnery.

EUGENE. (*Laughing.*) No.

MRS. ROGERS. What do you mean, *ha! ha!* no?

EUGENE. I mean it wasn't full of nuns.

MRS. ROGERS. Perhaps it could have done with a few.

EUGENE. Don't start.

MRS. ROGERS. Don't what?

EUGENE. I couldn't tell you who was there and who wasn't. It was too dark.

MRS. ROGERS. Dark? How dark?

EUGENE. It was –

MRS. ROGERS. Pitch dark?

EUGENE. It was –

MRS. ROGERS. Or just murky?

EUGENE. Look . . .

MRS. ROGERS. And did a girl turn to you at the table, scream loudly and say that you weren't Charlie?

EUGENE. Now lay off.

MRS. ROGERS. No?

EUGENE. I wasn't at a table, I was at the bar. All I went in for was a drink. I saw nothing and nobody except a big stained-glass mural which was some artist's impression of the destruction of Sodom.

MRS. ROGERS. (*Sneering.*) You're quite sure it wasn't Gomorrah?

EUGENE. How would I know one place from the other? Maybe you're an authority. I'm not. There was a wigger in it, a woman that was made of salt. I drew me own conclusions. Jasus, what do I know about the Crimea?

MRS. ROGERS. (*Sceptically.*) And that was all you saw?

EUGENE. I had a quiet jar, and the only person I spoke to was the barmaid . . . (*Correcting himself.*) the barman.

MRS. ROGERS. You said a barmaid.

EUGENE. That was a slip.

MRS. ROGERS. Yes, it was.

EUGENE. Every Thursday night it's the same (*Stands, moves to bar.*) thing. Me one night off.

MRS. ROGERS. You said a barmaid. (*Stands.*)

EUGENE. I never laid a finger on her.

MRS. ROGERS. Liar! Lecher!

EUGENE. You're making me life a misery.

MRS. ROGERS. So that's how you spend your time and my money . . . leering into an abyss of decolletage.

EUGENE. Oh, God.

MRS. ROGERS. The valley of the shadow of lust.

EUGENE. Will you stop, will you quit?

MRS. ROGERS. (*Standing in front of sofa.*) I shall lower my eyes unto the hills from whence cometh my lechery.

EUGENE. 'I am never, never jealous, ill-tempered or possessive. I aim to please.'

MRS. ROGERS. You do what?

EUGENE. (*From behind sofa.*) Not me – you. That was what you said to me. Your words: 'I aim to please.' Aim to please who?

MRS. ROGERS. (*Moving to Down Right of green chair.*) Whom.

EUGENE. Whom or who, you have bloody bad aim. Because I'm not pleased.

MRS. ROGERS. Aren't you . . . oh, dear.

EUGENE. Never jealous, never possessive. That's a load of Friar's Balsam for a start. (*Crossing Downstage to pouffe.*)

MRS. ROGERS. *How dare you!* You have been treated like a king.

EUGENE. Like a what?

MRS. ROGERS. Figure of speech. I meant a duke.

EUGENE. Is that how you treat a duke, then? . . . spy on him, smell his breath, sniff his shirt, search his pockets, send his drawers to the public analyst?

MRS. ROGERS. How dare you mention drawers to me? (*Turns and looks Upstage.*)

EUGENE. Where were you, who with, up to what and for how long? I can't even pass on the same side of the street as a ninety-year-old one-legged wigger with a long mustache. Climb into me skin, why don't you? (*Tries to sit and falls off pouffe.*)

MRS. ROGERS. (*Moving behind green chair.*) You are as ungrateful as your predecessor. Your mind was a blank page and I wrote my name on it.

EUGENE. You've scribbled all over me. (*Lying on floor next to pouffe.*)

MRS. ROGERS. Scribbled?

EUGENE. I'm one big blot. (*Covering his head with coat.*)

MRS. ROGERS. Is it my fault if the paper is porous? I did my best. Who was it cured your diction? Who introduced you to the diphthong? (*Crossing Upstage of* EUGENE *and puff.*)

EUGENE. Here we go . . .

MRS. ROGERS. Say 'violence.'

EUGENE. Voilence.

MRS. ROGERS. As I taught you!

EUGENE. Voilence.

MRS. ROGERS. 'This,' 'that,' 'these,' 'those!'

EUGENE. Dis, Dat. Dese. Dose.

MRS. ROGERS. You're doing it deliberately – may God forgive you. This is my thanks. I showed you how to dress, eat, drink, move, stand, sit and breathe . . . to behave so that people who knew no better would take you for a gentleman. Like a fool, I hoped that nature might come to imitate art; but, no . . . the same lazy, vulgar mind exists under the veneer like a maggot in a monument. But what else could (EUGENE *curved around green chair and head Upstage of large table.*) I expect? Le Notre took thirty years to create the gardens of Versailles, and *he* had real grass to work with! (*A pause.*) If I seemed jealous and possessive, it is because you are not to be trusted.

EUGENE. Me?

MRS. ROGERS. (*Crosses to sofa, sits and starts going through his vest pockets.*) You come in like a thief. You tell lies without reason.

EUGENE. That's a laugh. If I as much as mention a –

MRS. ROGERS. (*Stands, crosses to green chair, sits.*) Eugene, you and I are friends, isn't that so? Then we must know all about each other so that we can share out – (EUGENE *picks up his jacket.*)

EUGENE. G'night, now. (*Crossing Downstage of green chair on way to Stage Right.*)

MRS. ROGERS. Where are you going?

EUGENE. Bed. (*She trips him as he passes her. He falls.*)

MRS. ROGERS. Oh, dear. I'm afraid you're still a wee bit tipsy.

EUGENE. (*To the audience.*) She's mad.

MRS. ROGERS. Don't lie on the floor: it's slovenly. Sit up. (*She bends over and rubs shoulder lovingly.*) Listen to me. (*Pulls his tie. He emits a strangled gasp.*) Shhh . . . listen. (*Gently.*) When you behave furtively, when you lie to me, it harms our friendship. I feel hurt, I become annoyed. I try to catch you out, and you mistake that for jealousy.

EUGENE. (*Hoarsely.*) Like hell. (MRS. ROGERS *pulls tie hard.*)

MRS. ROGERS. How could I possibly be jealous? Are you suggesting that some kind of emotional involvement exists between us, between you and me? I do hope not . . . because we don't want to commit folie de grandeur, do we, my darling?

EUGENE. (*Struggling.*) Get off. (MRS. ROGERS *pulls tie hard.*)

MRS. ROGERS. Do we?

EUGENE. No.

MRS. ROGERS. We are separate islands. I am lush and crammed with amenities, a green and pleasant land; you have good fishing (EUGENE'S *head falls over.*) but are sadly underdeveloped. We aren't even in the same archipelago. (MRS. ROGERS *lets go.* EUGENE *rolls over to Stage Left like he is dead.*)

EUGENE. You were jealous.

MRS. ROGERS. (*With utter sincerity.*) No.

EUGENE. A little bit. (*Takes off tie and throws it down.*)

MRS. ROGERS. No. (*A pause.*)

EUGENE. Well, that's all right, then. (*Picks up tie.*)

MRS. ROGERS. Now I've wounded your vanity.

EUGENE. Haven't got any.

MRS. ROGERS. Liar. You seethe with it.

EUGENE. (*Airily.*) Okay. (*Crosses Upstage of green chair.*)

MRS. ROGERS. (*Up and crosses in circle to Left of sofa and then behind it to head off* EUGENE.) But I *am* your friend. Aren't we friends?

EUGENE. Oh, sure.

MRS. ROGERS. And we must confide in each other. You shall tell me everything . . . the most intimate details. I shan't be offended.

EUGENE. I bet!

MRS. ROGERS. (*Pulling* EUGENE *to curved area.*) Truly. I want you to discover the sheer fun of having someone to really talk to.

EUGENE. (*In triumph.*) Ah?

MRS. ROGERS. What?

EUGENE. '. . . someone to really talk to.'

MRS. ROGERS. Well?

EUGENE. (*Laughing hard, jumps up in air goes over and puts hand in seat of green chair.*) Split infinitive.

MRS. ROGERS. I never. Did I? (MRS. ROGERS *sits.*)

EUGENE. Caught you.

MRS. ROGERS. You wicked boy. You've been paying attention after all.

EUGENE. (*Shaking his head.*) '. . . someone to really talk to.'

MRS. ROGERS. Yes, careless of me. Now where was I?

EUGENE. '. . . someone to really − '

MRS. ROGERS. Shall I wear sackcloth?

EUGENE. Pardon?

MRS. ROGERS. Don't gloat.

EUGENE. Gloat?

MRS. ROGERS. It's rude.

EUGENE. You said 'Now where was I?' I'm telling you . . . 'Someone to really −'

MRS. ROGERS. '. . . talk to.' Oh. (*Contrite:*) Dear Eugene . . .

EUGENE. (*To the audience.*) I'll kill her.

MRS. ROGERS. Forgive me. Be friends.

EUGENE. (*Snapping.*) All right. (MRS. ROGERS *stands and gets* EUGENE, *pulls him to her and they sit on Upstage curved bench. They sit close.*)

MRS. ROGERS. And friends, as I was saying, should have no secrets. Yes?

EUGENE. Ah, now . . .

MRS. ROGERS. Try it. Tell me something.

EUGENE. Such as?

MRS. ROGERS. About this evening.

EUGENE. I did.

MRS. ROGERS. Fibs. I shan't be angry, not if it's the truth. And it would make me so happy. On your evenings out, for example, why do you drink so much?

EUGENE. No reason.

MRS. ROGERS. Are you unhappy?

EUGENE. No, I . . .

MRS. ROGERS. Yes?

EUGENE. When I'm jarred I go back home . . . that's all. It's like standing on a hill and seeing the two bays.

MRS. ROGERS. The . . .?

EUGENE. Bays, there's two bays next to one another, like a pair of spectacles cut across the middle. There's a hill between them, and I get a couple of jars in me and I'm on it. (*Pointing to his right and left:*) Lovely view, city . . . country. (*They pull apart.*) All the places of me life, all at once, and all the people. I miss them − even the fat, shy, silly wiggers at the half-crown hops.

Girls off the farms, stronger than I am, bristlin' with safety pins and miraculous medals; little tarty ones from the towns with hair like flex.

MRS. ROGERS. You mean like flax. Flaxen.

EUGENE. (*Shaking his head.*) Like flex. Flexen. You couldn't stroke hair like that, you'd have to strum it. Gedoink. Oh, them half-crown hops.

MRS. ROGERS. You told me you couldn't dance.

EUGENE. Novelty numbers. Hokey-Pokey, military two-step.

MRS. ROGERS. I don't think I . . .

EUGENE. (*Singing.*)

'All of a sudden a lump of black pudden came floatin' through the air.'

MRS. ROGERS. (*Recognizing the tune.*) Oh, yes. What else did you see?

EUGENE. When?

MRS. ROGERS. From your drunken hill.

EUGENE. (*Sits on Downstage arm of green chair.*) The lot. Behind the school I used to go to there's this field –

MRS. ROGERS. Where wild oats grew?

EUGENE. Smarty.

MRS. ROGERS. I don't think I care much for this field.

EUGENE. (*Turns and crosses Downstage of pouffe to shoes.*) It was where we used to have drill on Wednesdays. I was at the school on a scholarship, fifty-fifth place out of seventy, the upstart of our road, purple and gold cap, tie and blazer, 'Pax Super Omnes.' Nice crowd of fellas, if you didn't let them find out where you lived, the sort of house it was, the size of the house, (*Sits next to puff on floor putting on shoes.*) bed next to the gas stove, kill yourself in comfort. On Wednesdays the whole school jumped up and down in this lousy field. All morning you'd pray for rain, 'cause if it was fine you had to march out with the rest of them and take yout coat off. The shirt I was wearing, the sleeves of it had been cut in two, and a piece of stripey foreign material had been . . . insinuated, so as to add a couple of inches, 'cause I was a growing lad and the shirt was as old as the drunken hills. I'd be there with this stripey band around each arm, and before it could attract comment from elsewhere, I'd roar out: 'Hey, lads: how about this for glamour!'

MRS. ROGERS. How ingenious of you.

EUGENE. I was a cunning whoor.

MRS. ROGERS. (*Up and crosses to pouffe, sits on it.*) But why not remove your shirt altogether?

EUGENE. Ah, on hot days, when the sun shone, then you had to. And that was horrible, because the tail of the shirt had been lengthened the same way. From here down it was all thick . . . stripey . . . cloth off some abandoned shirt of me dad's. And no matter how quick you were, they'd be ready. You'd get it pulled up over your head, but some little get would hang on to the tail and this cheering would start, and you'd die in there, inside that mockery of a shirt. The whole school fell around like drunkards.

MRS. ROGERS. Embarrassing.

EUGENE. It was, a bit.

MRS. ROGERS. Stripey.

EUGENE. What?

MRS. ROGERS. Was that what they called you . . . your nickname?

EUGENE. No. (*Stands.*)

MRS. ROGERS. I think it was. Stripey?

EUGENE. I don't like to be called that. (*Moves to sofa and sits.*)

MRS. ROGERS. But it no longer applies.

EUGENE. Even so.

MRS. ROGERS. (*Stands and crosses to sofa, sits to Right of* EUGENE, *close.*) After all, how many of your derisive schoolmates now get their shirts from Jermyn Street? If they knew, think how your friends would seethe with fury. You should revel in your nickname, bear it proudly like a captured banner. Stripey.

EUGENE. Cut that out.

MRS. ROGERS. All I'm saying –

EUGENE. Don't.

MRS. ROGERS. My, aren't we prickly. What happened? Has someone been unkind to you?

EUGENE. (*Heartfelt.*) The women in this town are a terrible crowd of whoors.

MRS. ROGERS. You're so bitter. Tell me.

EUGENE. You'll raise the roof.

MRS. ROGERS. Never.

EUGENE. Right, then. After the picture I did a bit of foraging around the pubs, but there was nothing doing.

MRS. ROGERS. Foraging?

EUGENE. For wiggers . . . women.

MRS. ROGERS. (*Pleasantly.*) I see.

EUGENE. You're livid, aren't you?

MRS. ROGERS. I'm *pleased*. This is what I've wanted from you. But couldn't you find any wiggers?

EUGENE. Oh, sure: no shortage, W1 was crawling with them. Trouble is, when it comes to the push, when I'm all set, poised for action, a little man up here (*Tapping his head.*) says: You don't want her, are you mad? . . . you don't want that one . . . the kind of girl who'd let herself be picked up by the likes of you.

MRS. ROGERS. That must narrow one's field of choice.

EUGENE. It does.

MRS. ROGERS. What sort *do* you want?

EUGENE. Who? Don't ask me, how should I know? If she exists, she'll turn out to be the horrendous twit of all time . . . I know my luck. Whatever happened to Donna Reed? Anyway, there was nothing doing. Pubs closed and I went on to the Incest-a-Gogo, nothing there either. About an hour ago, I was weaving homewards across the park. There she was.

MRS. ROGERS. Oh?

EUGENE. Girl in a uniform.

MRS. ROGERS. A night nurse?

EUGENE. Not a nurse – tunic, buttons . . . red hair, nice trim little figure. The description fitted, this could be the particular person. I introduced myself, trotted along beside her, gave her the old poetic prose. She didn't say much, quiet girl, eyes dead ahead. Well, the park gates were getting nearer and it was a bit late to be subtle, two in the morning. So I pinned her against a tree, an oak.

MRS. ROGERS. Oh, yes?

EUGENE. She struggled a bit, flashed her eyes, told me to let go . . . all the usual etiquette. I didn't want her to think I was out of control or rapacious; so, just to make conversation before the final holocaust, I said, chattily: 'Which of the services are you in?' She said: 'I'm not in the services, I'm in the police.' Then the louser blew her whistle.

MRS. ROGERS. I hope you apologized. (*Separate from him.*)

EUGENE. I did, yes . . . on the hoof, as you might say. My mistake, so I . . . walked off.

MRS. ROGERS. Walked?

EUGENE. Mm.

MRS. ROGERS. (*Stands and crosses to her chair.*) And she went on blowing her whistle. (*He shakes his head.*) No? (EUGENE *takes a whistle from his pocket. Attached to it are a length of chain and a piece of blue serge material. He blows the whistle experimentally.*) Oh, do you have one, too?

EUGENE. It's hers.

MRS. ROGERS. (*In back of her chair.*) You took it? Eugene, that was wrong of you. Rape is bad enough . . .

EUGENE. I never tried to –

MRS. ROGERS. (*Left of her chair.*) Although even at its worst it is no more than pressing an unwanted gift upon another person. Theft is something else again. You must return the whistle. (EUGENE *blows it again.*) Don't do that, dear. It gives me a headache, and it isn't yours to blow.

EUGENE. You mad at me?

MRS. ROGERS. Disappointed.

EUGENE. About looking for wiggers?

MRS. ROGERS. About the whistle. Your carnal proclivities do not concern me.

EUGENE. Great. (*Stands.*) Goodnight, so.

MRS. ROGERS. (*In back of her chair.*) Although I confess myself saddened. I should never have taken you for a creature of the night, prowling sadly around the pleasures of others.

EUGENE. I say, I'm off.

MRS. ROGERS. Are you? Goodnight . . .

EUGENE. 'Night, 'night.

MRS. ROGERS. (*Forcing* EUGENE *in curve back to desk, in art nouveau pose.*) . . . Stripey.

EUGENE. Now lay off. Quit it.

MRS. ROGERS. The name still suits you . . .

EUGENE. Dry up.

MRS. ROGERS. . . . striped, like a tatterdemalion tiger.

EUGENE. I knew you'd be jealous, I knew it, I said so.

MRS. ROGERS. Stripey, stripey, burning bright, in the bordellos of the night.

EUGENE. (*Menacing.*) I told you: cut that out. (*Downstage Right of desk.*)

MRS. ROGERS. (*Downstage Left of desk.*) And if I don't, will you do me a . . . (*He makes as if to hit her, stops and tears up stamps and tosses them to floor. Mocking his pronunciation.*) voilence? He's nearer than you thought, isn't he, that runny-nosed little scholarship boy with the shame burning his face. He's in this room. Poor Eugene: you possess one great sad virtue. Without it, life could be so pleasant for you.

EUGENE. (*Nodding.*) I'm too honest for my own good. (*Crosses to Upstage Left of chaise.*)

MRS. ROGERS. No, no: not honesty. You possess taste.

65

EUGENE. (*Admitting it.*) Well, yes.

MRS. ROGERS. The rich, good taste to despise yourself.

EUGENE. (*Incensed; picks up whip and advances on* MRS. ROGERS.) Right. Once more. Once more will do it.

MRS. ROGERS. Your classmates, the girl in the cinema, the policewoman, the hundreds in between: you rush from one to the other, a pimply boy begging to be liked . . .

EUGENE. (*Throws whip to floor.*) Carry on, keep it up.

MRS. ROGERS. . . . And each one, with a discrimination to match your own, looks at you and runs off shrieking.

EUGENE. Press on. (*Crosses to Left of pedestal table and tosses magazines and fan to floor.*)

MRS. ROGERS. Probably because the poor dears see in you the griminess of their own carefully bandaged needs. You induce the same mixture of disgust and guilt as a famine relief poster. (EUGENE *then opens all the music boxes.*)

EUGENE. (*Hissing; as* EUGENE *opens gold music box.*) Thank you, Beatrix Potter. (*He starts towards the bedroom.*)

MRS. ROGERS. Where are you going?

EUGENE. To pack.

MRS. ROGERS. (*After* MRS. ROGERS *closes second music box.*) Pack? What for? We're in our U.D.I. mood, are we? (MRS. ROGERS *closes music boxes.*) Eugene, come out here. Being farouche doesn't suit you. Where is your celebrated Celtic sense of humour? (*Irately.*) This is flagrant Sinn Feinery. (*She picks up magazines.*) you can't leave here without giving me notice. I won't allow it. (*Picks up whip.*) I shall impose mandatory (*Hits tiger with whip.*) sanctions. Besides, where will you go? (*Puts whip back in place.*) The time is three in the morning: it's dark out, the streets are filled with Australians. (*Crosses Upstage to bookcase and looks in. Silence.*) Eugene: what are you doing? (*He returns. He is carrying a copy of 'Playboy' with the gatefold hanging down, a statue of the Infant of Prague and some articles in a carrier bag from Safeways.*)

EUGENE. I'm packed.

MRS. ROGERS. *Un*pack.

EUGENE. (*Crossing in curve to Upstage Left of pouffe.*) And so it is with genuine reluctance that we say: farewell, Glorious Guatemala, gem of the –

MRS. ROGERS. (*Crossing in curve around Upstage Right of green chair.*) No. I forbid you. Not. Out. There. You'll become one of them. They are the sort of people my father had crucified.

None of them sees our point of view: they still bear us a grudge.

EUGENE. (*Passing her.*) 'Scuse me.

MRS. ROGERS. Stay.

EUGENE. Can't: there's too much been said.

MRS. ROGERS. Supposing I were to apologize humbly.

EUGENE. You can smile radiantly for all I care.

MRS. ROGERS. And, as reparation, I might have a little treat for you. (*A pause.*)

EUGENE. Wiggers?

MRS. ROGERS. Where would I get wiggers?

EUGENE. (*Moving to leave.*) . . . gem of the Caribbean.

MRS. ROGERS. A coat of arms. (*He stops.*) Why don't we devise you a coat of arms?

EUGENE. For me?

MRS. ROGERS. Would you like that? Yes!

EUGENE. Illustrated?

MRS. ROGERS. Of course, illustrated.

EUGENE. (*Stepping back away from her.*) I won't be bought off.

MRS. ROGERS. No.

EUGENE. Only if the thought is there. I wouldn't like to be surly. I could put it on my letterheads.

MRS. ROGERS. You must.

EUGENE. And buy a blazer.

MRS. ROGERS. Come and unpack.

EUGENE. What sort of picture? (*She looks at him blankly.*) On the, uh . . .

MRS. ROGERS. (*Leading* EUGENE *Upstage around green chair to stairs.*) Oh. Tomorrow we'll think of an appropriate design, something nice and heraldic. We – (*She breaks off, smiling.*)

EUGENE. What?

MRS. ROGERS. (*Beginning to laugh.*) It was just a fancy.

EUGENE. Tell us.

MRS. ROGERS. I daren't, I mustn't: it's too –

EUGENE. (*Blocking her way on the steps. Smiling.*) Say it. (*She nods. Laughter prevents her from speaking. It is infectious:* EUGENE'S *voice trembles.*) I won't let you go to bed.

MRS. ROGERS. I can't.

EUGENE. Yes.

MRS. ROGERS. (*Coming back down the steps.*) I shan't tell you. Oh, my God: yes, I will. I can't help it: I'm going to. It's high in my throat already. Stop me. Your coat of arms . . . You'll take offence.

67

EUGENE. (*Following her and standing to her Right.*) Not if it's a joke.

MRS. ROGERS. I mustn't. An upstart rampant on a field of striped calico. (*A pause.*) You said if it was a – (*He goes to the wall unit and kicks it. One of the legs flies off.* MRS. ROGERS *screams. Flakes of plaster come fluttering down.*) Eugene! I forbid – (*She takes up the police whistle. She blows on it twice, piercingly and at length.*)

BLACKOUT

ACT THREE

It is daytime, coming on for evening. The wall unit is now buckled and misshapen from the increasing pressure of walls and ceiling.

The room is empty. EUGENE *appears outside, dressed in a business suit and a bowler hat. He carries an umbrella and a briefcase. He presses the bellpush.*

MRS. ROGERS. Ohhh!

EUGENE. (*Stepping into room.*) I tried the doorbell, but it —

MRS. ROGERS. (*Crossing up to* EUGENE.) Here you are then. You came.

EUGENE. It seems to be out of order.

MRS. ROGERS. 'How shall I get him here?' I asked myself. I thought of sending a gunboat, but an invitation proved just as effective.

EUGENE. I was going to pay you a visit in any case.

MRS. ROGERS. Aren't you nice to say so.

EUGENE. No, truly: you took the thought out of my mind. I was flicking through my date-a-day diary, just reaching for my fountain pen, when your embossed envelope arrived.

MRS. ROGERS. Great minds think alike.

EUGENE. How did you know where to find me?

MRS. ROGERS. But you look so well. (EUGENE *turns in circle so* MRS. ROGERS *can see his new clothes better.*) Let me take your accessories. (*He retains the briefcase.* MRS. ROGERS *takes umbrella, gloves, hat, she puts them on side chair.*)

EUGENE. I'll keep this.

MRS. ROGERS. Do. And how deliciously plump you are.

EUGENE. It must be all the serenity I've been getting.

MRS. ROGERS. And how smart. Not just the kind of smartness that comes from clothes and washing and combing. It's subcutaneous.

EUGENE. Is it?

MRS. ROGERS. Definitely.

69

EUGENE. I try to keep my pores open.

MRS. ROGERS. (*Upstage Right of pedestal table*.) That's evident. Now what shall you have to drink?

EUGENE. (*Crossing to bar*.) Sherry, I think. A drop of the by-appointment. But let me. (*She watches him as he pours the drinks with effortless aplomb*.) Like I say, when your invitation came you could have knocked me over with a corgi.

MRS. ROGERS. Could I?

EUGENE. Nobody knows my address.

MRS. ROGERS. *I* do.

EUGENE. How?

MRS. ROGERS. (*Watching him pour*.) Aren't you proficient! What expertise. Where has my fumbling boy gone?

EUGENE. There's a bit of plaster in this one. (*He tips a fragment of plaster out of a glass, which he then wipes clean with his immaculately white pocket handkerchief*.) Are you going to tell me?

MRS. ROGERS. Yes: when I've teased you a little. But what steadiness. Nary as much as a crystalline tinkle. Have you been taking lessons?

EUGENE. When?

MRS. ROGERS. A post-graduate course? Evening classes?

EUGENE. You taught me.

MRS. ROGERS. Liar. (*He returns to her with the drinks*.)

EUGENE. Yes, you did. I'm a slow learner, couldn't fasten my shoelaces till I was twelve. The stuff you taught me, one day after I left here, it all suddenly . . . (MRS. ROGERS *sits in her chair. He hands her a drink*.) . . . crystallized.

MRS. ROGERS. Oh, I am pleased.

EUGENE. Happened in a flash; (EUGENE *sits on sofa*.) just like with St. Paul.

MRS. ROGERS. I can't tell you how pleased (MRS. ROGERS *moves to sofa and sits to Left of* EUGENE.) I am. It means we've succeeded.

EUGENE. Yep.

MRS. ROGERS. You and I.

EUGENE. (*Raising his glass*.) Cheers.

MRS. ROGERS. In a flash, you said?

EUGENE. I was in this restaurant in Damascus Street. Couldn't get served: sitting there in Alopecia Corner; Hartigan of Molokai. Then there was this voice saying 'Waiter': saying it, not shouting, no annoyance, calm as Summer. My voice: from the diaphragm, audible only to bats and waiters, man calling to menial. 'Waiter!' (EUGENE *stands and moves in curve to Upstage of green chair.* MRS. ROGERS *claps her hands in admiration.*) I wish you had been there to see him: frozen in flight, then coming at me like a shot bird. 'Sir?' This was what he'd been born for. H.M.V. A great moment.

MRS. ROGERS. And then?

EUGENE. Never looked back.

MRS. ROGERS. Come and sit by me.

EUGENE. Where's your husband?

MRS. ROGERS. Abroad. Where else should he be?

EUGENE. Selling stamps?

MRS. ROGERS. Selling them, giving them away, being robbed: he has no head for business. The man's a fool. Luckily for me, I have my own income. This house . . .

EUGENE. It's looking a bit dilapidated. Since I was here.

MRS. ROGERS. Nonsense.

EUGENE. All the plaster . . .

MRS. ROGERS. Plaster? A few flakes.

EUGENE. (*Looks at wall unit.*) The wall unit is —

MRS. ROGERS. Don't touch it. (*Stands.*) Have your drink. Structurally, this house is a fortress. All it needs is redecorating.

EUGENE. If you look at it from the outside —

MRS. ROGERS. I never do.

EUGENE. (*Crossing to Right of green chair.*) It leans sideways.

MRS. ROGERS. (*Crossing to back of her chair.*) My house?

EUGENE. There's a bulge in the walls you could shove twenty West Indians into.

MRS. ROGERS. That is war damage.

EUGENE. Which war?

MRS. ROGERS. (*Leaning on back of her chair.*) *Which?*

EUGENE. It looks like Ben Hur had a nasty skid.

MRS. ROGERS. Don't be pert. If we've come here to criticize, then we can't have progressed quite as far as we think.

EUGENE. But go outside and look. There are wooden buttresses —

MRS. ROGERS. (*Crossing to desk chair.*) Well?

EUGENE. . . . oak beams, holding up the walls like a drunkard's wife.

MRS. ROGERS. So? (*He produces a spirit level from his pocket and places it on the floor.*)

EUGENE. (*Crossing to Downstage Right of desk.*) Look. Give you an example. Look at the bubble.

71

MRS. ROGERS. Is that a pen?

EUGENE. No, no. Spirit level.

MRS. ROGERS. Then get up.

EUGENE. The bubble has gone out of sight: it's around the back somewhere! No wonder I staggered when I came home at night; I wasn't drunk at all: walking on this floor is like being at a tea dance on the 'Titanic.' (*Picking up level.*)

MRS. ROGERS. Is it some kind of fad? This baroque obsession of yours with my architecture.

EUGENE. Yes?

MRS. ROGERS. What prompts it?

EUGENE. (*Getting up.*) Ah. The reason I came here –

MRS. ROGERS. (*Crossing to Upstage Left of chaise.*) . . . was because I invited you.

EUGENE. Ye-es . . .

MRS. ROGERS. For a chat.

EUGENE. I know . . .

MRS. ROGERS. From day to day I see no one. I live alone at the top of a high building. I never go out, and my friends are all too (*Sits on Upstage side of chaise.*) moribund to climb the stairs. (EUGENE *starts in again with level.*) So I swallow my pride, and invite you to come and tell me how you have fared out there, gadding among the Gadarene swine. You arrive, and then what? You lie on my floor and play with a tradesman's appliance.

EUGENE. (*Still on knees with level at Downstage Right of desk. He gets up on line.*) Sorry.

MRS. ROGERS. It isn't manners.

EUGENE. No.

MRS. ROGERS. A woman starved for companionship merits more appetizing company.

EUGENE. You're not fixed up, then?

MRS. ROGERS. Fixed?

EUGENE. Domestically.

MRS. ROGERS. No: I advertise daily for an au pair, but it seems to be a dying genre. I'm afraid you were inimitable, my dear: of the few young men who came to be interviewed, not one has had the proper . . . (*She smiles sadly.*) . . . disqualifications.

EUGENE. (*Turning to sofa, sits.*) Ah.

MRS. ROGERS. (*Stands.*) Now what have you been up to?

EUGENE. Nothing.

MRS. ROGERS. The coyness of him. The sapling I fertilized has become an oak tree, and he calls that nothing.

EUGENE. (*Modestly.*) Well . . .

MRS. ROGERS. Tell me how many little birds have been building their nests in your branches. (*He shakes his head.*) Don't blush.

EUGENE. Just the one. (MRS. ROGERS *sits.*)

MRS. ROGERS. Oho?

EUGENE. She's – (*He stops, shy.*)

MRS. ROGERS. Brightly plumaged?

EUGENE. Her name is Rose. It . . . um, suits her.

MRS. ROGERS. A flamingo!

EUGENE. (*Teased.*) Don't. If you're going to be all ornithological, well, her colouring (EUGENE *stands, crosses to Upstage of desk chair, leans on it.*) is so nice, you could say she was more of a goldfinch.

MRS. ROGERS. (*Quoting.*) 'Collects in family parties or small flocks. Twitters constantly.'

EUGENE. Ha-ha.

MRS. ROGERS. 'In size, rarely exceeds four and a half inches, in common with the tit family.'

EUGENE. Ah, now, wait –

MRS. ROGERS. No, I mustn't. I'm sure she's charming.

EUGENE. Quiet-spoken, a bit on the crisp side, you'd like her. Her people move around a lot.

MRS. ROGERS. In the nomadic sense?

EUGENE. Ah, no, no, they have houses: (*Leans on back of* MRS. ROGERS' *chair.*) two or three mansions, an abbey of some sort and a couple of turreted jobs. They commute between them: kind words to the servants, baskets for the cottagers, then they get a whiff of buckshot and they're off.

MRS. ROGERS. Buckshot?

EUGENE. They exterminate vermin. It's their hobby. (*Crossing to Upstage of green chair.*) Rabbits, foxes, stags, pheasants, partridge, plover, ducks and quail. They're doing a grand job.

MRS. ROGERS. They seem wealthy. Are they in trade?

EUGENE. No, I'm told they have a rich relation.

MRS. ROGERS. Who supports them?

EUGENE. Some woman.

MRS. ROGERS. Ah.

EUGENE. (*Crosses to chaise and sits.*) And they – People give them money.

MRS. ROGERS. People?

EUGENE. Everyone sort of chips in.

MRS. ROGERS. Why?

73

EUGENE. (*Crosses to green chair, sits.*) I don't know. It's like the Salvation Army gone mad. They just go rolling around from house to house, exterminating vermin and (*Waves like Royalty.*) waving out of the train.

MRS. ROGERS. How very feudal of them.

EUGENE. Rose is different from the others. She thinks they're wasters.

MRS. ROGERS. Silly child, doesn't she realize doing nothing is not only an exhausting occupation, but a thankless one. (*Stands and crosses to bar, puts glass on it.*) Mm. The bones of the young take time to form, and the backbone hardens last of all. Perhaps maturity and marriage will restore this Wild Rose to the path of duty. (*Crosses to her chair, leans on it.*)

EUGENE. I hope so.

MRS. ROGERS. Under your guidance.

EUGENE. Ah, now . . .

MRS. ROGERS. You must have . . . aspirations.

EUGENE. I'm fond of her.

MRS. ROGERS. Well, then!

EUGENE. She's a bit out of my class.

MRS. ROGERS. Decadence knows no frontiers. What truly matters is that you have the sacrificial zeal of a missionary. Ask yourself: for the sake of this girl, are you prepared to prey on others for their own spiritual good, to devote your life unstintingly to sloth, to forsake the primrose path of toil for the barren rock-face of indolence?

EUGENE. I could (*Stands, crosses to sofa, sits.*) give it a try.

MRS. ROGERS. Brave heart. (*Sits on her chair.*)

EUGENE. For Rose's sake.

MRS. ROGERS. Then bless you both.

EUGENE. Ta.

MRS. ROGERS. What credit you reflect on me. A lifetime of subsidized amorality: it's more than I could have dared hope for.

EUGENE. (*Leans in* MRS. ROGERS' *direction.*) I'm not there yet.

MRS. ROGERS. Patience; it will come. Dear heaven, look at him: shrieking for martyrdom. You make Thomas More seem like a hit-and-run victim.

EUGENE. I think I must have a death-wish.

MRS. ROGERS. (*Stands, moves between chair and sofa.*) What is more to the point, have you employment?

EUGENE. Me?

MRS. ROGERS. Even uselessness requires certain standards. Well, have you?

74

EUGENE. A job? Yes.

MRS. ROGERS. Tch-tch-tch.

EUGENE. Rose insisted. She says she'd only marry a man who had a job and was a success in it.

MRS. ROGERS. And do you perhaps live by your pen? (*Sits on sofa close to* EUGENE, *to his Left.*)

EUGENE. I haven't used it in months.

MRS. ROGERS. Ah.

EUGENE. These days I do it all by dictation.

MRS. ROGERS. Unwise.

EUGENE. I didn't know!

MRS. ROGERS. Don't whine.

EUGENE. Rose said it would help save time.

MRS. ROGERS. No matter. For whom do you work then? Not those odious people, Weatherby and . . . (*Stands, crosses to desk.*)

EUGENE. (*Stands, crosses to green chair and sits.*) . . . Fitch. God, no. I'm with Loman and Selway.

MRS. ROGERS. Who?

EUGENE. They're estate agents.

MRS. ROGERS. Oh yes?

EUGENE. A very old and well-established firm.

MRS. ROGERS. And your position with this firm?

EUGENE. Junior.

MRS. ROGERS. Prospects?

EUGENE. Yes.

MRS. ROGERS. What?

EUGENE. I think I'm due for a promotion.

MRS. ROGERS. Ah.

EUGENE. I could tell them to stick it.

MRS. ROGERS. No. (*Stands, crosses behind sofa to Upstage of green chair.*)

EUGENE. I'm to take it?

MRS. ROGERS. You must work hard, rise like a meteor. Get advancement at all costs. Make it seem effortless.

EUGENE. Right.

MRS. ROGERS. Then, at your zenith and with the world to lose, throw the position aside as if it were some petty skill you had mastered and then became bored with.

EUGENE. But . . .

MRS. ROGERS. Work is the hobby of gentlefolk.

EUGENE. A hobby; yes. Yes. I grasp you.

MRS. ROGERS. The reason you took the employment in the first place was because –

75

EUGENE. . . . because it was there.

MRS. ROGERS. How well you turn a phrase.

EUGENE. It's my own.

MRS. ROGERS. I believe you. (*Sits on puff.*)

EUGENE. (*Crosses over to whips, picks one up.*) I took on a hobby. Yes: say no more: I have you, I'm with you, I'm a mile past you down the road. From dogsbody to prince of commerce, then abdication. Tell them it's for the woman I love. (*Waving whip around.*)

MRS. ROGERS. This promotion . . .

EUGENE. That'll shake them.

MRS. ROGERS. How certain is it?

EUGENE. Advancement at all costs. Hand me my cut-throat razor.

MRS. ROGERS. Is your promotion certain?

EUGENE. As good as; and then Rose!

MRS. ROGERS. Oh?

EUGENE. I'm on this – (*He looks at her.*)

MRS. ROGERS. This?

EUGENE. (*Puts whip down.*) Initiative test.

MRS. ROGERS. Another one?

EUGENE. They're all the go. (*Downstage Right of green chair.*)

MRS. ROGERS. (*Crosses to green chair, knees in seat.*) And your future depends on the outcome?

EUGENE. Sort of.

MRS. ROGERS. In that case, you must succeed.

EUGENE. At all costs?

MRS. ROGERS. Ruthlessly.

EUGENE. Right.

MRS. ROGERS. What is it you have to do?

EUGENE. You'll laugh.

MRS. ROGERS. Something valorous?

EUGENE. Well . . .

MRS. ROGERS. Bring back the Golden Fleece? Kill a Cyclops? Find an honest socialist?

EUGENE. I'm to get you out of here. (*A pause.*)

MRS. ROGERS. (*Harshly.*) Ha-ha.

EUGENE. I said you'd laugh.

MRS. ROGERS. Get? Me? Out? (*Stands and backs out of chair.*)

EUGENE. Loman and Selway, they're your landlords, and . . .

MRS. ROGERS. My . . . (*Both cross to front of sofa.*)

EUGENE. I mean they act for the landlord, agents.

MRS. ROGERS. I own this house.

EUGENE. The . . . um, land it's built on is . . .

MRS. ROGERS. Freehold.

EUGENE. Well, not exact . . .

MRS. ROGERS. Mine in perpetuity.

EUGENE. I'd sooner kill a Cyclops than get you out.

MRS. ROGERS. What do you mean, 'Get me out'.

(EUGENE *turns to green chair in which his briefcase is.* MRS. ROGERS *retreats to her chair.*)

EUGENE. Not in the handcart sense. Not for Loman and Selway, nothing savage. No, wait. Let me tell you. It's good news, you'll turn cartwheels. Where is it? (*He delves into his briefcase and takes out a batch of papers.*)

MRS. ROGERS. Eloi, Eloi: lama sabacthani? (*Leaning on Upstage side of her chair.*)

EUGENE. (*Following* MRS. ROGERS *as she retreats around desk.*) Don't be outraged; this is nice. A trouble-free removal to superior split-level fully-furnished accommodation in semi-pastoral surroundings. There's a new development at Runnymede. Patios, barbecue pits, wastemasters, Californian kitchens, Scandinavian sideboards, French windows, double-glazed. (*He shows her a brochure.*) None of your Jerry-built rubbish: this is modern living. Double sinks. Two-car Tudor garages. Your own personalized moorings on the timeless Thames. My God, it's gorgeous.

MRS. ROGERS. (*From Downstage side of chaise.*) Are you deranged?

EUGENE. (*From Upstage side of chaise.*) You can buy a boat.

MRS. ROGERS. Ingrate. Renegade.

EUGENE. Now you're being testy.

MRS. ROGERS. Traitor.

EUGENE. Who just now told me to get the promotion? Who said 'at all costs'? Listen: they're giving you a chance to go in style. (MRS. ROGERS *tries to pull brochure away from* EUGENE.) Don't tear up the good brochure. Go to Runnymede; you won't know yourself.

MRS. ROGERS. Guards! (*Running to Upstage of clock.*)

EUGENE. What guards? (*Turning Upstage and taking four steps. She goes to a scabbard which hangs on the wall and draws from it an ornate rusty sword.*)

MRS. ROGERS. (*Pointing sword at* EUGENE.) By God, for this I will make you shorter by a head.

EUGENE. What's that for? (*Jumps in air and runs to Downstage side of chaise.*)

MRS. ROGERS. (*She takes three swings at him in air, hitting tiger head with sword. Advancing on him.*) Little man, little man . . .

EUGENE. No, be serious. (*Retreating to Stage Right of desk using brochure as shield.*)

MRS. ROGERS. God may forgive you, but I never can. (*She strikes at him with the sword. She runs brochure through and from Downstage of* EUGENE *takes two swings at him. He leaps out of the way.*)

EUGENE. Are you trying to give me tetanus? What's (*Hiding behind her chair.*) so awful about Runnymede? (*She aims a series of blows at him. She tries to stab again through the Upstage side of its decoration then takes two swings across the top of the chair.* EUGENE *runs up bedroom steps to front of Kitchener poster.*) Will you stop clowning before I'm hurt. It's not my fault, it's not even Loman and Selway's. It's the landlord: he wants you out. (*She flails at him. She makes three attempts to stab him to the Left, Right, Upstage Left, into small picture on wall. The sword goes plunging into the wall. She pulls at the handle, but it is stuck fast.*) There, you see, and that's one of the reasons. Dry rot. (EUGENE *is leaning against wall as if slain,* MRS. ROGERS *retreats down steps.*)

MRS. ROGERS. Rubbish.

EUGENE. That wall is like butter. (*Stands Stage Right of sword.*)

MRS. ROGERS. The keenness of the blade has penetrated the stone. (MRS. ROGERS *staggers Upstage of large table to rib chair.*)

EUGENE. What stone? There's nothing in there but disembowelled death-watch beetles.

MRS. ROGERS. (*Crossing to Stage Left of pedestal table.*) Fiend. Devil. Estate agent.

EUGENE. (*Coming down steps.*) I'm not surprised the landlord wants you out; it's a deathtrap. Soggy walls, slanty floorboards, ceilings like snowstorms, rotten rafters: even the doorbell won't work.

MRS. ROGERS. One of the electric wires is – (*Leaning on pedestal table.*)

EUGENE. They cut you off.

MRS. ROGERS. They – (*Affecting amusement.*) Oh, yes?

EUGENE. Off. You're a chronic defaulter. We found out. You don't pay your way, you pay (MRS. ROGERS *crosses to Upstage of her chair and takes snuff on 'you pay.'* EUGENE *has crossed to Upstage Right of green chair.*) no one. You're drowning in money, you could have had the house fixed, now it's too late;

woodworm, dry rot and wet rot. It tilts. People walk on the far side of the street and try not to cough; drivers change into neutral; when there's a breeze, the slates come down like sycamore pods.

MRS. ROGERS. (*Hand extended.*) I'm sorry you have to go now. (*Crossing to Upstage Left of side chair.*)

EUGENE. The house has rabies and the neighbourhood's caught them. Go outside. Mini-steak bars. Striporamas. Magazine swap shops. Sauna baths. You let them happen.

MRS. ROGERS. Your accoutrements! (*She fetches his hat and umbrella, handing* EUGENE *his hat, gloves and umbrella. He just puts them on green chair.*)

EUGENE. You're not . . . much . . . use.

MRS. ROGERS. Goodbye, Mr. Hartigan.

EUGENE. Are you? (*He ignores the proffered hat and umbrella.* MRS. ROGERS *moves with them to the door, opening door and takes it in her hand.*) The landlord's a nice man, but he can't afford you. He's not rich, and you're dragging down the local values.

MRS. ROGERS. (*Smiling warmly, at door.*) Do go carefully on the stairs.

EUGENE. He doesn't want to have to put you out. (*Her smile ceases to be.*)

MRS. ROGERS. Put? (*She closes the door.* EUGENE *takes new lease from his briefcase.*)

EUGENE. You've had a good innings. Go to Runnymede. (*He puts the new lease on the desk and stands Upstage of desk.*)

MRS. ROGERS. Did you say 'put'?

EUGENE. Sign the form. Take any house you like. All of Magna Carta Model Village to choose from.

MRS. ROGERS. No one can put me out. (*Crossing to her chair.*)

EUGENE. Use my pen.

MRS. ROGERS. No one.

EUGENE. You broke the lease.

MRS. ROGERS. I broke the . . .!

EUGENE. Like a P.T.'s promise.

MRS. ROGERS. The lease? Of a freehold?

EUGENE. (*Crosses to green chair.*) I may just so happen to have it with me. Say nothing. (*He rummages in the briefcase. The lease consists of several tattered pages, handwritten and yellow with age. Each page is framed and under glass. The frames are hinged to each other like a folder of picture postcards.*) You're

79

in luck. I slipped it in as an afterthought. (*He 'plays' the frames like an accordion. Singing.*) 'Martha, rambling rose of the wild wood . . .' Ha-ha.

MRS. ROGERS. What is that contrivance?

EUGENE. Your lease.

MRS. ROGERS. I have never seen it. (*Crosses to desk to get her glasses.*)

EUGENE. Well, it was before your time. (*They do take, she is at desk, he Downstage Right of green chair. Pause.*) Oh, I don't know.

MRS. ROGERS. (*Crosses up to him, reaching for it, he pulls lease away from her, she sits in her chair, he stands in front of sofa to her Left.*) Show me.

EUGENE. I'll read you an excerpt. (*He peruses the lease for a particular section.*) '. . . with your fragrance divine.' Where am I? Yes. 'Ye lands and ye edifice thereon and pertaining thereunto shall by God's grace and these Acts be vested in and enjoyed by ye Lessee and his heirs, yea even unto ye end of time.'

MRS. ROGERS. End of time! In perpetuity!

EUGENE. Hold on: we're coming to the small script. (*Reading.*) 'Caveat. Ye Lessee shall diligently forfend ye lands from ye incursions of foreign persons, rogures, vandals, poets and hawkers of treasonous broadsheets; and shall preserve ye edifice to ye envy, discomfit and most splenetic despair of ye neighbouring dwelling-places, that it may continue beauteous of aspect, sound of mortice, and rendered free from ye pestilence, ye plague, ye wall-sweat and ye timber-pox. If ye Lessee or his heirs shall most villainously fail in any part of this, then shall ye lands and ye edifice thereon and pertaining thereunto pass into ye hands of ye landlord for ye enjoyment and ye merry disport of ye common townspeople, yea even unto ye planning permission.' (*Pause.*)

MRS. ROGERS. Are you sure that's not a forgery?

EUGENE. With all those 'ye's'?

MRS. ROGERS. Even so.

EUGENE. No, to me it has the unmistakeable pong of more spacious days. I admit medievalism isn't my field, but I know what I like; and at Loman and Selway's we have a saying that a well-written lease never dates. Take that bit about ye wall-sweat and ye timber-pox: it's as fresh today as when this was new.

MRS. ROGERS. Obsolete, I would have thought.

EUGENE. The words, maybe: not the meaning.

MRS. ROGERS. That is hardly for you to say. (*He snaps lease shut and puts it in green chair.*)

EUGENE. I just so happen to have with me an attested glossary of medieval wood-fungi and their current equivalents, specially prepared for Loman and Selway by a fellow of Jesus College, Oxford. (*He produces the glossary from the briefcase.*)

MRS. ROGERS. A glossary; (*Stands.*) aren't you thorough. And the meaning of timber-pox is . . .?

EUGENE. Woodworm.

MRS. ROGERS. I thought it might be.

EUGENE. (*Puts glossary in green chair and takes out reports.*) I also just happen to have reports from the borough surveyor and the various departments which deal with public health, sanitation, fire prevention and urban development.

MRS. ROGERS. (*In back of her chair.*) Is this a conspiracy?

EUGENE. Efficiency drive at the Town Hall: nothing sinister. But I'm afraid the reports are unanimous: demolition is hotly recommended. (*He puts reports in green chair.*)

MRS. ROGERS. Of this house?

EUGENE. Best thing for it.

MRS. ROGERS. Never.

EUGENE. Put it out of its misery.

MRS. ROGERS. Not while I have breath. I shall appeal, I shall go to the courts.

EUGENE. You're an astute woman, you know they've got you. The shortest of the short hairs. By the stubble. (*She does not reply. She crosses to Upstage of desk chair and leans on it,* EUGENE *is to her Left with lease in hand.*) But don't give them that satisfaction. Tell you what they're after, what they want. Defiance. They'd like that. Barricades. Front door nailed up. Bailiffs abused. Crowds on the footpath, heads back, gobs open, baby birds waiting for worms. You being lowered on a rope. The politeness of policemen. You don't want that. Spike their guns. Think British. Surrender. (*He puts new lease on desk from Upstage side in front of her.* MRS. ROGERS *looks at it.*) Sign it. They think you won't, that's why they made the offer. Drive them mad: choose an end house, southern aspect.

MRS. ROGERS. If I do . . .

EUGENE. They'll be livid.

MRS. ROGERS. If I should go to Runnymede . . .

EUGENE. No 'ifs'. Gorgeous district, never regret it.

MRS. ROGERS. Shall you then get your promotion?

EUGENE. Never mind me: let's get you fixed.

MRS. ROGERS. Shall you?

EUGENE. I'll manage somehow.

MRS. ROGERS. And at all costs.

EUGENE. Ah, no. The main thing is to see you snug and settled. The ruthlessness is secondary.

MRS. ROGERS. Is it? Dear Eugene. (*Sits,* EUGENE *is Upstage of desk.*)

EUGENE. (*Proffering his pen.*) Use this. Keep it. Rose is buying me a Parker.

MRS. ROGERS. (*Reflectively; she ignores offered pen.*) Rose.

EUGENE. (*Pointing.*) Along the dots.

MRS. ROGERS. Have you ever grown flowers? (EUGENE *tries to stab her with pen.*)

EUGENE. No, but I'd like to. Just there . . .

MRS. ROGERS. I have heard that it can take years − generations, even, horticulturally speaking − to produce a new, quite perfect bloom. One cuts, prunes, divides, fertilizes, pollinates and propagates, cross-breeds and inter-breeds, creates a special environment of soil and weather. (EUGENE *takes lease and moves Downstage of* MRS. ROGERS *and kneels: offering his back as a writing table.*)

EUGENE. Ah, you're dreaming of your little garden.

MRS. ROGERS. Do you believe that with care and time, one flower may be superior to others?

EUGENE. Sure.

MRS. ROGERS. Yes?

EUGENE. Flowers win prizes.

MRS. ROGERS. Yet people cannot. A flower is encouraged to be perfect; so are animals, dogs, cattle. But not humans. An infant may win a cup for the ingratiating sickliness of its smile, just as a soldier may be rewarded for valour, or a young woman feted for a mammalian deformity. But to claim superiority by right of birth and behaviour is to utter blasphemy. We are members of a vast trades union which demands equal imperfection for all, which denies us the same rights as a flower or a beast, which prohibits excellence, lest in the company of a paragon lesser beings might see themselves as they are, instead of as they could be. It is easier to destroy what is perfect than to raise yourselves to its level. Anarchy is laziness.

EUGENE. You forgot to sign. (*Offers her lease again.*)

MRS. ROGERS. They want me to go, not because the house is crumbling, but because it stands. Envy, envy. (*Sticks pen in her hand.*)

EUGENE. I'll witness it. (*Crosses to Upstage side of desk.*)

MRS. ROGERS. Apres moi le deluge. (*She signs.* EUGENE *whips the form away. He takes his pen and scribbles his signature, then begins to gather up his papers.*)

EUGENE. Good, fine, splendid. (EUGENE *blots her signature.*) I'll go and ring Pickford's. This time tomorrow (EUGENE *sighs.*) you'll be up to your chops in gracious living.

MRS. ROGERS. So soon?

EUGENE. Why deprive yourself (EUGENE *blots his signature, gathers lease and starts to cross to green chair.*) unduly? Runnymede beckons. (EUGENE *is putting pen in his pocket.*)

MRS. ROGERS. You said I might keep the pen.

EUGENE. I'll . . . get you a better one. (*He puts the pen in his inside pocket.*)

MRS. ROGERS. Ah.

EUGENE. You're a rarity among women. (*He shakes her hand.*)

MRS. ROGERS. Not rare. Extinct.

EUGENE. (*At green chair.*) It's been a pleasure. We'll meet in heaven. (*He has not bothered to replace the various papers in the briefcase. He stands, holding all his belongings to his chest, anxious to be gone.*)

MRS. ROGERS. Have some more sherry.

EUGENE. Sorry, must rush, arrangements to be made, all your fault.

MRS. ROGERS. But –

EUGENE. (*Crossing Upstage to door.*) Expect the van-men crack of dawn. They like it if the breakables are laid out. Have a go, it'll kill the evening.

MRS. ROGERS. What will –

EUGENE. Can't stay, it's all happening.

MRS. ROGERS. What will Rose think?

EUGENE. (*Stopping.*) Who?

MRS. ROGERS. Your goldfinch.

EUGENE. Rose? (*Crossing back to Upstage Left of green chair.*)

MRS. ROGERS. Shall you tell her about this?

EUGENE. Why?

MRS. ROGERS. Idle topics. The day's little triumphs recounted during a carnal lull. Shall you?

EUGENE. I might.

MRS. ROGERS. Won't it upset her?

EUGENE. Rose?

MRS. ROGERS. Rather badly?

EUGENE. Why should – (*Pause.*)

MRS. ROGERS. Yes? (*He does not speak.*) You did mention that she has a rich relative. (*A pause. One by one, the various papers begin to slip, unheeded, through* EUGENE'S *arms to the floor.* EUGENE *starts dropping his things: brochure, new lease, reports, briefcase, glossary, umbrella, hat, gloves.*) For whom her youthful disapproval her never clouded her fondness. As you of course know, she has an affectionate nature. When Rose learns, as she's bound to, that her very favourite relative has been dispossessed, and by you, well, she just may be rather cross about it. You know how righteous and unbending young people can be. Yes? We expect great things of Rose in the mellowness of time: no one ever conforms so prettily as a lapsed rebel, don't you find? (EUGENE *kneels.* EUGENE *opens his mouth to speak. He emits a croaking noise.*) Dry throat? Do have a glass of sherry. (MRS. ROGERS *stands, and crosses to sofa.*) You have time. (*She sits. He goes to the drinks table. As he pours, the decanter rattles against the lip of the glass.*) Oh, dear. Do I hear the sound of a relapse? I hope not. (*She faces him.*) None for me? (*He pours a second glass of sherry.*) Rose is my favourite, a sweet child. When I told her how worried your abrupt departure had made me, how I fretted about you, out there on your own and friendless, she volunteered to take you under her . . . finch's wing, as it were. I heard all about your first meeting. Charming. (*He goes to her with it.*) And won't it be nice to have you in the family. (EUGENE *sits to Right of* MRS. ROGERS.) Rose takes after me, you know, in spite of her plebeian aspirations. In ten years from now you won't be able to tell us apart. There's something to look forward to. Yes? But why such a long face? You mustn't (MRS. ROGERS *stands and crosses to chaise and sits on Upstage side, she then reclines.*) feel that you have been led up the garden path just because you find me at the end of it. For a certain kind of traveller, such as you are, all roads lead to me. Would you take that sword out for me, dear? It looks unsightly. I hope you don't mind my saying that. You are at rather an impasse, darling. (EUGENE *pulls the sword out of the wall with apparently no effort.*) Aren't we Arthurian today. (EUGENE *crosses with sword Upstage of sofa to head of chaise.*) On the other hand, if I don't go to this little house you have so kindly set aside for me in the country, well, it doesn't augur brightly for your prospects, material and marital, does it? What do you think?

EUGENE. (*Accusingly*.) You –

MRS. ROGERS. Yes?

EUGENE. It . . . isn't cricket.

MRS. ROGERS. No, it isn't. Life can be so unfair: it seems that whichever course you choose, poor Rose will remain a spinster. We're having such trouble getting that girl settled. I know: (*Stands.*) you must stay to dinner. You must stay, and we shall put our heads together and think. There, that's arranged. Yes, you must stay. Don't run off. (*Setting down her glass, she crosses Upstage to* EUGENE *and hugs him.*) Perhaps after dinner we can refresh our memories on the correct way to pour sherry. And you may even have time to help with the correspondence: it's piled up so since you left. (MRS. ROGERS *crosses Upstage of sofa and out of room into bedroom.* EUGENE *takes a moment, then heads for front door, with sword, stops and goes to steps, sword raised as if to kill. She returns, carrying the metal waste bin.*) Oh, good: you're still here. I wonder, might I ask you to tidy those papers? The floor is rather littered. (EUGENE *looks at the papers, then at the bin, which she has set down in front of him. He goes on his knees and picks up the forms, legal documents, brochures and the lease, and puts them into the bin.* MRS. ROGERS *smiles down at him. She takes up her glass.*) Dear Eugene, what would I do without you? Cheers. (*She drinks. The clock strikes the hour. The chimes are drawn out like a gramophone record which is running down.*)

CURTAIN

85

THE
PATRICK PEARSE MOTEL

CHARACTERS

DERMOD GIBBON

GRAINNE GIBBON

FINTAN KINNORE

HOOLIHAN

NAIMH KINNORE

JAMES USHEEN

MISS MANNING

ACT I

The living-room of Dermod and Grainne Gibbon in Foxrock
– a suburb in Dublin's vodka-and-bitter-lemon belt.
A winter's evening in 1966.

ACT II

Scene 1   The Motel. Fifteen minutes later

Scene 2   The same. A few minutes later

Time – the present

NOTE – pronunciation — Niamh is pronounced 'Neeve'
Grainne is pronounced '*Graw*-nyeh'

This play was first produced at the Olympia Theatre, Dublin, for
the Dublin Theatre Festival, on 15 March 1971, with the following
cast:

DERMOD GIBBON   Frank Kelly

GRAINNE GIBBON   Rosaleen Linehan

FINTAN KINNORE   Godfrey Quigley

NIAMH KINNORE   May Cluskey

JAMES USHEEN   John Gregson

MISS MANNING   Angela Vale

HOOLIHAN   Derry Power

Director: James Grout   Designer: Patrick Murray

Later presented at the Queen's Theatre, London, with the following cast:

DERMOD GIBBON   Patrick Laffan

GRAINNE GIBBON   Moira Redmond

FINTAN KINNORE   Godfrey Quigley

NIAMH KINNORE   May Cluskey

JAMES USHEEN   Norman Rodway

MISS MANNING   Rosemary Martin

HOOLIHAN   Derry Power

Director: James Grout   Settings by Patrick Murray

88

THE PATRICK PEARSE MOTEL

ACT ONE

The living-room of DERMOD *and* GRAINNE. *A winter's evening.*
The room is an object lesson in gracious living. The rugs match the window-curtains and the curtains harmonize with the covers and cushions. The coffee-table is marble. There is a mini-chandelier. On the walls are a Yeats, a Keating and an O'Sullivan. A handsome antique cabinet houses the most expensive hi-fi system in Foxrock; huge loud-speakers stand at opposite ends of the room. There are two doors: one leads to the hall, the other into a small bar with stools. The bar is a recent conversion: it is under the stairs, so that the ceiling slopes down sharply, the result being that no-one who is more than five foot two inches in height can stand erect in it.
For ten seconds before the Curtain rises we hear the amplified sound of a game of ping-pong in progress. When the Curtain rises, DERMOD, GRAINNE, NIAMH *and her husband* FINTAN KINNORE *are seated on the floor with their backs to the audience. They are listening to a stereo demonstration disc. The ping-pong ball seems to travel from one end of the room to the other. They turn their heads in perfect unison as if at a tennis match. The track comes to an end, and an American voice is heard from one of the speakers.*

COMPÈRE. Anyone for ping – (*from the other speaker*) – pong?
FINTAN (*getting up*). What'll they think of next?
DERMOD. No, stay there – there's more.
GRAINNE. Isn't stereo wonderful – we're thinking of buying another record.
DERMOD. Sssh! This is fantastic. Can you guess what this it?
NIAMH. Is it someone throwing up?
DERMOD. It's sea-lions.
FINTAN. Certainly it's sea-lions. (*To the others*) She hears them every day!
(*The recording ends.* DERMOD *rises and switches off the power. The others get to their feet.*)
(*A quick look at them.* DERMOD *and* GRAINNE *are youngish and attractive. He is thirty-five or so, watches his weight, is go-*

89

ahead, wears horn-rims, which give him a deceptively earnest look. His clothes are well-cut; he wears a 'dress' sweater and an ornate medallion. GRAINNE *is petite. Her friendliness and beauty attract men; her poise and faintly goddess-like air tend to keep them at their distance. She speaks well. She and* DERMOD *might have been born for affluent living; there is no trace of the parvenu about either of them. They hold hands and hug each other a great deal – always a dangerous sign.* FINTAN *and* NIAMH *are older: God knows they try hard, but prosperity sits on them both like a donkey on a thistle.* FINTAN *is big, suspicious, inflammable.* NIAMH *is the kind of woman on whom an expensive piece of haute couture would resemble a canvas awning. She does her best, but even her walk suggests a dignified gallop.)*

NIAMH. That was beautiful, Dermod.

FINTAN. Highly impressive.

DERMOD (*modestly*). It's not bad.

NIAMH. I love the gramophone.

FINTAN. How much did it run you?

DERMOD. Five-seven-five.

FINTAN. That's not bad.

DERMOD. What about this, though? (*He operates another switch.*)
(FINTAN *and* NIAMH *listen intently. Utter silence.*)

FINTAN (*impressed*). Will you listen to that!
(NIAMH *looks at him, decides that she is in the wrong place, moves down and sits on the floor.*)
Oh, leave it to the Japs.

DERMOD. It's on in the master bedroom.

FINTAN (*who is nobody's fool*). Oh, I knew it was somewhere.
(*He notices* NIAMH. *In an embarrassed whisper*). Get up.

DERMOD (*operating another switch*). Now it's on in the sauna.

FINTAN. By God, what?

NIAMH (*on her hands and knees*). Such things as they invent. It's a great improvement on the old horny gramophones.
(FINTAN *looks at her.*)
Grainne, do you remember the old horny gramophones?

GRAINNE. No.

FINTAN. Will you get up!

NIAMH. Why, is it off?

DERMOD. Yes.

FINTAN. Yes!
(NIAMH *gets to her feet.*)

90

DERMOD. Who's for a drink?

FINTAN. (*looking at his watch*). Ummm . . .

GRAINNE. Shouldn't you and Mr Kinnore be off soon?

NIAMH. Fintan! Fintan!

GRAINNE. Fintan. Shouldn't you?

DERMOD. No rush. If we leave at nine we'll still be in Cork by midnight.

GRAINNE (*with a hint of alarm*). Nine? You said you were leaving at eight-thirty.

DERMOD (*shrugging*). Give or take. (*Putting his arms round her*) She can't wait to be rid of me.

GRAINNE (*playing his game*). You're right.

DERMOD. Got a boy-friend in the loft, haven't you?

GRAINNE (*shaking her head*). In the hot press.

DERMOD (*nuzzling her*). Hope he smothers.

NIAMH (*watching their display of affection*). It's like an advertisement for glue.

(FINTAN, *who is easily moved to passion, strokes her bottom.*) Stop that.

FINTAN. Some people might do well to show a quarter as much affection.

NIAMH. If you mean me, I don't have to. You've got enough in you for an orgy.

GRAINNE (*to* DERMOD). Love. I hate to think of you drinking and then driving all that distance.

DERMOD. We'll be careful.

GRAINNE. And the weather is so awful.

FINTAN. Is it still raining?

NIAMH. I'll see. (*She walks with dignity to the window, pulls the curtain aside and looks out.*)

FINTAN. Well?

NIAMH. It's urinating.

GRAINNE. There!

NIAMH (*to* FINTAN, *who is glaring at her*). You told me not to use the other word.

DERMOD. We have time for just the one. If you'll all step into the consulting room . . . !

(*They all go into the bar. The height of the ceiling obliges them to remain half-crouching while they are there.* DERMOD *goes behind the bar and begins to open a bottle of champagne.*)

GRAINNE. Wouldn't we be more comfortable in the living-room?

DERMOD. What's the point of having a bar put in if we don't drink in it?

NIAMH. Oh, this is very snug.

DERMOD. It's not bad, is it?

FINTAN. How much?

DERMOD. Twelve-fifty, with fittings.

NIAMH. It's so original. I love sunken ceilings.

GRAINNE. Believe it or not, that part of it was accidental.

NIAMH. Go 'way!

DERMOD. Absolutely.

FINTAN. By God.

(NIAMH *begins to climb up on a bar stool, facing it as if it were a ladder. She is trying to avoid hitting her head.*)

GRAINNE (*pointing upwards*). It's the stairs, you see. We thought of having them raised slightly, but . . .

NIAMH. Don't do that, you'll spoil it. (*She tries to turn into a sitting position on the stool.*)

FINTAN (*taking hold of her by the thighs*). Do you want a hand?

NIAMH (*a mite tetchy*). I'm all right, I'm all right. (*To* GRAINNE) Don't touch it, it's perfect.

(*A 'pop' is heard from behind the bar as* DERMOD *uncorks the champagne. The bottle comes into sight.* NIAMH *sees it.*)

Oh, Jay, looka . . .

(FINTAN *glares at her.*)

Champagne – how lovely.

DERMOD. Well, it's an occasion. Fintan, here's to a long partnership and a successful day in Cork.

GRAINNE. And prosperity.

DERMOD. Same thing, love.

FINTAN. No, here's to friendship – friends through and through, and to hell with money. (*He drinks.*) Good stuff. How much?

DERMOD. Ten-ten a half-doz.

FINTAN. That's with discount?

DERMOD. Sure.

FINTAN. I'll buy a gross.

GRAINNE. Darling, must you go to Cork?

DERMOD (*fondly*). Now, now . . .

GRAINNE. Don't. Stay home with me.

DERMOD. Can't.

GRAINNE. Yes!

FINTAN (*tolerantly*). Women, women! I'll have him back to you this time tomorrow night, with the deeds to a brand new motel.

DERMOD. What'll we call this one?

FINTAN. It's in Cork. Who's the most famous patriot from there?

DERMOD. Michael Collins?

FINTAN. The 'Michael Collins'!

NIAMH. Gorgeous.

DERMOD (*refilling* FINTAN'S *glass*). Fintan, you're a genius.

FINTAN (*crowing*). Our second motel – and the first one not even open yet!

DERMOD. Only one week to go!

GRAINNE. Stay here tonight.

DERMOD. I can't. We . . .

GRAINNE. I'll be all on my own.

DERMOD. No, you won't, you'll be staying with Niamh.

GRAINNE. It's not the same thing. I want to here *here*, with you.

DERMOD.Fintan, tell her . . .

GRAINNE. I don't care. You're mean. Where are my cigarettes?

(GRAINNE *goes into the living-room. Her peevishness at once disappears. She makes a dive for her handbag, fishes out her spectacles and peers myopically at her wristwatch.*)

FINTAN. By God, that girl is mad about you.

NIAMH. Can't bear to let him out of her sight.

DERMOD (*modestly*). I know, I know.

NIAMH. Lovebirds!

GRAINNE (*with a howl of anguish*). Half-past eight – is the rotten pig going to stay here all night? (*Hissing towards the bar.*) Get out, get out, go to Cork, go to Cork! Oh God, will you make the stupid, useless maggot go to C . . . (*She breaks off, suddenly noticing the presence of us, the audience. She holds her glasses to her eyes, just to make sure, then hastily puts them back in her handbag. She smiles at us charmingly, now the perfect hostess.*) Welcome, welcome to our home. I do wish you could see all of it. You'd adore my kitchen: it's eighteenth-century English and all-electric. And the master bedroom is a dream: in white, everything built-in, and the carpet so deep, if you lost an ear-ring you'd need a safari to find it. (*She laughs at her little joke.*) And there's a sunken bath – Dermod got the idea from *Spartacus* – all done in tiles inspired by the graffiti at Pompeii: daring, but nice. And I can just see you all sitting in our sauna. (*She looks at us for a moment, imagining this. Then, anxious for our good opinion.*) I hope I don't seem to boast? Dermod and I couldn't always afford little extras. But he worked so hard

93

— well, I won't bore you, but we were in this teeny flat, and there was this government contract, because the Department of Defence had sold their aeroplane. *You know* — the jet. But they shouldn't have, because the Department of Agriculture had nothing to spray crops with. A-a-nnnd, they wanted it back, and there was this purchasing contract. A-a-nnnd there was this man who seemed certain to get it, only some awful person reported him for diddling the income tax, so he didn't get it; and it turned out that the poor man hadn't been — diddling, I mean, but by then Dermod had the contract, and that was the beginning. And now we have all this, and we're so happy and grateful and sincerely humble. Because we're still simple people who sit home and look at colour television, just like you do. *Some* things are different: we swopped our old parish priest for a Jesuit; and *he* told us that the bit about the rich man and the camel going through the eye of a needle doesn't apply in areas where poverty has been eradicated — such as Foxrock. Does money bring happiness? Well, I have my ring and my brooch (*showing them*) and nice clothes — you'll see my coat later — and my car, and, of course, Dermod; and I can assure you — (*her voice quavers as she descends further into abject misery with each*) — that I'm the most — contented and the happiest — girl in the whole — wide — world. (*She dissolves into tears and gropes for her handkerchief.*)
(DERMOD *comes from the bar. He heads for the telephone and dials a number.*)
(*Coldly*). Who are you phoning?
DERMOD (*his joke*). My girl-friend.
GRAINNE (*with a snort of derision*). Huh!
DERMOD. No, that's one thing that'll never come between us, love. You'll always be the only girl for me. (*He blows her a kiss.*)
(GRAINNE *blows him a kiss back, then turns away.*)
GRAINNE. (*in utter disgust*). Yeccch!
DERMOD. Fintan reminded me that our new manageress is due in town. I don't want her ringing here and getting no answer, with us in Cork and you staying with Niamh. (*Into the phone.*) Come on, come on . . .
NIAMH (*in the bar*). Fintan, help me down, I'm getting a nose-bleed.
(FINTAN *helps her down.*)
And will you stop feeling me — you've been at it all night.
FINTAN. I can't help it.

NIAMH. Yes, you can.

FINTAN. You're so lovely.

NIAMH. You must be as blind as a bat.

FINTAN. Fifteen years, and every time I look at you I go mad inside. I don't know what I'm going to do in Cork without you.

NIAMH. I know what I'm going to do tonight – sleep! Oh, just to lie in an empty bed, to be able to roll over without a voice roaring in me ear, 'Good girl, good girl, here I am!'

FINTAN (*sure of himself*). Not at all: you'll cry yourself to sleep without me. Ah, don't fret, girl, I'll make it up to you tomorrow night on the double.

NIAMH (*hollowly*). Oh, God!

DERMOD (*into the telephone*). Hello, Royal Shamrock Hotel? . . . You might answer your switchboard – do you call this efficiency? . . . I want no lip, thank you. Has Miss Manning checked in yet? . . . Yes, she is: I myself made the reservation . . . But she must be; she was due at six from London . . . You did what? . . . That was damned officious of you . . . Oh, yes? Well, will you kindly tell your manager he'll be hearing from me. The name is Gibbon. Dermod Gibbon of Mother Ireland Motels, Limited. (*He hangs up.*) Bloody nerve.

GRAINNE. What is?

DERMOD. She hasn't turned up, so they've cancelled her room.

GRAINNE. So?

DERMOD (*angrily*). I made that reservation.

GRAINNE (*feigning horror*). And they cancelled it? Oh, the fools.

DERMOD. Not funny, love. I'll ring the airport.

GRAINNE. You haven't time.

DERMOD (*mildly amused*). Haven't time? What's the matter with you? (*He dials. Through the following he gets his number and talks into the phone.*)

NIAMH (*in the bar*). I'll tell you what's the matter with you. You're so randy that you can't even look at a wasp without imagining it with its stripes off.

FINTAN. 'Randy' – that's exquisite language from a woman's mouth.

NIAMH. And what's more, you're twisted.

FINTAN. Me?

NIAMH. Anyone who likes ugly women *must* be twisted.

FINTAN. What ugly woman? (*Pointing out of the bar.*) Do you mean her? That ugly article out there?

(GRAINNE, *who looks anything but an 'ugly article', idly smoothes her dress over her thighs, her head thrown back: the effect is definitely erotic.*)

95

Sure a man would be mad to look at her twice!

NIAMH (*half to herself*). It's true, I knew it – he's woman-blind.

FINTAN. I know what your game is; you're trying to get me confused. There's another man.

NIAMH (*stunned*). A what?

FINTAN. I'm not enough for you. You want to use that body of yours to drag other poor unfortunates to their destruction.

NIAMH. What body?

FINTAN. And that face. Beside you, Cleopatra was a camel. (NIAMH *stares towards the audience, her face numb with stupefaction.*)
Well, you're not going to get the chance to exercise your lust while I'm in Cork. That ugly article out there is going to stay with you – that was *my* idea. And if I ever catch you looking crossways at a man I'll crucify you and I'll tear him to bits. Do you hear me?

NIAMH (*frightened by his towering rage*). Yes, Fintan.

DERMOD (*on the telephone*). Closed down completely? Nothing getting off at all?
(NIAMH, *drink in hand, makes to move out of the bar.*)

FINTAN. Come back here. You mind your manners, because that bugger is putting me up for the country club, and men of substance who get into the country club do not have wives who at the first sight of a bottle of champagne say, 'Ah, jay – looka!'

NIAMH. You're always telling me to be myself.

FINTAN. At home – not when you're out. Go on, now.
(NIAMH *and* FINTAN *moves out of the bar as* DERMOD *hangs up.*)

NIAMH (*emerging at a half-stoop*). We thought we'd come out before we were left this way.

FINTAN (*glaring at her; to* DERMOD). What's the news of your Miss Manning?

GRAINNE (*to* NIAMH, *in an urgent whisper*). I've got to talk to you.

DERMOD. London Airport is closed for the night. Fog.

FINTAN. Well, there's no rush, she'll . . . (*Seeing that* NIAMH *has not straightened up*) You're out now, pet. (*To* DERMOD) She'll be here tomorrow.

DERMOD. I promise you, she's a jewel. I met her at a cocktail party in London. Grainne's old boy-friend was there – James Usheen.

96

NIAMH (*excitedly*). Oh, you don't mean the one on television? (*To* GRAINNE) You don't known *him?*

GRAINNE (*with a tight smile*). I used to.

DERMOD. Before he was famous. Her first love, yes?

GRAINNE. Something like that.

NIAMH. You and him? Oh, Jay – mes Usheen, how interesting for you.

GRAINNE (*wishing the subject had not come up*). It was twelve years ago. I haven't seen him since – except on the box.

NIAMH. I watch him every Sunday. I love him when he's insulting people.

FINTAN. Is he in colour?

NIAMH. Yes.

FINTAN. I'd have seen him, so.

NIAMH. He's here now.

GRAINNE (*whirling round, her hand on her throat*). Where?

NIAMH. Here in town. He's opening a supermarket. I saw it in the *News of the World* . . .

(FINTAN *looks at her.*)

. . . *The Times.* Do you remember how he got famous? When he made that remark on the television -- 'Homosexuality is only a pain in the a . . .'

FINTAN. That'll do!

NIAMH. I'm only saying what he . . .

FINTAN. Well, don't – (*for the benefit of the others*) – pet. Yes, I know him now. Didn't some husband get costs off him in a divorce case? And he's on every Sunday, belittling his own country and running down the sacrament of marriage. Oh, a credit to us – if he was in black-and-white I'd switch him off.

GRAINNE. They say he's a horrid person; let's not talk about him. (*Feigning surprise*) Look at the time! Where does the evening go to? Now – coats!

(GRAINNE *goes out, humming to herself and trying not to hurry.*)

FINTAN. You've got a fine girl there.

DERMOD. I know.

FINTAN. She's a monument to your good taste. Not many men appreciate that beneath a plain exterior there often beats a heart of gold.

DERMOD (*at sea*). Pardon?

NIAMH (*softly*). You can take him nowhere.

FINTAN. It was a very beautiful woman that first said that to

me. Did you ever meet my ex-secretary, Miss Shanahan? Oh, a
smasher. She was the spitting image of that Robert Morley.

DERMOD. Is that so?

FINTAN. She went into a convent.

NIAMH. I wonder why.

FINTAN. A shocking waste. (*Business-like*) Partner, I'll be honest
with you. There are women and women – man-eaters like this
one – (*indicating* NIAMH) – and decent plain creatures like
your wife. But I don't like the sound of this new manageress of
yours.

DERMOD. Miss Manning?

(GRAINNE *returns, carrying overcoats and scarves.*)

GRAINNE. Here we are. Now both of you wrap up well.

DERMOD. Because she was at a cocktail party? Fintan, she is the
dowdiest, dullest, most . . .

FINTAN. I accept that.

DERMOD. Then why?

GRAINNE. Let me help you.

(GRAINNE *helps the men into their coats and scarves. They
are too involved in their argument to notice.* NIAMH *looks
at her empty glass and goes into the bar for a refill.*)

DERMOD. If it's her qualifications . . .

FINTAN. No, it's her nationality.

DERMOD (*disbelieving*). Because she's English? Oh, Fintan . . . !

FINTAN. Don't misunderstand me: I'm not a bigot. Ordinarily I
wouldn't care if she was a black. (*On second thoughts*) Well, if
she was a – Norwegian.

DERMOD. But . . .

FINTAN. We decided, you and I did, to run our motels on patriotic
principles as a tribute to the men who died for Ireland. We owe
it to them.

DERMOD. Absolutely. (*To* GRAINNE) Thanks, love. But I don't
see . . .

FINTAN. Next week, five miles up those mountains – (*he points
out*) – we'll have our first grand opening. The motel will be
named after the greatest patriot of all time. The Tricolor and
the Plough and the Stars will float over the swimming-pool,
there will be an oil painting of a different patriot in every
bedroom. Look – look at the menu. (*He produces a sheet
of paper.*) 'Battle of the Boyne Salmon – Vinegar Hill
Mayonnaise – Black and Tan Pigs' Feet – I.R.A. Bombe
Surprise . . .'

DERMOD. Yes, and 'Remember Limerick Ham'. But what has that to . . .

FINTAN. It has this to do with it. With all the patriotism I wouldn't feel right having a manageress who was English.

DERMOD. I disagree. (*To* GRAINNE, *absently*) Thanks, dear. (*To* FINTAN) I think we've more than done our bit. There's a night-watchmen out there now who served in the nineteen-sixteen rising. He's too old to be efficient but we hired him. We advertised for a manageress, and you saw the applicants. Any one of them would have ruined us in a month. Ireland first, Fintan, and at all costs. But it is not patriotic to lose money. It is a betrayal of the economy.

FINTAN. My answer is still no.

DERMOD. Miss Manning has a contract. She could sue us.

FINTAN. Let her.

DERMOD. And she'll win.

FINTAN (*after a pause*). I am a patriot. But I don't want to look like a fanatic – we'll give her a try.

DERMOD. Fintan, you have greatness in you.

GRAINNE. There – you're weather-proof! (*She kisses* DERMOD.) Good-bye, my darling. Think of me and drive carefully. I'll miss you.

FINTAN. But I'd like to see her references.

GRAINNE. And I wish you every success in Cork.

DERMOD. They're upstairs in my workroom. I'll get them.

FINTAN. I'll go with you. I need to use the amenities.

(DERMOD *and* FINTAN *go out.* GRAINNE *has been too intent on getting rid of them to pay heed to what has been said.*)

GRAINNE (*calling musically*). Niamh, Fintan is go-ing! (*It dawns on her that they have merely gone upstairs.*) Dermod, Cork is *that* way! Oh, my God.

(NIAMH *comes out of the bar.*)

(*Ashen-faced*) They're still here.

NIAMH. I know. Before Fintan goes anywhere he always mauls me good-bye.

GRAINNE (*shoving her wristwatch under* NIAMH'S *nose*). What time is it?

NIAMH. Quarter to.

GRAINNE. I'm done for. They're going to stay on and on, and when he comes they'll still be here.

NIAMH. When who comes?

GRAINNE. Who? Who? Who do you think? James Usheen!

NIAMH. *Him?*
GRAINNE. Yes!
NIAMH. Shaggin' hell.
GRAINNE. Have you got the letter?
NIAMH. What?
GRAINNE. The *letter!*
NIAMH (*in a daze*). It came yesterday. (*She takes an envelope from her handbag and glances at the printed heading.*) The Royal Anna Liffey Hotel.
GRAINNE. That's the one.
NIAMH. He's – coming here?
GRAINNE. He's due now.
NIAMH. And Dermod doesn't . . .
GRAINNE. Sssh! No.
NIAMH. Will I see him?
GRAINNE. You'll do much more than see him. I need your help.
NIAMH. What for – to jump on him? (*She laughs.*)
GRAINNE (*grimly*). If there's any jumping to be done, I'll do it.
(NIAMH *gapes at her, realizing she is in earnest.*)
If only they'd go to Cork! Niamh, do you know what it's like, living in England? Over there women have affairs.
NIAMH. Do they?
GRAINNE. For God's sake, love, don't you read your *Nova?* They have freedom. In a big city a woman is like a needle with a haystack to hide in, and she's never caught.
NIAMH. Some are.
GRAINNE. Not so many. The *News of the World* never goes more than thirty-two pages.
NIAMH (*nodding*). And eight of those are sport.
GRAINNE. I have never looked at any man except Dermod. Where's the point? A man can take one look at a woman and love her for the rest of his life. But we women are different. We're realists.
NIAMH. I know. Just looking at a steak won't fill your stomach.
GRAINNE. You expressed that very well, Niamh.
NIAMH. Ta.
GRAINNE. I've tried to be a wife, not a vegetable. I take guitar lessons, I've studied Irish art, and I read Harold Robbins. In this country women are bond-slaves. I love Ireland. I believe that whatever English women have, we owe it to our pride as a nation to let Irish women have some of it, too.
NIAMH. There's an awful lot of patriotism around here this evening.

100

GRAINNE. God has given me so very much. But it's the little things
we can't have that turn us into monsters. I want to spare Dermod that, Niamh.

NIAMH (*touched*). Aren't you good to him!

GRAINNE (*with sudden passion*). Apart from which, he is so
bloody dull, and this house is dull, and I would love to have a
man just once, just once before my throat gets wrinkles and
people look at my brooch first and my ring, and then me, and
I swear, I swear I will never ask for another thing so long as I
live – just one short fleeting night of harmless innocent
adultery. Oh, God, is that too much to ask for?

NIAMH (*after a pause*). Have you tried St Ann?

GRAINNE (*calmly*). I had almost given up hope, then Dermod met
James Usheen at the party. He introduced himself as my husband. Next day, James rang me. He said he was coming over
to open a supermarket, and could we meet? He sounded so
affectionate.

NIAMH (*half horror, half awe*). You wouldn't!

GRAINNE. When Dermod said that he and Fintan were going to Cork
this evening, I knew it was a sign from heaven. I booked a double
room in your name at the Royal Anna Liffey Hotel. (*Hugging the
letter*) That's why I had them send you the confirmation.

NIAMH. In my name?

GRAINNE. Yours and Fintan's.

NIAMH. He'll slaughter me.

GRAINNE. He won't know. I've planned every little detail, and if
only they'll stop dithering upstairs and go to Cork, then nothing
– positively nothing – can go wrong. (*She looks at the letter
and emits a shriek of horror.*)

NIAMH. What is it?

GRAINNE. The hotel's full up.

(DERMOD *returns.*)

NIAMH. Ah, no.

GRAINNE. They can't take us.

NIAMH. Well, isn't that the . . .

DERMOD. Who can't take you?

(GRAINNE *and* NIAMH *swing around to stare at him.*
GRAINNE *thrusts the letter behind her back.*)

GRAINNE. The hairdresser.

NIAMH (*simultaneously*). The chiropodist.

DERMOD. Both full up, are they? Hard luck. Say good-bye, love.
We're off.

(*He moves towards* GRAINNE *to kiss her good-bye. She backs away, comes up against the table on which is* NIAMH'S *handbag and, operating by touch, shoves the letter blindly into it.*)

(FINTAN *enters to say his good-bye.* NIAMH *looks apprehensively at him and so does not see what* GRAINNE *is doing with the letter.*)

DERMOD. Take care, darling. I'll miss you.

GRAINNE. I'll miss you, too. Now be good.

DERMOD (*fondly*). *You* be good.

GRAINNE (*lovingly, groping for the handbag*). What do *you* think?
   (FINTAN *advances on* NIAMH.)

NIAMH. Keep away from me.

FINTAN. I want to say good-bye.

NIAMH. The only thing worse than you saying good-bye is you saying hello. (*As he closes with her*). Now get off!

FINTAN (*to the others, struggling with* NIAMH). It's our little game, isn't she great?

GRAINNE. Don't go.

DERMOD. Must. (*A last kiss*). 'Bye. Fintan . . . ?

NIAMH. Oh, you messer.

FINTAN (*thickly*). Right. (*He manages to plant a kiss on* NIAMH's *face*). Now remember what I said.

NIAMH. Yes!

FINTAN (*as a threat*). And mind yourself – pet. Good-bye, Mrs Gibbon.

GRAINNE. Grainne.

DERMOD. 'Bye, Niamh.

   (DERMOD *and* FINTAN *go out.* GRAINNE *sees them to the front door, off.*

   (NIAMH, *exhausted by her battle with* FINTAN, *sags into a chair.*)

DERMOD (*off*). Don't come out in the rain, love, 'bye!

GRAINNE (*off*) Drive carefully!

   (GRAINNE *comes back into the living-room.*)

NIAMH. In bed or out of it, he's the same. He comes at me like a threshing machine.

GRAINNE. Sssh! (*She listens.*)

   (*Car doors are slammed off. There is the sound of the engine starting up, then the noise of wheels on gravel.*)
   Gone! (*She gives a broad smile.*)

NIAMH. What are you looking so happy about? If the hotel is full
up . . .

GRAINNE. There's one other place we can go to.

NIAMH. At this hour?

GRAINNE. It came to me while I was kissing Dermod good-bye.
What does P.P. stand for?

NIAMH. The parish priest's house? You wouldn't!

GRAINNE. I mean the Patrick Pearse.

NIAMH. The motel?

GRAINNE. Why not? It's furnished, the heating's on, and there are
eighty-four bedrooms, all empty. There's even a swimming-
pool, in case James turns out to be kinky.

NIAMH. But the night watchman . . .

GRAINNE. He doesn't know me by sight; Dermod engaged him.
And next week, when the motel is open, he'll be let go, he'll
never see me again. It's perfect.

NIAMH. If men only knew what goes on inside women's heads
while they're kissing them! But, Grainne, you can't – not in
Dermod's motel.

GRAINNE. In a way, it's appropriate. When a ship is launched it's
always the owner's wife who christens it. Now I must go
upstairs and change.

NIAMH. Out of *that* dress?

GRAINNE. For James – nothing but the best. Niamh, be a love
and fetch me a drink, I'm shaking with nerves. Oh, when he
finds out what I've got in store for him!

NIAMH (*stunned*). He doesn't know?

GRAINNE. How could he? Do you take me for the kind of woman
who would tell a man she intends to go to bed with him? He'd
think I was fast.

NIAMH. Yeah – I'm sorry.

GRAINNE (*beginning to unzip her dress*). The drinks, love – and
have one yourself.

(*Again the sound of car wheels on gravel is heard.*)

It's too late, he's here! (*Babbling*) I left the door off the catch,
I told him to come straight in. One never looks one's best on
a doorstep. Niamh, I want the first thing he sees to be me,
alone, waiting, So would you . . . ?

NIAMH. Would I what?

GRAINNE (*pointing to the bar*). Please?

(NIAMH *nods, crosses herself resignedly, and goes into the
bar.* GRAINNE *braces herself for the great moment. As*

103

footsteps are heard in the hall, she shuts her eyes dreamily and extends her arms towards the open door, ready to be embraced.)
Darling –
(*But it is* FINTAN *who appears.*)
– is it really you?
FINTAN. No, he's out in the car.
GRAINNE (*staring at him*). Oh.
FINTAN. Niamh's Mini is blocking the drive. (*Yelling*) Niamh!
NIAMH (*in the bar*). What?
GRAINNE. I was just going upstairs to – pack a suitcase.
(GRAINNE *goes out.*)
NIAMH (*yelling from the bar*). What do you want?
FINTAN. Your car is in our way. Where are the keys?
NIAMH. In my handbag. (*She pours a drink for herself and for* GRAINNE.)
(FINTAN *finds her handbag, rummages inside it, takes out the letter, looks at it, puts it back, finds the key, shuts the handbag, and starts for the door. Halfway across the room he comes to a shuddering stop. He goes racing back to the handbag, takes the letter out again and reads it. Disbelief gives way to a convulsion of sheer, towering rage. He growls like an animal and raises his hands above his head, the letter crushed in his fist.* NIAMH *comes from the bar, a glass of champagne in each hand.*)
(*Coldly*) Why don't you go to Cork – you're not wanted here. And leave my keys in the dashboard.
(*He reaches for her as if about to strangle her.*)
And don't paw me with my hands full.
(NIAMH *goes out.*
(FINTAN *sits brokenly and begins to sob.*
DERMOD *comes in.*)
DERMOD. What's the delay for? (*Looking at him*) Why are you laughing?
(FINTAN *holds out the letter.* DERMOD *takes it.*)
What is it? (*He smoothes out the letter and reads it.*) So? You and Niamh tried to book into the Royal Anna Liffey tonight and it's full up. What's so . . . (*He looks at the letter again.*) *Tonight?* But . . .
(*A heartrending sob from* FINTAN.)
Fintan, stop that.
FINTAN. It was – in her handbag.

104

DERMOD. Yes?

FINTAN. Her and some bollix.

DERMOD. Good God.

FINTAN. Me in Cork, and her in her element.

DERMOD. Niamh? I don't believe it.

FINTAN (*with a terrible roar*). I'll kill her! (*He lurches towards the door, blind with rage.*)

DERMOD (*grabbing him*). Fintan, no.

FINTAN. Let go of me.

DERMOD. Not until you control yourself. The state you're in, now, you might kill her.

FINTAN. I will, I will.

DERMOD. Yes, and then what?

FINTAN. What do you mean, then what? We'll have it hushed up, what do you think? Now get your hands off.

DERMOD. Fintan, listen to me. We're going to Cork . . .

FINTAN. To hell with Cork, I'm not going to Cork, I never liked Cork.

DERMOD (*quietly, in charge*). We are going to Cork, because whatever Niamh was up to, it's fallen through. (*Showing* FIN-TAN *the letter*) The hotel is full up. Furthermore, Grainne will be with her tonight in your house, and there'll be no monkey business with her there. In Cork, you can think things over calmly, and tomorrow you can sort it all out with Niamh in a civilized manner.

FINTAN. You're right.

DERMOD. Good man.

FINTAN. I'll kill her tomorrow.

DERMOD. Have you her car keys? (*He sees that* FINTAN *is holding the keys and takes them from him.*)

FINTAN. Maybe I ought to kill her now.

DERMOD. No!

FINTAN. I didn't get where I am today by putting things off. Can you wait five minutes? (*He makes for the door.*)

DERMOD. Fintan!

FINTAN. Why did I have to marry a raving beauty? Do you know what I'm going to do? I'll choke her till there's just enough breath left in her gizzard to gasp out the name of the man. And when I find him . . . !

DERMOD. (*shaking him violently*). Fintan!

(FINTAN *looks glassily at him.*)

Cork.

FINTAN (*childlike*). Cork?

DERMOD. And money.

FINTAN. Money . . .

DERMOD. That's the man! (*He leads the suddenly docile* FINTAN *by the hand to the door*).

(*As they reach the door,* NIAMH *enters, passing them, with her own glass of champagne.* FINTAN *emits a terrible roar and is about to spring at her, but* DERMOD *yanks him out into the hall. By the time* NIAMH *turns around they are both gone.*)

NIAMH (*assuming that the roar was a sneeze*). Bless you. (*Calling*). Grainne, they're –

(GRAINNE *enters. She has changed into her newest, most stunning dress, and carries the other glass of champagne.*) – gone.

GRAINNE. I know, I saw them. Zip me up?

(*We hear the sound of the car moving off.*) How do I look?

NIAMH. In that dress you won't have time to get to the motel. It'll happen out there, in Galloping Green.

GRAINNE (*coolly*). No, it won't. It's all going to be beautiful.

NIAMH. But it's a sin.

(GRAINNE *laughs.*) Yes, yes, it is.

GRAINNE. Father Semple, our Jesuit, said to me that if there was no sin there would be no need for priests, and if there were no priests everybody in the country would be committing adultery. Well, if we're going to turn into a race of degenerates it won't be my fault. That's why there's that bit in the Bible about a man laying down his life for his friend. So it's . . .

NIAMH. No, stop. You've lost me, and if I'm confused I won't sleep – and tonight I am going to sleep. (*Ecstatically*) When I stretch out in that big bed it's going to be like lying in a field, and not a bull in sight.

GRAINNE. You poor thing.

NIAMH (*hastily*). I don't want you to think badly of Fintan. He's the kindest man in the world – yes, he is. And it's not even the night after night I object to. You'll think I'm too sensitive, but what I've come to dread, what turns me into a nervous wreck, is waiting for the very last minute, when he roars 'Up the rebels!'. What the English did to the Irish for seven hundred years Fintan's been doing to me for the past fifteen. How is Dermod that way?

106

GRAINNE. Nothing.

NIAMH. Do you mean he doesn't roar?

GRAINNE. I mean nothing, nothing.

NIAMH. But he's never done hugging you.

GRAINNE. That's for visitors.

NIAMH (*nodding*). I *thought* you looked very fresh. But why?

GRAINNE (*shaking her head*). I'm not a disobliging wife, I know my duty. Every night I lie on my bed with my face smothered in the cream I wear to keep my pores open, just for him. And he sits on *his* bed totting up figures and looking at me as if I were the Man in the Iron Mask.

NIAMH. Twin beds. Oh, Jay.

GRAINNE. His new Jensen gets more affection than I do. At least *it* gets driven. But when James Usheen walks through that door . . . !

NIAMH. I don't want to hear. What'll you do?

GRAINNE. Not a thing. He'll take one look and sweep me into his arms.

NIAMH. Oh, Jay, don't go on.

GRAINNE. Did you read what the judge called him in that divorce case? A dedicated philanderer. And yet, when I knew him, he was all pimples and damp hands. I used to scream whenever he touched me. But *now*, oh, when I look at that man on television! So debonair, so beautifully dressed, and that low-pitched sexy voice!

(*The door bursts open and James Usheen staggers in. His overcoat and most of his face are caked with mud.*)

USHEEN (*croaking*). Where's the fucking brandy?

GRAINNE
NIAMH } (*Speaking together*). In the bar.

(*Without pausing for a moment, USHEEN goes into the bar, hitting his head on the ceiling.*)

USHEEN. Shite!

GRAINNE. James!

NIAMH. It's him!

(*They rush into the bar, where USHEEN is nursing his head with one hand and pouring himself a drink with the other.*)

GRAINNE. James, what's happened to you? You . . .

USHEEN. Belt up, will you – I think I may drop dead.

(*They watch as he knocks back a brandy.*)

That's better. Who owned this house before you did – pygmies?

107

GRAINNE. James, your clothes . . .

USHEEN. I'm lucky to be alive. Two raving maniacs in a Jensen nearly ran over me at your front gate.

NIAMH. But that must have been –

GRAINNE (*shutting her up*). – terrible for you.

USHEEN. They ought to be locked up. Then I fell into a bloody great hole out there.

GRAINNE. That's going to be our swimming-pool.

USHEEN (*coldly*). Oh, yes?

GRAINNE. Heated.

NIAMH. You're lucky – next month you would have drowned.

USHEEN (*eyeing her bleakly*). Have we met?

GRAINNE. Excuse me – this is Niamh Kinnore. Niamh is my very dearest friend – we've known each other a week.

USHEEN. Charmed.

NIAMH. I watch you every Sunday, Mr Usheen. I don't know how you think up all the –

USHEEN. Could we move out of here, or are we rehearsing for a Japanese wedding?

GRAINNE. Of course, James.

NIAMH (*lamely*). – all those funny rude remarks you make. (*They move back into the living-room. Usheen brings the brandy bottle with him.*)

USHEEN. Have you just had visitors?

GRAINNE. Why do you ask?

USHEEN. That Jensen was coming out of your drive.

GRAINNE. Was it? Sometimes cars use our gateway to turn in. Did you get the number?

USHEEN. No –

GRAINNE. What a pity.

USHEEN. – but just before I threw myself into your flower-bed I saw the ugly red face of the bastard who was driving. He said, 'I'll kill her, I'll kill her' . . .

NIAMH. Why would Fintan want to . . .

GRAINNE. Heavens, look at your coat. Take it off, James. (*She assists him.*)

USHEEN. I suppose he mistook me for a woman. I never forget a face, and I won't forget that one.

NIAMH (*a golden-tongued flatterer*). I would never mistake you for a woman, Mr Usheen.

USHEEN. You're a perceptive little thing, aren't you? Yes, I'll remember that git. And if I ever meet him . . . !

GRAINNE. My goodness, what a beautiful coat.

USHEEN. Think so? I bought it to spite Eamonn Andrews. Now it's ruined.

GRAINNE. No, it's only mud. It'll brush out. The important thing is, you got here.

USHEEN. Where's your husband?

GRAINNE. He – went to Cork.

USHEEN. Oh?

GRAINNE. Unexpectedly.

USHEEN. I'm sorry to have missed him.

GRAINNE. So I'm afraid we're all alone.

USHEEN. You and I?

GRAINNE. Yes.

USHEEN. What's *that*, then?

(*They both look at* NIAMH, *who has been drinking in every word.*)

Niamh, why don't you take James's coat somewhere and see what you can do with it?

NIAMH. Will I hang on here until it's dry?

GRAINNE. No, dear.

NIAMH. Well, will I come straight back?

GRAINNE (*shaking her head slowly and deliberately*). Of course come straight back.

(NIAMH *reluctantly takes the coat and goes to the door.*)

(*To* USHEEN, *smiling*). Well!

NIAMH. Pssst!

GRAINNE (*to* USHEEN) Excuse me. (*Going to* NIAMH) What?

NIAMH. Be careful.

GRAINNE. Clean the coat.

NIAMH. I suppose, coming from England, he's on the Pill?

GRAINNE. The coat, Niamh.

NIAMH. Make sure.

(NIAMH *goes out unwillingly.*

GRAINNE *comes down to* USHEEN. *They face each other.*)

USHEEN. Well!

GRAINNE (*smiling*). Well?

(*He starts towards her. She prepares herself for a blissful encounter, but he bypasses her. His destination is the brandy bottle.*)

Do please help yourself.

USHEEN. Do you realize, this brandy has probably been in cask since the last time I saw you?

GRAINNE. Twelve years.

USHEEN. Is it? (*Sniffing the brandy*) You're right, you know!

GRAINNE. You've said hello to it twice – you might say hello to me. How do I look?

USHEEN. Superb.

GRAINNE (*pleased*). Liar.

USHEEN. The prettiest brunette on our road. You still are.

GRAINNE. There's mud on your glasses.

USHEEN. Is there? (*He takes them off.*) Oh, my God!

GRAINNE (*touching her hair*). I wouldn't have changed it, but Dermod likes me in red.

USHEEN. Oh, yes?

GRAINNE. He says it'll remind us of the days when we had an overdraft. God has been so good to us since then.

USHEEN. I do congratulate Him.

GRAINNE. Do you, James? Some men might be disappointed. Some men might wish that a girl hadn't done quite so well for herself without him.

USHEEN. I couldn't be more thrilled.

GRAINNE. Thank you, James.

USHEEN. And that dress!

GRAINNE. This old thing? It's my newest.

USHEEN. It'll be a knockout when it's finished.

GRAINNE. I like your suit.

USHEEN. Good.

GRAINNE. One of dozens?

USHEEN. I have six . . .

GRAINNE. Dermod has ten.

USHEEN. Beige, that is.

GRAINNE. Speaking of handmade shoes . . .

USHEEN (*looking at a painting*). That is beautiful.

GRAINNE. What? Oh yes, we like that.

USHEEN. I love it.

GRAINNE. It's a Paul Henry. (*Or whatever.*)

USHEEN. I know. I have the original.

GRAINNE. Oh?

USHEEN. Somewhere.

GRAINNE. Well, we've both come a long way.

USHEEN. Would you say?

GRAINNE. You, especially.

USHEEN. Yes, I suppose I have.

GRAINNE. But then, of course, I didn't have nearly so far to travel.

110

USHEEN. You're beautiful when you smile.

GRAINNE. Am I, James?

USHEEN. What dentistry!

GRAINNE. Seriously, James, Dermod and I are two of your most devoted fans. We've watched every programme of yours right from the very beginning.

USHEEN. All of them?

GRAINNE. I swear.

USHEEN. Good God.

GRAINNE. Except one.

USHEEN. How super.

GRAINNE. Yes.

USHEEN. Fantastic.

GRAINNE. Mmmm.

USHEEN. How come you missed one?

GRAINNE. We switched over to Eamonn Andrews. More brandy? (*She sails into the bar.*) I got him, I got him, I got him!

USHEEN. Grainne!

GRAINNE. Coming!

USHEEN. I am going home.

GRAINNE. He's going home.

USHEEN. Good-bye.

GRAINNE. Good – bye!

(USHEEN *stomps out.*)

Good-bye? My God, I must have been mad. James, come back. (USHEEN *returns.*)

USHEEN. Where is my overcoat?

GRAINNE. I was joking.

USHEEN. You were not.

GRAINNE. I was.

USHEEN. There are two things one does not joke about – death and Eamonn Andrews.

GRAINNE. So it was a joke in poor taste.

USHEEN. Sick.

GRAINNE. The reason I missed your programme just that once was because the children had tonsilitis.

USHEEN. And that is your excuse?

GRAINNE. We thought they were dying.

USHEEN. That's better.

GRAINNE. Of course it is.

USHEEN. I'll buy that.

GRAINNE. So sit, have your drink and talk to me.

111

USHEEN. Yes, when I met your husband in London he mentioned you had children.

GRAINNE. Two. Emer and Ronan.

USHEEN. Where are the little bug – beggars?

GRAINNE. They're convalescing at the moment with friends of ours who have a house in Greece.

USHEEN. I like Greece.

GRAINNE. So do we.

USHEEN. For week-ends.

(*There is a moment of strain.*)

GRAINNE. Pax, James.

USHEEN. Pax. Your husband seems a nice fellow.

GRAINNE. Yes, doesn't he!

USHEEN. I suppose you're mad about him.

GRAINNE. I adore him. But let's not talk about what's-his-name – Dermod – and me. Especially not me. All I am is just a plain, dull, boring housewife.

(USHEEN *smiles to himself and nods his head. When she looks at him, the nod turns into a shake.*)

Tell me what you've been up to. (*Playfully*) I've heard the most shocking stories.

USHEEN. About me?

GRAINNE. And women. I'm afraid you're a wicked man.

USHEEN. Ha-ha.

GRAINNE. And here I am alone in the house at your mercy.

USHEEN. Isn't your friend still here?

GRAINNE. She won't come in – not unless she heard me screaming the place down.

USHEEN. Well, then!

GRAINNE (*eyeing him firmly*). I never scream.

(*For a moment* USHEEN *is stunned by the implications of this.*)

USHEEN. I see! What you mean is, there won't be any need for you to scream, because you can trust me. Thank you – and yes, yes, you can!

GRAINNE. Can what?

USHEEN. Trust me.

GRAINNE. Yes?

USHEEN. You are the one woman I will always respect.

GRAINNE. Oh, shit. (*She bursts into tears.* GRAINNE *is a noisy weeper.*)

USHEEN. Why, I'd sooner lose my Sunday-night TAM ratings than harm a hair of your head. (*He pats her head*). There, there, there! No need to snivel. To me, you'll always be the shy little girl who used to shudder with virginal passion whenever I touched her. You're as safe with me now as you were then. Of course, I'm only human. The best of men sometimes commit the most horrible deeds.

(*At this ray of hope,* GRAINNE *stops crying.*)

They kill the things they love — perhaps through frailty, perhaps in a fit of drunkenness.

(GRAINNE *at once pours him a drink and puts it firmly in his hand.*)

But if I were to utter one lustful word to you, drunk or sober, I hope I should drop dead. Thanks. (*He drinks.*) I'm not a virtuous man. You may as well know that what they say about me is true. I have had women — in a way.

GRAINNE. How interesting. (*Delicately*) Which way did you have them?

USHEEN. And yet, through the whole ugly, sordid mess, there was always one woman I truly loved.

GRAINNE (*overwhelmed*). Do you mean . . . ?

USHEEN. One person who meant everything to me.

GRAINNE. Oh, James.

USHEEN. A love that stayed fine throughout the years.

GRAINNE. Don't . . .

USHEEN. Her name was Venetia.

(*He misinterprets* GRAINNE'S *stunned reaction.*)

And you're right   bloody stupid name for a woman. The silly cow liked to pretend she'd been conceived in a gondola. You read about the divorce case I was mixed up in? She was the woman. Afterwards, we lived together. Openly. Convention thrown to the winds, lost to all sense of shame, God no longer existed.

GRAINNE. Why didn't you marry her?

USHEEN. Are you mad? Marry a divorced woman — and be excommunicated? You're not paying attention, are you? Get the wax out, there's a good girl. Where was I?

GRAINNE. Venetia.

USHEEN. Don't mention that woman's name to me.

GRAINNE. But didn't you love her?

USHEEN. I curse the day I first laid hands on her. Three o'clock in the morning — 'James, do you love me?' I reply tenderly (*snarling*). 'I'm in bed with you amn't I?' Do you think that satisfies

113

her? No, she wants more endearments, and then it's 'You don't love me, you don't. And I broke up my marriage for you.' Her marriage! Her husband was a fifty-three-year-old alcoholic who narrowly escaped prosecution on a charge of attempted misconduct with a pillar-box while under the impression that it was a Chinese streetwalker. And that's the kind of anatomical education you pick up at Eton! Oh, those four words – 'You don't love me!' – the great digestive belch of a woman who's been feeding on your entrails. Then, after the recriminations, the threats. 'I'll give myself to the first man I meet.'

GRAINNE (*taking his empty glass*). Did she?

USHEEN. She tried it once. Disappeared. Of course I knew where to find her. Seven a.m., and she was in Chiswick, walking up and down outside Eamonn Andrews' gate. Silly cow, didn't even know he'd moved. And after the threats, the worst part.

GRAINNE. What was that? (*She begins to refill his glass.*)

USHEEN. She . . . (*His voice breaks.*)

GRAINNE. She tried to kill herself.

USHEEN. Worse. She did what was unforgiveable.

GRAINNE. Tell me.

USHEEN. If you'll shut up for a minute, I will. She was rude to me.

GRAINNE. Oh.

USHEEN. Insults, sarcasm, nasty little gibes. She said I had a big head and a small – oh, but some people have wicked tongues. Do you know what that woman did? She castrated me.

(GRAINNE *considers this, then regretfully begins to pour his brandy back into the bottle.*)

Figuratively speaking.

(GRAINNE *pours the brandy back into the glass.*)

GRAINNE. Did you leave her?

USHEEN. Regularly. I took up with those other women you just now mentioned. I didn't need her, and I'd prove it. The trouble was, when it came right down to the nitty-gritty – I couldn't.

GRAINNE. You couldn't what?

USHEEN. I just – couldn't. Perhaps I'd had too much to drink at the time. Perhaps that was why.

(GRAINNE *sighs, looks at the brandy and once more pours it from the glass back into the bottle.*)

No – no, it wasn't.

(GRAINNE *gives him both bottle and glass and lets him do his own pouring.*)

At the moment of truth, the same thing always happened. I kept seeing her mole.

114

GRAINNE. Her what?

USHEEN. She had a large mole right here – (*he prods his chest then prods* GRAINNE'S) – there. I beg your pardon.

GRAINNE. My pleasure.

USHEEN. I kept seeing her mole – her beauty spot, she called it. Ugly-looking thing. It ruined my life. Three weeks ago, I made up my mind, left her for good. It's over now.

GRAINNE. Venetia and you?

USHEEN. Everything. Involvements, emotions, sex. I've finished with it all.

(NIAMH'S *voice is heard off.*)

NIAMH. Oh, Jay.

(USHEEN *opens the door and reveals* NIAMH *kneeling at the keyhole.*)

Excuse me. The television set in the kitchen isn't working.

GRAINNE (*stunned, still looking at* USHEEN). Try the one in the loo.

(USHEEN *closes the door.*)

USHEEN. I'm sorry – this must be distressing for you.

GRAINNE. You have no idea.

USHEEN. It's my own fault. I should have fallen in love with an Irish girl.

GRAINNE. An Irish girl might have had a mole, too.

USHEEN. Yes, but I'd never have seen it.

GRAINNE. If you believe that, you've been away for longer than you think.

USHEEN (*shaking his head*). Some things never change. That's why I came to see you – my first love. The girl who longed to be a nun.

GRAINNE. Did I say that?

USHEEN. Have you forgotten? That was the reason you gave for not wanting to see me any more.

GRAINNE (*remembering*). So it was.

USHEEN. If I'm going to embark upon a life of celibacy, I thought I should begin here, with the only truly pure girl I ever knew.

GRAINNE. Me?

(*Tongue-tied with emotion, he cocks a finger at her like a pistol and fires an imaginary shot by way of an affirmative.*) Did you really love me, James?

USHEEN. I adored every black hair on your red head. I mean I . . .

GRAINNE (*swallowing this*). And I was fond of *you*, James. I still am, and I'm not going to stand by and watch you let a tiny mole ruin your life.

USHEEN. It was a brute of a mole. And what can you do?

GRAINNE. Supposing you were to slip on our imported Hong Kong marble bathroom floor and break your back? You'd expect me to help, wouldn't you? You'd expect me to – to do whatever it is you would do for a broken back.

USHEEN. Yes, but . . .

GRAINNE. This is the same thing. You're still moping over that awful woman, and I think what you need is a – love transplant. (USHEEN *is about to speak.*)
Don't argue – I am a woman, and that means I'm wonderfully wise, and I know that perfect love, and perfect love alone, casteth out moles. James, I have something to show you.

USHEEN (*nervously*). Oh?

GRAINNE. Right now.

USHEEN (*his eyes on her bosom*). I don't think I want to . . .

GRAINNE. You'll love it. It's the most beautiful mo –

USHEEN. I won't look.

GRAINNE. – motel in the world. Dermod owns it – at least he owns half of it. Let's go there.

USHEEN. To a motel? What for?

GRAINNE. I'll tell you on the way. It's only up the mountains.

USHEEN. Up the . . . ?

GRAINNE. The view is marvellous.

USHEEN. It's pitch dark out, it's pouring rain and there's a gale blowing.

GRAINNE. Irish weather, James – what they call a soft night. (*This strikes her as humorous, she giggles.*)

USHEEN. But what has you showing me a motel got to do with Venetia's mole?

GRAINNE. No questions. You must put yourself completely in my hands. Don't move, I'll get my coat.

USHEEN. Couldn't we just sit here and . . .
(GRAINNE *goes out.*
USHEEN *remains seated, looking baffled.*)
A motel? Why does she want us to . . . (*The truth dawns.*) She wouldn't (*Discarding the idea as preposterous.*) Don't be a fool, James, lad – she's an Irish Catholic wife and mother. The only thing she's got left is her virginity. (*He rises and takes a step towards the door, calling.*) Grainne, I . . . (*He stops. A look of physical discomfort comes over his face. He touches his trouser-legs.*) Damn.
GRAINNE *swings back into the room, now wearing a mink*

coat. She remembers to model it for us briefly, humming 'A Pretty Girl is like a Melody'. She passes the stricken USHEEN *on her way to be bar.*)

GRAINNE. I threw on just any old thing.

USHEEN. Grainne . . .

(GRAINNE *resumes humming and goes into the bar. Ducking expertly, she picks up two bottles of brandy and comes out at once, ducking again.*)

USHEEN. Grainne, I can't go.

GRAINNE. Yes, you can.

USHEEN. There's something you don't know.

GRAINNE. About Venetia?

USHEEN. About me. (*Indicating his upper leg*) Touch me here.

GRAINNE. Later, James.

USHEEN. I mean I'm soaked to the skin.

GRAINNE. For heaven's sake, a little dampness . . . !

USHEEN. Oh, if ever I get my hands on that red-faced bastard in the Jensen . . . !

GRAINNE. Take off your trousers.

USHEEN. I beg your pardon?

GRAINNE. You can borrow a pair of Dermod's.

USHEEN. But . . .

GRAINNE. Or do you *want* to catch cold? (*She goes to the door and calls off*) Niamh, is Mr Usheen's overcoat dry yet? (*To* USHEEN) Will you do as you're told? Take them *off*.

(GRAINNE *goes out.* USHEEN *broods for a moment, then reluctantly removes his trousers. He begins to empty the pockets.* NIAMH *comes in with his overcoat. The sight of* USHEEN, *trouserless, stops her dead in her tracks.*)

NIAMH. *Already?*

USHEEN. My trousers got wet.

NIAMH (*with a forced smile*). Ah, sure why wouldn't they!

(*There is an embarrassed pause.* USHEEN *toys with his drink.* NIAMH *tries unsuccessfully to keep her eyes away from his shorts. Their eyes meet.*)

Terrible weather.

USHEEN (*shortly*). Yes.

NIAMH. You'd need those on you this evening.

USHEEN. I'm sure.

NIAMH. I like blue.

(USHEEN *contrives to hide his shorts from view.*)

117

Fintan won't wear them. He says they're unmanly. So I'm
always at him.

(USHEEN *looks at her.*)

To wear drawers, I mean. If you were him now and I was
another woman, there'd be a court case. Can I ask you
something, Mr Usheen?

USHEEN. No.

NIAMH. I might never get the chance again, so just as a favour
would you say something insulting?

USHEEN (*losing his temper*). Bugger off.

NIAMH. Ah, thanks.

(Grainne *comes back with a pair of trousers.*)

GRAINNE. These are just back from the cleaners. Put them on.

USHEEN. Grainne, perhaps we should give the motel a miss for this
evening. It's getting late, and . . .

GRAINNE. Late? The night is still a pup. Now put them on. We
won't look – (*to* NIAMH) – will we?

(GRAINNE *and* NIAMH *retire to a position behind* USHEEN
*and watch fascinated as he puts on the trousers. Through
the following they keep their eyes on him.*)

NIAMH. Grainne . . .

GRAINNE. What?

NIAMH. Be good, will you?

GRAINNE. I'll be magnificent.

(NIAMH *moans feebly.*)

Now listen. Leave his wet trousers on the radiator in the
kitchen.

NIAMH. Right.

GRAINNE. And when we're gone, ring up the motel. Tell the
caretaker you're me. Say that two married friends of yours are
on their way there. They need a room, and he's to let them in.
Got that?

USHEEN. Blast.

GRAINNE. What's wrong?

USHEEN. The zip's stuck.

GRAINNE. That's what dry cleaning does. Pull it.

USHEEN. I am – it's stuck.

GRAINNE. Soap will fix it. Wait . . .

(GRAINNE *goes out.*

USHEEN *pulls on the zip.* NIAMH *kneels down in front
of him and peers closely at the zip.*)

USHEEN. What are you doing?

NIAMH. Let me have a go − I'm great with lids. Hold still.

(*As* NIAMH *wrestles with the zip, still kneeling in front of* USHEEN, FINTAN *appears outside the french windows. He clutches his face in horror at what he thinks he sees, then bangs on the glass with his fists.*)

Do you hear the wind?

USHEEN. That doesn't sound like . . .

NIAMH. There, I've got it.

(FINTAN, *grabbing his hair in fury, goes tearing off around the side of the house.*)

(*Yelling.*) Grainne, come back, I've got it!

USHEEN. Thank you, and bless your little frankfurter fingers. My overcoat?

NIAMH. It's here. (*She helps him on with his coat..*

(GRAINNE *returns.*)

GRAINNE. Is he unfastened?

NIAMH. Yes.

GRAINNE (*picking up the brandy*). Then let's go. Niamh, you know what to do.

NIAMH. Yes. No, I don't know the number of the − (*looking at* USHEEN) − M-O-T-T-E-L.

USHEEN. Mottel?

GRAINNE. It's in Dermod's address book. In the study, across the hall. (*Taking* USHEEN's *arm*) 'Bye, now.

USHEEN. Are you sure this excursion is necessary?

GRAINNE. I'll be the judge of that, James. You just keep on repeating as we drive − 'There are no moles on Grainne'.

USHEEN. Pardon?

GRAINNE. You heard.

(GRAINNE *crosses herself and pushes* USHEEN *out ahead of her.*)

NIAMH. 'Bye, 'bye, now. Have a nice . . . (*Getting on safer ground*) 'Bye!

(*The front door slams.*

NIAMH *wavers for a moment.*)

Address book!

(NIAMH *goes out at the very moment when* FINTAN *reappears at the window, now brandishing a hatchet. He smashes the lock on the french windows with one blow, then bursts into the room waving the hatchet. His hair is flattened by the rain.*)

FINTAN (*triumphantly*). Gotcha! (*He realizes that the room is empty. Then his eyes focus on the bar. He emits a growling noise and rushes in. We expect him to bang his head, but he*

119

ducks just in time and stands inside the bar, crouching. DERMOD *comes in by the french windows, noting the shattered lock.*)

DERMOD. (*sharply*). Fintan!

(FINTAN *jerks upright and bangs his head on the ceiling.*)

FINTAN. Jasus.

DERMOD. Come out here. Did you break the lock?

FINTAN (*dazed*). What?

DERMOD. And where did you get that hatchet?

FINTAN. In your shed.

DERMOD. That shed was locked.

FINTAN. I broke the lock.

DERMOD. What for?

FINTAN. To get the hatchet to break *that* lock. (*He indicates the french window*.) Why else do you think I broke the branch off the tree?

DERMOD. What tree?

FINTAN (*pointing out*). *That* tree!

DERMOD. My cherry tree?

FINTAN. God, didn't I need the branch to break the lock of the shed to get the hatchet to break *that* lock? (*To the audience*) He's so thick. And she's upstairs now.

DERMOD. Who is?

FINTAN. Niamh. I saw her through the window. She was . . .

DERMOD. She was what?

FINTAN. Kneeling down.

DERMOD. Praying?

DERMOD. Praying?

FINTAN. If she was, it wasn't for a mild winter.

DERMOD. What was she doing?

FINTAN. I won't tell you. I wouldn't tell anyone. It's a mortal sin even to *know* what she was doing. There was this man . . .

DERMOD. What man?

FINTAN. And I know his face from somewhere. He . . .

DERMOD. Niamh and a man? You're raving.

FINTAN. I tell you they're upstairs. My God, if they'd do what I saw them doing in a living-room, what are they not perpetrating in the presence of a bed? I'll kill her.

DERMOD. Fintan, your wife is not in this house.

FINTAN. She's bouncing on your springs.

DERMOD. She's gone.

FINTAN. Get stitched.

120

DERMOD. While you were pulling up my good tree, Grainne's car went out the gate. She and Niamh have gone to your house for the night, as they were supposed to.

FINTAN (*hollowly*). He's taken her off to some whorehouse!

DERMOD. There was no man here with Niamh.

FINTAN. I saw him.

DERMOD. You saw Grainne.

FINTAN. Your wife is ugly, but I wouldn't mistake her for a man.

DERMOD (*blinking*). My wife is ugly?

FINTAN. I know, but don't dwell on it.

DERMOD (*losing his temper*). That does it!

FINTAN. Does what?

DERMOD. I let you drag me back, all the way from Terenure, because it's either end up in bits on the Naas Road or let you see for yourself that Niamh is here and up to no harm. So I wait in the car, and what's my thanks? You break my cherry tree, you smash the lock on my shed, you butcher my french windows, and now you insult my wife. And all because your brain in unhinged.

FINTAN. Say that again!

DERMOD. You're having hallucinations.

FINTAN. You pup, you.

DERMOD. There was no man in this room.

FINTAN (*almost dancing with fury*). I saw him, I saw him!

DERMOD. You saw your reflection in the glass.

FINTAN. I saw my . . . (*He breaks off. It occurs to him that* DERMOD *may be right.*)

DERMOD (*having won his point*). And now I'm going to have a drink. (*He goes into the bar*).

(FINTAN *looks from the french windows to the spot where he saw* NIAMH *and* USHEEN.)

Do you want one?

FINTAN (*convinced*). He was a handsome bugger, right enough. Funny, the way your mind plays tricks. I could have sworn that I saw her kneeling down . . . (*He starts towards the bar, then sees* USHEEN'S *trousers on the back of a chair. He picks them up, discovers that they are wet and drops them with a gasp of revulsion. He heads into the bar.*) So I'm imagining things, am I?

DERMOD (*wearily*). Oh, God.

FINTAN. Am I imagining a pair of trousers? A pair of *wet* trousers?

DERMOD. You're demented.

FINTAN. Is that so? Come out and look.

(NIAMH *returns with the address book. She goes towards the telephone, then notices the trousers. She picks them up and goes out with them.*)

DERMOD. Look at what?

FINTAN. The trousers.

DERMOD. Whose?

FINTAN. His. They're in there, and they're sopping wet.

DERMOD. Trousers?

FINTAN. He couldn't even wait to drop them till he got upstairs.

DERMOD. Why are they wet?

FINTAN. Don't ask me. Will you come and look?

DERMOD. Damn sure I'll come and look.

(NIAMH *disappears with the trousers a split second before they emerge from the bar.*)

FINTAN. Now we'll see who's demented. (*He points to the chair*). There!

DERMOD. Where?

FINTAN. *There* – are you . . . (*He stares at the empty chair. He goes on his knees and looks under it, then runs his hands over the chair, as if the trousers were still on it, but had turned invisible.*) They were here ten seconds ago.

DERMOD. Fintan, see a doctor.

FINTAN. I saw them, I touched them. They were wet. Feel my hand.

DERMOD (*doing so*). Your hand is dry.

FINTAN. Of course it's bloody dry – I wiped it!

DERMOD. Fintan, go home, go to bed.

FINTAN (*jumping up and down, almost weeping with rage*). I saw the bugger's trousers, I saw them, I saw them.

DERMOD. Fintan, stop that.

FINTAN. I did, I did, I did. (*He gives three more mighty jumps as he speaks.*)

DERMOD. You'll upset all the thermostats.

FINTAN (*with sudden cunning*). I know what it is. It's a plot to drive me mad.

DERMOD. Now, look . . .

FINTAN. You're behind it – you and that ugly wife of yours. You want the Cork motel for yourself.

DERMOD (*coldly*). I think we should forget about the Cork motel for the time being. Perhaps our partnership wasn't such a good idea after all.

FINTAN. There's no perhaps about it.

DERMOD. Seeing trousers that aren't there, I can understand. But *wet* trousers – that's sick.

FINTAN. *You'll* be sick in a minute. (*He looks about wildly for the hatchet.*)

(DERMOD *sees the hatchet at the same time, and they both make a rush for it.* DERMOD *gets there first.*)

DERMOD (*loftily*). My hatchet, I believe.

FINTAN. What else could I expect from a get who got where he is by informing on people to the Income Tax.

DERMOD. Earlier, you said you wished you'd thought of it first.

FINTAN (*massively*). *That* was common politeness.

DERMOD (*dignified*). Fintan, I wish you good night.

FINTAN. There's no harm in wishing.

DERMOD. I mean good-bye.

FINTAN. The only place I'm going is up your stairs. That's where my wife is, and there's a man with her with his trousers off.

DERMOD. If I go up and look, will that convince you?

FINTAN. I wouldn't believe you if you told me that Paisley was a Protestant. Give me that hatchet.

DERMOD. I'll keep the hatchet, Fintan.

(DERMOD *goes out.*

(FINTAN *is on the point of following him, but decides that he needs a weapon. He goes into the bar and picks up a bottle which he strikes viciously into the palm of his hand. He discards it in favour of a heavy decanter which he holds like a cudgel!*

NIAMH *comes in carrying the address book and humming loudly to herself. She goes to the telephone and dials.*

(FINTAN, *hearing the humming, looks puzzled and rotates a finger in his ear to get rid of it.*)

NIAMH (*shrilling*). 'Let me call you sweetheart, I'm in love with you; let me hear you whisper that you love me too . . .' (*Into the phone*) Hello, is that the Patrick Pearse Motel? . . . Are you the caretaker? This is Mrs Dermod Gibbon speaking.

(FINTAN *sticks his head around the door of the bar to look at* NIAMH.)

I'm well, and how are you? . . . Aren't you great. The thing is, there are two friends of mine who need a room for tonight, and I'm sending them up to the motel . . . Yes, so it's all right to let them in . . . A lady and a gentleman, yes . . . No, not a twin, I think they'd like a double. The main thing is, you'll be ready for them?

(FINTAN *nods slowly, and with emphasis.*)
Thanks very much . . . Not at all. Good-bye.
(NIAMH *hangs up, looks heavenwards for forgiveness, and goes out, humming again.*
(FINTAN *emerges from the bar.*)

FINTAN. Oh, the rip. Lust under the Plough and the Stars – there's not a jury in the country will convict me. What are you talking about? You'll be made a Papal Count. But the rip!
(DERMOD *returns.*)

DERMOD. There's no-one upstairs, not a soul. Go and see for yourself.

FINTAN. Your word is good enough for me.

DERMOD. I'm not accustomed to being called a . . . Pardon?

FINTAN (*elaborately casual*). It seems I was mistaken. I'll go home, so – home to bed.

DERMOD. Fintan, are you all right?

FINTAN. Me? How can I be all right? I imagine things. I'm demented, so I'm sick.

DERMOD. If I said anything in haste . . .

FINTAN (*airily*). Don't give it a thought. I dare say we'll meet again. And if we don't, sure our solicitors will.
(FINTAN *gives* DERMOD *a nod from a great height and goes out.*)

DERMOD. Solicitors? I always knew he had a slate loose. Failure has gone to his head. (*He removes his coat, aware that he is in for a solitary evening. He goes up to the hi-fi unit and sets about selecting a record.*)
(*As* DERMOD *puts the record on the turntable,* NIAMH *comes in, dressed for home. She is about to switch off the lights when she sees* DERMOD *with his back to her. She emits a hoarse cry of shock, then goes haring out again.*
(DERMOD *turns, just in time not to see her. He goes towards the door.*)

DERMOD. Who's that? Who is it, who's there? (*Looking into the hall*) You? What are *you* doing here?
(MISS MANNING *comes in, smiling the smile of modest achievement. She wears spectacles, her hair is drawn back severely into a bun. Her coat and galoshes are sensible. She has the habit of saying 'Ai' and 'mai' instead of 'I' and 'my'.*)

MISS MANNING. How nice to see you again, Mr Gibbon. Wasn't I expected?

DERMOD. Not tonight, Miss Manning. They told me London Airport was closed.

124

MISS MANNING. It is. I took a train to Manchester and an aeroplane from there. A good employee can always find a way.

DERMOD. I congratulate you.

MISS MANNING. Might I compliment you, Mr Gibbon, upon the vigour of your friends?

DERMOD. Pardon me?

MISS MANNING. I was almost bowled over in your driveway by a gentleman who was running like billy-o.

DERMOD. That would have been my partner, Mr Kinnore. Running, did you say?

MISS MANNING. And again in your hall by a lady in a tizz.

DERMOD. A lady?

MISS MANNING. I'm sure you know best, Mr Gibbon.

DERMOD. Do sit down, Miss Manning. Did you have a good journey?

MISS MANNING. Beastly. On the train, I had to move my seat three times. Men with roving eyes, you know. No roving eyes here, Mr Gibbon.

DERMOD (*with a forced smile*). Well, just a few.

(*She gives a genteel little laugh, which turns into a no less genteel cough.*)

MISS MANNING. Hem! Might I have a glass of water?

DERMOD. Of course. Perhaps something a little stronger?

MISS MANNING. Well . . . ?

DERMOD. Whiskey?

MISS MANNING. Brandy?

DERMOD (*taken slightly aback*). Certainly. (*He goes to the bar.*) Odd – the brandy seems to have disappeared, Miss Manning. There's only Scotch.

MISS MANNING. I'm not fussy. (*She looks at him appraisingly as he pours her drink.*) I went directly to my hotel, but they seem to have cancelled my reservation. So I'm open to suggestions.

DERMOD. Well, I . . .

MISS MANNING. Such a charming home. Perhaps I might impose on Mrs Gibbon and you for the night?

DERMOD. My wife is staying with a friend.

MISS MANNING. Oh? (*Receiving her drink*) 'nk yow!

DERMOD. So it would hardly be proper if . . .

MISS MANNING. Quite. We must be proper, mustn't we? (*She knocks back half her drink in one go.*) I seem to be a little problem.

DERMOD. Not at all.

MISS MANNING. All I ask for is a bed. Then, first thing in the morning, I can begin my duties.

DERMOD (*inspired*). But of course!

MISS MANNING. Yes?

DERMOD. The motel! You'll be staying there tomorrow anyway when the staff arrive. Why not tonight?

MISS MANNING. How super.

DERMOD. The only thing is, it's a bit isolated.

MISS MANNING. I don't mind loneliness. I was married for five years.

DERMOD. Oh, yes?

MISS MANNING. Horrid man. I shall adore being at the motel. Tomorrow morning I shall say to myself, 'Here you are in Ireland, the land of creamery butter, little boggy roads, and religious mania.' I've done my homework, you see!

DERMOD. Ha-ha.

MISS MANNING. Might we go now?

DERMOD. To the motel? Yes. Have you luggage?

MISS MANNING. I left it on the doorstep.

DERMOD. It'll get soaked there. I'll put it in the car. You finished your drink?

MISS MANNING. Too kind.

(DERMOD *takes his coat and goes out.*

MISS MANNING *knocks back her drink, then helps herself to a refill, a hefty one. Carrying her glass, she drifts over to the hi-fi unit. She switches on the record player. The music is modern, sensuous.*)

MISS MANNING. Irish music — how super! (*She continues her tour of the room, drinking as she goes. Gradually, and apparently without realizing it, she begins to move in rhythm with the music. She opens a button of her coat, then shrugs one shoulder free, then the other. The coat falls to the floor and she steps out of it. She undoes the bow holding her hair in place, then shakes her head and lets her hair fall about her shoulders. Her mind seems to be a thousand miles away, but her body is getting into the spirit of the music. She takes off her glasses. She begins to unbutton her blouse*).

(DERMOD *comes in and stands stock still.*

Swaying sinuously, MISS MANNING *now unzips her skirt. She sees* DERMOD *and zips it up again, taking her time and not the least embarrassed. She switches off the record player.*)

126

MISS MANNING. I find music ever so restful, don't you?

DERMOD. (*croaking*). Yes.

MISS MANNING. Is something not right?

DERMOD. No. You don't seem quite the same as you did in London.

MISS MANNING. Gentlemen often say that about me – that I'm different. I don't know why. I hope I won't be a disappointment to you, Mr Gibbon.

DERMOD. I'm sure you won't.

MISS MANNING. And I know *I'm* going to enjoy working for *you*. I haven't had an interesting position since before my marriage, and it's so impo. 'ant to a girl as to whom she is under.

DERMOD. Oh, yes?

MISS MANNING. Will Mrs Gibbon be away *all* night?

DERMOD. Yes.

MISS MANNING. Oh, poor thing.

DERMOD. I'm supposed to be in Cork.

MISS MANNING. And amn't I glad you aren't!

DERMOD. Shall we go now?

MISS MANNING. Super. I can't wait. (*She gives him her coat to hold, and puts it on.*) 'nk yow! Now I'm all yours.

(*She turns so that she is very close to him. He is on the point of losing control, when she moves away from him abruptly and goes towards the door.*)

Are you partial to animals, Mr Gibbon?

DERMOD. Animals, Miss Manning?

MISS MANNING. Call me Venetia. I have the prettiest mole you have ever seen.

MISS MANNING *goes out as* DERMOD *takes a step to follow her, and* –

the CURTAIN *falls.*

ACT II

Scene 1

The Motel. Fifteen minutes later.
We see two bedrooms and a section of corridor. Seen from above, the corridor would resemble a letter 'H' lying on its side. it runs from R *to* L *up stage, and parallel to this down stage. A connecting length of corridor* C *cuts the stage in two and separates the two bedrooms. These are the Emmet room and the Parnell room. Each room is a mirror image of the other, except that one contains a large oil painting of Charles Stewart Parnell, and the other one of Robert Emmet. Each room contains a double bed, built-in wardrobe, easy chair and chest-of-drawers. Bathrooms are situated off down stage on either side.*
As the Curtain rises,. HOOLIHAN, *the night watchman, appears in the corridor, followed by* GRAINNE *and* USHEEN. *He is in his late seventies.*

HOOLIHAN. Now this, sir and missus, is what they call the Nineteenth Century wing. (*He indicates the doors at the rear*) There's a lovely room, the Isaac Butt room. And next to it, the Manchester Martyrs' room, with three single beds. You don't want that.

USHEEN. He's made a mistake. Tell him we're not staying.

HOOLIHAN. Yes, sir, sure they're all lovely rooms. And this one, excuse me, sir and missus − is the Chief's room . . .

USHEEN. The old eejit thinks we're staying the night.

(HOOLIHAN *goes into the Parnell room, salutes the painting, and stands before it at attention.*)

HOOLIHAN. Charles Stewart Parnell!

USHEEN. This isn't a motel. It's Madame Tussauds.

GRAINNE. Be respectful, James. He was out in nineteen-sixteen.

USHEEN. By the look of him, he hasn't come in yet. Let's get away from here now.

GRAINNE. James, it's time you and I had our little talk.

USHEEN. Right, we can have it back at your place − I've got to pick up my trousers anyway.

128

GRAINNE. But . . .

(HOOLIHAN, *having again saluted, comes out.*)

HOOLIHAN. Now I'll show you another lovely room. Named after bold Robert Emmet, sir, the darlin' of Erin. (*He goes into the Emmet room, salutes the portrait and stands before it in homage.*)

USHEEN. He's doing it again. My God, it's a political Stations of the Cross. How many rooms in this madhouse?

GRAINNE. Eighty-four.

USHEEN. We'll be here all bloody night.

GRAINNE (*with a catlike smile*). Mmmm . . .

USHEEN What does that mean?

(HOOLIHAN *comes out.*)

We're obliged to you for your trouble. This lady and I must be off now.

HOOLIHAN. It is, it is. The next room is the Wolfe Tone room and then there's the O'Donovan Rossa room . . .

USHEEN. He's senile.

GRAINNE. Well, he's old.

USHEEN. That's no excuse.

HOOLIHAN (*tottering forward*). Hup, two, three three, four! Hup, two, three, four!

GRAINNE. We'll give him the slip in a minute — you just be ready.

(HOOLIHAN *turns, waiting for them.*)

We're coming!

HOOLIHAN. Then there's the Thomas Davis room and the Michael Davitt room.

(HOOLIHAN *goes out of sight down left, followed by* USHEEN *and* GRAINNE.)

(*Off*) All lovely snug rooms. Hup, two, three, four!

(*There is a pause.*)

GRAINNE (*off*). Now, James.

(GRAINNE *comes back into view, pausing for a moment, apparently leading an unseen* USHEEN *by the hand.*)

Don't hang back, he'll see us. (*She pulls, not* USHEEN, *but* HOOLIHAN *into view and drags him after her at an agonized trot.*) Any room will do us. In here — quickly. (*She drags him after her into the Parnell room and shuts the door.*)

(HOOLIHAN *looks dazedly at his hand.*)

There, we did it. (*She turns and sees him.*) Oh, my God.

HOOLIHAN. You squezz me hand.

GRAINNE. I what?

HOOLIHAN. The modern girls is very rough.

(USHEEN *comes into view looking for* GRAINNE.)

USHEEN *(calling)*. GRAINNE?

(He goes off, right.)

HOOLIHAN. You'd no call to go pulling and hauling at an old man and give him a squezz hand. I'm seventy-eight, I have to be careful.

GRAINNE. Yes, I'm sorry.

HOOLIHAN. I have to go to the lav now over you.

(HOOLIHAN *shuffles into the bathroom.* GRAINNE *goes out and comes down stage.)*

GRAINNE. James, here I am. I made the silliest . . . *(She sees that he is gone.)* James, where are you? James?

(GRAINNE *hesitates, then goes off left.* NIAMH *appears at the rear, wandering along the corridor and carrying* USHEEN'S *trousers. She is looking for a sign of life and comes down stage.)*

NIAMH *(in a timid whisper)*. Grainne? Mr Usheen? *(Very loudly)*. Wooo-ooo!

(NIAMH *goes out of sight up stage.*
GRAINNE *and* USHEEN *enter down stage from opposite sides.)*

GRAINNE
USHEEN } *(together)*. *There* you are!

GRAINNE. Really, James, must you wander around? *(Going to him)* And if you want me, you know my name. There's no need to go 'woo-ooo'.

USHEEN. I didn't go 'woo-hoo'.

GRAINNE. Come in here. *(She pushes him ahead of her into the Robert Emmet room.)*

USHEEN. You're the one who went 'woo-ooo'.

GRAINNE. Who did?

USHEEN. You did.

GRAINNE. I did?

USHEEN. Just now, like a yak in labour.

GRAINNE *(bridling)*. Wives of Members of the South Dublin Country Club are not in the habit of sounding like yaks in labour.

USHEEN. Then they must regard *you* as something of a novelty.

GRAINNE *(losing her temper)*. James, I did not go . . .

(NIAMH *appears up stage.)*

NIAMH. Wooo-ooo!

(NIAMH *goes off.)*

GRAINNE. Exactly. So . . . *(She breaks off.)*

(They look in the direction whence the cry came, then at each other.)

USHEEN. Then what the hell was it?

GRAINNE. I don't know.

USHEEN (*looking into the bathroom*). Perhaps it was the wind whistling through the bidets.

GRAINNE. There aren't any bidets – Irish plumbers won't handle them.

USHEEN. In that case . . .

GRAINNE. Well?

USHEEN. Do you think it could have been a yak?

GRAINNE. James, there are no yaks in the Dublin Mountains.

USHEEN. There's *something* out there.

GRAINNE (*heatedly*). It isn't a yak.

USHEEN. Listen to me. I am a city boy. Where the footpaths stop, so do I, and I now wish to return to civilization.

GRAINNE. James, we're fifteen miles from Foxrock. You can't *get* more civilized than that.

USHEEN. Did you hear that 'woo-ooo'?

GRAINNE. The wind.

USHEEN. It was not the wind. What a way for James Usheen to finish up – in a concrete tomb high up in these God-forsaken mountains, torn limb from limb by some kind of Abominable Bogman!

GRAINNE (*becoming frightened*). Now stop that.

USHEEN. It's out there now.

(*They hear the sound of* HOOLIHAN *as he emerges from the bathroom and passes through the Parnell room, clearing his throat loudly. Then he marches off up stage.*)

HOOLIHAN. Hup, two, three, four – hup, two, three, four!

(GRAINNE *and* USHEEN *breathe more easily.*)

GRAINNE. James, what's got into you?

USHEEN. I see it all with dreadful clarity. He hates me, he wants to kill me.

GRAINNE. Who does?

USHEEN. So he sends two of his henchmen to run me down with a Jensen. Then I fall into a carefully dug pit. I survive that, and then, for no apparent reason, you take me up the mountains in a storm to a deserted bunker guarded by a madman. You work for Eamonn Andrews, don't you?

GRAINNE. No!

USHEEN. Then why was I brought here?

GRAINNE (*decisively*). I'll show you. (*She removes her coat and lies on the bed invitingly.*)

131

USHEEN (*through this, to himself*). They all hate me.

GRAINNE. Look at me, James. *Now* do you know why you were brought here?

(*He looks at her. Realization finally dawns.*)

USHEEN. You're having me on.

GRAINNE. Exactly.

USHEEN. You wouldn't.

GRAINNE. I meant what I said, James. You've seen your last mole.

USHEEN. You'd do that for me?

GRAINNE (*simply*). What are friends for?

NIAMH (*baying in the distance*). Wooo-ooo!

GRAINNE (*catching her breath*). There it is again.

USHEEN. Ignore it. (*Looking at her*). This is the nicest thing anyone ever offered to do for me.

GRAINNE. It's purely medicinal.

USHEEN. Even so – I couldn't.

GRAINNE. Why not?

USHEEN. You – who wanted to be a nun?

GRAINNE. I wouldn't dream of enjoying it.

USHEEN. I know that, love.

GRAINNE. I'm not immoral.

USHEEN. Sure.

GRAINNE. Don't you find me attractive?

USHEEN. I'm mad about you. I always have been, but how could I do such a thing in your husband's trousers?

GRAINNE. Silly – you won't be wearing them.

USHEEN. Besides, I've decided to return to my religion.

GRAINNE. How soon?

USHEEN. Tomorrow.

GRAINNE. Well, that gives us all night.

USHEEN. That's true. You really mean this?

GRAINNE. Don't look so amazed. You'd do as much for me if I kept seeing moles on Dermod. Try thinking of it as laying a ghost.

USHEEN. When did you decide?

GRAINNE. Quite on the spur of the moment. In the car.

USHEEN. It's ridiculous. I haven't even a toothbrush.

GRAINNE. I have two in my handbag.

USHEEN (*wiping his eyes*). What can I say, but that I accept gratefully, knowing that a refusal often gives offence.

GRAINNE (*kindly*). You need a drink. Where's the brandy?

USHEEN. You had it last.

GRAINNE. I left it in the car. You wait here – I'll go out the back way, it's shorter.

USHEEN. Run.

(GRAINNE *hurries out.*

USHEEN *picks up her handbag, opens it and takes out the two toothbrushes. His eyes moisten with affection. Then he sees something else in the handbag. He pulls into view what looks like several yards of rolled-up, see-through black nylon nightdress. He holds it up, picturing* GRAINNE *in it.*

NIAMH, *footsore by now, comes into view, down stage, still carrying* USHEEN'S *trousers. She cups her hands over her mouth for another mighty yell.*

USHEEN *beats her to it. The sight of the nightdress causes him to emit a cry of sheer anticipation.*)

USHEEN. Wooo-*ooo!*

(NIAMH *looks puzzled.* USHEEN *gleefully rolls up the night-dress and puts it back in the handbag. He takes off his over-coat and hangs it on a hook on the back of the half-open door.* NIAMH *decides to investigate the source of the yell. She comes to the threshold of the Emmet room and looks in. She and* USHEEN *are hidden from each other by the door. Seeing an apparently empty room, she goes out again, closing the door behind her.* USHEEN *sees the door and his overcoat swinging from him.* NIAMH *turns her attention to the Parnell room. She goes in, just as* USHEEN *looks around the door of the Emmet room and sees nothing.* NIAMH'S *feet are killing her and she is dispirited. She sits on the bed and takes her shoes off. Simultaneously, in the other room,* USHEEN *sits on the bed and removes his shoes. They emit independent sighs of relief and begin to massage their toes.*

FINTAN *appears up stage and stations himself between the two rooms. He is in a murderous mood.*)

FINTAN (*hissing off, impatiently*). Come on, come on, come on! Will you hurry up. I'm not paying you to sleep on your feet. (HOOLIHAN *comes into view carrying a lethal-looking shillelagh.*) Is that the biggest shillelagh we have in the gift shop?

HOOLIHAN. It's crooked.

FINTAN. It's meant to be crooked. What room did you say she pulled you into?

HOOLIHAN. Funny-lookin' walkin'-stick.

133

FINTAN. For God's sake, man, can't you understand plain Irish? I'm talking about the woman.

(HOOLIHAN *looks at him blankly*.)

Who pulled you into a bedroom?

HOOLIHAN. She squezz me hand.

FINTAN. The whoor.

HOOLIHAN. Hard.

FINTAN. Describe her to me.

(HOOLIHAN *merely holds up his hand*.)

Would you call her a raving beauty?

HOOLIHAN. I had to go to the lav over her.

FINTAN. I know that feeling – it's her all right. Which room did she go into? (*Grabbing him*) Which room?

HOOLIHAN (*saluting*). Charles Stewart Parnell.

FINTAN. Parnell. Of course – where else for adultery? Oh, the slut.

(USHEEN *starts removing his jacket*. FINTAN, *gripping the shillelagh, advances on tiptoe towards the Emmet room*.)

HOOLIHAN. Bold Robert Emmet.

FINTAN. Shut up. (*Then he sees the nameplate on the door*.) Oh.

(NIAMH *puts her shoes on again and goes towards the bathroom*. FINTAN *changes course for the Parnell room*. NIAMH *enters the bathroom, closing the door*. FINTAN *pounces in*.)

Gotcha! (*He stops in frustration*.)

HOOLIHAN *comes in behind him*. USHEEN *goes into the bathroom*.)

Gone.

HOOLIHAN (*looking at the portrait of Parnell*). Gone – all of them gone.

FINTAN. Wait! (*He sees* USHEEN'S *trousers on the bed where* NIAMH *has left them*.) The same trousers I saw seven miles away – and they're still sopping wet! I don't know what it is, but there's a perverted act going on here somewhere.

(GRAINNE *reappears with the brandy. She goes into the Emmet room and opens one of the bottles, humming to herself*.)

I'll search every room in the place from Brian Boru to De Valera, and when I find them . . . !

(*Still holding the trousers, he hustles* HOOLIHAN *out ahead of him and off downstage. In his anger he has left the shillelagh on the bed*.

(NIAMH, *attracted by* FINTAN'S *final shout, comes out of the bathroom, dabbing at her face with a towel*.)

NIAMH. Mr Usheen? (*She is about to return to the bathroom when she notices that* USHEEN'S *trousers have gone. She looks for them with mounting panic, but can find only the shillelagh.*)

(*In the Emmet room,* GRAINNE *taps on the bathroom door.*)

GRAINNE. James, dear, are you in there?

USHEEN (*off*). No.

GRAINNE. Well, really, haven't you ever heard of ladies first? Never mind, I'll use one of the other bathrooms. (*She takes her handbag and goes out. She enters the Parnell room.*)

(NIAMH *is on her hands and knees looking for the lost trousers.*

GRAINNE *goes into the bathroom without seeing* NIAMH. NIAMH *gives up the search and returns to the bathroom. She screams off,* GRAINNE *comes in, dragging* NIAMH *after her with one hand and holding her nightdress in the other.*)

GRAINNE. Of all the mean things. How dare you come here and spy on us. Don't you know I'd have given you all the details tomorrow?

NIAMH. There's not going to be any details. Dermod's come home.

GRAINNE. He's what?

NIAMH. I saw him.

GRAINNE. The rotten thing.

NIAMH. And if he's at home, you may depend on it so is Fintan. There goes my night off.

GRAINNE. Men! You can't trust them out of your sight.

NIAMH. So since you're supposed to be staying at my place, I came to collect you and give Mr Usheen back his trousers. Where is he?

GRAINNE (*pointing*). In there.

NIAMH. This will be a terrible let-down for him.

GRAINNE (*wincing*). Don't.

NIAMH (*indicating the nightdress*). What's that?

GRAINNE. My nightie.

NIAMH (*fascinated by it*). A hell of a let-down.

GRAINNE. I've been saving it for a rainy night.

NIAMH (*examining it*). I suppose it's the same as sun-glasses; you can see everything through it, but it takes away the glare.

GRAINNE. I'm furious with Dermod – my first evening out in ages, and he has to go and spoil it. Well, I won't let him. I've been to too much trouble, and waste is sinful.

NIAMH. You can't stay the whole night here – not now.

135

GRAINNE. I'm aware of that. James will just have to put up with the abridged version.

NIAMH. Grainne, come home now.

GRAINNE. *You* go home.

NIAMH. Without you.

GRAINNE. Tell Fintan I'm following in my car. When I get there I'll say I had a puncture. Yes?

NIAMH (*fearing the worst*). Oh, Jay.

GRAINNE. And to prove I'm grateful, you can have that (*the nightdress.*) tomorrow as a present. You can wear it for Fintan.

NIAMH. I'd never see the sun come up.

GRAINNE. But please go *now*. Where are James's trousers?

NIAMH. They were here five minutes ago.

GRAINNE. Well?

NIAMH (*holding the shillelagh*). Now all I can find is this.

GRAINNE. The night watchman must have taken them – what a funny old man. I'll find them. You go on home.

(GRAINNE *leads* NIAMH, *still holding the shillelagh, into the corridor.*)

NIAMH. How soon will you be after me?

GRAINNE. As soon as I decently can. Now go. (*She goes into Emmet's room.*)

NIAMH. The trousers might be under the bed.

(GRAINNE *closes the door.* NIAMH, *left on her own, has no choice but to head for home. She comes down stage.*)

(*Decisively*) Adultery can't be a sin – you go through so much suffering to commit it.

(NIAMH *goes off.*)

(GRAINNE *pours herself a brandy then goes to the bathroom door.*)

GRAINNE. James, are you still in there?

USHEEN (*off*). The bloody zip is stuck again.

GRAINNE. Well, do hurry. There's been some bad news. We're not playing a full eighteen holes any more. It's been changed to pitch-and-putt. Trousers . . . (*She takes her glass of brandy into the Parnell room, puts down the glass and looks under the bed.*) (NIAMH *appears in the corridor, now in a state of yammering terror.*)

NIAMH. Fintan's here, Fintan's here. (*She rushes into the Emmet room, assuming that* GRAINNE *is still there.*) Grainne, we're nackered, it's F . . . (*She realizes that* GRAINNE *is no longer there. She tries the bathroom door. It is locked.*)

136

(FINTAN *and* HOOLIHAN *appear in the corridor.*)
(NIAMH *hammers on the bathroom door.*)
Fintan's here — let me in.

FINTAN. The shillelagh was in your charge; do I have to see to everything myself?

NIAMH (*hearing this*). He'll slaughter me.

FINTAN (*close at hand*). It was this room. I know exactly where I left it.

(NIAMH *assumes that he is about to enter the Emmet room. She utters a moan of 'Oh, Jay,' and begins to run around in circles like a decapitated hen, finally collapsing into the built-in wardrobe. At the same time,* FINTAN *and* HOOLIHAN *go into the Parnell room, where* FINTAN *looks wildly about him for his shillelagh, and* HOOLIHAN *comes to attention in front of the portrait of Parnell.*)

(*In the Emmet room,* USHEEN *comes out of the bathroom, his flies half undone.*)

USHEEN (*ranting*). What kind of a Communist country is this? Can't a man undo his fly in peace? (*Looking about him*) Grainne . . . ?

FINTAN. Gone — the shillelagh's gone. I'm going mad. I left it here, you saw me. (*He turns and sees* HOOLIHAN.) Stop saluting that adulterer! Wait — I know where they are — (*pointing to the bathroom*) — in there! Easy now, Fintan, he's got a shillelagh.

(*Observed by* GRAINNE *from under the bed,* FINTAN *charges into the bathroom.*)

(GRAINNE *reaches for her nightdress which is lying on the floor. She draws it towards her.* HOOLIHAN *sees it moving. He tries to jump on it, and misses. He tries again and succeeds. He picks it up. At first he does not know what it is. Then dawn breaks.* USHEEN *is meanwhile attacking the stuck zip with such fury that he is whirling about the room. He begins to cry with childish rage.* HOOLIHAN *holds the nightdress in front of himself and stands before the mirror.*)

HOOLIHAN (*cackling*). Hih, hih, hih, hih!

USHEEN. Bugger it, bugger it, bugger it!

(FINTAN *comes out of the bathroom, holding* GRAINNE'S *fur coat.*)

FINTAN (*quietly; nothing else can happen*). Now I know. Now at last I know why she's doing it — for a mangy piece of rabbit skin.

(*The bed rocks violently.* FINTAN *sits on it heavily.*)
And for this she's willing to throw away a woman's most
precious possession – her husband's social status. Well, I'll say
this much in her favour – at least she's not doing it for love.

HOOLIHAN (*enjoying himself*). Hih, hih, hih, hih!

FINTAN. (*snarling*) What are you sniggering at? (*He sees the
nightdress.*) Show me that. (*He snatches it from* HOOLIHAN.)
(*In the Emmet room,* USHEEN *calms down.*)

USHEEN. Steady, James love! You don't want to use up all your
strength on a zip. Treat it as you would a studio audience.
That's it – soap!
(USHEEN *goes into the bathroom.*)

FINTAN (*examining the nightdress*). My God, she'd wear this for
him, but I'm only let see her in her skin! It's so thin she must
have paid a fortune for it. The faggot – spending my good
money on clothes that are only meant to put on so as they can
be ripped off. (*To* HOOLIHAN) Look at it. Jasus, what's wrong
with flannelette? (*He throws it over* HOOLIHAN'S *head.*)
(USHEEN *comes hopping out of the bathroom, happily removing his trousers. Humming a snatch of 'Does your Mother
Come from Ireland', he begins to fold them neatly.*)
We'll wait here – she'll be back. (*He slumps down on the bed
again, knocking the breath out of* GRAINNE.)

USHEEN. What the hell am I doing? They're not *my* trousers. (*He
opens the wardrobe door wide, rolls the trousers into a ball,
throws them in and closes the door. He comes down, takes up
the brandy bottle and the remaining glass and begins to pour
himself a drink. Suddenly he realizes what he has seen in the
wardrobe. The neck of the bottle beats a frenzied tattoo against
the lip of the glass. Almost in a whisper*) Grainne? Grainne,
there's a corpse in the wardrobe.
(*The wardrobe door begins to creak open of its own accord.*
USHEEN'S *nerve goes.*)
(*With a loud cry*). Grainne!
(FINTAN *leaps to his feet.* USHEEN *grabs his overcoat and
shoes and goes tearing out of the Emmet room and
dashes off down the corridor.*)
(*As he goes*) Grainne, where are you?

FINTAN. It came from outside. Follow me.

HOOLIHAN (*doing so*). Hup, two, three, four.

FINTAN. Shut up or I'll kill you.
(FINTAN *and* HOOLIHAN *go into the Emmet room, just*

missing the sight of USHEEN *galloping down the corridor in his shorts.* FINTAN *makes a quick reconnoitre, looking first into the bathroom.* GRAINNE *extricates herself from under the bed and goes cautiously into the corridor. In his lightning tour of the room,* FINTAN *slams the wardrobe door shut.*)

Someone's been in here. Look at this, a man's coat and tie, brandy and a shillelagh. This can only mean sex. Sit down, Hoolihan; they're gone now, but when they come back we'll be ready for them. Bring me that brandy.

(GRAINNE, *now at the door of the Emmet room, mouths the word 'gone?' in puzzlement. She realizes that* USHEEN *must be somewhere. She tiptoes along the passage.*)

GRAINNE. (*in a whispered shout*) Jay-ames, where are you? It's me-ee!

(GRAINNE *goes off up stage.*)

(*Softly*) Woo-ooo?

(FINTAN *and* HOOLIHAN *sit on the bed. A silence, broken only by* FINTAN *thudding the shillelagh into his hand. On the fourth thud the shillelagh breaks neatly in two. He looks at it. There is a pause.*)

FINTAN. Effin' Japanese shillelaghs. (*He helps himself to* USHEEN'S *brandy.*)

(*The door of the wardrobe opens and* NIAMH *crawls out, bent double. She practically walks into* HOOLIHAN, *who is looking at her. He salutes her. She returns the salute, turns and goes back into the wardrobe, closing the door.*)

HOOLIHAN (*after a pause; conversationally*). Them is grand spacious wardrobes, sir.

(FINTAN. *grunts.*)

I was up here in nineteen-sixteen. No motor car hotels up here then. No houses up here then. Nothing up here then, except me. Shot through the lung.

(FINTAN *looks at him.*)

Couldn't see the city with the smoke from the fires. Can't see it now with the rain.

FINTAN. You were shot?

HOOLIHAN. 'Is it rainin'?' some gobshite says to me in the South Dublin Union. So I look through the winda. Out in the yard there's a shagger in a tin helmet pointin' a gun at me. I seen the flash, but I didn't hear the bang. They say you don't, on account of the bullet gets to you before the bang does, and once

139

the bullet gets to you you're not interested in listenin'. So I sit down on the floor. 'Is it rainin'?' says the same gobshite to me. 'No,' says I, 'but I am.' Wasn't I quick, but?

FINTAN. How did you get up the mountains?

HOOLIHAN. Yis.

FINTAN. I said how did you . . .

HOOLIHAN. So they brung me up the mountains. This Volunteer puts me lyin' in the field and goes off to look for milk. Never cem back. 'The sunlight'll do you good,' he says. I have a bad chest ever since. He was another gobshite.

FINTAN. I'd offer you a drink, but there's only one glass.

(HOOLIHAN *unscrews the lens cap from his flashlight. He holds it out, and* FINTAN *pours brandy into it.*)

HOOLIHAN. The brother got shot in nineteen-twenty, shot in the ankle. They gev him a pension, only he was in a motor-bike accident in nineteen-thirty-six and he lost his leg. The ankle went with it, so they stopped the pension. (*He drinks.*) Thanks. Good job I didn't lose the lung. I do like walkin' around this wing, and I do like bein' in the restaurant with the big paintin's on the wall . . .

FINTAN (*with pride*). The Famine room – best steaks in Ireland.

HOOLIHAN. But I don't like the nineteen-sixteen wing. I don't like real things. But wasn't Mr Pearse full of ou' codology, wha'? (FINTAN, *his glass half-raised, stares at him.*) The rubbidge he used to come out with. 'Never tell a lie. Strength in our hands, truth on our lips, and cleanness in our hearts.' Jasus, what sort of way is that to run a country?

FINTAN. Nice talk from a man who fought in nineteen-sixteen!

HOOLIHAN. Yous lot has more sense. I do like to see the big motor cars and the women with all the rings, and to feel the heat comin' out of the doors of the hotels. I do like to see everybody buyin' things and batin' the lard out of the other fella. Money is great, though.

FINTAN. How dare you criticize Pearse to me? You don't deserve to have been shot in the lung.

HOOLIHAN. Decent man. 'Freedom!' says he. They wouldn't have shot him if they'd a known what we were goin' to do with it when he got it for us. They were gobshites, too.

FINTAN. You ought to be ashamed of . . .

HOOLIHAN (*with dignity*). I have to go to the lav now. If I hadda had brains, I'd be rich too, because it's the best nationality. (HOOLIHAN *goes into the bathroom.*

140

FINTAN *follows him and stands in the doorway.*)

FINTAN. You wouldn't be in the cushy job you're in today if it wasn't for men like Pearse, Emmet and me. You're in a free country, and all you can think of is money. And that carpet is new, and you're splashing it! (*He comes back into the room in disgust and sits on the bed.*)

(MISS MANNING appears in the corridor upstage, followed by DERMOD. *She comes down to the Parnell room.*)

DERMOD. Miss Manning, you don't have to inspect every room in the building.

MISS MANNING. But I do, it's my job. Besides, my quarters, as charming as they are, really do quite reek of paint . . .

DERMOD. I'm sorry about that . . .

MISS MANNING. So we must find me another little nest, hmm? Who is in this room?

DERMOD. Parnell.

(*She waits for him to open the door. He does so. She goes in.*)

MISS MANNING. 'nk yow!

DERMOD. The rooms are really all the same.

MISS MANNING. This one isn't. I spy with my little eye something beginning with 'n'.

DERMOD. 'N'?

MISS MANNING (*holding up* GRAINNE'S *nightdress*). For night attire.

DERMOD. How did that get there?

MISS MANNING. Oh, innocent Amy. As if you didn't know!

DERMOD. I don't.

MISS MANNING. You mean you haven't been entertaining young ladies here on the sly?

DERMOD. Miss Manning, what an idea!

MISS MANNING. Yes, isn't it! (*Examining the nightdress.*) I call this quite saucy.

DERMOD. If that night watchman has been letting couples in here for immoral purposes, I'll kick him the length of the building. That's funny . . .

MISS MANNING. What is?

DERMOD. I – once bought my wife a nightdress like this.

MISS MANNING. Silly man. Of course she didn't wear it.

DERMOD. How do you know?

MISS MANNING. Wives never do. They can't bear the disappointed look on a man's face when he realizes that underneath the mint sauce is the same old mutton. (*She coughs modestly.*)

141

DERMOD (*stiffly*). As it happens, Miss Manning, my wife is an attractive woman.

MISS MANNING. Saddle of lamb? How nice.

DERMOD. And the nightdress was accidentally set fire to.

MISS MANNING. You were there?

DERMOD. She showed me the ashes.

MISS MANNING (*drily*). There's no fooling you, is there, Mr Gibbon?

DERMOD. So if this room is to your liking . . .

MISS MANNING. I'm not sure. (*Pointing to the portrait*) Who is he?

DERMOD. Charles Stewart Parnell. My partner didn't want a room named after him, but we ran short of patriots. He destroyed himself because of a woman – an English woman.

MISS MANNING. This room will do nicely.

DERMOD. Good. I'll get your suitcase from reception.

MISS MANNING. It's been such a day. I can't face the thought of unpacking. And all my pretties are at the bottom.

DERMOD. Oh, yes?

MISS MANNING. Of my suitcase, Mr Gibbon. (*Holding the nightdress.*) I know – why don't I wear this?

DERMOD. That?

MISS MANNING. Finders keepers, losers weepers. And as you can see, I'm the kind of woman who will wear any old thing. Let's hope this one won't go on fire.

DERMOD. Why, do you smoke in bed?

MISS MANNING. I was thinking of spontaneous combustion. Mr Gibbon, would you be so kind as to fetch me my little vanity case . . .

DERMOD. Certainly.

MISS MANNING. And then I hope you won't be in a hurry to be off.

DERMOD. Well, I . . .

MISS MANNING (*reclining on the bed*). Because it's lonelier here than I had imagined. Also, there is such a thing as loneliness of the soul. Did I mention that my gentleman friend has left me?

DERMOD. I'm sorry to hear it.

MISS MANNING. 'nk yow! It happened after the party – the night you and I met. Mr Gibbon, you see before you a woman scorned. I gave that man the best nights of my life – and of his, too – and he threw me aside like an old bedsock. In my bitterness – (*all in one breath*) – I even thought of yielding my body to the first man with whom I should happen to find myself alone

142

in a bedroom in a deserted building on a mountain-side at dead of night, but of course that would have been silly. (*She looks at him inquiringly.*)

DERMOD (*his voice trembling*). Not necessarily.

MISS MANNING (*kneeling up on the bed*). No? Mr Gibbon, I hope you're not about to make an erotic proposal.

DERMOD (*retreating*). I wasn't.

MISS MANNING. I mean, just because we happen to be alone in a bedroom in a deserted building on a mountain-side at dead of night . . .

DERMOD. Are we?

MISS MANNING. Aren't we?

DERMOD (*hoarsely*). Yes.

MISS MANNING (*seizing him*). So kindly don't come any closer.

DERMOD. I won't.

MISS MANNING (*pulling him on to the bed*). You aren't listening, are you? I mean it – not another step. (*She is now as close to him as she can get. She puts her arms around him, as if on the point of fainting.*) There now. I knew I shouldn't be safe with you. Mr Gibbon, this is madness. Think what Mrs Gibbon would say –

DERMOD. I am.

MISS MANNING. – if you were silly enough to tell her.

(DERMOD *attempts to return her embrace. At once she breaks away.*)

(*Firmly*) No, it's too soon. The wounds go too deep. I shall need time.

DERMOD. (*crestfallen*). Of course.

MISS MANNING. Five minutes?

DERMOD. I'll get your vanity case.

(DERMOD *goes out and hurries off up stage towards Reception.*)

(*Miss Manning heads for the bathroom. On the way she sees the fur coat, which is on the floor where* FINTAN *dropped it and has hitherto been hidden by the bed. She picks it up.*)

MISS MANNING (*casually*). Oh – nice. (*Carrying it into the bathroom*) James Usheen, I will be revenged on you this night? (*Miss Manning goes off.*

HOOLIHAN *emerges from the bathroom.*)

HOOLIHAN. I enjoyed that.

FINTAN. You've been in there long enough to float a rowboat. In future use the staff lavatory down the hill.

143

HOOLIHAN. Yis. (*He starts out.*)

FINTAN. Not now, you've just been. Listen to me. I want you to go to the souvenir shop. (*Carefully, gripping* HOOLIHAN *by the lapels.*) Get me another shillelagh. One that won't break. Do it now.

HOOLIHAN (*saluting Emmet*). Gone – all of them gone.

FINTAN. I said get out. And remember about that lavatory. I didn't lay out ten quid for corrugated iron for my own amusement.

HOOLIHAN *goes out.*

GRAINNE *appears from down stage with* USHEEN, *still trouserless, in tow.*)

GRAINNE. Dead women in wardrobes – I never heard such nonsense.

USHEEN. I tell you she . . .

GRAINNE. Quiet! (*She starts violently as she comes face to face with* HOOLIHAN.) Oh. (*Standing in front of* USHEEN.) Hello, we were just . . .

HOOLIHAN. Gone.

GRAINNE. Pardon me?

HOOLIHAN. All gone now.

GRAINNE. Do you mean that the gentleman who . . .

HOOLIHAN (*rubbing a window in the downstage 'wall'*). How does water soak through glass? You don't know? (*Going*) He's another gobshite.

(HOOLIHAN *goes off.*)

GRAINNE (*to* USHEEN). Did you hear what he said? Fintan is gone. I'll just make sure. Shhh . . . (*She tiptoes to the door of the Emmet room.*)

(*Inside the room,* FINTAN *suddenly stands up.*)

FINTAN. Shag him. Now he has *me* wanting to pee.

USHEEN. I refuse to set foot in that . . .

(FINTAN *goes to the bathroom.*)

(GRAINNE *motions* USHEEN *to be silent, puts her ear to the door, then opens it cautiously just as* FINTAN *disappears into the bathroom. She looks into the room, then turns to* USHEEN.)

GRAINNE. We're safe. He's gone.

USHEEN. I'm not going in there. I tell you there was a dead woman in the wardrobe. She was huddled on the floor, a shapeless lump – her eyes were turned up. It was horrible. Funny thing is, she looked familiar.

144

GRAINNE (*nastily*). Are you sure she didn't have a mole on her breast?

USHEEN. If you're going to be rude I'll go home.

GRAINNE. I'll tell you your trouble. You've been watching too much television.

USHEEN. I never watch television. I still have my pride.

GRAINNE. What you don't have is your trousers, and they're in the wardrobe.

USHEEN (*craven*). You get them.

GRAINNE. First I have a question. Out of common Christianity, I offered to commit adultery with you tonight. Now – yes or no, James. Has rain stopped play?

USHEEN. I knew there was something I was trying to remember from twelve years ago. You're insane.

GRAINNE. Thank you.

USHEEN. Have you forgotten? Your husband's partner is on the premises.

GRAINNE. He'll have gone home by now. And it was Niamh he was after, not me – I can't think why. Luckily for her, she's miles away.

(NIAMH *comes crawling out of the wardrobe again. She grabs the bedclothes and hoists herself on to her knees.*)

So are we or aren't we?

USHEEN. I know you'll think me hypersensitive, but with a corpse under the same roof I doubt if my performance would be at its peak.

GRAINNE. (*icily*). Very well, James, there's no more to be said. I'll get your trousers my husband's trousers. Would you kindly fetch my nightie and mink – they're in there. (*She half opens the door of the Emmet room.*)

NIAMH. (*seeing the door opening*). Oh, shag. (*She wearily returns into the wardrobe.*)

GRAINNE. And, James – don't blame me if wherever you go from now on you keep seeing your precious Lucretia. (*She goes into the Emmet room, shutting the door, and stands trying to fight back tears of fury.*)

USHEEN (*to the closed door*). Her name is Venetia. And I do not suffer from hallucinations.

(MISS MANNING *comes in from the bathroom of the Parnell room dressed in the nightdress and mink coat.*)

(USHEEN *opens the door of the Parnell room just as Miss Manning enters it from the bathroom. They see each other and scream.* USHEEN *slams the door shut.*)

145

MISS MANNING \
USHEEN { *(together)*. Oh, my God.

(GRAINNE *hurries out.*)

GRAINNE. Now what? (*Looking at* USHEEN'S *stricken face.*) What is it?

USHEEN. Forgive me. You were right and I was wrong. It's all in my mind. I'll do anything you say, only cure me, I'm sick. Where's the bed? (*He pushes past her into the bedroom.*)

GRAINNE. But what's happened?

USHEEN. I'm losing my sanity and she asks stupid questions. Are you coming to bed or aren't you?

GRAINNE. I'll get my nightie. (*She stands for a moment, confused by this change of mind*).

(MISS MANNING *is still reeling from shock in the Parnell room.*)

MISS MANNING. I shall never eat British Rail mushrooms again.

(MISS MANNING goes into the bathroom.)

(GRAINNE *enters the Parnell room.* USHEEN, *in the Emmet room, picks up his jacket and tie from the bed. He goes with them to the wardrobe and opens it.*)

NIAMH (*from within*). Hello, Mr Usheen.

(USHEEN *looks at her blankly, then writes her off as an hallucination. He makes a dismissive gesture, hangs his jacket over her head, and closes the door. He gets into bed.* GRAINNE *cannot find her nightdress. She attempts to enter the bathroom but is surprised to find that the door is bolted.*)

MISS MANNING (*off*). Be patient, you impetuous man. I'll be out in a minute. And I've had rather a nasty shock, so you will be gentle with me, won't you, Mr Gibbon?

(GRAINNE, *facing down stage, is rigid with shock. She looks towards the audience and mouths 'Mr Gibbon?'. In the Emmet room,* USHEEN *moves over in the bed so that there is space for* GRAINNE. *He plumps up her pillow. There is the sound of the toilet being flushed.* USHEEN *looks towards the bathroom door, puzzled.*)

(FINTAN *comes out, drying his hands. He nods to* USHEEN.)

FINTAN. Evening. (*He sits on the edge of the bed, his back to* USHEEN. *Very slowly, he realizes that the bed has an occupant. He stares at us with the same disbelief as is manifested by* GRAINNE *in the other room. Emitting a low animal growl, he turns slowly and points at* USHEEN.) Uhhh – hhh – hhh . . .

USHEEN (*clutching the bedclothes around him*). I'm the first of the English visitors.
(FINTAN *advances on him*. USHEEN *gets out of bed on the far side*.)
Is there anything I can do for you? Cup of sugar?
FINTAN (*in a terrible voice*). Where is she?
USHEEN. She?
FINTAN. My adulterous trollop of a wife!
USHEEN (*avoiding him*). I don't think I know the lady, but if I see anyone answering that description I'll . . .
FINTAN. Whoremaster!
USHEEN. Who came in?
FINTAN. Tell me where she is, and I'll give you the mercy of a swift death.
USHEEN. Keep away from me. I don't know where she is or . . .
FINTAN. Stop! I know your face.
USHEEN (*seeing a way to safety*). Yes, most people do. And when you realize who I am, I think you'll change your tune, my man.
FINTAN. Wait – I know who you are!
USHEEN. I thought it would come to you.
FINTAN. You're Lester Piggott.
USHEEN. Try again.
FINTAN. Where was it? Where did I see you?
USHEEN (*confident now*). I presume you watch television?
(*A wild, drawn-out shriek fron* FINTAN.)
Oh, God, an Andrews fan.
FINTAN. You! The atheist, the adulterer. And my wife says she's mad about you.
USHEEN. Everybody is – don't take it personally.
(HOOLIHAN *appears in the corridor at a senile jogtrot, carrying another shillelagh*.)
(*Meanwhile* GRAINNE *is now pacing up and down the Parnell room like a tigress waiting for mealtime*.)
USHEEN. Sir, if any harm comes to me, I have twelve million devoted fans who will . . .
(*As* FINTAN *raises his hands as if in prayer*. HOOLIHAN *enters behind him and slides the shillelagh into his fist*. FINTAN *makes a gesture of thanks towards heaven*.)
FINTAN. A time-honoured Irish weapon!
USHEEN (*wearily*). Why did I ever come back?
FINTAN. *Now! (He raises the shillelagh on high. This one does not break. Instead, it droops like a withered flower.)*

147

(*All three men look at it.*)
Never mind. I'll kill him with my bare hands. And no-one will
hear your screams – there's not a soul within five miles.
(DERMOD *appears in the corridor, singing loudly to himself
and carrying* MISS MANNING'*s vanity case.*)
DERMOD (*singing*). 'There's a small motel
              And a wishing well,
              I wish that we were there
              Togeth-er . . .'
(FINTAN *and* GRAINNE *both react in their respective rooms.*
FINTAN *goes to the door in time to see* DERMOD *entering the
Parnell room.* GRAINNE, *hearing him approaching, stands
against the wall so that the opening door will conceal
her.*)
(*Entering*). I'm ba-ack!
(*At once,* MISS MANNING *appears from the bathroom, every inch
the man-eater in mink and nylon.*)
MISS MANNING (*archly*). Well, Mr Gibbon?
DERMOD (*stunned*). Miss Manning, you're . . .
MISS MANNING. I'm what?
DERMOD. You're beautiful.
MISS MANNING (*modestly*). You're blind.
GRAINNE. (*appearing from behind the door*). You're banjaxed!
DERMOD (*thunderstruck*). Grainne . . .
GRAINNE. Who is this faggot?
MISS MANNING. Oh, very nice.
DERMOD. Now, don't jump to conclusions . . .
GRAINNE. I know – you can explain everything! You, the man I
    trusted. I turn my back on you for an evening, and I find you
    here with that . . .
USHEEN (*from the other room*). Grainne, save me!
GRAINNE. Alone in a bedroom with that woman wearing my . . .
DERMOD. Who was that?
GRAINNE (*smiling brightly*). No-one, dear. (*Resuming her tirade.*)
    Wearing my fur coat and my – my . . .
USHEEN (*yelling*). Grainne!
DERMOD. No-one, eh? Well, let's see what no-one looks like! (*He
    marches out and into the Emmet room.*)
    (GRAINNE, *now frantic, follows him.*)
GRAINNE. Wait – I can explain everything.
    (DERMOD *comes face to face with* FINTAN. GRAINNE *comes
    in.* MISS MANNING *straggles after them as far as the doorway.*)

148

DERMOD (*to* FINTAN). What are you doing here? (*He sees* USHEEN) And who is he?

GRAINNE. I never saw him before.

DERMOD (*taking a closer look*). It's Mr Usheen.

USHEEN. Hello. Lovely to see you again.

MISS MANNING. It *wasn't* the mushrooms!

DERMOD (*with hand outstretched*). Forgive me, I didn't recognize you with your . . . (*He takes in* USHEEN'S *state of undress.*) You! You and my . . .

GRAINNE. Now don't jump to conclusions.

DERMOD. Him – the man you said you can't stand . . .

USHEEN (*to* GRAINNE). Did you say that?

DERMOD. Yes – now I see it all.

GRAINNE. Never mind what *you* see. (*Pointing at* MISS MANNING) What about what *I* see?

USHEEN. What about what *I* see?

FINTAN. Yes, who the hell is that?

MISS MANNING (*explaining everything*). I'm the new manageress.

HOOLIHAN. Hih-hih-hih-hih!

DERMOD⎱
FINTAN⎰ (*together*). Shut . . . up!

FINTAN. My God – you and her and her and him. Orgies under the Plough and the Stars – the Patrick Pearse Motel turned into a knocking shop. What sort of savages am I living with? And me – I'm the worst of the lot. I thought bad of the only decent, pure, honest woman left in the country. Niamh, Niamh – say you forgive me!

NIAMH (*coming out of the wardrobe*). I do! – I do!

(FINTAN *looks at her and screams. The Lights black-out and* –

The CURTAIN *falls.*)

149

Scene 2

The same. Five minutes have passed.

When the Curtain rises, DERMOD, GRAINNE *and* USHEEN − *still without his trousers* − *are sitting on what transpires to be* FINTAN *spreadeagled on the bed.* HOOLIHAN *is sitting on the floor in a corner of the room with the brandy bottle, from which he helps himself during the scene.* NIAMH *is standing as far away from* FINTAN *as she can get.*

There is a pause, then MISS MANNING *comes out of the bathroom in the Parnell room. She is dressed as in the previous scene. She picks up her vanity case and returns to the bathroom.*

GRAINNE. We can't go sitting on him all night.

USHEEN. If we get off now he'll go berserk again.

DERMOD. He's been quiet for a while now. Should we chance it?

NIAMH. Don't. He's the same at home; not a stir out of him in bed, and when you think he's asleep, that's when he turns into a madman.

DERMOD. We've got to let him up some time. (*He lifts the pillow which he has been holding over* FINTAN'S *head.*) Fintan, are you all right?

FINTAN (*gasping*). Get off me.

DERMOD. If we do, will you promise to be good? No more trying to strangle Niamh?

NIAMH. If you're going to let him up, at least give me a ten-minute head-start.

DERMOD. Fintan, we want your word that you'll behave.

FINTAN (*hoarsely*). Yes.

DERMOD. You swear as a gentleman?

FINTAN. I swear as a gentleman.

NIAMH (*hollowly*). Oh, Jay.

DERMOD. All right. (*To* GRAINNE *and* USHEEN) Slowly now . . . (*They get up as gingerly as if they were sitting on nitroglycerine.* FINTAN *arises like a whale surfacing. He bestows a baleful glance upon* NIAMH.)

150

NIAMH. Watch him!

FINTAN (*with massive dignity*). I intend to prosecute everyone here for assault and being sat down on. (*Indicating* USHEEN.) I intend to sue *him* for enticement and loss of a housekeeper. (*Indicating* NIAMH) As for her, I intend to get a Papal annulment. You'll be hearing from my bishop in the morning.

NIAMH. And now for the *bad* news.

DERMOD. She won't be the only one who'll be hearing from a bishop.

GRAINNE. Meaning me?

DERMOD. (*addressing the ceiling*). I'd say the Vatican is in for a profitable year.

USHEEN. That'll be a change!

(DERMOD *glares at him*).

I suppose we should be thankful he doesn't intend to have us up for G.B.H.

FINTAN. What's G.B.H.?

DERMOD. It stands for Grainne Being Had.

GRAINNE. How dare you? You can accuse me after I saw you with that sex-mad rip wearing my – (*amending*) – wearing a disgusting see-through nightdress.

USHEEN. That's unfair. Venetia is definitely not sex-mad. I've known her to go without it for hours on end.

DERMOD. At least Miss Manning was here by right. She's the manageress.

GRAINNE. She certainly goes in for room service in a big way.

USHEEN. That's not bad.

DERMOD (*pointing at* USHEEN). Does *he* belong here? Look at him. He's in his underwear.

FINTAN (*scowling*). Pansy.

USHEEN. There's a very simple explanation for that . . .

FINTAN.
DERMOD. } Yes?

USHEEN. (*to* GRAINNE). Tell them.

GRAINNE. Certainly. Niamh, tell them.

NIAMH. Me? (*Taking a deep breath*) Well, when a ship is launched, it's always the owner's wife who . . .

GRAINNE. (*panic-stricken*). Don't listen to her. If you want the truth, James couldn't find a hotel room in town, so I brought him here.

DERMOD. You're lying.

GRAINNE. Ask James.

151

USHEEN. Ask me.

GRAINNE. James and I were good friends once. What more natural than that he should ring up and ask if I knew of a place where he could stay?

DERMOD (*almost convinced*). I see.

GRAINNE. And Niamh came along as my chaperone. You know how people talk.

FINTAN (*to* NIAMH). Is this true?

NIAMH. May I drop down dead.

DERMOD (*to* FINTAN). It sounds plausible.

GRAINNE. Do I offer him a room in our house, with you away? No, I bring him here, seven miles up a mountain road. I try to protect my good name, and this is the thanks I get.

DERMOD (*now contrite*). Grainne, I . . .

USHEEN. (*heading for the door*). Well, now that that's cleared up . . .

FINTAN. Where are you going?

USHEEN. Back to my hotel. (*He comes to a shuddering standstill.*)

FINTAN }
DERMOD } (*together, to* NIAMH *and* GRAINNE *respectively*). Liar!

USHEEN. No, no, what I mean is to *look* for a ho . . .

DERMOD (*coldly*). The best thing you can do at the moment is to put your trousers on.

FINTAN. Yes, there are whores present.

GRAINNE (*to* FINTAN). Are you calling me a . . .

NIAMH. Don't contradict him, it puts him in a bad humour.

GRAINNE (*to* DERMOD). Are you going to let him insult your wife?
    (DERMOD *turns his back on her.*)
I swear on my mother's grave I'm innocent.

DERMOD. Your mother's alive.

GRAINNE (*snapping*). Her grave is paid for.

DERMOD (*losing his temper*). By me, more fool that I am. And may she never live to climb into it.

GRAINNE. That's it; now abuse my mother, a woman in constant pain.

DERMOD. She's worse than in constant pain, she's in a council house in Crumlin.

GRAINNE. How dare you throw Crumlin in my face, with your own parents slobbering in the shadow of a brewery? And if my mother's in Crumlin, who left her there to rot?
    (USHEEN *takes his* [DERMOD's] *trousers from the wardrobe and puts them on, having trouble with the zip.*)

152

DERMOD. I wish I'd left more than your mother to rot in Crumlin.
  I wish I'd . . . (*He laughs derisively at* USHEEN'S *trouble with
  the zip.*) Ha! Ha-ha!

GRAINNE. What?

DERMOD. Your fancy-man's taste in trousers is well in keeping
  with his taste in women. Yech!
  (GRAINNE *emits a loud, shrill laugh.*)
  What's so funny?

GRAINNE. I'll tell you after the annulment.

USHEEN (*struggling with the zip*). Bugger it! Excuse me . . .

NIAMH. Can I help you with your fly, Mr Usheen?
  (*An anguished growl from* FINTAN.)
  Now what?

FINTAN (*starting forward*). I'll kill her, I'll kill her!

DERMOD. Fintan, you promised . . .

FINTAN (*picking up an easy chair*). Only not to strangle her.

NIAMH. I only offered to . . .

FINTAN. I know what you were offering to do for him, I've seen
  you in action. You didn't learn that at your Oratorio practice.

NIAMH. Learn what?

FINTAN. I curse that hour and a half we spent in the airport in
  Paris on our way back from Lourdes.

NIAMH (*to the others; reasonably*). His own mother told me not to
  marry him.

USHEEN (*who has been thinking*). 'I'll kill her, I'll kill her!'
  (*The others look at him.*)
  (*To* FINTAN) I know where I've seen you before. The bastard
  in the Jensen.

FINTAN. The what in the what?

USHEEN. That face, that voice. Sir, allow me to inform you that
  you are without doubt the most wantonly irresponsible driver
  since Ben Hur. Where did you learn to drive, anyway — reform
  school? Do you know I could have you prosecuted?

FINTAN. First he depraves my wife, now he criticizes my driving.
  Get him out of here.

DERMOD (*to* USHEEN). You'd better go.
  (USHEEN *points a denunciatory finger at* FINTAN. *This in-
  volves his letting go of his trousers, which fall down. He
  picks them up, turning his attention to* DERMOD.)

USHEEN (*to* DERMOD). You were in the car with him, weren't you? In
  which case, you can whistle for your trousers. And furthermore . . . ! (*He kisses* NIAMH, *then goes out and into the Parnell room.*)

153

(FINTAN *roars with rage*.)

DERMOD. I wouldn't be seen dead in those . . . (*Staring at* GRAINNE) He's wearing my . . .

GRAINNE. His got wet.

DERMOD. You gave him my good fifteen-guinea . . .

NIAMH. She had to.

DERMOD. *Had* to?

NIAMH. Fintan nearly ran over him. (*To* FINTAN) What if he does go to the police?

FINTAN. I can't be prosecuted. I'm out of that income group.

DERMOD (*to* GRAINNE). You gave him my . . .

GRAINNE. Oh, shut up. And before you start throwing more sand in my eyes about your trousers, my semi-invalid mother and James Usheen, let me remind you that *I* was not the person who was caught red-handed with a nymphomaniac wearing a nightdress you could see the Hell-Fire Club through.

DERMOD. Yes, *about* that nightdress . . . !

GRAINNE (*knowing what is coming*). Don't change the subject.

DERMOD. When Miss Manning walked into that room, the nightdress was already there. So where did it come from?

GRAINNE. How do I know where it . . .

DERMOD. It was yours.

GRAINNE. Mine?

DERMOD. I bought it for you.

FINTAN. For *her*? (*With an incredulous laugh*) You madman.

GRAINNE. That nightdress was set fire to.

DERMOD. So you said. I remember I bought it at Chez Siobhan's. Why don't I go and get it, and we'll have a look at the label? (GRAINNE *and* NIAMH *look at each other in horror.* DERMOD *starts towards the door.*)
Good idea, yes?

FINTAN (*magisterially*). Wait just one minute!
(*In the Parnell room,* USHEEN *taps on the door of the bathroom.*)

USHEEN. Venetia? My zip is stuck.

MISS MANNING (*off*). I don't give a fig. Kindly go away.

DERMOD. (*to* FINTAN). Well?

FINTAN. Man, are you so blind that you can't see the truth? That nightdress isn't hers . . .

GRAINNE. Of course it isn't.

FINTAN (*indicating* NIAMH). It's *hers*, and your wife is protecting her. Look at those two women, compare them. Now to hell with loyalty, own up. If you were a dirty anglicized renegade Irishman looking for his oats, which one of them would you go to bed with?

NIAMH. He's off.

(DERMOD *looks dumbly at* FINTAN.)

FINTAN. I see by your face you agree with me. But don't think your wife is innocent. The ugly ones always encourage the good-looking ones.

GRAINNE (*indignantly*). I beg your p . . .

FINTAN (*to* NIAMH; *brokenly*). How could you do it to me? Have I ever neglected you?

NIAMH. No, not once.

FINTAN. Was the sight of me raking in money not happiness enough for you? And if you had to commit adultery, why did you disgrace me by choosing *him?* Why couldn't you have pick-ed a decent, good-living Catholic? Why? Why? (*He kneels before her.*)

NIAMH (*stroking his head; kindly*). I will, next time.

FINTAN. A man who gets on the television and belittles us in col-our. He was the one who said that the Irish are under the in-fluence of L.S.D. – laziness, slander and dirt. How dare he say that we're lazy? I'll get up early one of these days and kill him for that. (*Still on his knees, he 'walks' to the door and shouts, for* USHEEN'S *benefit*) What's more, I'm going to sue him and expose him!

USHEEN. Venetia, he says he's going to sue me and expose me.

(MISS MANNING *comes out of the bathroom, now dressed. She gets ready to leave.*)

MISS MANNING. High time, too.

DERMOD. Fintan, get up. (*He attempts to help* FINTAN.)

FINTAN. Get your hands off me! You're as bad as they are – the first member of the staff to arrive, and you have her in her pelt before she has time to count the towels. You don't fool me.

GRAINNE. Nor me.

DERMOD. Fintan, I want a private word with you.

FINTAN. I have nothing to say to any of you.

DERMOD. This is about money.

FINTAN. I couldn't care less.

DERMOD. A lot of money.

FINTAN. I said I don't want to talk to you.

DERMOD (*curtly*). Very well.

FINTAN. But if you're going to nag at me, I'll listen.

DERMOD. If the ladies would excuse us . . . ?

GRAINNE. Leave you? With pleasure. Excuse you? Not if you were
to come begging on your hands and knees, and wearing a see-
through nightdress! Come, Niamh, now that we're free women
again, we have plans to make.

NIAMH (*following her*). Oh, Jay.

(GRAINNE *and* NIAMH *go into the bathroom and shut the
door.*)

(DERMOD *goes to the door and listens.*)

FINTAN. I'm done with you.

DERMOD. Shhh!

FINTAN. Don't you tell me to shush. Thanks to you, my marriage
is in flitters, the motel is a mockery, and the cost of the Papal
annulment will put me in the poorhouse.

DERMOD (*impatiently*). Will you wait . . . (*He listens..*

(*In the Parnell room,* MISS MANNING *is ready to be off.*)

USHEEN. Venetia, where are you going?

MISS MANNING. Kensington High Street.

USHEEN. Good, I'll go with you.

MISS MANNING. I'll feel safer on my own — 'nk yow!

USHEEN. You silly cow, you'll drown in a boghole. Don't you
know that it's pouring with rain and you're on top of a
mountain?

MISS MANNING. Kindly move to one side.

USHEEN. At least help me get this fastened.

MISS MANNING. I've pulled up your last zip, James. And now I intend to give myself to the first gentleman farmer I meet on my
way down the mountain.

USHEEN. If this is because of what happened tonight, I'm as innocent as you are.

MISS MANNING. How do you know I'm innocent?

USHEEN. Because this bloody country hasn't changed. They can't
even commit adultery properly. Venetia, don't leave me alone
with the one they call Fintan.

MISS MANNING. I won't say good-bye, James. You said it in London when you sent me out to buy my trousseau, and then
changed the locks.

(MISS MANNING *goes off, heading towards Reception.*)

USHEEN. Venetia, wait. (*To his zip*) Come up, come up . . .

(*In the Emmet room,* DERMOD *comes away from the door
of the bathroom.*)

DERMOD. I knew it. They're trying to think up a good story.

USHEEN (*in triumph*). Got it!

DERMOD. Grainne is asking Niamh to . . .
(USHEEN *emits a scream of agony. He doubles up, his arms folded across his thighs. The pain continues.*)
USHEEN. Aaaaah . . .
DERMOD. My God, what was that?
FINTAN. Hah! The decent man has cut his throat.
(USHEEN, *still bent double, stumbles across the corridor and into the Emmet room. He stares at* DERMOD *and* FINTAN, *too agonized to speak.*)
USHEEN. Aaaaah . . .
DERMOD. What do you want?
USHEEN (*begging for help*). Aaaaah . . .
DERMOD. That's a bloody funny place to cut your throat.
FINTAN. Go away, we're not talking to you.
(USHEEN *utters another 'Aaaaah . . .' and staggers across the room and into the bathroom.*)
Where's he going? Come back here!
(*There are loud screams from* GRAINNE *and* NIAMH *off.*)
(USHEEN *is thrown out of the bathroom. His first loud cry has brought* MISS MANNING *hurrying back along the corridor.* GRAINNE *and* NIAMH *reappear.*)
GRAINNE. Filthy beast.
NIAMH. But thanks for the compliment.
(NIAMH *and* GRAINNE *return to the bathroom and close the door.*)
(USHEEN *is as much in agony as ever.* MISS MANNING *looks into the Parnell room.*)
DERMOD. You! Did you attack my wife?
FINTAN. Of course he did. The state he's in, he'd attack any old thing. Look at him – that's what television does.
DERMOD (*advancing on* USHEEN). You animal. But God, I'll . . .
MISS MANNING (*coming in*). James!
USHEEN (*seeing her*). Aaaaah . . .
MISS MANNING. Are you ill?
USHEEN (*negative*). Aaaaah . . .
MISS MANNING. Is it your zip?
USHEEN (*affirmative*). Aaaaah . . .
MISS MANNING (*to the others*). I'm afraid he's done himself a little mischief. Come with Venetia, dear. (*She takes* USHEEN *and leads him, still bent double, into the Parnell room and towards the bathroom.*)
(*On the way,* USHEEN *attempts to speak to her.*)

157

USHEEN. Aaah . . . aaah . . . aaah.

MISS MANNING. I know, pet. That's why I enjoy being a girl.
(MISS MANNING *and* USHEEN *go into the bathroom.*)
(FINTAN *stares after them from the Emmet room.* DERMOD
gets down to business.)

DERMOD. Fintan, we must make it up with the girls.

FINTAN. To hell with them.

DERMOD. And with each other.

FINTAN. Get stitched.

DERMOD. If we don't make it up, there'll be a scandal.

FINTAN. Damn sure there'll be a scandal. If I've got to be the innocent party, I'll have something to show for it. I'll spread these
goings-on all over town like jam on bread.

DERMOD. Right. Then you can say good-bye to the motel.

FINTAN. Don't threaten me, you pup.

DERMOD. Fintan, this is no ordinary enterprise. (*Mistily.*) Our motel
is the fulfilment of the dreams of the men who died for this green
island. Do you want to insult their memory? Do you want to make
their deaths meaningless? Do you want us to go bankrupt?

FINTAN (*grabbing him*). You know something – tell me.

DERMOD. I'm telling you that if there is one whisper of scandal
there'll be no grand opening next week. Think of it, Fintan. No
cabinet minister to unveil the bust in the De Valera Snackery,
no bishop to bless our Kitchen Garden of Remembrance, no
guard of honour to fire a salute over the swimming pool. Is that
what you want?

FINTAN. Don't go on.

DERMOD. We may as well put a note in the brochure: 'Unmarried
Couples Welcome – Fornicate in Comfort.'

FINTAN. Stop, stop . . .

DERMOD. 'Wine, Dine and Have it Away by Candlelight.'

FINTAN. Stop, or I'll kill you.

DERMOD. If you won't think of us, think of the employment we're
giving. What's going to happen to the staff who'll be depending
on us?

FINTAN. They'll all have to go back to Cyprus.

DERMOD. Exactly. Our wives are in there now, going through hell
to think up a tissue of lies. Fintan, what kind of men are we that
we won't meet them half-way?

FINTAN. I'm a patriot: that means I'll believe anything.
(MISS MANNING *and* USHEEN *come out of the bathroom into the
Parnell room.* USHEEN *is visibly shaken after his experience.*)

MISS MANNING. A little soreness won't harm you, James. None of this would have happened if you'd married me.

USHEEN. I've already explained to you why I can't.

MISS MANNING. For religious reasons?

USHEEN. Yes.

MISS MANNING. What a bigot you are in this day and age. After all, it's the same God we all disbelieve in, isn't it?

USHEEN. There's another reason.

MISS MANNING. Might I know it?

USHEEN. I can't stand you.

MISS MANNING. You sillikins, that's not a reason. You've simply found out before marriage what other husbands and wives find out afterwards.

USHEEN. Venetia, there are two men in there who are prepared to sue me and cause a scandal.

MISS MANNING. They won't cause a scandal.

USHEEN. They're Irish-Catholic business men. They'd cut your head off and charge you for corkage.

MISS MANNING. They won't cause a scandal, because I can stop them.

USHEEN. How?

MISS MANNING. If I did, would you marry me?

USHEEN. No.

MISS MANNING. Not ever?

USHEEN (*firmly*). I'd sooner spend the rest of my life caught in a zip.

MISS MANNING. Oh (*With a strange smile.*) Never mind, perhaps I'll help you all the same. (*Tapping his cheek.*) I'm so fond of you.

USHEEN (*facing front*). Why do I suddenly feel so frightened?

(NIAMH *and* GRAINNE *come from the bathroom.* GRAINNE *has a coolly defiant look on her face;* NIAMH *is downcast.*)

(FINTAN *and* DERMOD *rise expectantly.*)

FINTAN
DERMOD } (*with welcoming smiles*). Well?

GRAINNE. Perfectly.

NIAMH. We're grand, thanks.

DERMOD (*warmly*). What Fintan and I mean is, have you anything to tell us?

(*The women look at him blankly.*)

We know you were both innocent, don't we, Fintan?

FINTAN (*non-committal*). Ugh.

DERMOD. We were just naturally wondering how you came to be up here with him. Not that we're in the least bit suspicious. (*Silence.*)

FINTAN (*appealingly*). Niamh?

NIAMH. When a ship is launched, it's always the . . .

GRAINNE (*silencing her*). Quiet, Niamh! (*To the men.*) We have nothing to say.

DERMOD. Nothing?

FINTAN. Any old rubbish would do us.

DERMOD. Try us with anything.

GRAINNE (*turning on him*). All right then, you sarcastic devils. All right, if you want the truth, you can have it!

FINTAN (*in dismay*). The truth?

DERMOD. Who said anything about the truth?

FINTAN (*wheeling on* DERMOD). Now look what you've done!

GRAINNE. I *planned* to come up here with James Usheen. We were going to make . . .

(MISS MANNING *is in the room with* USHEEN *in her wake.*)

MISS MANNING. . . . going to make this nice motel of yours famous! (*She goes straight to* GRAINNE, *as if they were long-lost sisters.*) You poor thing – having to keep silent for James's sake and mine. But I've spoken to James, and it's not a secret any more. (*To* USHEEN) Is it, dear?

(USHEEN *looks at her, open-mouthed.*)

Now we can let it be known what a brave, good wife you are. Shall I tell them, or will you?

(GRAINNE *and* NIAMH *look at each other blankly, then at* MISS MANNING.)

GRAINNE⎱
NIAMH ⎰ (*together*). You tell them.

MISS MANNING. Hem! (*Indicating* GRAINNE). This lady – may I call you Grainy? – wrote to Mr Usheen some weeks ago and asked if he would interview her husband and this charming gentleman – (*indicating* FINTAN) – on his programme. To publicize the motel, you know.

FINTAN. Us? Him and me? On colour?

DERMOD. Grainne, is this true?

GRAINNE (*staring dazedly at Miss Manning*). Every word.

MISS MANNING. That was why Mr Usheen asked me to apply for the position of manageress. I haven't been honest with you, Mr Gibbon – I'm really here as a kind of spy – a snooper.

NIAMH (*to* GRAINNE). She's very good.

160

MISS MANNING. Mind, what I've seen, I like. And to make doubly
    sure, Mr Usheen came up here this evening with Mrs Gibbon to
    inspect the premises for himself.
    (USHEEN *is oozing relief. He puts an arm around* MISS
    MANNING.)
USHEEN. And I can't tell you how impressed I am.
FINTAN. Stop right there – I believe everything.
DERMOD. Grainne, can you forgive me?
GRAINNE. (*'wounded'*). Not if I live to be thirty.
MISS MANNING. Hem! Now you may ask, why should Mr Usheen
    and I visit the motel separately on the same night? Shall we tell
    them, Grainy?
GRAINNE. (*being big about it*). Yes, why keep it to ourselves!
MISS MANNING. James?
USHEEN (*squeezing her; lavishly*). Tell them everything!
MISS MANNING. I mean to. You might say that James and I are
    combining business with pleasure. After all, what better place
    than this for a quiet honeymoon?
USHEEN. Absolutely. It's peaceful, it's secluded – it's a lie.
MISS MANNING (*playfully*). Now you did say I could tell them.
    You're the first to know. James and I were married yesterday.
USHEEN (*appalled*). Venetia, you b . . .
    (*A peal of hysterical laughter from* GRAINNE.)
MISS MANNING. We told Grainy, of course. As you can see, she's
    so happy for us.
NIAMH. Oh, Jay.
GRAINNE. I think I'm going to choke.
MISS MANNING. So, as we're newly-weds, James would hardly be
    interested in another lady, now would he? Nor I in another
    gentleman. Although I did rather flirt with Mr Gibbon, just to
    keep him from suspecting.
USHEEN (*feebly*). Look this is all a –
MISS MANNING. – a dead secret – until Sunday. That's when
    James is going to make it public on television. Aren't you, pet?
USHEEN. And if I don't?
MISS MANNING. Eamonn Andrews will.
DERMOD (*bounding forward*). Mr Usheen – congratulations.
FINTAN (*hand outstretched*). I was always a fan of yours. Put it
    there.
    (*It is all too much for* USHEEN. *His shoulders begin to heave.*)
MISS MANNING. (*touched*). Ahhh – he's so sentimental deep
    down. (*She chucks him under the chin.*) Yes, he – is!

161

USHEEN. You . . .

(USHEEN'S *hands begin to reach for* MISS MANNING's *throat, but* FINTAN *wraps a massive arm around his shoulder.*)

FINTAN. Come here to me, me old son. You won't forget about putting us on TV?

MISS MANNING. I'll remind him.

FINTAN. And you'll give us the full treatment? I mean, the few little friendly insults?

(USHEEN *looks at him. At once his rage finds an outlet.*)

USHEEN. Yes! Yes, just to begin with, I think I'll call you an overstuffed upstart, who drives like a drunken Seminole Indian, and who combines the brains of a brontosaurus with the manners of a mongoose.

FINTAN (*wildly*). I like it, I like it!

MISS MANNING. And now, who would like to kiss the bride? Mr Gibbon?

(DERMOD *kisses her and is kissed back.*)

'nk yow! (*She sees that* FINTAN *is next in line.*) Oh, I like them big. Just a peck now! (*She leaves* FINTAN *gasping.*) 'nk *yow!* Well, now, who's next? Oh, no!

(*This is a reaction to the appearance of* HOOLIHAN *beside her. He has risen from the floor, and* MISS MANNING *assumes that he wishes to kiss her.*)

HOOLIHAN. I only want to get past. I have to go to the lav. I have sudden kidneys.

(MISS MANNING *stands back.*)

Thanks. (*He heads for the bathroom.*)

FINTAN. The outside lavatory!

HOOLIHAN. Oh, yes.

(HOOLIHAN *goes out and off down stage.*)

FINTAN (*good-humouredly*). You should have given him a kiss. It'd probably have been his last.

DERMOD. Fintan, the day we appear on English television we'll be set up for life.

GRAINNE. And all thanks to me.

DERMOD. No man ever had a better wife.

FINTAN. I told you all along the girls were innocent. Niamh, when we get home I'm going to make it up to you.

NIAMH. I think I'll slash my wrists.

(*They all come out in a group and move down stage,* FINTAN *carrying the brandy bottle.*)

MISS MANNING. Do try to smile, James. After all, marriage is only another form of entertainment tax.

162

FINTAN. Will you look at this? The old get drank the lot. (*He holds up the bottle.*)

DERMOD. We should get rid of him.

FINTAN. I'll give him the boot first thing in the morning. (*To* USHEEN). Now about this television lark . . .

MISS MANNING. Somebody's just gone past the window.

DERMOD. Where? (*He comes down stage and peers out.*) It's Hoolihan. He's gone off up the mountain.

FINTAN. There's so much brandy in him he can't see straight.

NIAMH (*to* FINTAN). Maybe you ought to go after him.

FINTAN. Who, me?

NIAMH. It's as black as pitch out, and it's teeming.

GRAINNE (*not too concerned*). He's nearly eighty.

DERMOD. If he goes over that rise he won't even see the lights of the motel.

USHEEN. He could die of exposure.

NIAMH. Or the wind could blow him over or he could get pneumonia or fall into a . . .

FINTAN. Nag, nag, nag! If we go out there, we could all get lost. I want to talk to James about this interview. (*To* USHEEN) Will we need dress suits?

NIAMH (*upset*). Fintan!

FINTAN. All right! We'll give the old drunkard twenty minutes. If he's not back by then, I'll drive down to Foxrock, pick up a couple of flash-lamps, wellington boots and raincoats, and we'll go and look for him. Fair?

DERMOD. More than fair.

NIAMH. But by then he could be . . .

FINTAN. Don't spoil the evening for us. We won't see him stuck. He was out in nineteen-sixteen – he's one of us.

(FINTAN, MISS MANNING, USHEEN, DERMOD *and* NIAMH *go off up stage, talking. The following is played very fast, with speeches overlapping.*)

Now about our other motel in Cork – the Michael Collins . . .

DERMOD. Hey, we might accept an investment.

USHEEN. Really?

FINTAN. If you're interested.

USHEEN. I could get my hands on twenty thousand . . .

FINTAN. You're in!

(GRAINNE *disengages herself from* DERMOD'S *arm and comes down to us, again with her warm hostessy smile.*)

GRAINNE. Hello, again. Please don't think we're not worried

about Mr – I forget his name – because we really are. So, as you can see, money hasn't spoiled us one bit. We're still very humanitarian. And Dermod and I do hope you'll drop in on us – at the motel, that is, not at the house. I'm afraid we have so many close friends. But – and we sincerely mean this – if you happen to be in town and you see our Jensen, do wave to us as you jump clear.

(GRAINNE *blows us a kiss, as –*

the CURTAIN *falls.*)

DA

TO MY DAUGHTER

CHARACTERS

CHARLIE
OLIVER
DA
MOTHER
YOUNG CHARLIE
DRUMM
MARY TATE
MRS PRYNN

A kitchen and, later, places remembered. May 1968 and, later, times remembered. There are several playing areas. The main one is the kitchen. This is the kitchen–living room plus small hallway of a corporation house. An exit at the rear to the scullery. A hint of stairs running up from the hall. There are two areas at either side of the kitchen and a series of connecting steps and ramps which climb up and over, behind the kitchen. One of the two areas is the sea-front; it includes a park bench. Behind the sea-front, on the rising platforms, is the hilltop. On the other side of the stage is a neutral area, defined by lighting. This can be a number of locales as the script requires. (In the Second Act there is an ornamental bench there; the park bench is removed.) The kitchen, however, is the womb of the play.

This play was first produced outside the U.S.A. at the Olympia Theatre, Dublin, for the Dublin Theatre Festival, on 8 October 1973, with the following cast:

CHARLIE	Kevin McHugh
OLIVER	Frank Kelly
DA	John McGiver
MOTHER	Phyl O'Doherty
YOUNG CHARLIE	Chris O'Neill
DRUMM	Edward Golden
MARY TATE	Dearbhla Molloy
MRS PRYNN	Pamela Mant

166

DA

ACT ONE

CHARLIE, *overcoat on, is at the kitchen table, sorting letters, family papers, old photos, etc., into two piles. He finds one paper of interest and puts on his glasses to examine it. He then goes to the range and pours boiling water from the kettle into a teapot. He then picks up the teapot as* OLIVER *comes to the door.*

He is CHARLIE's *age — early 40s. His clothes are too neat for him to be prosperous; youthful bouncy step, handkerchief exploding from his breast pocket. He sees that the door is ajar. He knocks all the same.*

CHARLIE. Yes?
  (OLIVER *is about to come in, but stops to remove a crêpe bow from the door.*)
  Yes, who is it?
  (OLIVER *steps into the hall and coughs.*)
  (*Half to himself*) I didn't ask how you are, but who you are.
  (*Then, seeing him*) Oliver!
OLIVER. Instant recognition. Oh — yes, full marks.
CHARLIE. You . . . good God.
OLIVER (*careful speech, equal emphasis on each syllable*). Well, I'm still a native-you-know. Not a globe-trotter like some. (*Almost wagging a finger*) Oh, yes.
CHARLIE. Well, today's the day for it.
OLIVER. Par-don me?
CHARLIE. Old faces. They've turned up like bills you thought you'd never have to pay. I'm on my own . . . come in. (*He puts the teapot down on the table.*)
OLIVER. Won't intrude. Thought I'd offer my . . .
CHARLIE. Sure.
OLIVER. For your trouble. (*Holding up the wreath*) I took the liberty.
CHARLIE. That's damn nice of you, Oliver. Thank you.

167

OLIVER. It was –

CHARLIE. He would have liked that.

OLIVER. It's from the door.

CHARLIE. From . . . ? (*A loud laugh*) I thought it was a . . . gift-wrapped Mass card. I mean, Masses in English, the priest facing you across the altar like a chef at a buffet luncheon . . . I thought it was one more innovation. (*Taking it purposefully.*) Yes, by all means. (*He drops it into the range.*)

OLIVER. Gwendolyn – the wife-you-know – saw the notice in the 'Press'. I would have gone to the funeral –

CHARLIE. What for!

OLIVER. But business-you-know.

CHARLIE. It's nice to see you. It must be ten . . . I don't know, fifteen years? Sit down . . . the mourners left a soldier or two still standing. (*He takes a bottle of stout out of a crate.*)

OLIVER. It's seldom I take a drink.

CHARLIE. I've made tea for myself, do you mind? I never drink in this house. Every Christmas the Da would say: 'Will you have a bottle of stout, son?' Couldn't. It was the stricken look I knew would come on my mother's face, as if I'd appeared in my first pair of trousers or put my hand on a girl's tit in her presence.

OLIVER (*dutifully*). Ho-ho-ho.

CHARLIE. So I . . . (*Blankly*) What?

OLIVER. Joll-y good.

CHARLIE. My God, Oliver, you still think saying 'tit' is the height of depravity. You must find married life unbearably exciting.

OLIVER (*beaming*). Haven't changed, haven't changed!

CHARLIE (*pouring the stout*). Anyway, I kept meaning to take that Christmas drink and send her upstairs in tears with a frenzied petition to St Ann. Next thing I knew, there I was aged thirty-nine, the year she died, a child on my lap who was capable of consuming the dregs of everyone else's tawny port to wild grandparental applause, and my wife sitting where you are, looking with disbelieving nausea at the man she had half-carried home the previous night, as he shook his greying head virtuously and said: 'No, thanks, Da, I still don't.' (*He hands the stout to* OLIVER.) After she died, the not altogether frivolous thought occurred to me that the man who will deliberately not cause pain to his mother must be something of a sadist. I suppose I could have had a drink since then, but why spoil a perfect . . . (*Looking down at* OLIVER) You've got a bald spot.

OLIVER. Me? No . . . ha-ha, it's the wind. (*Producing a comb*)
Breezy out. No, no: fine head of hair still-you-know.
(CHARLIE *smiles and pours his tea, using a pot-holder.*)
(*As he combs*) Warm for a coat, but.

CHARLIE. Yes.

OLIVER. Month of May-you-know.

CHARLIE (*an evasion*). I was halfway out the door when I
remembered this lot. Rubbish mostly. HP agreements, rent
books, insurance, broken pipe . . . (*He moves them to the
bureau.*)

OLIVER. Now!

CHARLIE. What?

OLIVER (*bowing his head for inspection*). Look, you see . . . see?

CHARLIE. Mm . . . you were right and I was wrong. Hair care is
not an idle dream.

OLIVER. The old massage-you-know.

CHARLIE. Ah-hah.

OLIVER (*firmly*). Oh, yes. (*Stroking his hair, he picks up his glass
and drinks.*)

CHARLIE. Have you children?
(*Drinking,* OLIVER *holds up four fingers.*)
Ah?
(OLIVER *jabs a finger towards* CHARLIE.)

CHARLIE. Um? (*Takes a sip of tea.* CHARLIE *points interrogatively
towards himself and raises one finger.*)

OLIVER. Ah.

CHARLIE. What else?

OLIVER. What?

CHARLIE. Is new.

OLIVER. Oh, now.

CHARLIE. Long time. So?

OLIVER. Oh, now. (*He thinks.*
Pause. CHARLIE *waits, then is about to go back to his
sorting.*)
Yes, by Jove, knew I had something to tell you. Six years
ago . . .

CHARLIE. Yes?

OLIVER. I finally got the theme music from 'King's Row'.

CHARLIE. Is that so?

OLIVER. Only electronically-simulated stereo-you-know. But
still . . .

CHARLIE. Still . . .

OLIVER. That was a good fillum.

CHARLIE. Wasn't it.

OLIVER. I got billy-ho for going with you to that fillum. My mother wouldn't let me play with you over that fillum.

CHARLIE. Why?

OLIVER. Oh, pretend he doesn't know!

CHARLIE. Remind me.

OLIVER. You made me miss my elocution class.

CHARLIE (*remembering*). So I did.

OLIVER. Ah, sappy days. Do you remember that expression we had, ah, sappy days? I was glad I kept up with the old elocution-you-know. A great stand-by. Always pronounce properly and look after your appearance: that's how you get on.

CHARLIE. *Did* you get on?

OLIVER. Oh-well-you-know.

CHARLIE. How fantastic.

OLIVER. No harm being ready and waiting.

CHARLIE. None.

OLIVER. That's why I was always smart in myself.

CHARLIE. And you got all the best girls.

OLIVER. I did, though, did-n't I?

CHARLIE. Betty Brady . . .

OLIVER. Oh, now.

CHARLIE. And that one who lived in the maze of buildings behind Cross Avenue. What was it we called her?

OLIVER. The Casbah.

CHARLIE. The Casbah. And Maureen O'Reilly.

OLIVER. Maureen . . . oh, don't-be-talking. There was a girl who took pride in her appearance. With the big — well, it was-you-know — chest.

CHARLIE. Tits.

OLIVER (*as before*). Ho-ho-ho.

CHARLIE. She once told me . . . she said: 'Oliver is going to be a great man.' Believed it.

(OLIVER *'s smile crumples; it is as if his face had collapsed from inside.*)

Mad about you. They all were. What's up?

(OLIVER *shakes his head. He affects to peer closely at a wall picture.*)

All I ever seemed to get was the kind of girl who had a special dispensation from Rome to wear the thickest part of her legs below the knees. (*Looking for reaction*) Yes?

OLIVER (*face unseen*). Oh, now.

CHARLIE. Modelled yourself on Tyrone Power, right? I favoured Gary Cooper myself, but somehow I always came across as Akim Tamiroff. Jesus, Oliver, us in those days! We even thought Gene Autry could act.

OLIVER (*turning*). He could sing 'Mexicali Rose', still and all.

CHARLIE. Least he could do.

OLIVER. Your drawback was you didn't take the Dale Carnegie course like I done.

CHARLIE. Too lazy.

OLIVER. Very worthwhile-you-know. Then, after you went over the Pond, as they say, I joined the Rosicrucians. That was a great comfort to me the time the mother died. It's all about the soul surviving-you-know in the Universal Consciousness. Do you think I should keep on with it?

CHARLIE. Of course if it helps.

OLIVER. Your da-you-know came to the mother's funeral. I never forgot that to him.

CHARLIE. Well, he was always fond of you.

(DA *comes in from the scullery and looks at* OLIVER.)

DA. Fond of him? Fond of that one? Jasus, will you give over, my grave's too narrow to turn in. (*He goes out again.* CHARLIE, *in whose mind this has happened, winces.*)

CHARLIE. In his way.

OLIVER. In the end, was it . . . 'em, if you don't mind me asking . . .?

CHARLIE. No, it wasn't sudden. He got those silent strokes, they're called. Old age. What I mean is, it wasn't unexpected. He *went* suddenly.

OLIVER (*still delicately*). You weren't, em . . .

CHARLIE. I was in London: flew over yesterday, off tonight. Well, my middle-aged friend, now we're both parentless. We've gone to the head of the queue.

OLIVER. Queue for what? Oh, now. Long way to go yet, only getting started. (*He bounces to his feet.*) Well!

CHARLIE. Don't go. Finish your drink.

OLIVER. The wife-you-know.

CHARLIE. Let me finish here and I'll run you home.

OLIVER. No, must be riding the trail to the old hacienda.

CHARLIE (*a hint of urgency*). Ten minutes.

OLIVER. The little woman . . .

(OLIVER *moves to the door, takes gloves from his jacket pocket.*)

171

Queer-you-know how a house looks empty after a funeral.
What will happen to it now, do you think?

CHARLIE. This place? It'll be re-let, I suppose.

OLIVER. I wondered – what was it I wondered? – do you happen
to know anybody in the Corporation?

CHARLIE. Me?

OLIVER. Well, I hear you got on, so they tell me. Gwendolyn and
me are on the list for a house this long time. If you had a bit
of pull-you-know.

CHARLIE (*his manner cooling*). No, I haven't. Sorry.

OLIVER. Oh, now. Man who's up in the world . . .

CHARLIE. I haven't.

OLIVER. Oh. Well, ask not and you receive not.

DA. Dale Carnegie.

OLIVER. Ho-ho. Oh, now. Well, see you next time you're over.
Sorry for the trouble. Sappy days, eh?

CHARLIE. Sappy days.

(OLIVER *goes.* CHARLIE *closes the door.*)

Fucking vulture. (*He faces the empty room. He returns the
teapot to the range with* OLIVER*'s unfinished tumbler of stout.
He looks briefly at* DA*'s chair and then goes to the bureau and
begins to sort papers. He finds a wallet and puts on his glasses
to examine a photograph in it.*

DA *comes in. He wears workingman's clothes: Sunday best.*)

(*Refusing to look at him*) Hoosh. Scat. Out.

DA. That wasn't too bad a day.

CHARLIE. Piss off.

(DA *sits in his chair,* CHARLIE *looks at him.*)

Sit there, then! No one is minding you.

DA. I knew it would hold up for you. You were lucky with the
weather when you came over at Christmas, too.

(CHARLIE *ignores him and returns the papers to the table and
goes on sorting them.*)

Mind, I wouldn't give much for tomorrow. When you can see
the Mountains of Mourne, that's a sure sign it'll rain. Yis, the
angels'll be having a pee.

CHARLIE (*whirling on him*). Now that will do!

DA. That's a good expression. Did you ever hear that expression?

CHARLIE. Did I? Thanks to you, until I was twelve years of age
every time the rain came down I had a mental picture of a group
of winged figures standing around a hole in the clouds relieving
themselves. Go away; I'm working, I'm clearing up. (*Working,*

172

half to himself) Oh, yes, that was him. A gardener all his life, intimately associated with rainfall: i.e., the atmospheric condensation of warm air which, when large enough to fall perceptibly to the ground, constitutes precipitation. Hot air rises, the rain falls; but as far as he was concerned that kind of elementary phenomenon was . . .

DA. Codology.

CHARLIE. Codology. No, it was easier and funnier and more theologically orientated to say that the angels were having a pee. (*He goes to the range and drops a large pile of papers in.*)

DA. You ought to put that down in one of your plays.

CHARLIE. I'd die first.

(DA *rises and, without moving more than a step or two, takes a look at* CHARLIE'*s teacup, then turns towards the range.*)

What are you doing?

DA. Sitting there without a cup of tea in your hand.

CHARLIE. I've a cupful.

DA. It's empty.

CHARLIE. It's full.

DA (*dismissively*). G'way out that.

CHARLIE. Now don't touch that teapot. Do you hear me? For forty-two years I've been through this, you and that bloody teapot, and I know what's going to happen. So don't touch it!

DA. Not a drop of tea in his cup . . . no wonder he's delicate.

CHARLIE. LOOK, will you – (*He watches dumbly, almost tearfully, as* DA *picks up the teapot and starts with it across the room. Halfway across he sets the teapot down on the floor.*)

DA (*agonized*). Jesus, Mary and Joseph. (*He hugs his hand.*)

CHARLIE. I knew it.

DA, CHARLIE (*together*). That's hot.

CHARLIE. Too damn headstrong. Couldn't you have waited until my ma came in and let her – (*Softly*) Jesus.

(DA *begins to stalk the teapot.*)

DA. Bad cess to it for an anti-Christ of a teapot. The handle must be hollow. Whisht, now . . . say nothing. (*He takes* CHARLIE'*s cup from the table and looks contemptuously into it.*) Empty! (*He pours the contents – it is three-quarters full – into a scuttle, then kneels down, placing the cup in front of the teapot. He holds the handle of the pot between fingers and thumb, using the end of his necktie as a potholder, and pours the tea. Wincing*)

173

The devil's cure to it, but it's hot. (*Rising*) Oh, be the hokey. (*He sets the cup before* CHARLIE.) There you are, son.

CHARLIE. (*controlling himself*). Thanks.

DA (*hovering*). That'll put the red neck on you.

CHARLIE. Right!

DA. Where's the sugar?

CHARLIE. I have it. (*Beating him to the sugar and milk.*)

DA. Is there milk?

CHARLIE. Yes!

DA. If you don't want tea I'll draw you a bottle of stout.

CHARLIE. No! (*More composed*) You know I never . . . (*Correcting himself*) I don't want a bottle of stout. Now sit.

DA. Sure there's no shaggin' nourishment in tea. (*Returning to his chair, he is brought up short by the sight of the teapot.*) How the hell are we going to shift it? Hoh? If herself walks in on us and sees that on the floor there'll be desolation. The gee-gees let her down today, and if the picture in the Picture House was a washout as well she'll come home ready to eat us. That's a right conundrum, hoh?

CHARLIE (*coldly*). Cover it with a bucket.

DA. That handle is hot for the night. (*A solution.*) Don't stir. Keep your ear cocked for the squeak of the gate.

CHARLIE. Why? What . . .

(DA *goes to the range, picks up a long rusting pair of tongs and starts to use them to lift the teapot.*)

Oh, God. (CHARLIE *rushes over, grabs the teapot and puts it back on the range. He sucks his scorched hand.*)

Now will you get out and leave me be. You're dead. You're in Dean's Grange, in a box, six feet under . . . with her. I carried you . . . it's over, you're gone, so get out of my head.

(DA *sits in the armchair, unperturbed, filling his pipe with tobacco.*)

Or at least stay quiet. Eighty miserable years of you is in this drawer, and as soon as I've sorted out the odds and ends, I'm slamming that front door and that's *it*. Your nephew Paddy got the TV set, I gave the radio to Maureen and Tom, and Mrs Dunne next door got my sincere thanks for her many kindnesses and in consequence thereof has said she'll never talk to me again. The junkman can have the rest, because I've got what *I* want. An hour from now that fire will go out and there'll be no one here to light it. I'll be rid of you. I'm sweating here because I couldn't wait to put my coat on and be off. So what do you say to that?

DA (*amiably*). Begod, son, you're getting as grey as a badger.

CHARLIE. Old Drumm was right about you. The day he came here to give me the reference.

DA. Drumm is not the worst of them.

CHARLIE. He had *you* taped.

DA. Was he here today?

CHARLIE. He was at the Mass . . . next to the pulpit.

DA. Was that him? I wouldn't recognize him. God, he's failed greatly.

CHARLIE. You can talk.

DA. Decent poor bugger, but.

CHARLIE. Do you know what he called you? The enemy.

MOTHER. (*off*). Charlie! (*She comes in from the scullery. At this time she is in her late fifties; DA is four years older.*)
(*Looking towards the ceiling*) Do you want me to come up to you?

CHARLIE. I'd forgotten what she looked like.

MOTHER (*to* DA). Will you get off your behind and call him. He's in the lavatory with his curse-o'-God books again.

DA (*galvanized into action, yelling*): Do you hear your mother? Come down out of there. You pup, come when you're called. If I put my hand to you . . .

MOTHER. That will do.

DA (*now wound up*). Slouching around . . . skipping and jumping and acting the go-boy. Mr Drumm is halfway up the path!

MOTHER. I said that will do. Read your paper.

DA (*a grotesque imitation of a boy leaping about*). With your hopping and-and-and leppin' and your playing cowboys on the Green Bank. Buck Jones.

CHARLIE. You were always behind the times. I hadn't played cowboys in five years.

DA. Hoot-shaggin' Gibson, Tim McCoy and Randaloph Scott.

MOTHER. You'd give a body a headache.

DA (*subsiding*). And-and-and-and Jeanie Autry.

MOTHER. When Mr Drumm comes in this house you're not to say yes, aye or no to him, do you hear me?

DA. Sure *I* know Drumm. Who was it pruned his rose-trees?

MOTHER. No passing remarks. (*She picks up the teapot.*)

DA. Mag, that teapot is . . .

MOTHER. Say nothing. (*She takes the teapot into the scullery.*)

CHARLIE. I never knew how she did it.

DA. 'Tynan,' says he to me, ''clare to God, I never seen the beating of you for roses.' That's as true as you're standing there, Mag. Never seen the beating of me. (*Ruddy with pleasure*) Hoh?

CHARLIE. Throw you a crumb and you'd call it a banquet.

DA. 'I hear,' says he to me, 'you're a great man for the whist drives.' Do you know, I nearly fell out of my standing. 'Who told you that?' says I, looking at him. 'Sure,' says he, 'there's not a dog or divil in the town doesn't know you!' (*He laughs.* YOUNG CHARLIE *comes downstairs. He is seventeen, shabbily dressed. He carries a book.*)

(*To* YOUNG CHARLIE) Charlie, I was saying, sure I know old Drumm these donkey's years.

CHARLIE. Oh, God: not that little prick.

(YOUNG CHARLIE *looks at him, smarting at the insult. Their contempt is mutual.*)

You were, you know.

YOUNG CHARLIE. And what are you, only a big –

CHARLIE. Careful, that could lead to a compliment.

(YOUNG CHARLIE *sits at the table and opens his book.*)

DA. Oh, Drumm will give you a grand reference.

(MOTHER *returns with the teapot and pours boiling water into it.*)

And if he didn't itself, what odds? Aren't we all grand and comfortable, owing nothing to no one, and haven't we got our health and strength and isn't that the main thing?

CHARLIE. Eat your heart out, Oscar Wilde.

MOTHER. (*to* YOUNG CHARLIE). Don't lie over the table . . . You'll get a hump-back like old Totterdel.

DA. Old Totterdel was a decent man.

CHARLIE. What's the book?

YOUNG CHARLIE (*surly*). 'Story of San Michele'. (*He pronounces it 'Michelle' as in French.*)

CHARLIE (*Italian*). Michele, you thick.

MOTHER. The state of that shirt. I'll give you a fresh one.

YOUNG CHARLIE. It's only Tuesday.

MOTHER. Take it off.

YOUNG CHARLIE. How am I to wear one shirt all week?

MOTHER. You can go easy on it, can't you? Do as you're told.

(*Going into the scullery*) More you do for them, the less thanks you get.

(YOUNG CHARLIE *removes his shirt, under it is a singlet.*)

DA. You could plant seed potatoes on that shirt, son.

176

YOUNG CHARLIE (*muffled, the shirt over his head*). Ah, dry up.
DA (*singing to himself: the tune is 'The Girl I Left Behind Me'*).
'Oh, says your oul' wan to my oul' wan,
"Will you come to the Waxie Dargle?"
And says my oul' wan to your oul' wan,
"Sure I haven't got a farthin'." '
The Waxies were tailors and the Waxie Dargle was a fair they
used to have beyant in Bray in old God's time. You never knew
that. Hoh?
(YOUNG CHARLIE, *shivering, ignores him*.)
CHARLIE (*glaring*). Answer him.
YOUNG CHARLIE. (*to* DA). Yeah, you told me. (*To* CHARLIE)
You're a nice one to talk about being polite to him.
CHARLIE. Privilege of age, boy.
DA (*pinching* YOUNG CHARLIE*'s arm*). Begod, son, there's not a
pick on you. 'I'm thin,' the fella says, 'and you're thin'; but
says he: 'Your man is thinner than the pair of us put together!'
(MOTHER *has returned with the shirt*.)
MOTHER. This is new-ironed. Put it on. (*She holds it for him. It
has been lengthened by the addition of ill-matching pieces from
another shirt to the tail and sleeves*.)
YOUNG CHARLIE. What's that?
MOTHER. Put it on you.
YOUNG CHARLIE. Look at it.
MOTHER. There's not a brack on that shirt, only it's gone a bit
small for you. There's many a poor person 'ud be glad of it.
YOUNG CHARLIE. Then give it to them.
MOTHER. You cur.
YOUNG CHARLIE. God, look at the tail.
MOTHER. Who's going to see it?
YOUNG CHARLIE. I'm not wearing it.
MOTHER (*flinging the shirt down*). Leave it there, then, Don't.
(*Picking it up at once*) Put that shirt on you.
YOUNG CHARLIE. I won't.
MOTHER (*turning to* DA). Nick . . .
DA (*a half-feigned, half-real, rather frightened anger*). Do like the
woman tells you. Can we not have a bit of peace and quiet in
the house the one day of the week? Jasus Christ tonight, do you
want old Drumm to walk in on top of you?
MOTHER (*quietly*). That will do with your Sacred Name. (*To
YOUNG CHARLIE) Lift your arms.
YOUNG CHARLIE (*already beaten*). I'm not wearing that –

(*She slaps his face briskly and, almost in the same movement, thrusts the shirt over his head. She pulls his arms into the sleeves, jerks him to her and fastens the buttons.*)

DA (*relieved*). That's the boy. Herself cut up one of my old shirts for that, son: didn't you, Mag?

CHARLIE. You were always there with the good news.

MOTHER (*coldly, wanting to hurt back*). The day you bring money in, you can start being particular. Time enough then for you to act the gentleman. You can do the big fellow in here then, as well as on the sea front. Oh, it's an old saying and a true one: the more you do for them . . .

DA. Sure that looks grand.

MOTHER. How bad he is . . . And at the end of it they'd hang you. (YOUNG CHARLIE *puts his jacket on. He sits and picks up his book.*)

CHARLIE. You always gave in. Too soft to stand up to them. No guts.

(MOTHER *is at the door looking out.*)

It could have been worse. Like the time you had the date with Ita Byrne and you asked her (MOTHER) to press your navy-blue trousers: told her it was for the altar boys' outing. She'd never pressed a pair of trousers in her life, and she put the creases down the side. And every little gurrier in the town followed you and Ita that night singing 'Anchors Aweigh'. Remember?

YOUNG CHARLIE (*now grinning*). Sappy days.

(*The gate squeaks.*)

MOTHER. There he is now. (*To* YOUNG CHARLIE, *fearfully, the quarrel forgotten.*) God and his holy Mother send he'll find you something.

(DA *starts towards the door. She yanks him back.*)

Will you wait till he knocks.

DA (*almost an incantation*). Sure I know old Drumm.

MOTHER. And keep that mouth of yours shut. Have manners.

YOUNG CHARLIE. He's only a clerk, you know.

(*She looks at him venomously.* DRUMM *comes into view: he is in his mid-fifties, thin, acerbic. He knocks.* MOTHER *and* DA *go to the door. The greetings are mimed.*)

CHARLIE. He was a chief clerk.

(YOUNG CHARLIE *looks towards the door, anguish on his face, fists clenched.*)

Five-fifty a year . . . not bad for nineteen-forty . . . what?

YOUNG CHARLIE. Four . . . November.

CHARLIE. What's up?

YOUNG CHARLIE. Nothing.

CHARLIE. Don't be proud with me, boy.

YOUNG CHARLIE. Listen to them: they always *crawl*.

CHARLIE. Blessed are the meek: they shall inherit the dirt. The shame of being ashamed of them was the worst part, wasn't it? What are you afraid of?

YOUNG CHARLIE. Tell us . . . That day.

CHARLIE. When?

YOUNG CHARLIE. Then. Now. Today. Did they . . . say anything to him?

CHARLIE. About what?

(DRUMM *is shown in.*)

MOTHER. Still, we're terrible, dragging you out of your way.

DRUMM. Is this the young man? (*Shaking hands*) How do you do?

DA (*belatedly*). Shake hands, son.

DRUMM. A bookworm like myself, I see.

MOTHER (*to* DA). Move out and let the man sit down.

DA (*offering his chair, saluting with one finger*). Here you are, sir!

CHARLIE (*angry*). Don't call him sir.

MOTHER. Now you'll sit there and have a cup of tea in your hand. (*She sets about pouring the tea.*)

DRUMM (*quite sternly*). No, I will not.

DA (*aggressive*). Don't mind him. Yes, he will. You will!

DRUMM. You're a foolish woman. In these times we may take hospitality for granted. A ration of a half-ounce of tea per person per week doesn't go far.

MOTHER (*serving him*). Now it won't poison you.

DA. And them's not your tea-leaves that are used and dried out and used again, sir. Get that down you. There's your milk and there's your sugar.

DRUMM. Look here, my dear man, will you sit. I'm not helpless.

MOTHER. Nick . . .

DA. Sure what the hell else have we only for the cup of tea? Damn all . . . amn't I right?

DRUMM (*ignoring him, to* YOUNG CHARLIE). Your name is . . .?

MOTHER. Charles Patrick.

DRUMM. And you've done with school?

MOTHER. He's got a scholarship to the Presentation Brothers. There was many a one got it and took the money; but no, we said, let him have the education, because it'll stand to him when we're gone.

179

DA. Oh, Charlie's the boy with the brains.

DRUMM. Bright are you? Who's your favourite author?

YOUNG CHARLIE. Shakespeare.

CHARLIE. You liar.

DRUMM. And where do your talents lie?

YOUNG CHARLIE. Dunno.

DRUMM. An authority on Shakespeare shouldn't mumble. I asked, what kind of post do you want?

MOTHER. He'll take what he's offered. He's six months idle since he left school. He won't pick and choose.

DA. And if there's nothing for him, sure he can wait. There'll be any amount of jobs once the war's over.

DRUMM. Past history says otherwise. There's usually a depression.

DA. Not at all.

DRUMM. You're an expert, are you?

DA (*a stock phrase*). What are you talking about, or do you know what you're talking about? The Germans know the Irish are their friends, and sign's on it, when the good jobs are handed out in England they'll give us the first preference.

DRUMM. Who will?

DA. The Jerries, amn't I telling you . . . when they win.

DRUMM. You support the Germans, do you?

CHARLIE (*to* DA). Shut up. (*To* YOUNG CHARLIE) Don't go red. Smile.

(YOUNG CHARLIE *summons up an unnatural grin. He laughs. At once* DRUMM *looks at him bad-temperedly.*)

DRUMM. Is something amusing you?

YOUNG CHARLIE. No.

DA. Hitler's the man that's well able for them. He'll give them lackery, the same as *we* done. Sure isn't he the greatest man under the sun, himself and De Valera?

MOTHER (*not looking at him*). Now that will do . . .

DA. What the hell luck could the English have? Didn't they come into the town here and shoot decent people in their beds? But they won't see the day when they can crow it over Heil Hitler. He druv them back into the sea in 1940, and he'll do it again now. Sure what's Churchill anyway, bad scran to him, only a Yahoo, with the cigar stuck in his fat gob and the face on him like a boiled shite.

(*Pause.* DRUMM *just looks at him.*)

MOTHER. There's plenty more tea in the –

DRUMM. No, I must be going.

MOTHER (*with a false smile*). You oughtn't to mind him.

DRUMM. I don't at all. I thought the boy might walk with me, and I could ask him what it is I need to know.

MOTHER. Charlie, do you hear? Go and comb your hair and give your face a rub.

(YOUNG CHARLIE *goes upstairs, glad to get away.*)

I know you'll do your best for him. You will.

DRUMM. It would be a poor best. There's nothing here for anyone. Have you thought of letting him go to England?

DA. England!

DRUMM. There's work there.

MOTHER. Ah, no.

DRUMM. It might be for his good.

MOTHER. No, we'd think bad of losing him.

DA. There's good jobs going here if you keep an eye out. I'm gardening above in Jacob's these forty-six years, since I was a young lad . . . would you credit that?

DRUMM. Yes, I would.

MOTHER. What is there in England only bombs and getting into bad health? No, he'll stay where he's well looked after. Sure, Mr Drumm, we're all he has. His own didn't want him.

DRUMM. His own?

MOTHER (*bitterly*). Whoever she was.

DRUMM. Do you mean the boy is adopted?

(YOUNG CHARLIE *comes downstairs at a run, anxious to be off. He hears what* DRUMM *has said and hangs back on the stairs.*)

MOTHER (*purely as punctuation*). Ah, don't talk to me.

CHARLIE. And I listened, faint with shame, while you delivered your party-piece.

MOTHER. I took him out of Holles Street Hospital when he was ten days old, and he's never wanted for anything since. My mother that's dead and gone, the Lord have mercy on her, said to me: 'Mag, he's a nurse-child. You don't know where he was got or how he was got, and you'll rue the day. He'll turn on you.'

DA (*a growl*). Not at all, woman.

MOTHER. Amn't I saying! (*To* DRUMM) You try rearing a child on thirty shillings a week then and two pounds ten now after forty years of slaving, and see where it leaves you.

CHARLIE. Stand by. Finale coming up.

MOTHER. And a child that was delicate. She tried to get rid of him.

181

DRUMM. Get rid?

CHARLIE. Roll of drums, *and . . .*!

MOTHER. Before he was born. Whatever kind of rotten poison she took. Dr Enright told me; he said, 'You won't rear that child, ma'am, he'll never make old bones.' But I did rear him, and he's a credit to us.

CHARLIE. Band-chord. Final curtain. Speech!

MOTHER. He's more to us than our own, so he is.

CHARLIE. Thunderous applause. (*To* DRUMM) Hand her up the bouquet.

DRUMM. You're a woman out of the ordinary. The boy has cause to be grateful.

CHARLIE. Well done. House-lights.

(YOUNG CHARLIE, *his lips pressed tight together to suppress a howl, emits a high-pitched half-whimper, half-squeal, and flees into the garden.*)

And the scream seemed to come through my eyes.

MOTHER. Charlie?

DRUMM (*looking out*). I see he's leading the way. Goodbye, Mrs Tynan: I'll do what little I can.

MOTHER. Sure I know. God never let me down yet.

DRUMM (*looking at* DA *and then at* MOTHER). You surprise me.

MOTHER. Nick, say goodbye.

DA. Are you off? Good luck, now. (*Giving him a Nazi salute*) We shall rise again. Begod, we will.

DRUMM. You're an ignorant man. (*He nods to* MOTHER *and goes out.* DA *laughs softly and shakes his head, as if he had been complimented.*)

(*Off*) Young man, come here.

DA (*as* MOTHER *comes in from hall*). There's worse going than old Drumm. A decent man. 'I never seen the beating of you,' says he, 'for roses.'

(*She glares at him, too angry to speak, and takes* DRUMM's *teacup out to the scullery.*)

CHARLIE (*to* DA). You could have stopped her. You could have tried. You never said a word.

DA (*calling to* MOTHER). I think I'll do me feet tonight, Mag. I have a welt on me that's a bugger.

CHARLIE. All those years you sat and looked into the fire, what went through your head? What did you think of? What thoughts? I never knew you to have a hope or a dream or say a half-wise thing.

DA (*rubbing his foot*). Aye, rain tomorrow.

CHARLIE. Whist drive on Wednesday, the Picture House on Sundays and the Wicklow regatta every first Monday in August. Bendigo plug-tobacco and 'Up Dev' and 'God bless all here when I get in meself'. You worked for fifty-eight years, nine hours a day, in a garden so steep a horse couldn't climb it, and when they got rid of you with a pension of ten shillings a week you did hand-springs for joy because it came from the Quality. You spent your life sitting on brambles, and wouldn't move in case someone took your seat.

DA (*softly*). You're a comical boy.

CHARLIE (*almost an appeal*). You could have stopped her.

(MOTHER *comes in.*)

MOTHER. Ignorant, he said you were, and that's the word for you.

DA (*taken aback*). What?

MOTHER. With your 'Up Hitler' in front of him and your dirty expressions. Ignorant.

DA. What are you giving out about?

MOTHER. You. You sticking your prate in where it's not wanted, so's a body wouldn't know where to look. I said to you: 'Keep that mouth of yours shut,' I said. But no . . . it'd kill you.

DA. Sure I never said a word to the man, good, bad or indifferent.

MOTHER. You're not fit to be let loose with respectable people. I don't wonder at Charlie running out of the house.

DA. What? Who did?

MOTHER. It wouldn't be the first time you made a show of him and it won't be the last. God help the boy if he has you to depend on.

DA (*upset*). Ah now, Mag, go easy. No . . . sure Charlie and me is —

MOTHER. *Anyone* would be ashamed of you.

DA. No, him and me is —

MOTHER. He's done with you now. Done with you. (*She goes out.*)

CHARLIE. Serves you right. You could have stopped her.

(*The lights go down on the kitchen and come up on the promenade. The sound of seagulls.* DRUMM *and* YOUNG CHARLIE *appear. They stand in front of a bench.*)

DRUMM. The wind has moved to the east. Do you take a drink?

YOUNG CHARLIE. Not yet.

DRUMM. You will, please God. Do you chase girls?

YOUNG CHARLIE. Pardon?

DRUMM. Female persons. Do you indulge?

YOUNG CHARLIE. The odd time.

DRUMM. As a diversion I don't condemn it. Henry Vaughan, an otherwise unremarkable poet of the seventeenth century, summed it up happily when he wrote 'How brave a prospect is a bright backside.' Do you know Vaughan?

YOUNG CHARLIE. 'They are all gone into the world of light.'

DRUMM. So you do read poetry! Listen to me, my friend: if you and I are to have dealings you had better know that I do not tolerate liars. Don't try it on with me ever again.

YOUNG CHARLIE. I didn't . . .

DRUMM (*firmly*). Shakespeare is nobody's favourite author. (*He gives* YOUNG CHARLIE *a searching look.*) We'll say no more about it. Yes, chase away by all means and give them a damn good squeeze if you catch them, but be slow to marry. The maximum of loneliness and the minimum of privacy. I have two daughters myself . . . no boys.

YOUNG CHARLIE. I know your daughters.

DRUMM. Oh?

YOUNG CHARLIE. To see. Not to talk to.

DRUMM. I would describe them as . . . bird-like.

YOUNG CHARLIE (*trying to say the right thing*). Yes, I suppose they –

DRUMM. Rhode Island Reds. You may laugh . . .

YOUNG CHARLIE. I wouldn't.

DRUMM. I say you may. *I* do. No . . . no boys. (*He sits on the bench and motions for* YOUNG CHARLIE *to sit beside him.*) There will be a vacancy in my office for a filing clerk. I don't recommend it to you: jobs are like lobster pots, harder to get out of than into, and you seem to me to be not cut out for clerking. But if you want to sell your soul for forty-five shillings a week I daresay my conscience won't keep me awake at nights.

YOUNG CHARLIE. Do you mean I can have it?

DRUMM. If you're fool enough. My advice –

YOUNG CHARLIE. A job. A job in an office, in out of the cold. Oh, Janey, I think I'll go mad. (*He jumps up.*) Yeow!

(DRUMM *taps the umbrella on the ground.*)

God, I think I'll split in two. I'm a millionaire. Mr Drumm . . . any time if there's e'er an oul' favour I can do for you over this –

DRUMM. You can speak correct English.

YOUNG CHARLIE. Honest to God, Mr Drumm, I'm so delighted, if you asked me to I'd speak Swahili. A job!

184

DRUMM (*sourly*). And this is how we throw our lives away.

YOUNG CHARLIE (*grins, then*). Beg your pardon?

DRUMM. You'll amount to nothing until you learn to say no. No to jobs, no to girls, no to money. Otherwise, by the time you've learned to say no to life you'll find you've swallowed half of it.

YOUNG CHARLIE. I've been looking for a job since school, Mr Drumm. I couldn't refuse it.

DRUMM. To be sure.

YOUNG CHARLIE. I mean, I'm the only one at home . . .

DRUMM. I'm aware of that. (*Considers it settled.*) So be it. There's a grey look about your face: I suggest you begin to wash yourself properly. And I'll need a copy of your birth certificate. What's your name?

YOUNG CHARLIE (*surprised*). Tynan.

DRUMM. I mean your real name. You overheard what your foster-mother told me, didn't you? That you're illegitimate. Don't give me that woe-begone look. It's a fact, you're going to have to live with it and you may as well make a start. Bastardy is more ignominious in a small town than in a large one, but please God it may light a fire under you. Do your friends know? (YOUNG CHARLIE *shakes his head.*)

Probably they do. So don't tell them: they won't thank you for spiking their guns. What ails you? Look here, my friend: tears will get no sympathy from me. I said we'll have done with it . . . people will take me for a pederast. Your nose is running: wipe it.

YOUNG CHARLIE. I haven't got a handkerchief.

DRUMM. Well, you can't have mine. Use something . . . the tail of your shirt.

(YOUNG CHARLIE *is about to comply when he remembers.*) Well?

YOUNG CHARLIE. I won't.

DRUMM (*bristling*). Won't?

YOUNG CHARLIE. (*loftily*). It's a disgusting thing to do.

DRUMM. You think so?

(*They outglare each other.* YOUNG CHARLIE *sniffs deeply. Brass band music is heard in the distance.*)

Well, perhaps there's hope for you yet.

YOUNG CHARLIE. There's a band on the pier.

DRUMM (*rising to look*). Hm? Yes, the Artane Boys, by the sound of them.

(YOUNG CHARLIE *whips out his shirt-tail, wipes his nose*

185

and readjusts his dress as DRUMM *turns to face him.*)
Your . . . mother, shall we call her? . . . is a fine woman.

YOUNG CHARLIE. Yeah. Except she tells everyone.

DRUMM. About you?

YOUNG CHARLIE. All the old ones. Then they say to her: isn't she great and how I ought to go down on my bended knees. Even the odd time I do something right, it's not enough . . . it's always the least I could do. Me da is different: if you ran into him with a motor car he'd thank you for the lift.

DRUMM. I'm fond of him.

YOUNG CHARLIE (*disbelieving*). Of me da?

DRUMM. I can afford that luxury: I'm not obliged to live with him. You are. That's why he's the enemy.

YOUNG CHARLIE. The what?

DRUMM. Your enemy.

YOUNG CHARLIE (*straight-faced, trying not to laugh*). I see.

DRUMM. Don't be polite with me, my friend, or you'll be out of that job before you're into it. Once at a whist drive I heard him say that the world would end in 1940. It was a superstition that had a fashionable currency at one time among the credulous. Well, 1940 came and went, as you may have noticed, and finding myself and the county of Dublin unscathed, I tackled him on the subject. He was unruffled. He informed me that the world hadn't ended because the German bombs had upset the weather.

(YOUNG CHARLIE *laughs boisterously. He bangs his fists on his knees.* DA *enters the neutral area and rings a doorbell.*)
Yes, the dangerous ones are those who amuse us.

(*The bell is rung again.* DA *puts his pipe in his pocket and waits.*)
There are millions like him: inoffensive, stupid, and not a damn bit of good. They've never said no in their lives or to their lives, and they'd cheerfully see the rest of us buried. If you have any sense, you'll learn to be frightened of him.

(*A light is flashed on* DA*'s face as if a door had been opened.*)

DA (*saluting*). That's a hash oul' day, ma'am. Certainly you know me . . . Tynan, of Begnet's Villas, sure I'm as well known as a begging ass. And do you know what I'm going to tell you? . . . that back field of yours, the meadow: if you was to clear that field of the rocks that's in it and the stumps of trees and had it dug up with a good spreading of manure on the top of

it, begod, you wouldn't know yourself. There's bugger-all you
couldn't grow in it.

DRUMM. From people too ignorant to feel pain, may the good God
deliver us!

DA. The young lad, do you see, he's starting work. Oh, a toppin'
job: running an office, sure he's made for life. And the way it
is, I'd think bad of him starting off without a decent suit on his
back or the couple of good shirts. Sure you couldn't let him mix
with high-up people and the arse out of his trousers. Have you
me?

DRUMM. I'm advising you to live in your own world, not with one
foot in his.

DA. I'll come to you so on Sundays and do the field . . . sure it
won't take a feather out of me. (*Embarrassed by mention of
money*) Very good, yis . . . I'll leave that to yourself: sure
whatever you think. (*Saluting.*) Thanks very much, more power.
(*He starts off, then bobs back again.*) More power, says oul'
Power when young Power was born, wha'?
(*The door-light snaps off. As he moves away, the lights on the
neutral area go down.*)

DRUMM. Are we still on speaking terms?

YOUNG CHARLIE (*hating him*). Yes.

DRUMM. You aren't angry?

YOUNG CHARLIE. No!

DRUMM. Indeed, why should you be! Shall we stroll down and
listen to the Artane Boys?
(*They walk off. Lights come up quickly on CHARLIE and DA
in the kitchen as before.*)

CHARLIE. And I went off with him like a trollop.

DA. Drumm is a decent skin. Came in here once to see how I was
managing after herself died. Three years ago this month, yis.
Gev me a packet of cigarettes. 'No,' says I, 'I won't.' 'You
will,' says he; 'take them when you're told to.' So I did. Wait
now till I see where I have them.

CHARLIE. We listened to the band and I even made excuses for
you. Told him about your grandfather and two uncles starving
to death in the Famine.

DA. Oh, aye. Them was hard times. They died in the ditches.

CHARLIE. What ditches? I made it up!

DA. Fierce times they were. Where the hell did I put them? You
can smoke them in the aeroplane. (*Going to the dresser*)

CHARLIE. I don't want them.

187

DA (*searching*). Yes, you do.

CHARLIE. Don't make a – (*He takes a packet of 'Player's' from his pocket.*) It's all right . . . look, I found them.

DA. Hoh?

CHARLIE. Look.

DA. Good lad. Yis, it was in the month of – (*he breaks off.*) Drumm smoked 'Sweet Aftons' . . . that's not them. (*He resumes the search.*)

CHARLIE. Messer!

DA. It was in the month of May herself died, and it was in the month of May I went. Would you credit that? (*He climbs on a chair.*)

CHARLIE. Congratulations. I should have stuck up for you and told him to keep his job. Then I could have hated you instead of myself. Because he was dead on: he described you to a – (*Seeing him*) Oh, get down.

(DA *finds the cigarettes on top of the dresser. He begins to climb down.*)

You destroyed me, you know that? Long after I'd quit the job and seen the last of Drumm, I was dining out in London: black dickie-bow, oak panelling, picture of Sarah Bernhardt at nine o'clock: the sort of place where you have to remember not to say thanks to the waiters. I had just propelled an erudite remark across the table and was about to shoot my cuffs, lose my head and chance another one, when I felt a sudden tug as if I was on a dog-lead. I looked, and there were you at the other end of it. Paring your corns, informing me that bejasus the weather would hold up if it didn't rain, and sprinkling sugar on my bread when Ma's back was turned.

(DA *gives him the cigarettes as if he was passing on contraband.*)

DA. Say nothing. Put this in your pocket.

CHARLIE. So how could I belong there if I belonged here?

DA. 'Take them,' says Drumm to me, 'when you're told to.'

CHARLIE. And it was more than a memory. She was dead then, and at that moment I knew you were sitting here on your own while the daylight went. Did you think bad of me? I wish I were a fly inside your head, like you're a wasp inside of mine. Why wouldn't you come and live with us in London when we asked you?

DA. What would I do that for?

CHARLIE. You were eighty-one.

DA. Sure I was a marvel. 'Begod, Tynan,' says Father Kearney to me, 'we'll have to shoot you in the wind-up.' What a fool I'd be to leave herself's bits and pieces here where any dog or divil could steal them. And for what? To go to England and maybe land meself in an early grave with the food they serve up to you.

CHARLIE. No, you'd rather stay here instead, like a maggot in a cabbage, and die of neglect.

DA. I fended for meself. No better man.

CHARLIE. In sight or out of it, you were a millstone. You couldn't even let me lose my virginity in peace.

DA. Lose your what?

CHARLIE. Nothing. It's a slang word, now obsolete.

(MARY TATE *walks on. She is twenty-five, a loner.*)

DA. Who's that? That's a fine figure of a girl. What's she doing around here?

CHARLIE. She's not here: she's on the sea-front. And she wasn't a fine girl. She was known locally as the Yellow Peril.

(YOUNG CHARLIE *and* OLIVER – *younger now* – *are lounging in the neutral area.* MARY *walks by. They pay her no obvious attention.*)

YOUNG CHARLIE (*suddenly, singing*). 'Underneath the lamplight . . .'

OLIVER. 'By the barracks gate . . .'

YOUNG CHARLIE. 'Darling, I remember . . .'

OLIVER. 'The way you used to wait.'

YOUNG CHARLIE, OLIVER (*together*).

'I heard you walking in the street,
I smelt your feet,
My lily of the lamplight,
My own Lily Marlene.'

(MARY*'s step falters as she hears the lyrics. She continues on to the bench, where she sits and opens a copy of 'Modern Screen'.*

The two youths go on singing – quietly now and to themselves.

YOUNG CHARLIE *looks covertly at her once or twice.*)

CHARLIE (*to* DA). We all dreamed, privately and sweatily, about committing dark deeds with the Yellow Peril. Dark was the word, for if you were seen with her, nice girls would shun you and tell their mothers, and their mothers would tell yours: the Yellow Peril was the enemy of mothers. And the fellows would jeer at you for your beggarman's lust – you with your fine words of settling for nothing less than Veronica Lake. We

189

always kept our sexual sights impossibly high: it preserved us from the stigma of attempt and failure on the one hand, and success and mortal sin on the other. The Yellow Peril never winked, smiled or flirted: the sure sign of an activist. We avoided her, and yet she was a comfort to us. It was like having a trusty flintlock handy in case of necessity.

(YOUNG CHARLIE *and* OLIVER *both look at* MARY.)

YOUNG CHARLIE. They say she's mustard.

OLIVER. Oh, yes. Red-hot-you-know.

YOUNG CHARLIE. And she has a fine-looking pair.

OLIVER. Of legs-you-mean?

YOUNG CHARLIE. Well, yeah: them, too.

OLIVER. Oh. Ho-ho-ho. Oh, now. Joll-y good.

(MARY *looks up from her book as* OLIVER *raises his voice: a calm direct look, neither friendly nor hostile.*)

YOUNG CHARLIE. She's looking. (*To* MARY, *bravely*) 'Evening.

OLIVER. (*embarrassed*). Don't.

YOUNG CHARLIE. Why?

OLIVER. We'll get ourselves a bad name. Where was I? Yes . . . I was telling you about Maria Montez in 'Cobra Woman'. Now there's a fine figure of a –

YOUNG CHARLIE. They say she'd let you. All you have to do is ask.

OLIVER. Maria Montez? Is that a fact?

YOUNG CHARLIE (*pointing*). Her.

OLIVER. Ah, yes: but who is that hard up for it?

CHARLIE. I was.

OLIVER. I mean, who wants to demean himself?

CHARLIE. I did.

YOUNG CHARLIE. God, I wouldn't touch her in a fit. I'm only –

OLIVER. And she would make a holy show of you, you-know, like she done with the man who tried to interfere with her in the Picture House.

YOUNG CHARLIE. When?

OLIVER. I think it was a Bette Davis. The man sat down next to her and as soon as the big picture came on the screen he started tampering with her in some way. And she never said a word, only got up and dragged him to the manager by his wigger-wagger.

YOUNG CHARLIE (*stunned*). She never.

OLIVER. True as God. He felt very small, I can tell you.

YOUNG CHARLIE. Still, if she minded she can't be all that fast.

OLIVER. Oh-I-don't-know. If she wasn't fast she'd have dragged him by something else.

190

(YOUNG CHARLIE *looks at* MARY *in awe.*)

CHARLIE. Lust tied granny-knots in my insides. I wanted the Yellow Peril like I wanted no girl before or no woman since. What was worse, I was wearing my new suit for the first time and I had to do it now, now or never, before the newness wore off.

OLIVER (*who has been talking*). So will we trot up to the billiard hall?

YOUNG CHARLIE. You go.

OLIVER. Me?

YOUNG CHARLIE. I'll follow you. (*He looks almost tragically at* OLIVER.

Pause. Then OLIVER *stares from him to* MARY.)

OLIVER. Her?

YOUNG CHARLIE (*agonized*). Go on.

OLIVER. Ho-ho-ho-ho. Oh, now. (*Dismay*) You wouldn't.

YOUNG CHARLIE. Olly . . . fizz off.

OLIVER. But you don't want to chance your arm with her; she'd let you. (*Then*) Where will you take her?

YOUNG CHARLIE. I dunno: down the back.

OLIVER. I'll see you, then.

YOUNG CHARLIE. Yeah.

OLIVER. I suppose you know you'll destroy your good suit.

YOUNG CHARLIE. Will you go on. See you.

(OLIVER *does not move. Hostility forms on his face.*)

OLIVER. I was the one you came out with-you-know.

(YOUNG CHARLIE *waits for him to go.*)

They say it's very disappointing-you-know, very over-rated. (*Pause. Angrily*) Well, don't salute me in the town when you see me, because you won't be saluted back. (*He goes.*

YOUNG CHARLIE *goes towards the bench. He stops, suddenly panic-stricken.*

CHARLIE *has by now moved out of the kitchen area.*)

CHARLIE. Do you want a hand?

(*Still looking at* MARY, YOUNG CHARLIE *motions to him to be quiet.*)

If they think you're afraid to ask them they attack you. You said yourself, all you have to do is ask.

YOUNG CHARLIE. Dry up, will you.

(MARY *looks at him.*)

CHARLIE. Now . . . quick!

YOUNG CHARLIE. 'Evening.

191

MARY. You said that.

CHARLIE. Sit.

(YOUNG CHARLIE *sits beside her. What follows is ritual, laconic and fast.*)

MARY. Didn't ask you to sit down.

YOUNG CHARLIE. Free country.

MARY. Nothing doing for you here.

YOUNG CHARLIE. Never said there was.

MARY. Ought to have gone off with that friend of yours.

YOUNG CHARLIE. Who ought?

MARY. You ought.

YOUNG CHARLIE. What for?

MARY. Nothing doing for you here.

YOUNG CHARLIE. Never said there was.

(*Pause. Phase Two in conversation.*)

MARY. What's your name, anyway?

YOUNG CHARLIE. Bruce.

MARY (*a sceptical grin*). Yeah?

YOUNG CHARLIE. It is. (*He crosses his eyes and thumbs his nose at* CHARLIE *by way of defiance.*)

MARY. Bruce?

YOUNG CHARLIE. Mm.

MARY. Nice name.

YOUNG CHARLIE (*pointing off*). He's Oliver.

MARY. That so?

YOUNG CHARLIE. He's from the town.

MARY. Where *you* from?

YOUNG CHARLIE. Trinity College.

MARY. That right?

YOUNG CHARLIE. English Literature.

MARY. Must be hard.

YOUNG CHARLIE. Bits of it.

(*She goes back to her reading. A lull. End of Phase Two.*)

CHARLIE. Ask her.

YOUNG CHARLIE. She's not on.

CHARLIE. Ask.

(*Instead,* YOUNG CHARLIE *clamps his arm heavily around* MARY. *She does not look up from her magazine during the following.*)

MARY. Wouldn't Edward G. Robinson put you in mind of a monkey?

YOUNG CHARLIE. Let's see. Do you know, he does.

192

MARY. One of them baboons.

YOUNG CHARLIE. Yes. Yes, yes, yes, yes.

(*At each 'yes' he slaps her vigorously on the knee. She stares as if mesmerized at his hand as it bounces up and down and finally comes to rest on her knee in an iron grip. As she returns to her magazine he begins to massage her kneecap.*)

CHARLIE (*staring*). You insidious devil, you.

MARY. It doesn't screw off.

YOUNG CHARLIE. What?

MARY. Me leg.

(*His other hand now slides under her armpit, intent on touching her breast. He is unaware that he is kneading and pinching her handbag, which is tucked under her arm. She watches this hand, fascinated.*)

CHARLIE. I think you're getting her money all excited.

MARY (*having returned to her reading*). You needn't think there's anything doing for you here.

YOUNG CHARLIE. I don't.

MARY. Dunno what you take me for . . . sort of person who'd sit here and be felt with people passing. If you won't stop I'll have to go down the back. (*She looks at him directly for the first time.*) If you won't stop.

YOUNG CHARLIE (*not stopping; hoarsely*). All right.

MARY (*looking off*). Wait till that old fella goes past.

YOUNG CHARLIE. Who?

MARY (*fondling his knee*). Not that you're getting anything.

YOUNG CHARLIE (*dazed with lust*). I know.

CHARLIE. My silver-tongued eloquence had claimed its helpless victim. Defloration stared me in the face. My virginhood swung by a frayed thread. Then . . . !

DA (*off*).

'Oh, says your oul' one to my oul' one.

"Will you come to the Waxie Dargle?"

And says my oul' one to your oul' one.

"Sure I haven't got a farthin'." '

(YOUNG CHARLIE*'s kneading and rubbing comes to a halt. As* DA *walks on at a good stiff pace, he tries to extract his hand from under* MARY *'s but she holds it fast.*)

(*Passing*) More power. (*He walks a few more paces, stops, turns and stares.*) Jesus, Mary and Joseph.

YOUNG CHARLIE (*his voice cracking*). Hello.

MARY. Don't talk to him.

(DA *looks at* MARY*'s hand on* YOUNG CHARLIE*'s knee.*
YOUNG CHARLIE *removes her hand; she replaces it.*)

DA. Sure the whole world is going mad.

MARY. Don't answer him.

(DA *sits next to her.*)

DA. The whist drive was cancelled, bad scran to it. Only four
tables. Says I: 'I'm at the loss of me tram fare down, but I
won't be at the loss of it back, for I'll walk.' (*He looks at*
YOUNG CHARLIE*'s hand flapping helplessly.*) I dunno. I dunno
what to say.

MARY. He'll go away. Don't mind him.

CHARLIE. If my hand was free I'd have slashed my wrists.

DA. Oh, the young ones that's going nowadays would eat you. I
dunno.

MARY. He doesn't know much.

DA. He knows too shaggin' much. (*To* YOUNG CHARLIE) If your
mother was here and seen the antrumartins of you, there'd be
blood spilt.

MARY. Much she'd care.

DA. Much who'd care.

MARY. Me ma.

YOUNG CHARLIE. He's talking to me.

DA. Certainly I'm talking to him, who else? That's my young lad
you're trick-acting with.

MARY (*to* YOUNG CHARLIE) Is he your –

DA. Oh, that's Charlie.

MARY. Who?

YOUNG CHARLIE. Bruce is me middle name.

DA. That's Charles Patrick.

YOUNG CHARLIE. Oh, thanks.

DA (*to* MARY). You mind me, now. What is it they call you?

MARY (*a little cowed*). Mary Tate.

YOUNG CHARLIE. Leave her alone.

DA. You hold your interference. From where?

MARY. Glasthule . . . the Dwellin's.

(DA *makes a violent gesture, gets up, walks away, turns and
points at her dramatically.*)

DA. Your mother was one of the Hannigans of Sallynoggin. Did
you know that?

MARY. Yes.

DA. And your uncle Dinny and me was comrades the time of the

194

Troubles. And you had a sister that died of consumption above in Loughlinstown.

MARY. My sister Peg.

DA. And another one in England.

MARY. Josie.

DA. Don't I know the whole seed and breed of yous! (*To* YOUNG CHARLIE) Sure this is a grand girl. (*He nudges* YOUNG CHARLIE *off the bench and sits down next to* MARY.) Tell me, child, is there news of your father itself?

MARY (*her face clouding*). No.

DA. That's hard lines.

MARY (*bitterly*). We don't *want* news of him. Let him stay wherever he is – we can manage without him. He didn't give a curse about us then, and we don't give a curse about him now.

DA. There's some queer people walking the ways of the world.

MARY. Blast him.

(DA *talks to her. She listens, nods, wipes her eyes.*)

CHARLIE. And before my eyes you turned the Yellow Peril into Mary Tate of Glasthule, with a father who had sailed off to look for work in Scotland five years before, and had there decided that one could live more cheaply than seven. The last thing I'd wanted that evening was a person.

(DA *rises, about to go.*)

DA (*to* YOUNG CHARLIE). You mind your manners and treat her right, do you hear me. (*To* MARY) Don't take any impudence from him. Home by eleven, Charlie.

YOUNG CHARLIE. Yes, Da.

DA. 'Bye-'bye, so. Mind yourselves.

MARY. 'Bye . . .

(*They watch until he is out of sight.*)

Your old fellow is a gas.

YOUNG CHARLIE (*sourly*). Oh, yeah. A whole bloody gasometer.

MARY (*pause, then*). Well, will we go down the back?

YOUNG CHARLIE. Uh . . . down the back . . . yeah.

MARY. He's gone, he won't see us. (*Affectionately, mocking*) Bruce!

YOUNG CHARLIE. The thing is, I promised Oliver I'd see him in the billiard hall.

MARY. Oh, yeah?

YOUNG CHARLIE. Maybe some evening next week, if you're around, we can –

MARY. Mm . . . sure.

195

YOUNG CHARLIE. Oliver's holding a table for us. Got to run. Well
. . . see you.

MARY. Suppose you will. (*As he goes*) Y'ought to wrap yourself in
cotton wool. (*Chanting*) Daddy's little baby . . . Daddy's little
b—
(*She stops and begins to cry, then goes off.*)

CHARLIE. I stayed away from the sea-front for a long time after
that. (*He finds an object on the table in front of him.*) Is this
yours? (*He sees that he is alone. He looks at it more closely.*)
Tug-o-war medal. Nineteen . . . God almighty, nineteen-twelve.
It was different then. It was even different when . . . when?
When I was seven. You were an Einstein in those days.
(DA *comes in from the scullery. He is thirty years younger: in
his prime.*)

DA (*a roar*). Hup out of that! Put up your homework, get off your
backside, and we'll take the dog for a run around the Vico.

CHARLIE (*happily*). Yes, Da.

DA (*summoning the dog*). Come on, Blackie . . . who's a good
dog? That's the fella . . . hup, hup! (*He crouches as if holding
a dog by the forepaws, and allows his face to be licked.*) Give
us the paw . . . give. Look at that . . . begod, wouldn't he near
talk to you? Get down. Are you right, son? (*He extends his
hand.*

CHARLIE *takes it.*

MOTHER *comes in from the scullery with a woollen scarf.*)

MOTHER. No, he's not right. (*She puts the scarf around* CHARLIE*'s
neck, tucking it in tightly.*) You have as much sense in you as
a don't-know-what. Dragging him out with his chest exposed.
Do you want to get him into bad health?

CHARLIE. Ah, Ma . . .

MOTHER. Ah, Ma! Go on. Bless yourselves going out, the pair of
you.
(CHARLIE *and* DA *go into the hall.* DA *dips his fingers into a
holy-water font and flicks the water at* CHARLIE.)

DA (*opening the front door: to the dog, stumbling*). Blast you,
don't trip me up . . . hoosh owa that!
(*They stop on the doorstep,* DA *looking at the sky.
During this acene,* CHARLIE *does not attempt to imitate a
child. He is an adult re-enacting a memory. Trust is evident in
his attitude towards* DA.)
That's a fine mackerel sky. Sure isn't it the best bloody country
in the world!

CHARLIE. Da, say it.

DA. Say what?

CHARLIE. What you always say. Ah, you know . . . what the country mug in the army said. Say it.

DA (*feigning innocence*). What did he say?

CHARLIE. Ah, do . . .

DA. Yis, well, he joins up. And sits down to his dinner the first night, and says he . . .

CHARLIE. Yeah, yeah!

DA. Says he: 'Yes, sir; no, sir, if you please. Is it up the duck's arse that I shove the green peas?'

(CHARLIE *laughs delightedly.*

They walk hand in hand up and around the stage, both singing 'Waxie Dargle'.

Lights go down on the kitchen. They stop at an upper level. DA *reaches back to help* CHARLIE *up.*)

Come on, now . . . big step.

CHARLIE. I can't, Da.

DA. Yes, you can.

CHARLIE. I'll fall.

DA. You won't fall. Catch a hold of me hand. That's the lad . . . and there you go! Looka that, looka them mountains. There's a view, if you were rich enough you couldn't buy it. Do you know what I'm going to tell you? . . . there's them that says that view is better nor the Bay of Naples.

CHARLIE. Where's Naples, Da?'

DA. Ah, it's in Italy.

CHARLIE. What's Italy like, Da?

DA (*pause, then gravely*). Sticky, son . . . sticky.

CHARLIE. Da . . .

DA. What?

CHARLIE. Will I go to Italy when I grow up?

DA. (*comforting*). Not a fear of it . . . we wouldn't let you.

CHARLIE (*looking out and down*). There's a ship. Is that it, Da? . . . is that our ship coming in?

DA. Where? No . . . no, son, that one's going out.

CHARLIE. Will ours come in tomorrow, Da?

DA. Begod now it might.

CHARLIE. We'll be on the pig's back then, Da, won't we? When we're rich.

DA. We won't be far off it.

CHARLIE. And what'll we do?

197

DA. Do?

CHARLIE. When we win the Sweep.

DA (*the standard answer*). We won't do a shaggin' hand's turn.

CHARLIE (*awe and delight*). Gawny!

DA (*deadpan*). Sure the girl drew out me ticket the last time, and bad cess to her, didn't she drop it.

CHARLIE (*dismay*). She didn't?

DA. She did.

CHARLIE. The bloomin' bitch.

DA. The what? Where did you hear that expression?

CHARLIE. Sorry, Da.

DA. Women is different from you and me: y'ought to grow up to have respect for them. No, never call a woman a name like that, son, not even if she was a right oul' whoor. (*Pause*) Do you know where we are now?

CHARLIE. Dalkey Hill, Da.

DA. Not at all. In my day this was called Higgins' Hill, and oul' Higgins used to chase us off it and him up on a white horse. He never set foot in church, chapel or meeting, and sign's on it when he died no one would have him, and (*Pointing off*) that's where he's buried, under that stump of what's left of a cross after it was struck by lightnin'. Sure they say he sold his soul to the Oul' Fella himself.

CHARLIE. What oul' fella?

DA (*pointing down*). Your man. Isn't the mark of his hoof on the wall below on Ardbrugh Road where he tripped running down to the mailboat to go back to England?

CHARLIE. Da, let's go home.

DA. What ails you?

CHARLIE. I'm afraid of old Higgins.

DA. Are you coddin' me?

CHARLIE. And it's getting dark. I want to go home.

DA. Sure ghosts won't mind you if you don't mind them.

CHARLIE. Da. (*Reaching for his hand*).

DA. Wait now till I light me pipe and then we'll go.

CHARLIE. Da, you know the thing I'm worst afraid of?

DA. What's that?

CHARLIE. Well, you know me mother? . . . not Ma: me real one.

DA. What about her?

CHARLIE. Me Aunt Bridgie says when it gets dark she comes and looks in at me through the window.

DA. Looks in at you?

CHARLIE. And she says she's tall and with a white face and a black coat, and she comes out from Dublin on the tram, and she wants me back.

DA. Is that a fact?

CHARLIE. And me Aunt Bridgie says it wasn't true what you told me when I was small, about me mother being on Lambay Island where she wasn't able to get hold of me, and living on pollack and Horny Cobblers.

DA. Not true? Did I ever tell you a word of a lie?

CHARLIE. I don't believe she's on Lambay Island.

DA. No. No, she's not there. That wasn't a lie, son: it was . . . a makey-up. Because you were too young, do you follow me . . . you wouldn't have understood.

CHARLIE (*apprehensive*). Understood what? Why, where is she? (DA *looks impassively out to sea.*)
Da, tell us.

DA (*seeming to change the subject*). Do you see that flashing light?

CHARLIE. That's the Kish lightship.

DA. Well, that's where she is.

CHARLIE (*stunned*). On the Kish?

DA. God help her.

CHARLIE. What's she doing on the Kish?

DA. She . . . cooks.

CHARLIE. For the lightshipmen?

DA. Yis.

CHARLIE. What does she cook?

DA. Ah, pollack, son, and Horny Cobblers.
(CHARLIE *gives him a suspicious look, then peers out to sea.*)

CHARLIE. Gawny.

DA. So now you know.

CHARLIE. Da . . . what if she got off the Kish? What if she's at home now before us and looking through the window?

DA. Well, if she is, I'll tell you what we'll do. I'll come up behind her and I'll give her the biggest root up in the arse a woman ever got.

199

CHARLIE (*pleased*). Will you, Da?

DA. I will. And bejasus it'll be nothing compared to the root I'll give your Aunt Bridgie. (*Rising, brushing his trousers-seat*) Now where the hell is that whelp of a dog?

CHARLIE. Da, I love you.'

DA (*staring at him in puzzlement*). Certainly you do. Why wouldn't you? (*Moving away*) Blackie, come here to me!

(DA*'s reply has the effect of causing* CHARLIE *to revert to his present-day self*.)

CHARLIE (*fuming*). Why wouldn't I? I'll tell you why bloody wouldn't I. Because you were an old thick, a zombie, a mastodon. My God . . . my mother living on a lightship, trimming the wick and filleting Horn Cobblers. What a blazing, ever-fertile imagination you had – Cobblers aren't even edible!

DA (*whistles*). Blackie!

CHARLIE. And pollacks!

DA. You're right son, a bollix, that's what he is.

CHARLIE. The black dog was the only intelligent member of the family. He died a few years later. He was poisoned, and no one will convince me it wasn't suicide. God knows how Ma ever came to marry you.

(*Lights come up in the kitchen.* MOTHER *looks on while* YOUNG CHARLIE *is writing a letter.*)

Oh, I know how, sort of . . . she told me. I mean why.

MOTHER. He was called Ernie Moore. He used to be on the boats . . . the B and I. The 'Lady Hudson-Kinahan' it was. I was very great with him for a while. Then himself came to the house one day and said how he had the job above in Jacob's and he wanted to marry me. So that was that.

YOUNG CHARLIE. How?

MOTHER. It was fixed.

YOUNG CHARLIE. How fixed?

MOTHER. My father told him I would, so it was fixed. Things was arranged in them days.

YOUNG CHARLIE. Did you want to?

MOTHER. I had no say in it.

YOUNG CHARLIE. How well did you know him?

MOTHER. Well enough to bid the time of day to.

YOUNG CHARLIE. That was handy.

MOTHER. A body's not put into this world to pick and choose and be particular. I was seventeen, I done what I was told to.

YOUNG CHARLIE. What about Popeye the Sailor?

MOTHER. Who?

YOUNG CHARLIE. The other one.

MOTHER. Mr Moore in your mouth. When your time comes and you have to answer to God in the next world it makes no differ who you married and who you didn't marry. That's when everything will be made up to us.

YOUNG CHARLIE. You mean they hand out free sailors?

MOTHER. What? You little jeer, you. (*She aims a blow at him which he wards off.*) Well, God send that you never have to get married young for fear that if you stayed at home you might die, like many another died, of consumption for want of proper nourishment.

(YOUNG CHARLIE *affects to ignore her. He resumes writing and sings 'Popeye the Sailorman' under his breath in derisive counterpoint.*)

Waited on hand and foot, never wanting for nothing. Well, when you do get married, to whatever rip will have you, I only hope you'll be half the provider for her as himself has been for me. Is that letter done?

YOUNG CHARLIE. Yeah.

MOTHER. Read it out.

YOUNG CHARLIE. The Jacobs don't care whether I got a job or not.

MOTHER. It's manners to tell them, they ask after you. Go on.

YOUNG CHARLIE. 'Dear Nelson and Jeanette . . .'

(*She gives him a look. He amends.*)

'Dear Mr and Mrs Jacob. My father has told me how often you have been so good as to inquire as to whether I have yet found employment. I am grateful for your interest and am glad to say that I have now been given a clerical position. So, happily, I am no longer like Mr Micawber, constantly expecting something to turn up. Thanking you for your – '

MOTHER. What sort of codology is that?

YOUNG CHARLIE. What?

MOTHER. You're no longer like who?

YOUNG CHARLIE. It's an expression out of a book.

MOTHER. Write it out again and do it proper.

YOUNG CHARLIE. What for?

MOTHER. Because you're told to.

YOUNG CHARLIE. Look, there's this character in a book. He's always hard up, but he's an optimist. He –

MOTHER. Do as you're bid.

YOUNG CHARLIE. There's nothing wrong with it. Maybe you don't understand it, but the Jacobs will. It's meant to be funny, they'll laugh when they read it.

MOTHER. Aye, to be sure they will. At you, for setting yourself up to be something you're not.

YOUNG CHARLIE. It's my letter. You're not writing it: I am.

MOTHER. Then write it proper.

YOUNG CHARLIE. Proper-*ly*!

MOTHER. Don't you pull *me* up. Don't act the high-up lord with *me*, not in this house. They said I'd rue the day, and the gawm I was, I didn't believe them. He'll turn on you, they said. My own mother, me good neighbours, they all –

YOUNG CHARLIE. Oh, play another record.

MOTHER. Don't you back-answer me, you cur.

YOUNG CHARLIE. Whatever it is, if you don't understand it, it's rubbish. To hell with Charles Dickens and the rest of them: Nat Gould and Ruby M. Ayres made the world.

MOTHER. Are you going to write that out again, yes or no?

YOUNG CHARLIE. No, because there's nothing the –

MOTHER. Are you not! (*She looks up at* DA, *who with* CHARLIE *is still standing in the hill area*.) Nick . . .

DA. Ah, son, write it out the way she wants you to.

MOTHER. Don't beg him: tell him.

DA (*violently*). Will you do as you're bloody well told and not be putting the woman into a passion! Can we not have a solitary minute's peace in the house with you and your curse-o'-God Jack-acting?

MOTHER. Do that letter again.

YOUNG CHARLIE (*in a rage*). All right, all right! I'll do it. (*He crumples up the letter, takes the notepad and writes furiously*.) 'Dear Mr and Mrs Jacob . . . I am very well. My parents hope you are well, too, as it leaves them. I have a j-o-b now. I do not know myself, I am that delighted. Thanking you and oblige . . .' (*He signs it*.) Now are you happy?

MOTHER. Hand it here. I wouldn't trust you to post it. (*She takes the letter and puts it into an envelope. He cannot quite believe that she is taking it seriously*.)

YOUNG CHARLIE. You're not going to send –

DA (*turning to* CHARLIE). Begod, son, you always made a great fist of writing a letter.

YOUNG CHARLIE (*barely in control*). I'm going to the billiard hall.

MOTHER. Go wherever you like.

(YOUNG CHARLIE *storms out, loudly singing 'Popeye the Sailorman'. He emits a last mocking 'Boop-boop!' as he vanishes. We hear the far-off barking of a dog.*)

CHARLIE. It was a long time before I realized that love turned upside down is love for all that.

DA. There's the whoorin' dog gone down ahead of us in the finish. And the lights is on in the town. (*Pointing*) That's the Ulverton Road, son, where we frightened the shite out of the Black-and-Tans. And the lamp is lit in your uncle Paddy's window.

CHARLIE. If it is, he didn't light it: he's dead these donkey's years. Uncle Paddy, Kruger Doyle, Gunger Hammond, Oats Nolan – all your cronies – and old Bonk-a-bonk with his banjo and Mammy Reilly in her madhouse of a shop, with her money, so they said, all in sovereigns, wrapped up inside her wig. All dead. Like yourself . . . and, trust you, last as usual.

DA. That's a hash old wind starting up. We'll need a couple of extra coats on the bed tonight, son.

CHARLIE. We will.

DA. Mind your step now. If you slip and cut yourself she'll ate the pair of us. Give me your hand. Let the light from the Kish show you where the steps are.

CHARLIE. That's it, Mother: light us home. Least you can do.

CURTAIN

ACT TWO

CHARLIE *and* YOUNG CHARLIE *appear, walking towards the front door. There is a slightly exaggerated vivacity in* CHARLIE'S *manner: the result of having had a few drinks.*

CHARLIE. Ikey Meh? I remember the *name* . . .

YOUNG CHARLIE. The tram conductor. We used to yell Ikey Meh at him when the tram went past, and he'd pull the emergency stop and lep off after us —

CHARLIE. Leap off.

YOUNG CHARLIE. . . . And leave the passengers high and dry. God, he could run.

CHARLIE. Of course. Yes! Ikey Meh. (*'Meh' is drawn out in imitation of a goat.*) He — (*He catches sight of* DA, *who is trailing along behind them.*) I told you to stop following me. Now go away.

YOUNG CHARLIE. Leave him alone.

CHARLIE. I go out for a bite to eat and a quiet jar, to get away from him, and what happens? He's in the pub ahead of me. Fizz off.

(DA *hangs back and lurks in the shadows.*)

YOUNG CHARLIE. You might be civil to him. I mean, it's his day.

CHARLIE. It was. The funeral's over.

YOUNG CHARLIE (*coldly*). Oh, that's exquisite. You're a gem, you are.

CHARLIE. Don't get uppish with me, sonny Jim: you're as dead as he is. Come in and keep me company while I finish up.

YOUNG CHARLIE. I think I'll hump off.

CHARLIE (*aggressively*). You'll hump nowhere. You'll stay in my head until I choose to chase you out of it.

YOUNG CHARLIE. Oh, will I?

CHARLIE. There's only room in there for one of you at a time, and if I let you leave he'll come back like a yo-yo. Look at him, lurking. Get in there when you're told to. (*He has opened the front door with a key and pushes* YOUNG CHARLIE *in ahead of him.*)

204

YOUNG CHARLIE. Mind who you're shaggin' pushin'.

CHARLIE. Shagg*ing*. Push*ing*. Get in.

> (DA *comes up to the door, moving fast*.)
> Oh, no you don't. Out, and stay out. (*He shuts the door*.)
> (DA *promptly walks through the fourth wall and sits in his armchair filling his pipe*.)

YOUNG CHARLIE. Someone to see you.

CHARLIE. Who? (*He stares angrily at* DA.)

DA. God, they done wonders with that public house, son. I wouldn't recognize it. All the metally bits and the red lights . . . it'd put you in mind of a whoorhouse.

YOUNG CHARLIE. When were you ever in a –

CHARLIE. Say nothing. Ignore him. (*He searches through the bureau drawers*.)

DA. That pub used to be called Larkin's . . . you didn't know that. (*He fetches a jug from the dresser and empties it. It is filled with old keys, bits of yarn and thread, receipts, newspaper clippings, odds and ends*.)

YOUNG CHARLIE. If you hadn't gone out you could have been finished and away by now. But no, you couldn't wait to get maggoty drunk.

CHARLIE. Maggoty? On three small ones?

DA. I never seen you take a drink before, son. But sure what odds? Aren't you old enough?

YOUNG CHARLIE (*primly*). *I* never needed artificial stimulets.

CHARLIE. Stimulants.

YOUNG CHARLIE. Booze. Look at you.

DA (*placidly*). The way you swally-ed them. Begod, says I to meself, that fellow would drink Lough Erin dry.

CHARLIE. Shut up. (*To* YOUNG CHARLIE) What's wrong with me?

YOUNG CHARLIE. Well, you're a bit of a disappointment.

CHARLIE. Oh, yes?

YOUNG CHARLIE. I mean, I'd hoped to do better for meself.

CHARLIE. What had you in mind?

YOUNG CHARLIE. Don't get huffy. It's not that I amn't glad to see you: at least it means I'll live till I'm forty: that's something.

CHARLIE. Thanks.

YOUNG CHARLIE (*looking at* CHARLIE'*s wrist*). And I like the watch.

CHARLIE. Oh, good.

YOUNG CHARLIE. I suppose I could have done worse: but you can't deny you're a bit ordinary. It gives a fellow the creeps, seeing

205

himself at your age: everything behind him and nothing to look forward to.

CHARLIE. I get the old-age pension next year: there's that.

YOUNG CHARLIE. Yesterday I was thinking: I'm only eighteen, anything can happen to me . . . anything. I mean, maybe a smashing girl will go mad for me. Now I dunno.

(CHARLIE *puts on his glasses to read a receipt.* YOUNG CHARLIE *looks at him.*)

Ah, God.

CHARLIE. What?

YOUNG CHARLIE. Glasses. I'm blind as well.

CHARLIE. I'm sorry about that. The time I was castrated in a car crash, it affected my eyesight.

YOUNG CHARLIE (*horrified*). You weren't. (*Then*) You're so damn smart.

DA. Oh, them motor cars is dangerous.

YOUNG CHARLIE. Everything's a laugh, isn't it? Anyone I see who's your age . . . same thing. All lah-de-dah and make a joke of it. God if something good happens to me, I jump up in the air, I let out a yell, I run. Your sort just sits there.

CHARLIE. Arthritis.

YOUNG CHARLIE. You're dried up. Dead.

CHARLIE. I'm a seething torrent inside.

YOUNG CHARLIE. You? You're jizzless.

CHARLIE. I'm what?

YOUNG CHARLIE. There's no jizz in you. The fun's gone out of you. What's worse, you're no good . . . wouldn't even take him with you to London when me ma died.

CHARLIE. I asked him.

YOUNG CHARLIE. Instead of forcing him.

CHARLIE. Him? Who could force him to do anything?

YOUNG CHARLIE. Did you try?

CHARLIE. Don't get righteous with me, my pasty-faced little friend. It doesn't become you. Were *you* any good? Who was it once gave him a packet of six razor blades for Christmas?

YOUNG CHARLIE. I was broke.

CHARLIE. Yeah, and why? Because you'd bought a pair of nylons for that typist from Cappoquin who let you grope her up against the railings of the Customs House. Six Gillette blades!

DA. Oh, there was great shaving in them blades.

YOUNG CHARLIE. You weren't even here when he died.

CHARLIE. It was sudden.

DA (*rising*). I think I have one of them still. Hold on.

CHARLIE, YOUNG CHARLIE (*together*). Sit down.

CHARLIE. It was sudden. I'm not clairvoyant.

YOUNG CHARLIE. You were glad it was sudden, though, weren't you?

CHARLIE. Why not? It's the best way. No pain . . .

YOUNG CHARLIE. No pain for you, you mean. No having to go to him and wait and watch him and say things. All the dirty bits over with when you got here.

CHARLIE. Do you think I planned it?

YOUNG CHARLIE. No, but it suited you. Didn't it?

CHARLIE. I was . . .

YOUNG CHARLIE. Relieved.

CHARLIE (*nodding*). Mm.

YOUNG CHARLIE. Look at me, you with your lousy watch. I haven't got a tosser, but at least I've got a few principles. Where's yours?

CHARLIE. Principles? You mean like when you took that job Drumm offered you?

YOUNG CHARLIE. That's a stop-gap.

CHARLIE. I see.

YOUNG CHARLIE. I'll be out of it in a month and doing what I want to.

CHARLIE. A month?

YOUNG CHARLIE. A month!

(DRUMM *appears in the neutral area, a letter in his hand*.)

DRUMM. My friend . . . (*As* YOUNG CHARLIE *looks around*) Come in here.

YOUNG CHARLIE. Now what? (*He leaves the kitchen through the fourth wall and goes over to* DRUMM.) Yes, Mr Drumm?

DRUMM. How long have you been employed here?

YOUNG CHARLIE. Thirteen years, Mr Drumm.

DRUMM. In those thirteen years it may not have escaped your notice that there is one filing drawer for names with the initial letter 'M', and another for those which are adorned with the prefix 'Mac', whether written M-a-c, M-c or M-apostrophe. This letter pertains to one James Maguire. I found it, after a forty-minute search, in the 'Mac' drawer. Spell 'Maguire', would you?

CHARLIE, YOUNG CHARLIE (*together*). M-a-g-u-i-r-e.

DRUMM (*slowly, as if it were a death sentence*). M-a-g.

YOUNG CHARLIE. I must have −

207

DRUMM. M-a-g.

YOUNG CHARLIE. Yes.

DRUMM. You will concede that this was incorrectly filed?

YOUNG CHARLIE. Technically, yes . . .

DRUMM (*with venom*). Don't use words you don't know the meaning of. A barely literate child could have filed this letter where it belongs. But not, apparently, a man thirty years of age, with a wife, the beginnings of a family and pretensions towards intellectual superiority.

YOUNG CHARLIE. That has nothing to do with – (*He stops.*)

DRUMM (*dangerously*). With whom? (*He nods towards the other, unseen members of the staff.*) Get on with your work. (*To* YOUNG CHARLIE) With whom?

YOUNG CHARLIE (*a retreat*). With this place.

(DRUMM *smiles at him scornfully.*)

DRUMM. File this where it –

YOUNG CHARLIE. Or with you either, Mr Drumm.

DRUMM. Don't get insolent with me, my friend. If you don't like it here, be off with you. No one is holding you. But while you remain you will stay awake and do your work. Accurately. Do you understand?

(YOUNG CHARLIE *holds out his hand for the letter.*)

I asked if you understood.

YOUNG CHARLIE. Yes. (*He takes the letter.*)

DRUMM. We all know that you think your position here is beneath you. But you must try and put up with it and with us, Mr Tynan. Or whatever your name is.

(YOUNG CHARLIE *looks at him, then goes.* DRUMM *remains standing during the following.*)

DA. Oh, Old Drumm is a decent man.

CHARLIE. For years he'd taken me in hand like a Victorian father. He taught me, not by his enthusiasms – he had none – but by his dislikes.

DRUMM. Women, Mr Tynan, should be given a damn good squeeze at the earliest opportunity, and thereafter avoided.

CHARLIE. Perhaps he wanted a son or had a fondness for strays. He made me his confidant.

DRUMM. That man Kelly is known to be a pervert. Shun him. What's more, he spits as he talks. I move away from him, and he follows me and spits on me again.

CHARLIE. One evening, I was in a hurry somewhere – to meet a girl, go to a film: I don't know. I saw him coming towards me.

208

I didn't want to stop and talk, so I crossed over. He'd seen me avoid him. It was that simple. Except at work, he never spoke to me again.

(*The light fades on* DRUMM. DA *gets the razor blade from the bureau.*)

DA. Ah.

CHARLIE. What?

DA. I dunno is this one of the blades you gev me, son.

CHARLIE. Show. (*He sniffs at it.*) A Gillette, definitely. Sheffield, I'd say . . . nineteen-forty-three. An impudent blade, sharpish after-taste . . . precocious, but not presumptuous. Damn it, I bet this *is* one of them. Anything I ever gave you, you took and wouldn't use. Wouldn't be under a compliment to me.

(DA *slips the blade into* CHARLIE's *pocket.*)

DA. Say nothing . . . take them home with you.

CHARLIE. It's a wonder you cashed the cheques I sent you for tobacco.

DA. Certainly I cashed them. Wasn't that how I got thrun out of that home you put me into last January?

CHARLIE. Home? Blast your impudence, that was a private hotel.

DA. Whatever it was.

CHARLIE. I'm telling you what it was. An hotel.

DA (*carelessly*). Yis.

CHARLIE. Because you'd gone dotty. Shouting out to Ma, who was two years dead. Going around to my cousin Rosie for your Christmas dinner at two in the morning. Do you know how hard it was to get you into that hotel?

DA. Hotel my arse. Sure they wouldn't let me go up the bank to cash that cheque you sent me. But begod, says I, I'll bate them yet. Do you know what I done?

CHARLIE. I heard.

DA. I got out over the shaggin' wall. And these two big impudent straps of country ones cem after me. 'Come back,' says they. 'Leave go of me,' says I; 'The divil's cure to the pair of yiz.' Then doesn't one of them put her mawsy red hands on me be the collar. 'Be a good boy,' says she to me. Well . . . (*He laughs fondly.*) I drew out with me fist and I gev her a poke for herself in the stomach.

CHARLIE. They told me it was on the breast.

DA. It was in the pit of the stomach . . . I wouldn't poke a woman in the breast. Yis, I drew out with me fist . . . ! That wasn't bad for eighty-three, wha'?

CHARLIE. So they threw you out.

DA. And after that you had me put into the Union.

CHARLIE. Into the what?

DA (*ashamed to say it*). You know . . . the . . . the . . . the poorhouse.

CHARLIE. Oh, you malignant, lop-sided old liar. It was a private room in a psychiatric hospital.

DA. I know, I know.

CHARLIE. A hospital.

DA. Yis.

CHARLIE (*incredulous*). Poorhouse!

DA. Sure it's greatly improved since I was a young lad. You wouldn't know a bit of it.

CHARLIE (*beginning to shout*). It was not the p—

DA. I amn't saying a word again' it. Sure hadn't I the best of everything, and wasn't I better off there than I was where you put me before that − in the home?

CHARLIE (*giving up*). Jesus.

DA. Do you know what I'm going to tell you? If the oul' heart hadn't gone on me the evenin' before last, I'd be alive today.

CHARLIE. Is that so?

DA. It is.

CHARLIE. There are no shallows to which you won't sink, are there?

DA (*proudly*). There aren't! (*Reminiscent*) I drew out with me fist and I give her a poke. You never seen me when I was riz, did you, son?

CHARLIE. No. (*Then*) Yes . . . once.

DA. You did not.

CHARLIE. Nineteen-fifty-one. You were sixty-seven . . . She was sixty-three then, and I still don't believe I saw it happen.

(*There is a squeak of the gate and* MOTHER *appears. She is carrying a shopping bag.*)

DA (*looking out*). There she is at long last. It's gone half-past six; I thought she was run over. (*He opens the door.*

MOTHER *comes in. She is in a good mood, humming to herself.*)

I say, we thought you were under the wheels of a bus. Where were you at all? The boy is home before you, with his stomach roaring for his tea.

MOTHER (*unruffled*). He'll get it when it's put in front of him, not before. (*She takes off her coat and hangs it up, then puts on her apron.*)

210

DA (*grumbling*). We didn't know *what* happened to you. Was the picture any good itself?

MOTHER. It was an old love thing, all divorces and codology. A body couldn't make head or tail of it. Charlie, clear that rubbidge off the table and be a bit of help to me.

(CHARLIE *puts the odds and ends back into the jug.*

MOTHER *begins to lay the table.*)

DA. It's seldom we hear a song out of you.

MOTHER. I ought to cry to suit you.

DA. I'm only saying, any other time the picture is a washout you come home to us raging. (*Pause*) And your horse finished down the field today as well.

MOTHER. Did it? (*Nodding, not caring*) The going was too soft.

(*She goes on with her work, still humming.*

CHARLIE *and* DA *exchange puzzled looks.*)

DA (*curious, fishing*). I suppose Dun Laoghaire was packed.

MOTHER. Crowds.

DA. Nothing strange or startling, so?

MOTHER (*almost coyly*). Mm . . .

DA. Well, tell us or don't tell us, one or the other.

(MOTHER *turns. She cannot keep her adventure to herself.*)

MOTHER. I was treated to a glass of port in the Royal Marine Hotel.

DA. You were what?

MOTHER. Someone I met in Lipton's.

CHARLIE. The grandeur of you!

DA (*laughing*). Was he good-looking itself?

MOTHER. It wasn't a 'him' at all — don't be such a jeer. This woman comes up to me. 'Excuse me,' says she, 'for asking. Are you not Margaret Tynan . . . Maggie Doyle, that was?' 'I am,' says I; 'Do I know you?' 'You do,' says she.

DA (*in disgust*). Ah.

MOTHER. Well, to cut a long story, who was she but Gretta Moore out of the Tivoli in Glasthule.

DA. I never heard tell of her.

MOTHER. Ah, Gretta Nolan that married Ernie Moore off of the B and I.

CHARLIE (*remembering*). Who?

MOTHER. He's retired these two years.

CHARLIE (*it comes to him; singing*). 'I'm . . . Popeye the Sailorman!'

MOTHER. Hold your tongue.

(DA *is staring at her, numbed.*)

So in with the pair of us into the Royal Marine Hotel. Says she to me: 'Sure we're as good as the best of them.' And the style of all the old ones there, with their dyed hair and the fur coats on them. Tea, they were all having, and sweet cake. 'Sure,' says Gretta, 'we can have *that* at home in the house.' (*To* CHARLIE) So this waiter comes up in a swalla-tail coat. Oh, she was well able for him. 'We want two large glasses of port wine,' says she, and off he went like a hare to get them!

DA. Making a show of yourself.

CHARLIE. What show?

DA. High-up people looking at you.

MOTHER (*loftily*). Pity about them!

DA. The whole town'll have it tomorrow.

CHARLIE (*to* MOTHER).Then what?

MOTHER. Three shillings for two glasses of port wine you'd be hard put to it to wet your lips with . . . and sixpence on top of that for the waiter. Oh, it was scandalous. Says I to her –

DA. Sure Ernie Moore is dead these donkey's years.

MOTHER. What?

DA (*dogged*). I know he's dead.

MOTHER. How do you know?

DA. I know.

MOTHER. The man's wife says different.

DA. Oh aye, ask me brother am I a liar! Oh, she must be a right good thing. And you're worse. Pouring drink into you in the Royal Marine Hotel, and the crowds of the world looking at you and . . . and . . . laughing.

CHARLIE. What crowds?

MOTHER. Don't mind him.

DA. And I say he's dead and long dead.

MOTHER. Is he? Well, I'll soon tell you next Thursday whether he's dead or no.

DA. What's next Thursday?

MOTHER (*almost coquettishly*). I'm invited down for me tea.

DA. Down where, for your tea?

MOTHER. To the Tivoli. (*To* CHARLIE) Gretta was telling me her eldest is beyant in Canada, and she has a grandson nearly your age, and –

DA. Well, you'll go there by yourself if you go, because I'm staying where I am.

MOTHER. You can stay wherever you like, for you aren't invited.

DA. Am I not!

MOTHER. Your own tea will be left here ready for you.

DA. Well, it needn't be, because you're not going.

MOTHER. Why amn't I?

DA. You're not setting foot outside of here.

MOTHER. You won't stop me.

DA. Will I not!

MOTHER (*her fury mounting*). You were always the same and you always will be the same. The one time I'm invited to a person's house, you begrudge it to me. (*Beginning to shout*) Well, I'll go *wherever* I like and see *whoever* I like.

DA. Do, and you'll go out of this. I'm the boss in this house and I'll stay the boss in it.

CHARLIE. She's only going for a cup of tea.

DA (*wildly*). Oh aye . . . aye, that's what she'd like us to think. But it's to see him . . . *him*.

MOTHER. To see who?

DA. You faggot, you: don't let on you don't know. It's Ernie . . . Ernie . . . curse-o'-God Ernie! (*His fist crashes on the table.*) May he die roaring for a priest . . . curse-o'-God Ernie!
(*Even* MOTHER, *who knows him, is alarmed by the violence of his rage. She stares at him. He strikes the table again.*)

CHARLIE (*remembering*). And the floorboards barked like dogs, and the cups went made on their hooks.

DA. You set one foot in the Tivoli, you look crossways at a whoor-master the like of him, and be Jesus, I'll get jail for you, do you hear me? I won't leave a stick or a stone standing in the kip.

MOTHER (*recovering, still a little afraid*). Look at you . . . look at the yellow old face of you.

DA (*savagely, almost skipping with rage*). With your . . . your port wine, and your sweet cake, and your Royal Marine Hotel.

MOTHER. The whole town knows you for a madman . . . aye, and all belonging to you.

DA. Ernie . . . Ernie! You'll stay clear of him, Thursday and every other day.

MOTHER. Because you know I preferred him over you, and that's what you can't stand. Because I never went with you. Because you know if it wasn't for me father, God forgive him, telling me to –
(DA *makes a violent rush at her, his fist raised.*)

CHARLIE. Hey . . .

213

(DA's *fist comes down and stops, almost touching her face, where it stays, trembling, threatening.*)

MOTHER (*quietly*). Go on. Go on, do it. And that'll be the first time and the last. I'll leave here if I was to sleep on the footpath. (*Pause.* DA *starts past her towards the scullery.*)

(*Half to herself*) You went behind my back to him because you knew I wouldn't have you.

(DA *runs to the table and raises a cup as if to dash it to pieces. Instead, he takes his pipe from the table and throws it on the ground. It breaks. He goes into the scullery.* CHARLIE *stoops to pick up the pieces of the pipe as* MOTHER *faces away from him to wipe her eyes.*)

CHARLIE (*still stooping*). Will you go? On Thursday?

She faces him. Although tears are coming, there is a wry, almost mocking attempt at a smile.)

MOTHER. The jealous old bags.

(*The lights fade. Then we see a woman enter and sit on a rustic seat in the neutral area. She is* MRS PRYNNE, *50, Anglo-Irish accent, dressed for the country.*)

YOUNG CHARLIE (*off, singing: the tune is 'Blaze Away'*).
'Tight as a drum,
Never been done,
Queen of all the fairies!'
(MRS PRYNNE *opens her eyes. Through the following,* YOUNG CHARLIE *comes on carrying two quart cans.*)
'Bolicky Biddy had only one diddy
To feed the baby on.
Poor little fucker had only one sucker
To grind his teeth up . . .' (*He stops on seeing* MRS PRYNNE.)

MRS PRYNNE. Good evening. Do you know where Tynan is? The gardener.

YOUNG CHARLIE. He's in the greenhouse. Will I tell him you want him?

MRS PRYNNE. If you would.

YOUNG CHARLIE. Sure. (*He goes across the stage.*) Da! Hey . . . (DA *appears, carrying a basket of tomatoes.*)
You're wanted.

DA. Who wants me?

YOUNG CHARLIE. I dunno. Posh-looking old one.

DA (*a mild panic*). It's the mistress. Hold this for me . . . will you hold it! (*He thrusts the basket at* YOUNG CHARLIE *and getting his coat from offstage struggles to put it on.*)

YOUNG CHARLIE. Easy . . . she's not on fire, you know. (*Helping him*) How much do you think?

DA. How much what?

YOUNG CHARLIE. Money.

DA (*confidently*). I'll get me due. Poor oul' Jacob wouldn't see me stuck, Lord ha' mercy on him . . . no, nor none of us. Says he many's the time: 'Yous'll all be provided for.' The parlourmaid and Cook got their envelopes this morning. (*A sob in his throat*) A decent poor man.

YOUNG CHARLIE. Don't start the waterworks, will you?

DA (*voice breaking*). God be good to him.

YOUNG CHARLIE. Hey, is it true they bury Quakers standing up?

DA. Jasus, you don't think they do it sitting down, do you? Where's the mistress?

YOUNG CHARLIE. Yours or mine? (*As* DA *looks at him*) By the tennis court. (*He calls after him*) Da . . . how much was the cook left?

DA. A hundred.

YOUNG CHARLIE. Pounds? (*He emits a quiet 'Yeoww!' of pleasure. Exits.*

DA *makes his way painfully, carrying the basket of tomatoes. He salues* MRS PRYNNE.)

MRS PRYNNE. Oh, Tynan, isn't this garden beautiful? Mr Prynne and I shall hate not to see it again. I'm sure you'll miss it too. Sit down, Tynan: next to me.

(DA *salutes and sits beside her.*)

We loathe selling 'Enderley', but with my dear father gone and the family with homes of their own, there's no one left to live in it.

DA. I picked you the best of the tomatoes, ma'am.

MRS PRYNNE. Aren't you the great man. We'll take them back to Mountmellick with us in the morning. And the rose-trees.

DA (*authoritative, tapping her knee*). Yis . . . now don't forget: a good pruning as soon as you plant them. Cut the hybrids – the Peer Gynts, the Blue Moons and the Brasilias – cut them well back to two buds from the bottom, and the floribundas to five buds.

MRS PRYNNE. The floribundas to five buds.

DA. The harder you cut, the better the bloom: only don't cut into a stem that's more than a year old.

MRS PRYNNE (*attentive*). I'll remember.

DA (*slapping her knee*). I'll make a rose-grower out of you yet, so

I will. And feed the buggers well in July, do you hear, if you want a good second blush.

MRS PRYNNE. I do hope they take: my father loved the Enderley roses. Did you hear we have a buyer for the house, Tynan? A schoolteacher and his wife. She owns a fashion business in the city . . . I daresay that's where their money is. Catholics, I believe.

DA (*contemptuous*). Huh!

MRS PRYNNE. I'm sure they'll want a gardener.

DA. Let them. Catholics with money, letting on they're the Quality: sure they're the worst there is. No, I wouldn't work for me own: they'd skin you. The way it is, the legs is gone stiff on me, and the missus says it's time I gev meself a rest.

MRS PRYNNE. What age are you now, Tynan?

DA. I'm sixty-eight, and I'm here since I was fourteen.

MRS PRYNNE. Fifty-four years?

DA. The day yourself was born, the boss called me in. Nineteen-hundred-and-three, it was. 'Take this in your hand, Tynan,' says he to me, 'and drink it'. Begod, I never seen a tumbler of whiskey the size of it. 'And now,' says he, 'go off to hell home for the rest of the day.'

MRS PRYNNE. The world is changing, Tynan, and not for the better. People are growing hard; my father's generation is out of fashion.

(DA*'s eyes are moist again. She takes an envelope from her handbag.*

DA *gets to his feet.*)

In his will he asked that Mr Prynne and I should attend to the staff. We think you should have a pension, Tynan: you're entitled to it. We thought twenty-six pounds per annum, payable quarterly.

DA (*saluting automatically*). Thanks, ma'am; thanks very much.

MRS PRYNNE. Nonsense, you've earned it. Now, the lump sum. Poor Cook is getting on and will have to find a home of her own, so we've treated her as a special case. But I'm sure you and Mrs Tynan won't say no to twenty-five pounds, with our best wishes and compliments.

(DA *takes the envelope and again salutes automatically. He looks at it dumbly.*)

You're a great man for the work, and whatever you may say, we know you wouldn't give it up for diamonds. And there's that boy of yours. Once he leaves school he'll be a great help to you. You did well to adopt him.

DA. The way it is, do you see, the young lad is saving up to get married . . .

MRS PRYNNE. Married?

DA. So we'd think bad of asking him to –

MRS PRYNNE. How old is he?

DA. Sure didn't yourself send him up to get me.

MRS PRYNNE. Was that he? But he's a young man.

DA (*calling*). Charlie! Come here to me. (*To* MRS PRYNNE) Sure he's working these six years. Only every shilling he earns, do you see, has to be put by. So herself and me, we couldn't ask him to –

MRS PRYNNE. You mustn't encourage him to be selfish. Young people can live on next to nothing.

(*As* YOUNG CHARLIE *arrives*) Hello. How d'you do?

YOUNG CHARLIE. 'Evening.

DA. Shake hands now, son. (*To* MRS PRYNNE) He cem to pick the loganberries. Sure we couldn't leave them to go rotten.

MRS PRYNNE. You are thoughtful. I'll ask Cook to make jam and send it to us in Mountmellick. (*To* YOUNG CHARLIE) I hear you're getting married.

YOUNG CHARLIE. I hope to.

MRS PRYNNE. Well done. But you must look after this old man. Remember how much you owe him, so be good to him, and generous. (*She looks in her handbag and finds a five-pound note.*) Mr Prynne and I would like you to have this. A wedding gift. Perhaps you'll buy something for your new home.

YOUNG CHARLIE. No . . . thank you. I –

DA. Yoo, he will. Talce it.

YOUNG CHARLIE. Well . . . (*Taking it*) I'm sure we could do with a Sacred Heart picture for over the bed.

DA (*missing the sarcasm*). That's the boy!

MRS PRYNNE. I see you've reared an art-lover, Tynan. And now the most important thing. I know my father would want you to have a keepsake . . . one of his treasures. (*She picks up a loosely-wrapped package from the seat.*

DA *and* YOUNG CHARLIE *are intrigued.*)

(*To* YOUNG CHARLIE) Have you travelled?

YOUNG CHARLIE. Not much.

MRS PRYNNE. You must. In these days of aeroplanes, young people have no excuse. When my father was your age he'd been around the world. In nineteen-hundred-and-six he was in San Francisco at the time of the earthquake. That's on the west coast of America, you know.

217

YOUNG CHARLIE. Yes, I saw the film.

MRS PRYNNE. After the great fire, he was passing a gutted jewellery shop when he saw this, lying on the ground for the taking. A find in a thousand, Tynan. (*She reverently lifts the paper, unveiling a mass of tangled bits of wire mounted on a metal base.*) What do you think of that? Thirty or more pairs of spectacles, fused together by the heat of the fire. (*Pause*) My father had them mounted.

DA. Sure, what else would he do with them?

MRS PRYNNE. Extraordinary, yes?

DA. That's worth having.

MRS PRYNNE. It is, and there you are. (*She gives it to him; then shaking hands*) Goodbye, Tynan. Take care of yourself and we'll call to see you when we're in town. (*To* YOUNG CHARLIE) See that he doesn't overdo things, won't you? Goodbye . . . our best to your intended. (*She goes off, taking the various cans with her.*

DA *salutes her, tears in his eyes.*)

YOUNG CHARLIE. It's a miracle she didn't take the bench. When she said he found it in the ruins of a jeweller's shop, I thought for sure it was the Star of India. Thirty pairs of spectacles.

DA. You hold them: me hands is dirty. Don't drop them.

YOUNG CHARLIE. Don't what?

DA. They're worth money.

YOUNG CHARLIE (*irate*). Ah, for − What are you bawling for?

DA. A great man, she said I was. Sure I am, too.

YOUNG CHARLIE. How much did you get?

DA. Fifty-four years in the one place. I laid that tennis court . . . aye, and rolled it, too.

YOUNG CHARLIE. I don't care if you knitted the net. How much?

DA (*looking up*). And I planted them trees.

YOUNG CHARLIE (*realizing*). You've been diddled.

DA. What diddled? Sure she needn't have gev me anything. The work I done, wasn't I paid for it . . . every Friday like clock-work. I got me week off in the summer . . .

YOUNG CHARLIE. Give me that. (*He takes the envelope and opens it.*)

DA (*unheeding, ranting away*). And me two days at Christmas, with an extra pound note put into me fist, and the sup of whiskey poured and waiting for me in the pantry. Wasn't I −

YOUNG CHARLIE (*looking at the cheque*). Twenty-five?

DA (*snatching it back*). Don't go tricking with that.

218

YOUNG CHARLIE. Is that *it*?

DA. Isn't it money for doing bugger-all? And sure haven't I the offer of work from the people that's bought the house.

YOUNG CHARLIE. What work? You're giving it up.

DA. Ah, time enough to give it up when I'm going downhill. Catholics, yis. They own a dress shop. Sure if your own won't look after you, who will?

YOUNG CHARLIE. My God, she'll kill you.

DA. Who will?

YOUNG CHARLIE. She will, when you bring that home to her. (*Meaning the cheque*) Here, put this with it. (*He offers him the five-pound note.*)

DA. What for?

YOUNG CHARLIE. It'll save you a couple of curses.

DA. Go 'long out of that . . . that's for yourself and Polly, to buy the holy picture with. Are you off into town to see her?

YOUNG CHARLIE. Well, I'm not going home, that's for sure. Blast her anyway, and her twenty-five quid and her Californian wire puzzle.

DA. Sure the Quakers was the only ones that was good to us the time of the Famine. Oh, the mistress is a decent skin. (*He laughs.*) 'Tynan,' says she to me, 'aren't you the greatest man that ever trod shoe-leather!' And I planted them hyacinths, too. (YOUNG CHARLIE *has gone off, taking the parcel with him.* (DA *goes into the house.*) Mag . . . Mag. Do you know what the mistress said to me? (*Lights up.* CHARLIE, *his glasses on, is writing. The jug, with its contents, is back on the table.*)

CHARLIE. Twenty-five pounds divided by fifty-four. I make it that your gratuity worked out at nine shillings and threepence per year of service. No wonder she didn't talk to you for a week.

DA. Who didn't?

CHARLIE. She didn't.

DA. Are you mad? In fifty-nine years there was never a cross word between us.

CHARLIE. Oh, dear God.

DA. There was not.

CHARLIE. 'Ernie, Ernie, curse-o'-God Ernie!'

DA. Sure I was only letting on I was vexed with her. (*With relish*) Oh, I put a stop to her gallop, her and her . . . high tea! Son, do you remember them spectacles from San Francisco?

CHARLIE. Do I?

219

DA. Herself took them down to the pawn office. 'How much will you give me on these?' says she. 'I'll give you nothing at all on them, ma'am,' says he, 'for they're too valuable for me to keep under this roof.' And you saying I was diddled: you thick, you!

CHARLIE. Where are they?

DA. What?

CHARLIE. The spectacles.

DA (*shiftily*). I musta lost them.

CHARLIE. Liar. (*Searching*) They're in this house, and if I find them I'll pulp them and bury them. You ignorant, wet, forelock-tugging old crawler. (*Mimicking him*) 'Begod, ma'am, sure after fifty-four years all I needed to be set up for life was a parcel of barbed wire.' And then you put in another four years, toiling for the Catholic but somewhat less than Christian Diors of Grafton Street.

DA. 'Tynan,' says that bitch's ghost to me, and him only a schoolmaster, 'I want more honest endeavour from you and less excuses.' 'Do you see this fist?' says I to him –

CHARLIE (*still searching*). I asked you where they were.

DA. I disrecall.

CHARLIE. You probably had them buried with you. I can hear St Peter now – 'Hey God, there's an old gobshite at the tradesmen's entrance with thirty pairs of spectacle-frames from the San Francisco earthquake. What'll I tell him?' (*God's voice, with a Jewish accent*) 'Tell him we don't want any.' (*He scoops up the contents of the jug and moves to dump them in the range.*) Mind up: this is the last.

DA (*seizing on an article*). That pipe is worth keeping.

CHARLIE. It's in bits. You broke it.

DA. Sure a piece of insulating tape would –

CHARLIE. No. Move. (*He goes past DA and drops the lot in the range.*)

DA. You could have smoked that, and you'll folly a crow for it yet. What else did you throw out? (*He opens CHARLIE's dispatch case and goes through the papers.*)

CHARLIE. At the funeral this morning I heard one of your old cronies muttering what a great character you were and how I'll never be the man me da was.

DA. Don't belittle yourself: yes, you will. What's this?

CHARLIE. Death certificate. Tell me, what was it like?

DA. What?

CHARLIE. Dying.

DA (*offhand*). Ah, I didn't care for it. (*Peering at a document*) Eighteen-hundred-and-

220

CHARLIE. . . . Eighty-four. Birth certificate.

DA (*annoyed*). You kept nothing worth keeping at all. There was more to me than this rubbidge. Where's me old IRA service certificate? And the photograph of the tug-o'-war team? I still have the mark under me oxter where the rope sawed into it. And the photo herself and meself had took in the Vale of Avoca.

CHARLIE. I threw them out.

DA. And yourself the day of your first Communion with me beside you.

CHARLIE. I burned them. I don't want them around.

(DA *stares blankly at him.*

CHARLIE *waits, almost daring him to be angry.*)

DA. You wha'?

CHARLIE. I got rid of them. You're gone, now they're gone. So?

DA (*nodding*). Ah, sure what the hell good were they anyway.

CHARLIE. Eh?

DA. Bits of paper. Sure they only gather dust.

CHARLIE. I burned all that was left of you and you can't even get angry. You were a sheep when you lived: you're still a sheep. 'Yes, sir; no, sir; sir, if you please – '

DA (*chuckling*). 'Is it up the duck's arse that I shove the green peas?' Oh, that was a good poem. (*Singing*) 'Is it up the – '

CHARLIE. Where's my coat? I'm going to the airport.

DA. Yis. (*Calling*) Mag . . . Mag, the lad is off.

CHARLIE. She won't answer you. Goodbye.

(MOTHER *comes in quickly from the scullery. She pays* CHARLIE *no attention.*)

MOTHER (*briskly*). Where is he? (*Calling upstairs*) Charlie, you'll be late. (*To* DA) Call him.

DA (*yelling*). You pup, will you come down before the shaggin' aeroplane is off up into the air and you're left standin'!

MOTHER. Charlie!

DA. If he misses that aeroplane they'll be no whoorin' weddin' Then he'll be nicely destroyed. Jasus, come when you're called!

(YOUNG CHARLIE, *carrying a suitcase, is on the stairs, followed by* OLIVER.)

MOTHER. That will do. He won't miss it.

YOUNG CHARLIE (*coming in*). Will you quit roaring. I'm not deaf.

MOTHER. It's the last time you'll have to put up with it, so hold your tongue. Have you everything?

YOUNG CHARLIE. Yes.

MOTHER. Smarten yourself. Anyone'd think it was Oliver that was getting married.

OLIVER. Oh, now. Ho-ho. Oh, now.

YOUNG CHARLIE. I left Oliver's wedding present upstairs. Will you keep it for me?

OLIVER. It's just a bowl to float rose-petals in-you-know. Maybe your da will give you some of his roses.

DA. I only grow the shaggers. I don't learn 'em to swim.

MOTHER. You're to mind yourself in that aeroplane and bless yourself when it starts.

YOUNG CHARLIE. Yes.

DA. Oh, Charlie won't crash.

MOTHER (*half snapping*). No one is saying to the contrary.

DA. Divil a fear of him.

MOTHER (*aggrieved*). Going off to the other side of the world to get married.

YOUNG CHARLIE. Five hundred miles . . . !

MOTHER. It's far enough. Too far.

YOUNG CHARLIE. It's where she lives.

DA. Oh, Belgium is a great country.

MOTHER. It's little you or I will ever see of it. No matter.

YOUNG CHARLIE (*angrily*). Don't start. You were both invited –

MOTHER. Oh, aye. Aye, I'm sure we were.

YOUNG CHARLIE (*To* OLIVER). They damn well were. But no, it's too far, it's too foreign, his legs won't let him . . .

MOTHER. I said it's no matter.

(YOUNG CHARLIE *gives her a hostile look.*)

OLIVER. When he gets time during the honeymoon, Charlie is going to drop you a line and give me all the details.

(*As they look at him*)

About going in an aeroplane-you-know.

(*Pause.* YOUNG CHARLIE *is chafing to be off and trying to conceal it.*

CHARLIE *moves to be near him.*)

MOTHER. You may as well be off, so. There's nothing to keep you.

YOUNG CHARLIE (*Protesting*). I'll be back in a fortnight.

(*She nods, upset.*)

MOTHER. Please God.

CHARLIE. Now. Goodbye, and out.

YOUNG CHARLIE. Yeah, well, mind yourselves.

MOTHER. You mind yourself. (*She reaches for him blindly.*
He half-resists the kiss, half-accepts it.

222

She steps back and looks at him, eyes large.
He reaches for his case as DA *comes forward, hand extended.*)
CHARLIE. Hang on . . . one to go.
DA (*shaking hands*). Good luck now, son. Sure you'll get there in
great style. Oh, aeroplanes is all the go these days.
YOUNG CHARLIE. Yeah. 'Bye, now.
DA (*not letting go*). Have you your tickets?
YOUNG CHARLIE. Yes.
CHARLIE (*to* DA). Let go.
DA. Have you your passport?
YOUNG CHARLIE. Yes.
CHARLIE. It's the Beast with Five Fingers.
DA. Have you your –
YOUNG CHARLIE. I've got to go. (*He prises his hand free and starts
out.*)
MOTHER. Bless yourself!'
(*He dips his fingers in the holy-water font and hurries out.*
MOTHER *and* DA *come to the door.*
OLIVER *is caught behind them. He coughs.*)
OLIVER. I'm going with him. As far as the bus-you-know.
YOUNG CHARLIE (*agonized, waiting for him*). For God's sake.
OLIVER. Well, 'bye-'bye now and sappy days. That's an expression
him and me have-you-know. Oh, yes.
YOUNG CHARLIE (*half to himself*). Oliver!
OLIVER (*turning to wave*). Cheerio, now.
CHARLIE (*from the house*). Well, at least wave to them.
(YOUNG CHARLIE *raises a hand without turning and climbs
across to an upper level where he rests, waiting for*
OLIVER.)
OLIVER. That went well, I thought. I mean, they can get very
sentimental-you-know. Often with my mother I can't feel
anything because I'm trying to stop *her* from feeling anything.
How do *you* feel?
(YOUNG CHARLIE *makes a huge gesture of relief.*)
They're all the same-you-know. I dread the roars of my mother
when I get married. She cries even if I go to a late-night
dance.
YOUNG CHARLIE. Come on before we meet someone.
OLIVER. Oh-ho. Off to the altar. Can't wait.
YOUNG CHARLIE. Dry up.
OLIVER. The eager bridegroom. Oh, yes.
YOUNG CHARLIE. Well, it's the beginning, isn't it?

(*They go off.*)

MOTHER. Well, that's the end of him. (*She and* DA *return to the kitchen.*)

DA. Still and all, mebbe we ought to have gone, Mag, when we were asked.

(*She gives him a sour look.*)

Sure it'd have been a . . . a . . . a change for us.

MOTHER. I never hindered him. I wasn't going to start now.

DA. What hinderment? Weren't we asked?

MOTHER (*it is not a disparagement, but evasion*). You'd be a nice article to bring to a foreign country. (*Then*) I think I'll make his bed now and have done with it. (*She goes upstairs. She is in view during part of the following.*)

DA (*laughing, watching her*). Oh, a comical woman.

CHARLIE. She died an Irishwoman's death, drinking tea.

DA. Do you want a cup?

CHARLIE. No! Two years afterwards, I told a doctor in London about you, on your own and getting senile. I said you'd have to be made to come and live with us. He said: 'Oh, yes. Then he can die among strangers in a hospital in Putney or Wandsworth, with nothing Irish around him except the nurses.' But with your luck you'd probably have got Jamaicans. It's always pleasant to be told what you half-want to hear. So when I came to see you – the last time – there was no talk of your going to London. I was solicitous: asked you how you were managing, were you eating regularly . . .

(DA *is in his eighties, stopped and deaf.* CHARLIE's *attitude is paternal.*)

DA. Hoh?

CHARLIE. I said are you eating regularly?

DA. Sure I'm getting fat. I go to Rosie for me tea and Mrs Dunne next door cooks me dinner. Are *you* eating regular.

CHARLIE. She's a widow. I'd watch her.

DA. Hoh?

CHARLIE. I say I'd watch her.

DA. I do.

CHARLIE. You reprobate. Do you need extra cash, for whist drives?

DA. I gave up going. Me hands is too stiff to sort the cards into suits. The last time I went, oul' Drumm was there. Do you remember oul' Drumm?

CHARLIE. Yes.

DA. He accused me of renegin'. 'Why don't you,' says he, 'join the Old People's club and play there?' Says I to him back: 'I would,' says I, 'only I'm too shaggin' old for them!' (*He laughs.*)

CHARLIE. That was good.

DA. Sure I have the garden to do . . . fine heads of cabbage that a dog from Dublin never pissed on. I'm kept going. I say I blacked the range yesterday.

CHARLIE. You're a marvel.

DA. I am. How's all the care.

CHARLIE. They're great. Send their love.

DA (*rising*). I was meaning to ask you . . .

CHARLIE. What?

DA (*saluting him*). I do often see your young one in the town.

CHARLIE. What young one?

DA. Her . . . Maggie. Your eldest. 'Clare to God, Mr Doyle, I never seen such shiny black hair on a girl.

(CHARLIE *stares at him.*

Note: this is not a flashback to DA *as a young man; it is* DA *in his eighties, his mind wandering.*)

Sure she's like a young one out of the story books. The way it is, Mr Doyle, I'm above at Jacob's these six years, since I was fourteen. I have a pound a week and the promise of one of the new dwellin's in the square. I'd think well of marrying her, so I would.

CHARLIE. Da, no, she's –

DA. You can ask anyone in the town about me. And, and, and she wouldn't want for an'thing. The job is safe, we won't go short. I'm learning roses, do you see. To grow them. Oh, yis: Polyanthas and Belles de Crecys and Cornelias and Tuscanys and Amy Robsarts and Janet's Pride and –

CHARLIE. Da, stop.

DA. And, and, and Portlands and Captain John Ingrams and Heidelbergs and Munsters and Shepherdesses and Golden Jewels and Buccaneers and New Dawns and King's Ransoms and –

CHARLIE. Jesus Christ, will you stop. (*In despair*) You old get, what am I going to do with you?

DA. A rainbow of roses. I never seen a young one like her . . . so I know you'd think bad of refusing me. (*Looking at* CHARLIE) But sure you wouldn't.

CHARLIE. No.

DA. And you'll put in a good word for me? She wouldn't go again' you.

CHARLIE. I'll talk to her.

DA (*happy now*). I'm on the pig's back, so. On it for life. Oh, she won't be sorry. (*Looking up at the ceiling*) Mag! Mag, are you up there?

CHARLIE. Da, sh. (*He seats* DA.)

DA (*begins to sing aimlessly*).
'I've just been down to Monto Town
To see the bould McArdle,
But he wouldn't give me half a crown
To go to the Waxy –'

CHARLIE. Stop it: it's not then any more, it's now. (*Picking up a paper*) See that? Death certificate . . . yours.
(DA *nods and straightens up, returning to the present.* CHARLIE *puts the papers back into his dispatch case and closes it.*)

DA. I never carried on the like of that.

CHARLIE. How?

DA. Astray in the head. Thinking it was old God's time and you were herself's da.

CHARLIE. Oh, didn't you!

DA. And you not a bit like him. Begod, I don't wonder at you putting me into the poorhouse.

CHARLIE (*getting annoyed again*). You useless old man.
(*The gate squeaks.*)

DA. Sure it must have gev you a laugh, anyway.
(CHARLIE *is too angry to speak. He picks up his overcoat.*
DA *moves to assist him.*
DRUMM *appears outside the house carrying a briefcase. He is now seventy, still erect.*)
Are you off, so? Well, God send you good weather, son. Tell them I was asking for them.
(DRUMM *knocks at the front door.*)
That must be another Mass card. Do you know, I have enough of them to play whist with.
(*As* CHARLIE *goes to the door*)
Did you see the flowers on me coffin? . . . shaggin' weeds, the half of them. (*He sits.*
CHARLIE *opens the door.*)

CHARLIE (*surprised*). Mr Drumm . . .

DRUMM. I'm glad I caught you. Might I have a word?

CHARLIE. Of course . . . come in.

(*They go into the kitchen.*)

DA. Oh, old Drumm is not the worst of them.

DRUMM. It's been many years. Will you agree to shake hands? . . . It's a bad day for grievances.

(*They do so.*)

There, that's done . . . I'm obliged. Mind, I won't say it's generous of you: *I* was the wounded party.

CHARLIE. It was a long time ago.

DRUMM (*good-humoured*). Don't play word-games with me, my friend. Time doesn't mitigate an injury; it only helps one to overlook it. (*Indicating a chair*) May I?

CHARLIE. Please.

DRUMM (*sitting*). Years ago I made a choice. I could have indiscriminate friendships or I could have standards. I chose standards. It's my own misfortune that so few people have come up to them.

CHARLIE. Including me.

DRUMM. You tried. You had your work cut out.

CHARLIE. I had.

DRUMM (*being fair*). I daresay I was difficult.

CHARLIE. Impossible.

DRUMM (*bridling*). And you've become impudent.

CHARLIE (*unruffled*). Yes.

DRUMM. A beggar on horseback.

CHARLIE. It's better than walking.

DA. There was a young fella went to confession. 'Father,' says he, 'I rode a girl from Cork.' 'Yerra, boy,' says the priest, 'sure 'twas better than walking.'

(CHARLIE's *face twitches.* DRUMM *glares at him.*)

CHARLIE. I hope you're well.

DRUMM. Your hopes are unfounded.

CHARLIE. Oh?

DA. Didn't I tell you he was sick? Sure he has a face on him like a boiled –

CHARLIE (*hastily*). It's hard to believe. You look well.

(DRUMM *chuckles to himself as if at a private joke. He leans confidentially towards* CHARLIE.)

DRUMM. I have this . . . tummy trouble. I told a certain person – I don't know why, out of mischief, it isn't like me – I told him cancer was suspected. Quite untrue. Of course he told others, and since then my popularity has soared. I said to one man: 'I know you for a rogue and a blackguard.' Was he offended?

227

'You're right,' he said; 'come and have a drink.' (*With defiant pleasure*) I did.

CHARLIE. There'll be ructions when you don't die.

DRUMM. There will.

CHARLIE. False pretences.

DRUMM. Pity about them.

CHARLIE. Still . . .

DRUMM. They shun a man because he's intelligent, but get maudlin over a few supposedly malignant body-cells. I'm as bad. Ten years ago I wouldn't have given one of them the time of day, still less have taken pleasure in their approbation.

CHARLIE. Do you?

DRUMM. People like them, like the old man – your foster-father – they thank God for a fine day and stay diplomatically silent when it rains. They deride whatever is beyond them with a laugh, a platitude and a spit. They say: 'How could he be a dental surgeon? – his father was warned by the police for molesting women.'

DA. Who would that be? Old Martin Conheedy used to tamper with women. Is his son a dentist now?

DRUMM (*answering* CHARLIE'*s question*). They . . . amuse me.

DA (*derisive*). Who'd trust that fella to pull a tooth?

DRUMM (*picking up his briefcase*). When the old man was in hospital he sent word that he wanted to see me.

CHARLIE. My father?

DRUMM. Who lived here.

CHARLIE (*persisting*). My father.

DRUMM (*letting it pass*). He asked my advice. I told him that not being related by blood you would have no natural claim on his estate.

CHARLIE. What estate? He had nothing.

DRUMM. At his request I wrote out a will for him then and there. He signed it and I had it witnessed. (*He takes an envelope and hands it to* CHARLIE.) It'll stand up with the best of them.

CHARLIE. But he had bugger-all.

DRUMM. There was also the matter of an heirloom which he gave into my keeping.

CHARLIE. Heirloom?

(DRUMM *dips into his briefcase and takes out a familiar-looking brown-paper parcel.*)

DA (*jovially*). There now's a surprise for you.

CHARLIE (*staring at the parcel*). No . . .

228

DA (*crowing*). You won't guess what's in that!

DRUMM. He said it was valuable, so I asked my bank manager to keep it in his vault.

CHARLIE (*under stress*). *That* was in a bank vault?

DRUMM. I can see that the value was also sentimental. (*Rising*) Well, I'm glad to have discharged my trust.

CHARLIE. Thank you. (*Looking at the parcel*) His estate.

DRUMM. Oh, no. Whatever that is, it has nothing to do with what's in the will. And I'd be careful with that envelope. There's money involved!

CHARLIE. Money?

DRUMM. He mentioned the sum of a hundred and thirty-five pounds, with more to come.

CHARLIE. He never had that much in his life.

DRUMM. He thought otherwise.

CHARLIE. He was raving. I *know*. All he had was his pension and the cheques I sent him for – (*He breaks off and looks around at* DA.)

DA (*strategically*). That dog from next door is in the garden. Hoosh . . . hoosh, you bastard.

(CHARLIE *watches him murderously as he beats a retreat into the scullery.*)

DRUMM (*waiting for* CHARLIE *to finish*). Yes?

CHARLIE. I was wrong. I've remembered where it came from.

DRUMM. The money?

CHARLIE. Yes.

DRUMM. I imagined it was hard-earned.

CHARLIE (*grimly*). It was.

DRUMM (*sternly*). Now, my friend, no caterwauling. To whom else could he leave it? I once called him an ignorant man. I still do. And yet he may have been better off. Everything I once thought I knew for certain I have seen inverted, revised, disproved, or discredited. Shall I tell you something? In seventy years the one surviving fragment of my knowledge, the only indisputable poor particle of certainty in my entire life, is that in a public house lavatory incoming traffic has the right of way. (*Acidly*) It isn't much to take with one, is it?

CHARLIE (*smiling*). Well, now *I* know something.

DRUMM. I have always avoided him and his kind, and yet in the end we fetch up against the self-same door. I find that aggravating. (*Moving towards the door*) The old couple, had they children of their own?

229

CHARLIE. I was told once there were several. All still-born.

DRUMM. He didn't even create life – at least I have the edge on him there.

CHARLIE. How are the two Rhode Island Reds?

DRUMM. Moulting. (*He offers his hand.*) It was pleasant to see you. I enjoyed it. Goodbye.

CHARLIE. Mr Drumm, he never took anything from me, he wouldn't let me help him, what I offered him he kept and wouldn't use. Why?

DRUMM. Don't you know?

CHARLIE. Do *you*?

DRUMM. The Irish national disease.

CHARLIE. Bad manners?

DRUMM. Worse, no manners. (*He holds out his hand, inspecting the sky for rain, then goes.*)

CHARLIE *closes the door, returns to the kitchen.*)

CHARLIE. Where are you? (*Yelling.*) Come . . . in . . . here! (DA *comes in.*)

DA. Do you want a cup of tea?

CHARLIE. You old shite. You wouldn't even use the money.

DA. I did.

CHARLIE. How?

DA. Wasn't it something to leave you?

CHARLIE. I'll never forgive you for this.

DA (*not worried*). Ah, you will.

CHARLIE. Since I was born. 'Here's sixpence for the chairoplanes, a shilling for the pictures, a new suit for the job. Here's a life.' When did I ever get a chance to pay it back, to get out from under, to be quit of you? You wouldn't come to us in London; you'd rather be the brave old warrior, soldiering on.

DA. And wasn't I?

CHARLIE. While I was the ingrate. The only currency you'd take, you knew I wouldn't pay. Well, I've news for you, mate. You had your chance. The debt is cancelled, welshed on. (*Tapping his head*) I'm turfing you out. Of here. See that? (*He tears the black armband from his overcoat and drops it in the range.*) And this? (*He holds up the parcel containing the spectacle frames.*)

DA. You wouldn't. Not at all.

CHARLIE. Wouldn't I? You think not? (*He bends and crushes the frames through the paper with increasing violence.*)

DA. Ah, son . . .

CHARLIE. San Francisco earthquake!

DA. You'd want to mind your hand with them –

CHARLIE (*cutting his finger*). Shit.

DA. I told you you'd cut yourself.

(CHARLIE *gives him a malevolent look and very deliberately shoves the parcel into the range. He sucks his hand.*)

CHARLIE. Now wouldn't I?

DA. Is it deep? That's the kind of cut 'ud give you lockjaw. I'd mind that.

CHARLIE. Gone . . . and you with it.

DA. Yis. (*Taking out a dirty handkerchief*) Here, tie this around it.

CHARLIE. Get away from me. Ignorant man, ignorant life!

DA. What are you talking about, or do you know what you're talking about? Sure I enjoyed meself. And in the wind-up I didn't die with the arse out of me trousers like the rest of them – I left money!

CHARLIE. *My* money.

DA. Jasus, didn't you get it back? And looka . . . if I wouldn't go to England with you before, sure I'll make it up to you. I will now.

CHARLIE. You what? Like hell you will.

DA. Sure you can't get rid of a bad thing.

CHARLIE. Can't I? You watch me. You watch!

(*He picks up his case, walks out of the house and closes the front door. He locks the door and hurls the key from him. A sigh of relief. He turns to go, to find* DA *has walked out through the fourth wall.*)

DA. Are we off, so? It's starting to rain. The angels must be peein' again.

CHARLIE. Don't you dare follow me. You're dead . . . get off.

DA. Sure Noah's flood was only a shower. (*Following him*) Left . . . left . . . I had a good job and I left, right, left!

CHARLIE. Hump off. Get away. Shoo. I don't want you.

(*He goes to the upper level.*
DA *follows, lagging behind.*)

DA. Go on, go on. I'll keep up with you.

(CHARLIE *stops at the top level.*)

CHARLIE. Leave me alone.

(CHARLIE *slowly walks down as* DA *follows, singing.*)

DA (*singing*).

'Oh, says your oul' one to my oul' one:
"Will you come to the Waxy Dargle?"

231

And says my oul' one to your oul' one:
"Sure I haven't got a farthin'." '

CURTAIN

SUMMER

CHARACTERS

RICHARD HALVEY
TRINA HALVEY
MICHAEL, THEIR SON
STORMY LOFTUS
JAN LOFTUS
LOU, THEIR DAUGHTER
JESS WHITE
MYRA WHITE

The action takes place on a hillside overlooking Dublin.

ACT I
A Sunday in Summer, 1968

ACT II
A Sunday in late Summer, 1974

SUMMER

ACT ONE

A hillside. An afternoon in high summer, 1968.

An age-worn Celtic cross juts up at an angle near the summit. There is a suggestion of trees, and there is a wooden picnic table with flanking benches. The debris of the picnic has yet to be cleared up.
   The Curtain rises, and the Lights come up on eight people, of whom six are married couples in early middle-age. They are: STORMY *and* JAN LOFTUS *and their daughter* LOU, *aged seventeen;* JESS *and* MYRA WHITE; *and* RICHARD *and* TRINA HALVEY *and their son* MICHAEL, *who is eighteen. To begin with, the individual families are grouped together, but not markedly so.*
   Everyone is quite still, as if momentarily overcome by torpor or the warmth of the sun. STORMY *and* JAN *have brought folding stools on which they are sitting; the others are sitting or half-lying against the grassy slope. Then* MYRA *fans an insect away from her face.* JESS *lights a cigarette.* LOU *idly teases the back of* JAN's *neck with a frond;* JAN, *eyes shut, jerks her head.* RICHARD *looks up from his* Sunday Times *and squints forward.* MICHAEL, *who is cradling a guitar, plays one soft chord. As if this were a signal,* STORMY *speaks.*

STORMY. One day, some right little bastard at school filled the saddlebag of my bicycle with manure off the allotment behind the sports field. I knew it would pong for a month, couldn't afford a new one. So I'm crossing the school yard with murder on me face when one of the brothers, Brother Fergal, grabs hold of me. (*He takes hold of his ear. In a Kerry accent:*) 'Boy, if ye want to shtay out of trouble in dis world and Purgatory in de nexsht, take dat shtormy look off oor face.' That's how I got the nickname, Stormy. I became fond of it in time. It sort of suggests. . .
JESS. A dirty night.
STORMY. A tempestuous nature, I was going to say. It's a great

235

oul' standby. Fellows don't mess when your name is Stormy.

RICHARD. (*Not turning.*) What does Jan call you?

JESS. What do I call him? Not Stormy.

STORMY. 'Beloved'.

JAN (*in amusement*). Ha!

TRINA. No, what?

JESS. His name's Terence. (*To* STORMY) I didn't know you went to a Catholic school.

STORMY. The stepmammy was R.C.

RICHARD. You aren't?

STORMY. I'm a Prod. (*Indicating* JAN.) Like her.

JAN (*disliking the word*). Prod!

STORMY. Certainly. (STORMY *prods* JAN *in the ribs. She makes a bored face.*)

MYRA. Jess ought to have had a nickname.

JESS. Why ought I?

STORMY. What's it short for – Jessica?

MYRA. Jesse.

STORMY. That's as bad. (*To* JESS) Give us a dance.

JESS. No, I'm with someone.

MYRA. It's not even a saint's name.

STORMY (*on his feet*).

> 'Let's twist again,
> Like we did last summer,
> Let's twist again,
> Like we. . .'

JAN. Terry, sit down. It's too hot.

MYRA. I'm baking.

TRINA. It's like the summers we used to have.

LOU. The Twist is ancient.

STORMY. Who says?

LOU. It's years old. Prehistoric.

STORMY. Do you hear the arrogance?

RICHARD (*indicating* MICHAEL). Same with him.

TRINA. Stop running him down.

RICHARD. I'm not running him. . .

JAN. Louise, why don't you sit with Michael?

LOU. I'm fine.

JAN. They're so difficult.

MYRA. I hope ours are all right.

JESS. Don't worry.

MYRA. I thought bad of going off without them. I mean, picnics

236

are for children more than anyone.

RICHARD. Yes, that's because they wreck them for grown-ups.

MYRA. They do not.

RICHARD. Get off. They fall in nettles, they squabble, they bark their shins, slobber their food, wet their pants, get too much sun and cry to go home. Then they get sick in the car as a benediction.

TRINA. Now stop.

RICHARD. All I'm saying is that adults, Myra included, are entitled to one solitary hard-earned day's outing in the year without having to wipe runny noses and dig latrines. (*To the men*) See? Now I'm heartless.

TRINA (*lightly*). Oh, we all know that.

MYRA. I don't want a day off from the children. Poor little mites, sure they're only young the. . .

JAN (*ready to avert an argument*). You have how many, Myra? Three?

MYRA (*her eyes lighting up*). Four. Noreen is the eldest, she's twelve; then there's Brian and Laurence and Catherine. There were five altogether, but we gave one to Holy God.

STORMY. What's that, a school?

MYRA. I mean, one died.

STORMY. Oh. Sorry.

(MICHAEL *begins to smile*, RICHARD *darts him a warning look*.)

MYRA. That's what we tell the children when they ask. 'Little Elizabeth has gone to live with Holy God.'

JAN. Yes; of course they don't understand.

MYRA (*unsentimentally*). They do understand. What I mean is, it's true; she has. (MYRA's *matter-of-factness causes a moment of discomfort*.)

TRINA. Well, I wish I had as much. . .

STORMY. Yeah, well, that's it. None of us know, do we?

TRINA (*on cue*). No, no, we don't.

RICHARD. I do. (TRINA *glares at him*. MYRA *notices. Affecting innocence*) Pardon?

MYRA (*with affection*). I don't worry myself about Richard. He's not the worst. (*She smiles at him*.)

JAN. Shall we clear away? There's not much point waiting for the men to do it.

TRINA. Catch them!

(*The women go to attend to the remnants of the meal.* MYRA *stops for a moment near* RICHARD.)

MYRA (*in a half-whisper*). The longest way round is the shortest way home.

237

RICHARD. I wish I'd said that.

(MYRA *sticks her tongue out at him and joins* JAN *and* TRINA. JAN *is brisk, setting the pace at clearing up.*)

STORMY. I think that white wine is beginning to mull inside me. (*He holds back a belch, striking his stomach gently with his fist. At the same moment,* MICHAEL *strums another chord.* STORMY *looks at him, askance.* LOU *giggles.*)

RICHARD. Pity there's a haze. We lose the view.

STORMY. Yeah, I have a house going up down there.

RICHARD. To live in?

STORMY. No, I'm in the trade.

RICHARD. Ah, yes. Doing well?

STORMY. You know: fair. It'll pick up, there's a few quid in the country now. God, in my young day even the Protestants were poor. A builder gets a great satisfaction. You drive down a road, you go past a house and say: 'I put that up'.

RICHARD. Good.

JESS. The time I used to travel for Rosenthal's the wallpaper people, I'd get the same kind of satisfaction. I'd drive past one of Stormy's houses and say: 'My wallpaper's holding that up'.

STORMY. You bugger, you.

RICHARD. Is that how you met Jess? Business?

STORMY. I bought a roll or two off him out of kindness. He's a pathetic poor devil. (JESS *smiles.*) He knows how to keep his friends well-hidden all the same. I used to see you up in the pub, the Druid's Chair, Sunday mornings. Wondered who the fellow was with his eye on me wife.

RICHARD. Me?

STORMY. And of course never a word out of Jembo here that he knew you. Oh, a cute hawk.

RICHARD. Jess and I are old friends.

STORMY. Sorry for your trouble.

(TRINA *begins to scrape the contents of a plate on to the grass.*)

JAN. Do you mind, Trina, I brought plastic bags for the leftovers. Louise, be useful – fetch the plastic bags. The last thing we want is a swarm of wasps.

MYRA. You brought everything – even stools to sit on.

JAN. (*Nodding towards* STORMY) That was his idea. I felt ridiculous. What does Richard do?

TRINA. Books.

JAN. Oh, yes?

TRINA. Secondhand.

238

RICHARD (*overhearing*). Collectors' items, do you mind?

TRINA. Well, whatever. (*She winks at* JAN).

LOU (*finding the bags*). These, do you mean?

JAN. Thanks, dear.

(LOU *sits near the cross.*)

MYRA. They're so handy. Of course you can't have them in a house with children: they'd suffocate.

STORMY. Is there money in that? Books?

RICHARD. Some. People die; their libraries are sold off.

STORMY. Months since I read a book.

RICHARD. This isn't reading, this is owning. Or often they don't like the idea of their books outliving them. They say to me: empty the shelves, scatter them; nothing goes on after I die, here it ends.

STORMY. People do that?

RICHARD. Sure.

STORMY. Want to take it with them?

RICHARD. Right.

STORMY. Books, huh? Tell you something; the only thing I'd like to take with me is. . .

RICHARD. Go on.

JESS. Travellers' cheques.

STORMY. I've got to dig myself one of those latrines you mentioned. Stay there: I'll tell you.

(STORMY *goes off.*)

JESS. What do you think?

RICHARD. Of him? Amiable.

JESS. No, I mean. . . (*He jabs a thumb towards* JAN.)

RICHARD. What about her?

JESS. What do you think the form is?

RICHARD. You ought to know; they're your friends.

JESS. Not that I'd lay a finger. . .

RICHARD. How could you, when you even expect me to do your lusting for you? Do you know what you are? You're a vicarious lecher.

JESS (*prompting him*). Handsome woman, though.

RICHARD (*disparaging*). Good for a daydream.

JESS. Come on. . . (RICHARD *embarks on what is almost an established routine, with him as performer and* JESS *as delighted audience.*)

RICHARD. A professional Protestant. Wears black jersey dresses in the evening, no jewellery. Hasn't wept since Rajah, her horse,

239

died. Hon. treasurer and guiding spirit of the Old Folks Happy Christmas and Euthanasia fund. Highly accomplished: gives impromptu dinners for twelve in telephone booths and has a Ph.D. in flower arrangement.

JESS. Sex, sex – what about sex?

RICHARD. You're depraved, you know that?

JESS. Do you think she gives him a bit?

RICHARD. Sure,. as long as she doesn't know what he's at.

JESS (*like a schoolboy*). Heeee!

MYRA (*looking around*). What?

JESS. Nothing.

(STORMY *enters*.)

RICHARD. I'd as soon try to climb the north face of the Eiger. No vices; no flaws; no, thanks.

JESS (*warning him*). Watch it.

RICHARD (*quietly*). I know. Michael. . . (MICHAEL *looks at him*.) The reason you're with us is to keep Louise company. Now talk to her. Drown her with charm.

(*It is an order.* MICHAEL *slouches reluctantly to where* LOU *is sitting, near the cross.*)

STORMY. He's a fine-looking lad. Is he still at school?

RICHARD. He starts at Trinity in the autumn. He's studying to be a deaf mute.

JAN. There, all done!

MYRA. Aren't we great!

JAN. But there doesn't seem to be a litter bin. I'd better put this stuff in the car. (*She picks up the plastic bags, now filled, and starts up the slope.*)

MICHAEL (*having steeled himself to talk to* LOU). That Ogam writing on the cross, it's a fake, you know. Wrong part of the country.

LOU. That so?

MICHAEL. And – and the markings are too fresh. It probably dates from the eighteenth. . .

LOU. I'll take those, mum. (*sotto voce*) Please.

JAN (*sotto voce*). You're being rude.

(LOU *takes the bags from* JAN *and bears them off.*)

RICHARD. Well, help her.

LOU (*singing back*). No, thanks!

MICHAEL *shoots an unforgiving look at* RICHARD *and walks away.*)

JAN (*to* RICHARD). Were we like that?

240

RICHARD. Were you?

JAN. I hope not. But if the only reason a boy talked to me was because his father told him so, I daresay I might send him packing, too – yes.

RICHARD. Stick up for your own, don't you? (JAN *senses a faint antagonism beneath the joke.*)

JAN (*looking at him*). Yes.

STORMY. Well, there may not be a wedding in the family, but at least we're sure of tomorrow's lunch: it went that way.

IAN. Oh, you.

(MICHAEL *plays a third chord, an angrier one this time. Pause.*)

MYRA. Jess, sit beside me.

JESS. What for?

MYRA. We're married. (*Incredulously*) What for! (JESS *sighs and moves down to comply.*)

STORMY. See you around sometime. (*To* RICHARD) I'll tell you one thing: if Jan tried to come the hound with me in public I know the answer she'd. . . (*As* JESS *sits beside* MYRA *she clasps his hand in both of hers.*) Hey up, hang on: stand by for another christening.

TRINA. I'm getting a tan already. (*Holding up her arms*) Richard, look: am I?

RICHARD. Yes.

TRINA. I'd take my top off if I thought nobody'd mind.

STORMY. We wouldn't give you a passing glance. At our age, we're all beyond that sort of thing. (*To* RICHARD) Aren't we?

RICHARD. Sure.

STORMY. Certainly. (*He at once whips his fists up to his eyes, training them on* TRINA *like binoculars, and emits a slavering 'Duhhh!' of idiot lust.*)

TRINA. Sure who's to see! (*She begins to unbutton her blouse, half-shyly, half-provocatively.* JESS *begins to hum 'The Stripper'.* STORMY *goes through the motions of a strip-tease.*) (*Stopping*) No, I'd better not.

STORMY and JESS. (*speaking together*) Awwww!

RICHARD (*irritably*). If you're all that keen, go ahead.

TRINA (*in a whisper*). Michael. . .

RICHARD. What?

TRINA (*through her teeth*). Michael!

RICHARD. For God's sake, every year on holiday she galumphs around the kiddies' paddling pool in a bikini you couldn't

241

bandage a sore finger with, but she won't let her eighteen-year-old son see her wearing a dirty great bra.

TRINA (*embarrassed*). Shut up.

RICHARD. It's so stupid!

MYRA. Underwear is different, Richard.

RICHARD. How?

JAN. It is, you know.

RICHARD (*glaring*). Is it!

MYRA (*reasonably*). Of course there's underwear and underwear in it. I mean, if it's a modest kind of underwear, then I suppose there's no harm out in the country and in front of friends. I suppose. But in front of your children is something else.

RICHARD. You mean they're not meant to know that their mothers are equipped with breasts. I imagine that's the first thing they would have found out.

TRINA. He heard every word. Now that will do.

STORMY. Which reminds me: I wonder if they're open yet.

(JESS *squints at his watch.*)

JESS. Zero minus twenty.

JAN. Terry, it's very seldom we get weather like this, and we're not burying ourselves in a pub.

STORMY. I thought the lads might care to wander down for a libation.

MYRA (*to* JESS). You don't want to, do you?

JESS. No.

JAN (*settling back*). It's heavenly.

(LOU *enters carrying a book. She hesitates, then walks over to* MICHAEL.)

LOU. The *Shell Guide to Ireland* says that the cross is genuine sixth century.

MICHAEL. I never said it wasn't.

LOU. Yes, you did.

MICHAEL. I said the Ogam writing on it was fake.

LOU. Well, if you want to worm out of what you said I couldn't care less.

MICHAEL. Nobody is worming. . .

LOU. You distinctly. . .

MICHAEL. I said the cross is genuine, the marks are. . .

LOU. I'm really not interested.

MICHAEL. All right!

STORMY (*beaming upon them*). Now that's more like it!

(LOU *sits and affects to be absorbed in her guide book.*)

242

TRINA. Richard. . .

RICHARD. Hm?

TRINA. Over there, that red roof – is that the Tara Castle Ballroom?

RICHARD. Where?

TRINA. Down there.

RICHARD. No, the Tara Castle is miles that way, out of sight.

TRINA (*who knows where it is*). Oh. We went there once.

JAN. Yes?

TRINA. Years ago, didn't we? (*Silence*) Not since then. Just the once. (*Silence*) Years and years ago. Only the once.

RICHARD. Trina won a beauty contest there.

JAN (*interested*). Oh?

TRINA (*feigning annoyance*). What did you have to go and mention that for?

JAN. A beauty contest?

STORMY (*reappraising her*). Get away.

TRINA. It was so silly. I can't even remember the title they gave me.

RICHARD. It was a mountain, wasn't it? Miss Sugar Loaf.

TRINA. I think it was Miss Glen-of-the-Downs, Richard.

JAN. What a distinction!

MYRA. I remember. It was Holy Year.

TRINA. It was ludicrous. I had this buttercup dress, it showed my straps. Not quite lemon-coloured, sort of butter-cup – puff sleeves and a really tame scoop – (*with comic distaste*) – you know! I mean, today I'd have gone short. There were – how many other contestants?

RICHARD. Half-a-dozen?

TRINA (*overlapping*). Twelve at least.

RICHARD (*smiling*). More like twenty.

TRINA (*laughing*). We had to – walk up and down. Sunny Fitzgerald was there. I only got up because I thought she was sure to win.

RICHARD (*softly*). Oh, no.

TRINA. And I was just beginning with Michael at the time. I mean, it didn't show, but you feel –

JAN. Yes.

TRINA. – anything but graceful. Eighteen years ago, nineteen-fifty. And I burst into tears, didn't I, like one of those girls on the television – Miss World, all white teeth and high heels. We were out at the back of beyond – parading like cattle, big countrymen roaring at us.

243

RICHARD. 'More o' that! More o' that, you raving beauties, you!'

TRINA. So I got a cheque for ten pounds, and some county coun-
cillor put this crown on my head – fourteen carat tin! – and
a cloak, green velveteen, more like someone's tablecloth.

RICHARD (*in a rural accent, orotund*). 'And in crowning this lovely
young lady as the only sort of queen a good Irishman will
tolerate – a beauty queen! – I express the hope of all here present that her triumph on this St Patrick's Night will spur her on
to future endeavours and yield her the height of happiness as
through the world she goes.'

JAN. He never!

(RICHARD *removes a shoe and places it on* TRINA's *head.*)

RICHARD. 'I now crown you Miss Rocky Valley.'

TRINA. It was Miss Glen-of-the. . . My hair, Richard.
Glen-of-the-Downs.

MYRA. I have a photograph of that night. Trina looked gorgeous.

RICHARD (*singing*). 'A pretty girl –'

STORMY (*modelling*). Bumpety-bump, bumpety-bump!

RICHARD. ' – Is like a melody –'

STORMY. Hello, sailor!

RICHARD. ' – That haunts you night and day, Just like the
strain. . .'

TRINA (*coldly*). Don't jeer.

RICHARD. Who's jeering? (*Facetiously*) He's jeering; I'm not.
(TRINA *looks at him; his expression changes to a look of ill-
temper. She gives a couldn't-care-less smile to the others.*)

TRINA. He thinks I'm all dewy-eyed about it. That's the mistake he
makes: he's the one who's thick, not me. I mean, a dance-hall
out in the wilds – it was a panic.

JESS. You had a smashing old shape on you, Trina.

TRINA (*with mock anger*). Had? *Had*?

JAN. Well, I'm seething with envy. I always had a figure like a
hall-stand.

MYRA. It was the children destroyed me, God love them.

TRINA. Still, it doesn't last long, does it?

JAN. What?

TRINA. That time – then. It flew.

RICHARD. Here we go.

TRINA. It's nothing to be ashamed of. I liked being young. We had
fun.

STORMY. You were miserable.

TRINA. Who was?

JAN. How do you know?

STORMY. We all were. I was; you were. 'Oh God, will he ring me? Will she turn up? And if she does, will she let me?'

JAN (*good-humouredly*). Now, now.

STORMY. And I did ring her, and she did turn up, and mind your own business. We were so bloody wet, strutting into a hop as if you were George Raft. (*With motions of flipping a coin and chewing gum*) 'Okay, sister, let's you and me shake the torso.'

JESS (*to* TRINA, *in broad Dublin*). Are yeh dancin'?

TRINA. Are yeh askin'?

STORMY. And let one little chrissy off a backstreet with more gums than teeth turn up her nose at you, and instead of George Raft you were Quasimodo. You limped. (*Pointing to* LOU) They're cruel at her age: I used think they went home and practised on the cat. (*To* TRINA) And you: you take a look at that photograph she's got. I bet you you had a face like a doll: nothing in it.

JESS. Nice legs, but. (TRINA *winks and shows her knee, vamp-like.* JESS *releases his hand from* MYRA's *in turning to look.*)

MYRA. Jess.

JESS. Me hand's gone dead.

STORMY. In those days I thought I knew it all.

RICHARD. And now?

STORMY. Oh, now I'm wise.

JESS. I love him!

STORMY. Never having two ha'pennies to rub together. Slouching around the streets so's you could end the evening on a high note: in out of the cold, eating a plate of chips. No thanks.

RICHARD. I used think I had T.B.

STORMY. That right?

RICHARD. It was the time when everyone seemed to be dying of it. They called it 'The Captain of the Men of Death'.

JESS. He used to go around tapping his chest. (*He demonstrates.*) And he didn't know whether he ought to be listening for an echo or a muffled thud.

RICHARD. It's true. (*He clears his throat.*)

STORMY. Jasus, he's still got it.

JESS. We used to call him 'La Traviata'.

RICHARD. You can talk. This fellow got all his teeth pulled out in one go. For the next three months –

JESS. One month.

RICHARD. – he was subject to these fainting fits. On a bus, at the

245

pictures, anywhere. One day he and I were going into Dun Laoghaire baths. We were coming down the steps, just in sight of the girls displaying their two inches of bare midriff, and he hit the ground like a sack of turnips. When he came to, they called him a sex maniac and threw him out.

STORMY. Oh, them bare midriffs.

JESS (*protesting*). I had anaemia.

STORMY. When you saw a bit of skin in those days you knew what you were looking at. Now it's an optical illusion. The modern girdle has more bones in it then Dean's Grange cemetery.

MYRA. That puts me in mind of me mother.

STORMY. Does she wear one?

MYRA. She's in Dean's Grange.

STORMY. Oh.

MYRA. The house we lived in, the floorboards went rotten and we had to walk on the joists.

JAN. This seems to be becoming a poverty contest.

RICHARD. If it is, you lose.

JAN. Do I?

TRINA. Still, we were happy.

STORMY. You're happy now. (TRINA *smiles to herself*.) Prime of life, the real good times not here yet. Bellies full, cars to drive home in, and instead of poverty we've got debts – that's progress.

JESS. I'm too poor to be in debt.

JAN. Stop bragging.

STORMY. Although I suppose the young ones think we're ancient monuments.

RICHARD (*to* MICHAEL). Do you?

STORMY. Like the oul' cross.

RICHARD. Speak to us. (MICHAEL *shakes his head*) Why not?

MICHAEL. You only talk about the past.

LOU. What do we know about that?

STORMY. See, they're ganging up on us.

MICHAEL. You can't. . . (*He stops, nervous.*)

RICHARD. Yes?

MICHAEL (*stammering slightly*). . . .Can't expect us to work up a lather over where you've been; we have enough – worries about where we're going to. Maybe you were poor starting out; well, you aren't any more, so neither are we – so that makes us different, right? We're climbing another hill; that's why we don't b-bleed like you do.

246

STORMY. You don't. . .?

MICHAEL. Bleed, get. . .

LOU. Soppy.

MICHAEL. Show ourselves.

STORMY (*with a hint of aggressiveness*). Maybe you should.

MICHAEL. That's not for you to say, Mr. Loftus. (STORMY's *face
tightens.* MICHAEL *is afraid of him, but goes on*) It's the way
things are. Mum there cries at 'Random Harvest' on the telly.
I think it's a hoot, I fall about.

MYRA. Ah, not at 'Random Harvest', Michael.

STORMY. (*dismissing* MICHAEL) Did anyone see 'Dr. Zhivago' yet?
Now that's what I call a. . .

MICHAEL. Maybe she needs simple things, happy endings. I don't,
and it's thanks to them, my parents – and I mean it: thanks.
'Cause they let me see what b-brains I've got. So I can face it
that things may not end well, me included. I don't know what
to do about it, but I can face it, and I don't need to be tran-
quillized with old rubbish. (*Pause.* MYRA's *thoughts have
drifted away. She begins to sing.*)

MYRA. 'I'll be with you in apple-blossom time; I'll be with you. . .'

STORMY. Rubbish! (MYRA *breaks off and looks at him.*) No –
him. I know that if I criticized my parents' tastes. . .

MICHAEL. What's so terrible about that? Why shouldn't you
criticize them? You know more than they did.

TRINA (*not shocked; bored*). Michael, that will do.

MICHAEL. Same as one day we'll know more than you do. Can't
be helped – we will. (*Pause. He looks at* RICHARD.) Well, you
asked me. (*He slouches away and sits near* LOU. MYRA *has
resumed her song. She finishes.*)

STORMY. That was exquisite.

MYRA (*assuming he means her singing*). Thanks.

JAN. He's a boy.

STORMY. Making a jeer of 'Random Harvest'. What about them
and their Elvis the Pelvis?

MYRA. I loved Greer Garson.

TRINA. Poor James Dean is dead these thirteen years. Would you
credit it? Nineteen-fifty-five. I was mad for him. I still love
him.

RICHARD. Necrophilia.

STORMY (*absently, still smarting*).She was good, too. (JAN *and*
RICHARD *look at each other and burst out laughing.*) What's
up? (*Scowling at* MICHAEL) Did he upset you?

247

JAN (*incoherently*). No. . .

STORMY. What's the joke, then? (RICHARD *points at him, unable to talk.*)

TRINA. What?

JESS. I didn't hear it.

STORMY (*getting annoyed*). If it's so funny, let's in on it. (JAN *explodes into another paroxysm.* RICHARD *sits on the bank, laughing painfully.*) Ah, this is a cod. I'm asking you what's so . . . . (JAN *waves him away.*) Am I the joke, is that it? (MYRA *begins to giggle.*) What are you laughing at?

MYRA (*losing control*). I don't know.

> (*There is a sudden alarming shriek of falsetto laughter from* JESS.)

STORMY. Jasus, now what?

JESS (*pointing at* RICHARD). Him.

STORMY. What about him?

TRINA. Tell us.

JESS. What he's. . .

STORMY. What he's what?

JESS (*shrilly*). What he's. . .sitting in! (RICHARD *leaps up, feeling the seat of his trousers. Now it is* STORMY's *turn to laugh: great humourless gusts which are punctuated by* JESS's *Stan Laurel-like shrieks.*)

TRINA (*in revulsion*). Oh, Richard.

> (*Then she, too, joins in the laughter.* JESS *staggers over to one of the folding stools and sits. It collapses, pitching him to the ground. The laughter escalates.* MICHAEL *buries his head in his arms, while* LOU *faces away, her shoulders shaking.*)

JESS (*kicking his feet in the air*). Stop. . .oh, stop.

RICHARD. It's too much.

TRINA (*wiping her eyes*). Oh, my God.

STORMY (*holding his chest*). No – no – no no o o – OH! (*It is, finally, a cry of pain. His face registers alarm. He sinks to his knees, gasping for breath, his eyes bulging.*)

RICHARD (*still laughing*). Look, he. . . (*He realizes that* STORMY *is ill.*)

JAN. Terry? (*She goes to him.*)

MYRA. What is it? (JESS *emits another hoot of laughter.*) Jess!

JAN. It's all right. (*To* STORMY) Don't panic, darling. Take a deep breath. He gorges himself – all that French bread. You aren't going to die, but if you will eat like a pig this is what you must expect.

248

RICHARD. I think it's his heart.

JAN. Fat chance. His trouble is six inches further down. (*To* STOR-MY) Get some air in: gulp. Did you bring your tablets? (STOR-MY *shakes his head, agonizedly trying to belch.*)

MYRA. Has anyone any baking-powder?

(TRINA *looks into her handbag, then stares at* MYRA, *who shrugs helplessly.*)

JESS. He gave that potato salad a terrible death.

JAN. And the piccalilli, and the cheese. (*Wiping* STORMY'*s forehead*) You won't learn, will you? As greedy as a child – which you aren't any longer.

STORMY (*belching*). Excuse me. (*In relief*) Oh, God.

RICHARD. How is it now?

STORMY. I'm doing the breast-stroke in me own sweat. I'm okay.

JAN (*to* RICHARD). And you talk about taking children on a picnic!

MYRA (*to* JESS). See? We could have brought them.

STORMY Humblest apologies. But yous don't get rid of me that easy. I've got a ticker like a donkey engine.

JAN. Donkey is right.

LOU (*shaken*). I thought he was. . .

MICHAEL. He's fine. In middle-age the digestive system collapses, that's all.

STORMY (*looking at* MICHAEL). Lou, your dad will be around to give you a silver-wedding present. Now what we all need is a stretch of the legs.

JAN. He's mad.

STORMY. Through the woods to the top of the hill, down the grassy lane, turn right at the road and. . .

JAN. And look where we are. A pub! How did that get there?

STORMY. I need a soda water, Jan.

TRINA. I'm sure.

RICHARD. I don't mind, if you're up to it.

JESS. I'm on.

MYRA (*privately*). No.

JAN. At least let him rest for a minute. (*To* STORMY) Yes, you will. Now, please.

(STORMY *makes a martyred face. They subside.* MICHAEL *strums a chord. The Light changes so that the couples are separately key-lit by spots. The lighting of the unoccupied areas becomes muted. There is an effect of individual isolation.*)

249

STORMY. I feel like a wet dish-rag.

JAN. He looks awful.

MYRA (*to* JESS). I thought I was going to have to say an act of contrition into his ear. Except he's a Protestant. What do you do in that case?

JESS. Say it into his left ear.

TRINA. All that laughing has made my eye-black run. Ah, look at me: I'm a fright to the world. (*She begins repairing the damages.*)

RICHARD (*looking at* STORMY). Poor fellow: he's more frightened than ill. God, if he knew I'd been out with his wife he'd really have a heart attack.

(RICHARD *and* JAN *look at each other briefly.* JESS *surreptitiously counts his money.*)

JESS. I'll need a quid for petrol for tomorrow's calls. (*He tucks a pound note into his sock.*) If they don't drink shorts I'm not too bad. Wait now: Trina's on vodka, Jan is gin and tonic. So if Richard sticks to beer and Stormy takes soda water. . . Only he won't; he'll want brandy to recuperate.

JAN. I'm not going to see him again. I sat in that pub trembling in case one of our friends walked in. Not that they'd ever tell: it'd spoil their fun. The sense of power.

JESS (*retrieving the pound note*). I can get the petrol on tick, and if I have a good breakfast I can skip lunch. Yeah.

STORMY. What if it had been the old ticker? I'd hate to pop off on a summer's day: all that invigorating sunshine going to waste. The depth of winter, now, when the blood is thin and you can't lay concrete: that's different. I mean, for preference. Rain or shine, poor old Jan'd take it very hard.

JAN. I'm insane. A married woman going on forty, having her head turned like a schoolgirl because a man is interested. Well, no harm done, but not again: no, thank you.

MYRA. It's a sin. It's a sin to spend money in public houses with children's mouths to be fed and clothed. How can we expect God and His Holy Mother to help us if we won't help ourselves?

TRINA. (*to her mirror*) You'll do. You'll more than do. Men still look at you, do you know that? They squint at you sideways, think you don't notice. In the pub Sunday mornings, eyes like spiders. They strip you to your skin, but wouldn't give you an honest-to-God up and down look if it killed them. Too soon after Mass! But I see them. (*She laughs knowingly and puts her mirror away*.) Now I don't mind where we go. As long as the day lasts. I'm sick and tired of days ending. (*Instantly bored, she begins to hum 'A Pretty Girl is Like a Melody'.*)

MYRA (*through the humming*). I wish I was at home now tucking them in, and Jess telling them a story.

JESS. Once upon a time there was this princess, and she met a prince. And they were as keen as mustard. And one day she gave him a kiss, and he tasted smashin', so he did. So she ate him.

RICHARD. She sat in that pub, so bloody poised. Fine bones, posh accent – end of inventory. Thin as a lath and cold as January. The Queen chatting up a comedian: 'And when one falls arse over tip, does it hurt?' I bet it would be like kissing a cobweb. No, forget it.

STORMY. Back page of the *Irish Times*. 'The offices of T. E. Loftus and Co. will be closed today as a mark of respect to our late managing director, Mr. Terence-bracket-Stormy-bracket-Loftus, dearly beloved husband of Jan and father of Louise Hilary. Will those who think of him today, a little prayer to Jesus say.' (*He wipes his eyes*.)

JAN. Discreet, though: no-one would guess. Too damn discreet: he's been needling me all day. That wasn't pretending.

JESS. You've got to look prosperous. If I could afford a decent suit, I could get new customers. . .

RICHARD. I'll try to get her on her own later on and cancel Tuesday.

JESS. But until I get new customers I can't afford a decent suit. Every penny goes to the kids. One of these days, the girls will be the best-dressed nuns in the convent.

MYRA. I always liked Richard. He has a good heart, he'll turn to God in his own time. (*She looks at him*.)

TRINA. She wouldn't have that dawny look on her face if she had to live with him. All he's good for is finding fault. He thinks I'm some kind of joke just because I try to be a credit to him.

JAN. Tomorrow evening, the Victoriana society; coffee mornings on Wednesday; ways-and-means committee Thursday. And damn, the Gleasons for dinner on Friday.

RICHARD (*watching* JAN). Still, she's thinking about me.

JAN. I'll serve them a paella.

TRINA. He says I'm vain, when that aftershave he has on would knock out a horse. He's not eighteen years old any more either.

STORMY. That young pup upset me, saying all we ever talk about is what's past and done with. Is it! Give me ten years and all them fields and woods down there will be gardens. Then there'll be a view worth looking at from here.

TRINA (*looking at* MYRA). Maybe he'd like to be married to her. A house like a slum because all she bothers to keep clean in it is her soul. Look at Jess, the heels out of his socks. (JESS *catches her eye and winks at her. Brightly.*) Hi.

JAN. Louise isn't sticking to her diet. That child's so overweight, and she doesn't seem to care.

JESS. I can see up Trina's leg. I'd love to get off my mark with a fast bit of stuff. Just the once, to think back on. I keep meaning to, only I never get round to it. Maybe when I get the new suit.

(*The guitar strikes a chord. The Lights come up as before.*)

STORMY. Well, are we right?

JAN. Are *you* all right?

STORMY (*mock-lecherously*). Will I prove it?

JAN. I think I fed him too much red meat.

STORMY. Very active woman, the wife. She was going to leave me once, but she couldn't fit it into her week.

RICHARD. Here we go, then. Lead on. (*They all rise and start to march off.*)

JESS. Quick march. Hup! Hup!

MYRA. Jess, not so fast.

TRINA. My heel is caught – wait!

STORMY. Stragglers will be shot out of hand. Step it out – lift them! (*To* MICHAEL *and* LOUISE) The pair of you, come on.(*The group marches off, talking as they go.* MICHAEL *and* LOU *watch them as they walk away.*)

MICHAEL. Do you want to go with them?

LOU. No. You can.

MICHAEL (*shaking his head*). I don't think your dad fancies me.

LOU. That's odd.

MICHAEL. Yeah.

LOU. He's usually a bad judge of character.

MICHAEL. (*laconically*) Oh, devastating.

LOU. Another Einstein!

MICHAEL. Who is?

LOU. Saying you know more than they do.

MICHAEL. I said I will, one day. Not now. I don't know anything yet.

LOU. You said. . .

MICHAEL. What?

LOU. Those marks.

MICHAEL. Ogam.

LOU. That they were fake.

MICHAEL. They are.

LOU. Einstein!

MICHAEL. Sure, and I can tell you that Dublin is there – (*pointing out front*) – and Wicklow is that way (*to his right*). And Robert Kennedy was killed three weeks ago, and the atomic weight of mercury is two hundred point sixty-one, and in case you want to propose to me, this year is a leap year. But that's not knowing: I took someone's word for it. I haven't found out one thing for myself yet.

LOU. All right: what colour's my hair?

MICHAEL. Fairish.

LOU (*triumphantly*). See? You know that my hair is. . .

MICHAEL. No, I don't. Someone told me that colour is called fairish.

LOU. Oh, get shredded.

MICHAEL (*professionally*). Now of course you will argue that every so-called fact must have a given hypothesis –

LOU. I'm not going to argue. Go to Trinity. Persecute them.

MICHAEL. I will. At least there'll be people there I can talk to, because at home it's useless. It's the modern generation of parents. They don't listen, they're out till all hours, they rush around in cars. If they see a Porsche that's doing ninety, they have to pass it, but they can't pass a pub that's standing perfectly still. I dunno, they're too young for their years, they're missing their adulthood.

LOU. Let them.

MICHAEL (*pointing*). I mean, look at them now.

LOU. Where?

MICHAEL. There, are you blind? They're out of sight. (LOU *turns away wearily*.) We sit here calmly, conserve energy. They go rushing over precipices like lemmings.

LOU. Because they're older than we are. They can't be sure they can rush until they try.

MICHAEL. I asked my dad a question yesterday – just so's he wouldn't feel out of things. I said 'Do you believe man is by nature a monogamous animal?' Did I get the courtesy of an answer? He looked at me as if I was a red infiltrator and he was John Wayne.

253

LOU. I may go to Trinity this year.

MICHAEL. Waste of time.

LOU. Thank you.

MICHAEL. For girls it is. Any girl. You do four years' hard slog, take your degree, then go and get married. It's like saving up to buy a Maserati when all you want is the ashtray.

LOU. You're nasty.

MICHAEL. I'm a realist, what's wrong with that? Time enough to be a romantic when I'm middle-aged.

LOU. And for your information, I don't intend to get married.

MICHAEL. That so?

LOU. Not for diamonds.

MICHAEL. It's just as well.

LOU. Boys bore me. What do you mean, it's just as well?

MICHAEL (*backing down*). Nothing.

LOU. I suppose you mean I'm not likely to be asked.

MICHAEL. No! All sorts get. . . (*He stops, aware that he has made matters worse.*)

LOU (*unrelenting*). Do they?

MICHAEL. I mean, when you see some of the gargoyles who. . . (*He stops again.*)

LOU. A girl doesn't have to be as thin as a rake, you know.

MICHAEL (*conciliatorily*). Sure.

LOU. Or dye her hair, or have eye-lashes you could whisk eggs with. Pointy bosoms, that's what men are supposed to be mad for, isn't it?

MICHAEL. Are there pointy ones?

LOU. Not half.

MICHAEL (*politely*). That's worth knowing.

LOU. Fiona Mulligan, she's in fifth year, hers are like daggers.

MICHAEL. Get away.

LOU. You'd cut yourself.

MICHAEL. Deary me.

LOU. I really do pity that sort of girl. All the time rushed off their feet, never get a minute's peace and quiet. And the sort of creepy-crawlies they always go out with. Ugh.

MICHAEL. I know, yes.

LOU. And of course they get married years too soon and live in the same house till doomsday. I'd hate that. No, when I look at them I'm honestly and truly glad I'm the way I am.

MICHAEL (*feigning innocence*). What way is that? (*She gives him a knowing and bitter smile.*) I've seen worse than you.

Real clock-stoppers. (*As her smile congeals*) What?

LOU (*shaking her head*). I'm just so thrilled I came out today.

MICHAEL (*uneasily*). So what are you going to do?

LOU. Go for a walk.

MICHAEL. After Trinity.

LOU (*with unfeigned intensity*). I'll tell you one thing: I won't stay here, not in this hole. I'll get a working scholarship and go abroad. Places like Israel and America and New Guinea. Northern Labrador, maybe.

MICHAEL. What's in Northern Labrador?

LOU. Do you know – well, I forgot; you don't know anything, do you? – that some Eskimo women kill their second-born on account of in the Arctic there are no vegetable foods and the mother has to nurse her first child until it's three years old? Helping those people, that would be wonderful.

MICHAEL. They're real primitive, right?

LOU. Some are.

MICHAEL. Yeah, you see photographs of them. All in furs. And the Eskimo women. . .

LOU. Poor things.

MICHAEL. They're really fat. (*Meaning it kindly.*) You'll look thin when you go there. (*She stares at him in dismay; tears begin.*) You've got your life all parcelled up, haven't you? I'd hate that: no adventure. Hey, you ever play rugby? (*Hastily*) I mean tennis. When you can't even blink an eye, and your heart wants to stop, because if the ball comes and you're some place else, that's it: goodbye, now. Only with life, there's so much of it, and you don't know which bit is yours. (*Nudging her*) So?

LOU. So what?

MICHAEL. So you grab. All of it. (*Miming elaborately; he catches and discards.*) Is this mine? No. Is this? Is this? Maybe this is. (*On impulse, he seizes her breast.*)

LOU. What are you doing?

MICHAEL. Ow! (*Feigning pain, he puts his fingers to his mouth.*)

LOU. Are you mad?

MICHAEL. Daggers.

LOU. You oughtn't to be allowed out.

MICHAEL. First time I ever did that.

LOU. And the last.

MICHAEL. God, it's enormous. (*As she looks at her bosom*) No. . . life. And on a day like this there's nothing you can't do. (*Shouting*) Not. . .one. . .damn. . .thing!

255

LOU. Except whisper.

MICHAEL. There isn't.

LOU. Let's walk down.

MICHAEL. Think of you in Labrador, eating dog-meat sandwiches and doing your D.B. degree in an igloo.

LOU. What's D.B.?

MICHAEL. Doctor of Blubber.

LOU. I'll get further than you will.

MICHAEL. You've made your choice. I can be a rally-driver, an artist, a leader of men.

LOU. *You?*

MICHAEL. I can work for my dad in the bookshop or dig sewers or push a pen or pull teeth. Anything! I can marry a nice homely girl who's a credit to me, or I can ruin myself over a real bitch, the kind that effs and blinds and wears black net –
(*He breaks off.*)

LOU. What?

MICHAEL (*almost slavering*). Oh, Jesus. . . black net stockings.

LOU (*contemptuously*). I'm going to catch up with them.

MICHAEL. One thing's sure, when it begins I'll be ready.

LOU. When it begins?

MICHAEL. Living. Race you to the pub.

LOU. It's too far.

MICHAEL. On your mark, get set. . .

LOU. That's not fair. Wait.

MICHAEL. Go! (*He starts to exit.*)

LOU (*calling after him*). I don't know the way. I'll get lost.
(MICHAEL *and* LOU *exit. The Lights change to indicate a lapse of hours: the sun's rays are now oblique.* RICHARD *and* JAN *appear over the crest.* JAN *stays on the summit.*)

JAN. We shouldn't have left them so far behind.

RICHARD. Where are you going?

JAN (*as if he should know better*). To where they can see at least one of us. (*Looking off*) He's sitting down.

RICHARD. Who?

JAN. Jess (*Waving*) Coo-ee! (*To* RICHARD) Is he tight?

RICHARD. Pissed.

JAN. Yes?

RICHARD. Three pints and he's anybody's.

JAN. How many do you need?

RICHARD. Pints or women?

JAN. I've heard stories.

256

RICHARD. Where?

JAN. The village.

RICHARD. About me?

JAN. And women.

RICHARD. Anybody I know?

JAN. Joan Armitage.

RICHARD. Who?

JAN. They say you and she. . .

RICHARD. Joan Armitage?

JAN. You do it awfully well.

RICHARD. What?

JAN. Innocence. Years of practice, I expect. (*Looking off*) They're heaving him up.

RICHARD. I've never even been. . .

JAN. No, he's down again. Poor Jess.

RICHARD. Not once.

JAN. My dear man, I couldn't care less.

RICHARD. Nor could I.

JAN. (*A blank smile*) Oh, good. The children seem to be squabbling again. What a waste of fine weather.

RICHARD. The village is a gossip factory, you know.

JAN (*in the voice she uses for small-talk*). Yes, it's the most flourishing of our cottage industries. I wish they wouldn't.

RICHARD. Gossip?

JAN. Squabble.

RICHARD (*coldly*). I think I'll lend them a hand with Jess.

JAN. You said in the pub you wanted to talk to me in private. What about?

RICHARD. Yes, I did.

JAN. Well?

RICHARD. About Tuesday. . .

JAN. I think we should scrub Tuesday.

RICHARD. So do I.

JAN. It's mutual, then? How super.

RICHARD. Yes, jolly hockey-sticks.

JAN (*with a gesture*). So off you go to the rescue.

RICHARD (*hesitating*). Purely out of interest. . .

JAN. What?

RICHARD. Why are *you* cancelling Tuesday?

JAN. Purely out of lack of interest. (RICHARD *is offended. He opens his mouth to speak; instead he makes what he hopes is an ironic bow and starts off.*) Face it: we didn't exactly hit it off.

257

RICHARD. We were too close to home.

JAN. Oh, come on.

RICHARD. (*stubbornly*) If we had met nearer to town. . .

JAN. You must be touched.

RICHARD. How?

JAN. Because of all women, you pick on me. I'm thirty-nine – as my husband keeps reminding me, in five years' time I'll be for- ty. I have a home to worry about, and a daughter who's a recluse at seventeen. I do so much committee work, there aren't enough days in the week, and I promise you, you'd find that cross sexier than I am. And still you want me to skulk around bars and restaurants and sit mooning with you in a car after the pubs close. No, you go and find some nice unhappy lady who needs that sort of thing. Hm?

RICHARD. I thought I'd found her.

JAN (*smiling*). Oh, no.

RICHARD. Foiled again.

JAN. Yes, you are.

RICHARD. I just cannot resist a posh accent.

JAN. Is that the attraction?

RICHARD. Blue-bloods. Women who ooze refinement.

JAN. Me?

RICHARD. Unflappable.

JAN. And that excites you?

RICHARD. It's what my son would call a turn-on. As if I'd come across a rare first edition.

JAN. You mean something to curl up in bed with?

RICHARD. Too risky. In bed I stick to book-of-the-month.

JAN. At least this explains Joan Armitage.

RICHARD. Does it?

JAN. She's awfully grand.

RICHARD. Yes, if she were a lesbian she'd be a thorough gentleman.

JAN. Another rejection? Oh, poor man. (*Looking off*) Good, they're coming. Now there's someone who adores you.

RICHARD. Trina?

JAN. Wives don't count. Myra.

RICHARD. She thinks I'm a nice man.

JAN. You and she meet secretly.

RICHARD. When?

JAN (*tapping her head*). In here.

RICHARD. It would have to be. The nearest Myra ever comes to making a date with someone is when she says 'We'll meet in heaven'.

JAN. Purely out of interest. . .

RICHARD. What?

JAN. Why did you want to cancel Tuesday? (RICHARD *grins*).

RICHARD. Purely out of. . .

JAN (*as a challenge*). You dare!

RICHARD. Your reason is as good as any. What was it you said? Skulking around bars. Childish.

JAN (*in her small-talk voice*). Have you skulked much?

RICHARD. Beginner's stuff – nursery slopes kind of thing. I mean, my skulk never got as far as the slalom class.

JAN. Slalom? I thought that was a Jewish good-bye.

RICHARD. Only if you fall into a crevasse. (*She giggles; we see the girl underneath*). It just isn't worth it. Mind you, if it was a question of a great volcanic all-devouring passion. . .

JAN. You'd run for your life.

RICHARD. You reckon?

JAN. A man who takes jolly good care to chase after the kind of women who won't have him? You'd run ten miles.

(STORMY *and* TRINA *enter. In the distance a church bell is heard. It rings for about a minute.*)

STORMY. I couldn't run ten feet. I'm bunched.

RICHARD (*wondering if they have overheard*). You got here!

STORMY. Thanks for giving us a hand with Jess the Mess.

RICHARD. I'd no idea he was that bad. Where is he?

(STORMY *gestures off.*)

TRINA. His legs went all rubbery.

STORMY. Yeah, he wasn't so much drunk as vulcanized. The fresh air does it every time. I always say, if you go into a pub, stay in it for the sake of sobriety.

TRINA (*looking off*). Now Myra is on the ground. No, she's only praying; it's the Angelus.

JAN (*looking at her watch*). Six o'clock?

RICHARD. Your wife and I have decided to break off our affair.

STORMY. That a fact?

(JAN, *caught off guard, attempts to play up.*)

JAN. Yes, before it starts.

STORMY. Pity. There goes our mixed foursome.

(TRINA *slides her arm through* STORMY'*s. While the gesture is meant to seem mock-amorous, the afternoon's drinking has made her mildly lustful.*)

259

TRINA. Sure we can play a singles.

RICHARD. Oh, do.

TRINA (*warmly*). Can't we, Blowy?

STORMY. Stormy.

JAN (*sotto voce*). Is she. . .

RICHARD. No, just tipsy.

TRINA. You don't mind us at all. We're having an intimate conversation. (*To* STORMY, *hazily*) What about?

STORMY. Indoor toilets.

TRINA (*squeezing his arm*). Yeah. (TRINA *looks at* STORMY *with intensity. He either does not notice her unwavering stare or pretends not to.*)

STORMY. I was saying. I foresee the day when every home will have a minimum of three.

TRINA. That right?

STORMY. The ivy-coloured privy in the yard may have been good enough for our parents. These days people want a plurality of toilets to make up for their years of deprivation. Have you me?

TRINA. I have you.

STORMY. Or better still, invest in vitreous china. (*Including* RICHARD) Sanitation is a fact of life. If I had capital I'd sink everything I had in toilets.

TRINA. No flies on you.

STORMY (*to* RICHARD). It's worth a flutter.

TRINA. Talk to me. (*As* RICHARD *looks at her*) Is something up with you?

RICHARD. No, love.

TRINA (*antagonistic*). Love!

RICHARD (*to* JAN). Have you a busy week ahead?

TRINA (*in a mutter, mimicking*). Have you a busy week ahead?

JAN. Only frantic.

RICHARD. Committee work?

JAN. There's no end to it.

TRINA. I never got my tan. (*Lifting her skirt.*) Did I, Windy?

STORMY (*squirting skywards*). You won't get one now.

TRINA. I think maybe I have a little bit of one.

STORMY. Sun is too low.

TRINA. Would you say I have a bit of one?

STORMY (*absently*). What?

RICHARD (*snarling*). For Chrissakes, Windy, tell her she has a bit of one!

JAN. Now, now.

STORMY. Yeah, all she asked was. . .

TRINA. 'S all right. I don't mind him.

JAN. Hear, hear.

TRINA (*very grandly*). I don't give a shite.

STORMY. That's a good girl. (JAN *holds up a finger, forbidding* RICHARD *to speak*.) (*Chattily*) The haze is lifting. It's not often in this country our summer happens on a Sunday, what? (*To* TRINA) I say it's great weather for laying a cement path, as long as you damp it well.

TRINA. Not even allowed to flirt.

STORMY. 'Cause if you don't, it'll crack, as sure as shootin'.

TRINA. Like living with Hitler.

STORMY (*gently*). Ah, shush.

TRINA. A squeeze of the hand to let you know you're not dead – no harm in that. A bit of messing on a summer's day. Yeah? 'S nice. Different if it wasn't open and above board.

RICHARD. No one is. . .

TRINA. Old jealous-boots. You'd think I went in for hole-and-corner carryings-on like – like some.

STORMY. Now you're talking, Trina. Down in the town – Jasus, it's like the Roman empire: they're all at it. You'd think it was Judgement Day and the archangel had stood up and said: 'Good news, ladies and gentlemen – adultery doesn't count'.

TRINA. He's never done belittling me.

RICHARD. Belittling?

STORMY. Compared to them we're saintly.

RICHARD (*to* JAN). Show her a newspaper and all she reads is 'Mutt and Jeff' and 'The Wizard of Id.'

JAN. Oh, stop it.

STORMY. Playing with fire. What gets into people?

(JESS *enters,* MYRA *by his side. He is boisterous and affectionate, waving his arms.*)

JESS (*singing*).
>   'Those – were – the days, my friend,
>   We thought they'd never end. . .'

STORMY. Jess, me oul' flower!

JAN (*to* MYRA). Is he all right?

MYRA. I laddered a stocking saying the Angelus.

JESS. The angel of the Lord declared unto Myra. No better woman!

RICHARD. Are you well?

JESS. I'm in great form. Treen, come here to me. (*He embraces her clumsily.*)

261

TRINA. He was at me again.

JESS. I'd like to be at you, Treen — true as God.

MYRA. I love him when he jokes.

TRINA. Always when I'm enjoying myself.

JAN (*to* RICHARD). Yes?

JESS. Ah, life's too short. Enjoy it like I do.

TRINA (*bad-temperedly*). Jess, leave off! (*She breaks away from him, causing him to stagger. He grins fixedly to hide his bruised feelings. She smoothes her dress and hair.*)

JESS. I like to annoy her.

MYRA. Richard wouldn't upset Trina.

TRINA (*bridling*). You're the expert?

STORMY. She was saying about the goings-on down in the town. Ordinary lads — your Joe Soap that maybe grew up same as you did, in a house where he had to walk on the joists. Every second one of them at it like a fiddler's elbow.

MYRA. At what?

JESS. Ridin', what else.

MYRA. No.

STORMY. Look. (*On his fingers*) George Canaan going with Tim Corboy's wife. Dave Giffney and Finnuala-butter-wouldn't-bloody-melt-McArdle. Des Luby who's in church furnishings, at it as if there was no tomorrow with Chad Whelan's missus. . .

JAN. Stop gossiping.

STORMY. And what about your one with the teeth and the gold-embossed accent — Joan Armitage? If she moves and if it's male, she's under it. (RICHARD *stares at* STORMY. JAN *begins to laugh.* JESS *busily takes notes on the back of a cigarette packet.*) You'd want to have leprosy with complications before that one'd say no to you. (*To* JAN) You may laugh, but it'd take an IBM machine to keep up with them.

MYRA (*serenely*). One day you'll get sense, boy.

STORMY. Think so?

JESS. How do you spell Armit—

STORMY. What?

JESS (*as they look at him*). Nothing.

MYRA. It's play-acting, and sure what harm? God love them, they think they're great. It's like the children out on the road playing cowboys, with the badges on them and the toy guns.

STORMY (*sourly*). Yeah — bang, bang.

MYRA. Dressing up to be what they're not — all excited. And even if it was true, what you say they're doing, aren't we all children of Eve? They'll get sense.

STORMY (*a great arm-flapping gesture of resignation*). I give up.

RICHARD. There's a man called Joe Pettifer . . .

STORMY. He's a dipso.

RICHARD. He goes into Hogan's and stays clear of his wife. Her pub is the Mariner's. Pauline. She has a three-star rating in the local graffiti. Most nights at closing time some kind man gives her a lift home by way of a back road or a building site. God alone knows why she does it, maybe her looks went . . .

JAN. Does he know?

RICHARD. He weeps, he slobbers. He confides in total strangers, half of whom gallop straight down to the Mariner's. I used to think, if I were that man I'd walk into the sea. The kids have left home, he has nothing. One day Trina and I went to a wedding . . .

(MICHAEL *and* LOU *enter.*)

MICHAEL. Hi.

LOU. We came back by the . . .

(RICHARD *holds up a hand: a salutation and to get attention.*)

RICHARD. There was dancing afterwards. Ragtime. And there was Joe Pettifer playing a bloody banjo.

TRINA (*remembering*). Him? Was that . . .

RICHARD. Sweat pouring off him. And he was good: they cheered. Happiest man in the room . . . (*He pauses.* MICHAEL *strums a chord.*)

STORMY. Can you play that?

MICHAEL. Wish I could. It's ornamental.

TRINA. We ought all to go to a dance, the six of us. That's my idea of an evening. (*Indicating* RICHARD) He's hopeless. But Jess always asks me up.

JAN (*loftily*). Not any more.

(TRINA *makes a face at the others as if to say 'What's biting him?'*)

MYRA. We'll have to make a move soon. I want to get him to bed before the children come home from their granny's.

JESS. Bed?

MYRA. I'll tell them he has a toothache.

JESS. I've no teeth.

MYRA. Or a cold. We don't want them to see you.

JESS. Hide their glasses. (*To the others*) Four children – sixteen

263

eyes between them. Our youngest looks like Ben Turpin.

MYRA. Who?'

JAN. Myra, why don't I take our car, and Terry can drive you and Jess home in yours?

JESS. I can drive; no better man.

MYRA. Do you hear him? He'd give St Christopher a nervous breakdown.

STORMY. We'll stop by for a jar at our place.

MYRA. No – straight home.

RICHARD. Same here. Early start in the morning.

TRINA (*speaking from the side of her mouth*). I want to see their house.

RICHARD. I want to see ours. (RICHARD *crosses to* JESS *and speaks to him, a hand on his shoulder.* JESS *shakes his head stubbornly.*)

STORMY (*during the above*). Five past six – the day's only started.

JAN. Don't oblige them. (*She folds up a stool.*)

STORMY. One drink won't kill you.

TRINA. It'd kill him to be sociable. (*She starts to clear the picnic things.*)

RICHARD. Make it up with her.

JESS. I'm not dirt.

RICHARD. I know.

JESS. She made little of me.

RICHARD. She's squiffed.

MYRA. Jess. . .

JESS (*peering at* TRINA). She's never!

RICHARD. She's flying.

MYRA. We're going home.

RICHARD. So be big.

JESS (*solemnly*). Them that can hold their gargle make allowances for them that can't. Trina. . .

RICHARD. Attaboy.

(JESS *leads him over to* TRINA *and puts an arm about the shoulders of each*).

JESS. No hard feeling.

TRINA (*friendly, not knowing what he refers to*). Not a bit of it.

JESS. You're a livin' doll.

TRINA. Am I? Aw!

JESS. And you offended me, but I forgive you.

TRINA. Good.

JESS. 'Cause Richard has appraised me of your condition.
(TRINA's *smile fades.*)

RICHARD. Thanks, Jess!

JESS (*hugging him*). Me old comrade. Since we were that high.

RICHARD. Right.

JESS. The time we robbed old Threadgold's orchard. (*Indicating* JAN) And her da chased us.

RICHARD. Whose da?

JESS. Her da. Mick Goggins – the rozzer, the policeman. That lived in the Cottages.

RICHARD. (*To* Jan) You're one of the Gogginses?

JAN. I was.

RICHARD. From the Cottages?

JAN. What of it?

RICHARD. Where'd you get that accent?

JAN (*proudly*). Hard work!

RICHARD. Well, I'm. . .

JESS (*plucking at his sleeve*). Hey, hey. . .

JAN. You are, rather, aren't you? (*She skips away from him, humming 'The Rain in Spain'.*)

JESS. I say, I had a smashing day.

STORMY. We all had.

MYRA. (*To* JESS) No speechifying, now.

JESS. And I haven't a tosser. Do you know what that louser I work for did last week? Put me on straight commission. Times, he says to me, are hard. A man that can buy his wife a shagging Volvo for a run-around, telling me that times are hard! Catch him getting snotty letters from the nuns for school fees.

MYRA (*smiling*). Oh, you're in a bad way.

JESS. I am. I could pass through the eye of a needle with me arms extended. And you know what? . . . bugger it! I have me mates, and we still have the long evenings.

MYRA. Home now. Where's your jacket?

STORMY. I see it. (*He moves to fetch it.*)

JESS. We'll pull the divil be the tail somehow.

MYRA (*tidying his hair*). You have it pulled out of him. If you lowered less drink into you . . .
(STORMY *fumbles with* JESS's *jacket.*)

JESS. Yeah, yeah.

MYRA. The sun splitting the heavens, and us stuck in a pub.

JESS. Blame me! He drags us in and I get the . . . (*he stops, looking at* STORMY) What are you doing in my pocket?

STORMY. Nothing.

JESS. Gimme that.

STORMY. I wasn't in your . . .

JESS (*snatching the jacket*). You need watching, mate.

MYRA. Nobody was next or near your . . .

JESS. I had a few jars, but I'm not ossified. (*He pulls a dirty hand-kerchief from the jacket pocket*.) Here – here, all I've got.

RICHARD. Easy . . .

JESS. Do you want it? Have it.

(STORMY, *fists clenched, is holding his temper in check*.)

TRINA. Ah, Jess.

JESS. It's not safe to go out any more. Take it. Here. (*He tosses the handkerchief at* STORMY's *feet and turns his back on him*.)

STORMY. You pick that up. (*Dangerously*) Jess . . .

JAN. That's quite enough.

STORMY. No one is going to call me a . . .

JAN. The word wasn't said – don't you say it.

STORMY. He accused . . .

JAN. Today is not going to end with a row.

STORMY (*pointing*). That . . .

JAN (*furiously*). Will you shut up! (JAN *glares* STORMY *into silence, then bends, picks up the handkerchief and gives it to* MYRA.)

MYRA. It needs ironing.

JAN. Myra and Jess have to go home now. So do we.

STORMY. He can drive himself, then.

JESS. You watch me.

MYRA. No . . .

JESS. Downhill all the way, do it in neutral.

STORMY (*with a mirthless laugh*). Jasus.

JAN (*to* MYRA). Don't mature men make your toes curl?

MYRA (*earnestly*). Oh, yeah. 'Bye, Richard, we had a great time.

RICHARD. Safe home, Myra.

TRINA. 'Bye.

MYRA. (*To* JAN) It was the drink talking, don't mind him. (*To* LOUISE *and* MICHAEL) God bless, now.

LOU. 'Bye.

MICHAEL. Yeah, see you.⎱ (*Speaking together*)

STORMY. Mind yourself.

JESS. (*To* RICHARD) It was a . . .

RICHARD. A what?

JESS. A day you could frame. Give us a buzz. (*To* STORMY) All the best, so. (STORMY *looks away*.) Benny the Dip

266

is not talking to me. (STORMY, *still angry, finds himself trying not to laugh. He keeps his back to* JESS.) Aw, he's crying.

JAN (*mock-angrily, pointing off*). Jess, go home.

MYRA (*waiting for him*). Jess . . .

JESS. Have you got me hanky?

MYRA. Yes!

JESS. Another robbery thwarted! (STORMY *swings around.*) (*Singing*)
'Those were the days, my friend,
We thought they'd never end...'
(JESS *and* MYRA *go out of sight.*)

STORMY. Messer.

RICHARD. How much did you put in his pocket?

STORMY (*sheepishly*). Didn't get the chance. (*He unclenches his fist to reveal two crumpled pound notes.*)

JAN. Is that what the . . .

STORMY. Do a fellow a favour!

TRINA. Nice man.

STORMY. Now I'm Benny the Dip.

RICHARD. Serve you right.

TRINA. It's more than you'd do.

JAN. Terry, don't let him drive, go after him. (STORMY *is about to protest.*) Yes, you will. Louise and I will follow you.

STORMY. (*To* RICHARD) You'll notice I know better than to argue. I'm glad we got together. We ought to make a thing of it. (JAN *pushes* STORMY.)

JAN. Yes, come and have dinner.

RICHARD. Love to.

STORMY. (*To* JAN) You fix it.

JAN (*pushing him*). Yes – now hurry.

STORMY. I'm saving his life, and you know the thanks I'll get? By tomorrow he'll have it all around the town that I'm queer for dirty handkerchiefs. (STORMY *waves to them and goes.*)

TRINA. He's gorgeous.

JAN. Yes?

TRINA. So considerate.

JAN. When the humour takes him. I like this spot; we ought to come back, it's unspoiled. (*To* LOU *and* MICHAEL) Have a nice day, you two?

LOU. Super.

MICHAEL. Yeah.

267

JAN. Their eloquence is positively Shakespearian. Damn.

TRINA. What?

JAN. My considerate husband has gone off with the car keys. Louise, would you . . .?

(LOU *runs off. We hear her calling* 'Dad. . . the keys!' JAN *goes to the summit and watches her.*)

RICHARD. (*To* TRINA) You have a good day? (*She shrugs and starts clearing up again.*) No?

TRINA. You've been at me since we got up this morning. I can't do nothing right anymore.

RICHARD. Anything right.

TRINA. Christ almighty.

RICHARD (*martyred*). Sorry . . .

TRINA. I have to take every word out of my mouth and look at it.

RICHARD. Don't start a . . .

TRINA. Then telling Jess I was drunk.

RICHARD. You were mauling Stormy.

TRINA (*raising her voice*). Mauling?

(JAN *probably hears the following, but gives no sign.*)

RICHARD. Shh . . .

TRINA. A bit of affection.

RICHARD. Shout, why don't you?

TRINA. More than I get from you.

RICHARD. Yes, all right.

TRINA (*lowering her voice*). 'Act your age. Read this book. Don't wear that dress. Take up something, join something, do something.'

JAN (*looking off*). She's got the keys. Good girl!

TRINA. You'd like me to rot, that's what'd please you, isn't it?

RICHARD. Of course it would.

TRINA. To be like them, puffing themselves up with their sales-of-work and their meetings, making a noise to cod themselves that they're not dead and done for. Not me, no damn fear.

(LOU *enters with the keys.*)

JAN. Bless you, you're a jewel. (*To the others*) Shall we stroll down together?

RICHARD. Let's. (*To* TRINA, *a peace offering*) We could have dinner out this evening. If you like. At the Castle.

TRINA. I'm not mad keen.

RICHARD. It would save you from cooking.

TRINA. No, I don't want to.

JAN. Yes, about dinner — when can you come to us?

RICHARD. You say.

JAN. Tuesday? No, wait. (*Looking at him*) No, I'm meeting a girl friend on Tuesday, in town. So that's out.

RICHARD (*after a pause*). I see.

JAN. Of course I could cancel it.

RICHARD. Don't. I have to be somewhere on Tuesday as well. A late night.

JAN. Mine won't be. Home by eleven. (*Including* TRINA) We're having people over on Friday. Come then.

TRINA. That'd be great.

JAN. Eight for eight-thirty. Well, then . . . !

(TRINA, JAN *and* RICHARD *start up the slope*.)

TRINA. Richard . . .

JAN. Come along, young 'uns.

TRINA. I can't go into the Castle like this. I'm not dressed.

RICHARD. We'll go home first.

TRINA. I can wear my long black.

RICHARD. Sure.

TRINA. With the see-through top.

RICHARD. What else!

(TRINA *is childishly pleased. She takes* RICHARD's *arm as they start off*.)

JAN (*favouring* TRINA). I want to pick your brains. The Borough Council wants to take down a Victorian lamp-post in Harbour Road. It's of historical value, so of course we're going to stop them. Question is: how? Now, if we got up a petition, could I rope you in to . . .

(JAN, RICHARD *and* TRINA *exit. The attitude of* MICHAEL *and* LOU *during the following is of affectionate parents*.)

LOU. Do you think they enjoyed themselves?

MICHAEL. I'd say it did them good.

LOU. It makes a change.

MICHAEL. Mine had a row. (*He collects up the stools*.)

LOU. Oh. (*In the sense of 'What a shame!'*)

MICHAEL. Nothing drastic.

LOU. That's 'cause they got too much sun.

MICHAEL. Yeah?

LOU. It makes them bilious.

MICHAEL. How?

LOU. Too much of it.

MICHAEL. Queer. I mean, it's the smallest star known to man. It's big, but its density is only one-point-four-one times that of

water. You wouldn't think it could upset them, would you?
LOU. No.
MICHAEL. And its light takes four whole minutes to get here.
LOU. Yeah. . . it's a long way to come, just to start a row.
    (MICHAEL *strums a chord.* MICHAEL *and* LOU *go. Immediately, the stage fills with blinding light, followed by a Blackout, as* –

the CURTAIN *falls.*)

ACT TWO

The same. Six years later, August 1974.

*The Celtic cross is gone; in its place is a notice board. The trees —
if any were visible previously — have been chopped down. There
is a suggestion that the area is being cleared for 'development'. The
picnic area is substantially as it was, but we sense an encroachment;
soon it will be eaten up. The sunlight has a harshness which suggests a chill in the air.*
   *A young woman walks on and takes off her sunglasses to read
the notice board. It takes us a moment to recognise* LOU, *who is
now slim and self-possessed. After a moment,* STORMY *and* JAN
enter. He has put on weight and wears an expensive mohair suit.
JAN'*s clothes echo the rise in his fortunes, but now there are lines
of stress in her face that were not there previously.* STORMY *carries
a picnic hamper, a rug and an expensive cassette player. He stares
at the view.*

STORMY. This is not the place.

JAN. Why isn't it?

STORMY. Where's all the fields?

JAN (*looking front*). Someone's been busy.

STORMY. And I say we took the wrong turn.

JAN. You're so pig-headed . . .

STORMY. Straight on at Stepaside, I said, but no, she knew the
    way. Why did I listen?

JAN. You listened, my pet, because you hoped I was wrong, and
    you wanted to be —

LOU. There used to be a Celtic cross.

STORMY. Good girl. (*To* JAN, *crowing*) The cross, where's the
    cross?

LOU (*reading*). 'St Eanna's Cross, which stood on this spot, has
    been removed to the National Museum of Ireland.'

STORMY. It's been what? (*He reads the notice.*)

JAN. You see? I said this was —

STORMY. Yes, grand, full marks.

JAN. But no, 'Straight on at Stepaside.'

STORMY. Christ, I said I was wrong, you don't have to make your dinner and tea out of it. (*He looks, blinking, at the view.*) There's nothing left.

LOU. It's awful.

STORMY. Those are Bellavista Homes. I'd know them a mile off. How did the buggers get permission?

LOU. For what?

STORMY. To build. Down there used to be country.

LOU. Not now.

STORMY. Even this place is ear-marked – the cross's gone, national monument.

JAN. Who cares?

STORMY. You mean you don't?

JAN. I mean no one does.

STORMY. God almighty, that's a million quid's worth of land. Someone got his palm well-greased.

JAN. You missed the bus then, didn't you?

STORMY. You never saw me grease a palm.

JAN. No?

STORMY. When did I?

JAN. The houses at Churchtown.

STORMY. That was a favour, I didn't pay.

JAN (*drily*). Oh?

STORMY. Back-scratching's one thing. Paying money's corruption.

LOU. Two of them have swimming pools.

STORMY. In this climate? Snob jobs.

JAN. A bit out of your class.

STORMY (*coldly*). Get off my back.

JAN. Gladly.

STORMY. You know bugger all. (*Pointing*) It's them – your so-called executive hilltop houses, built by chancers and paid for by runners-in, bastards, and every one of them called Brendan or shaggin' Declan – that land your independent builder in Stubb's Gazette. And before you turn your nose up at Corporation houses, they're what paid for the clothes on your back and the bits of Georgian silver you're so fond of. No one is asking you to live there.

LOU (*lightly*). Bicker, bicker.

STORMY. Not that it'd be a come-down for you after the Cottages.

JAN. Thank you.

272

STORMY. Tit for tat.

JAN. Yes, well done.

STORMY. That house there isn't finished yet. I'm going down for a squint inside it.

JAN. Go.

LOU (*looking off*). Here's someone.

JAN. Who?

LOU. The Halveys, I think. There's three of them.

STORMY (*turning back*). Ah, the bold Richard. Good.

JAN. Lick his boots, why don't you?

STORMY. How?

JAN. Do you have to be at their beck and call? We've waited for them; now let them wait for us. (*Starting off*) Well, are we going to look at that house or aren't we?

STORMY. There's a wasp in you today.

JAN. I'm not going to sit and be trampled on. (*She goes.*)

STORMY. No one is –

LOU. I'll hang on.

STORMY. Yeah, say hello. And mind this stuff. (*Following* JAN) What the hell's up with you?

(LOU *looks up at the sun and hugs her arm as if chilled.* MICHAEL *appears. He is dressed as befits a trend-conscious young man on a picnic: suit of suede 'denims', perhaps. He carries a picnic hamper.*)

LOU. Hello.

MICHAEL. Afternoon. (*He makes to pass her.*)

LOU. Lovely day, isn't it?

(*He gives her an appraising look.*)

MICHAEL. Not bad. Cold for August.

LOU. But getting warmer. (*Her look is deliberately provocative. He's unable to cope and looks elsewhere, catching sight of* STORMY *and* JAN.) Look . . . I'm –

MICHAEL. Mr Loftus! Hello.

(*He waves and goes off with the hamper.* LOU *is immensely pleased with herself. She whirls around, crowing with delight.* RICHARD *and* TRINA *appear. There is no obvious change in him, but she has lost her previous petulance. Her clothes – perhaps an attractive trousers suit – are no longer too young for her.* RICHARD *carries two camp-stools,* TRINA *a freezer bag, cushion and rug.*)

RICHARD. I don't believe it. . . Louise!

LOU. Hi!

273

TRINA. Doesn't she look fab?

RICHARD. The word is 'blooming'.

LOU. No, the word is not. It makes me feel like a house plant.

RICHARD (*kissing her*). Here. Prerogative of age.

TRINA (*laughing*). Any excuse.

LOU. Trina . . . you look *younger*.

TRINA. Sure. Than your granny.

RICHARD. No one else here?

LOU. Down there. They went to look at one of the houses. Isn't it frightful?

RICHARD (*now noticing*). Yes. Yes, it is.

LOU. Ugh.

RICHARD. And not one of them Stormy's. He missed the bus.

LOU. That's what Mum says.

RICHARD. I know. (*Then*) Does she?

TRINA. Richard . . .

RICHARD. Right here.

TRINA. Look at all the lovely houses.

RICHARD (*a wink at* LOU). Breathtaking.

TRINA (*taking his arm*). Well, they are.

RICHARD. (*To* LOU) You home for long?

LOU. Just the weekend.

RICHARD. So how are things in foreign parts?

LOU. Oh, Cork doesn't change.

RICHARD. Fine city.

TRINA. We haven't seen you since . . .

LOU. The wedding.

RICHARD. Was it?

LOU (*brightly*). Black Saturday.

TRINA. And how is . . . (*Forgetting.*)

LOU. Pearse?

TRINA. Pearse!

LOU. Fine, thanks, sends his love.

TRINA. He's not with you? Say he is.

LOU. He wanted to, but if he doesn't work weekends this month there'll be no Costa del Wherever next month.

TRINA. Aw.

LOU. And of course there'll be fat chance of getting away in a year's time, what with a newborn bawling its head off. (*Giggling*) I must tell you . . .

TRINA. What?

LOU. Michael . . .

RICHARD. Our Michael? Where is he?

LOU. He walked straight past me.

TRINA. He never.

LOU. Said wasn't it cold for August, gave me a sexy look and – (MICHAEL *enters with the hamper. He makes an elaborate gesture of apology.*)

RICHARD. You're a right nit.

MICHAEL. It's been five years, do you mind?

LOU. Six.

MICHAEL. (*To* RICHARD) You've seen her since then.

RICHARD. When did the penny drop?

MICHAEL (*indicating off*). They told me. (*To* LOU) Sorry.

LOU. I'm thrilled.

MICHAEL. And I'm thrilled that you're thrilled. Except that where the sexy looks came into it, I was not the one who said (*grossly overdoing it*) 'But getting warmer!'

LOU. And you went crimson.

MICHAEL. Liar.

TRINA. Do you remember that day, Michael?

MICHAEL. When?

TRINA. Here. (*To* RICHARD) Hadn't we a great time?

RICHARD. It was pleasant . . .

TRINA (*fondly*). Head like a sieve. All of us as happy as Larry. Except poor Jess got this (*touching her chest*) upset. Bilious, like.

LOU. It wasn't Jess, Trina, it was –

TRINA. The fright he gave us. I don't forget one detail. (*To* RICHARD) You had to drive him home.

RICHARD. No, no, that was –

TRINA. Yes, you did. God, wasn't I there? The good old days.

LOU. No, it was –

RICHARD. Don't argue, she was there.

MICHAEL. You live in Cork?

TRINA. Happy as Larry.

LOU. Crosshaven. My . . . ah, Pearse is with the refinery at Whitegate.

MICHAEL. That's in . . . Northern Labrador?

LOU. You brat, you remember!

RICHARD. What's in Labrador?

MICHAEL. She isn't.

LOU. I was seventeen. (*Primly*) If everyone went where they'd set their hearts on going when they were fat and foolish –

MICHAEL. Then Ireland would be full of Eskimos.

275

(LOU *makes a face at him.*)

TRINA. Michael is a – (*The word escapes her.*)

RICHARD. Bio . . .

TRINA. Bio-chemist.

LOU. Not really? From know-nothing to know-all.

TRINA (*laughing*). Oh. . . !

MICHAEL. The Cork air is sharp.

RICHARD (*to* LOU). Do you like Cork?

LOU. I wish I could get home oftener. That way you don't notice
the changes. The bad ones. Do you think Mummy looks well?

TRINA. Who . . . Jan?

RICHARD. The thing is, Louise. . .

TRINA. We . . . ah . . .

RICHARD. We haven't seen them in –

TRINA. Haven't laid eyes on them –

RICHARD. . . .in a month.

TRINA. More. Nearer two.

RICHARD. Haven't had time.

TRINA (*about to argue*). Now. . .

RICHARD. Haven't.

TRINA (*mildly*). He doesn't go to the Druids any more on a Sunday. Says he's tired of it, wants a change. The times Jan and Stormy ask us out, it's yes at first and then no, he has work to do.

LOU. I'm sure he has.

MICHAEL. You *can* go off people. *I* do.

RICHARD. I went off no one. If I didn't have your mother's books
to keep, as well as my own. . .

TRINA. That excuse!

RICHARD (*to* MICHAEL). *You* may go off people; I do not.

TRINA (*amiably*). Now he blames me. Who was it bully-ragged me
into finding an interest?

RICHARD. I'm not disputing –

TRINA. Calling me a . . . a cabbage. Yes, you did. Whose idea was
'Treenager?'

LOU. Was what?

TRINA. That's the name of it. The shop.

RICHARD. Boutique.

TRINA. Whatever. 'Treen' for Trina – and then sort of like
'Teenager'. You come in tomorrow, Louise; I have a jersey
dress for you in Italian loose-knit will have the Corkmen's eyes
out on sticks. (*To* RICHARD, *soberly*) No, Stormy is fond of
you, and you're not a good friend to him.

276

RICHARD. I'll make amends.

TRINA. Do.

RICHARD. Give him a French kiss.

TRINA. Shut your mouth.

MICHAEL. Funny sort of French kiss that'll be.

TRINA. Oh, like father, like. . . Louise, don't laugh at them.

LOU. I'm not. I was picturing myself in an Italian loose-knit a few months from now.

TRINA. Won't it keep for after. You aren't going to be expecting for twelve months out of every year, surely to God, like – Myra, hello!

(MYRA *enters, followed by* JESS, *who instead of a picnic hamper carries a cheap papier-mâché attache case. She has happily embraced middle age; there are streaks of grey in her hair and her figure has thickened.* JESS *is a bit older, a bit scruffier; his mind seems to be focussed on something within himself.*)

MYRA (*catching her breath*). Woo! Thanks be to God, we got here.

RICHARD. The belle of the ball, let the good times roll!

MYRA (*looking around*). Jess?

JESS. I'm here. (*To the others*) How are yous?

MYRA. Hello. . . Richard . . . Trina . . . and Mich – (*Seeing* LOU, *she breaks off. Emotional*) Ah, and Louise!

LOU. How are you, Myra?

MYRA. Such great news.

LOU. Oh, you heard?

MYRA. Louise that was only a child. Jess . . . Jess, look at her.

LOU. Don't tell me it shows.

MYRA (*comforting*). Now have patience. You'll be out like a house in no time.

TRINA. Won't that be worth waiting for? (RICHARD *nudges her; she slumps against him.*)

LOU (*straight faced*). I can't wait.

MYRA. When's it due?

LOU. Early Feb.

MYRA. Winter – mind its chest.

LOU. I will.

MYRA. Have you morning sickness?

TRINA. My-ra!

MYRA. What?

TRINA. Don't talk shop.

LOU. And how's Jess?

277

JESS. Smashin'.

MICHAEL. You look great.

RICHARD. He *is* great.

MYRA. He's to mind himself.

JESS. I am.

MYRA. No catching colds.

JESS. It's August.

MYRA. Summer is treacherous. And no worrying.

JESS (*to* RICHARD). I've had a clean bill since las –

MYRA. It can come back.

RICHARD. Not a chance.

MYRA. It can, if he worries.

JESS. Then stop worrying me. (*To* RICHARD, *forcing a grin*) Bloody stupid thing to get at my age.

RICHARD. Who's 'La Traviata' now?

JESS (*not rising to the joke*). Yeah.

RICHARD. Have you noticed the new scenery?

JESS (*not looking*). Nice.

MYRA (*mainly to* LOU). We all had to go for X-rays. I couldn't credit it, I mean, you do your best. You toil and you moil and you go without. And then you have a thing like that in the family.

RICHARD. Myra, come out of the dark ages.

MYRA. When I heard that word. . . !

RICHARD. Probably you'll regard this as heresy, but a spot on the lung is now considered respectable. You carry on as if it were V.D. he had.

JESS. No such bloody luck.

(MYRA *looks sullenly at* RICHARD.)

MICHAEL. Myra, it's a bacillus, right?

MYRA. I suppose so.

MICHAEL. A bacterium called the tubercle bacillus. Yes?

MYRA. Yes.

MICHAEL. Good.

MYRA. Well, he didn't get it in our house.

(MICHAEL *gives up*.)

JESS (*suddenly*). I heard a riddle.

RICHARD. Tell us.

JESS. It's a good one.

(LOU *has espied a medal which* MYRA *wears around her neck on a chain*.)

LOU. Myra, that's gorgeous.

278

MYRA. It's the Blessed Virgin.

LOU. It's beautiful.

MYRA. I've had it these many years. Louise, if you're that taken with it –

JESS. I said, I heard a riddle.

MYRA. We're listening, pet.

JESS. You won't guess it.

LOU (*impatient*). Oh, Jess.

JESS. Not in a fit.

RICHARD. For God's sake, tell it.

JESS. Right. Are yous ready? (RICHARD *groans.* TRINA *shushes him.*) What do you call an uncircumcised Jewish child?

MYRA (*after a moment's pause*). A girl? (JESS *looks at her, his face thunderous. Innocent*) Is it?

RICHARD. Hey, not bad. Where'd you hear that?

JESS. A priest told me.

MYRA (*now laughing*). Oh, it's very funny.

LOU (*pointing*). Hey, I know those people.

TRINA. Who?

(STORMY *and* JAN *appear.*)

STORMY. The meeting will now come to order.

TRINA. Well, at long last. The dead arose!

STORMY. How are you, luscious?

MYRA. Hello, Jan.

JAN. Myra, don't you look summery. Hello, Michael.

MICHAEL. Hi.

JAN (*to* RICHARD, *a too bright smile*). How are you?

RICHARD. Hello.

JAN. And Jess!

STORMY. And fresh and well he's looking. (*He kneels before* JESS *and sings:* 'Your tiny hand is frozen. Let me warm it into li-ife!'

JESS (*retrieving his hand*). Bugger off.

STORMY (*to* RICHARD). And where in flames have you been?

RICHARD. Around.

STORMY. Well, we're black out with you. (*To* JAN) Aren't we?

JAN. Completely.

RICHARD. No reprieve?

JAN. None.

STORMY. That's your hash cooked. Once herself puts the knife in. . .

TRINA. Blame him.

JAN. We do. (*Ignoring* RICHARD) How's the boutique?

279

TRINA. Mmm . . . wait till you see our new Autumn range. We're showing it next month in Jury's.

JAN. Aren't you grand!

TRINA. Not at all: the only people not exhibiting are the pawn shops. (*In a stage whisper*) But I'm doing better than he is.

JAN (*politely*). Yes?

STORMY (*to* RICHARD). Are you raging?

RICHARD. Livid.

MYRA. Sure isn't it in the family?

TRINA. Oh, no, it is not. (*A catch phrase*) What's his is mine, and what's mine's my own.

RICHARD. Don't think she doesn't mean it.

JAN. I'd think ill of her if she didn't (*Turning to* MYRA) Are the children well?

MYRA. Grand, the whole six of them. And I have news.

TRINA. God, Myra, not again!

MYRA. Ah, wait. Noreen is getting married after Christmas.

JAN. Is she?

MYRA. She'll be the first to leave us. Well, we did our *best*. We made sacrifices for them, and they'll do the same for theirs.

JESS. And so on and so on.

MYRA. Please God.

JESS. Like a recurring decimal.

MYRA. A what?

JESS. Doesn't it ever end? Where's the pay-off?

MYRA. He's very morose.

STORMY. He's hungry. We're famished.

RICHARD. We can't eat here.

STORMY. Why can't we?

RICHARD. Look at it. By the time we're finished someone will have built a house around us.

MICHAEL. No chance, it's Sunday.

LOU. Don't say we're going to have to go tearing off into Wicklow.

STORMY (*to* JAN). What do you think?

JAN. Well, if it means we've got to drag this stuff all the way back to the cars.

MYRA. Jess has to take things easy.

MICHAEL. And the sun's going in.

STORMY. That does it. Out-voted.

RICHARD (*a gesture of surrender*). The noes have it. So we'll sit here and count garden gnomes.

STORMY. Girls, get weaving. I'm that hungry I could eat a baby's bum through a cane chair.

JAN. Charming, as ever. (*To* RICHARD, *smiling uncertainly*) Sorry about that. (*He shrugs*) Blame me. I thought what a good idea if we all came back here, seeing as Louise and Michael are with us. I mean, we've put it off for so long.

RICHARD. And now we're here. Good-o.

TRINA. Will we pool what we've got or stick to our own stuff? Jan?

JAN (*still looking at* RICHARD). Yes.

TRINA. Which?

JAN (*coming to*). Let's share.

MICHAEL. Can I help?

TRINA. Yes, you can. Do nothing.

STORMY. Young fella . . . (*He motions to* MICHAEL *to join the men.*)

MYRA. I'm awful: all I brought was sandwiches.

TRINA. Don't worry.

MYRA. I didn't even cut the crusts off.

(*The women unpack the food on the table. The business of serving it will take several minutes. There is chicken, ham, potato salad, French bread, cheese, pickles, etc. The men move well away from this activity.* STORMY *produces a nest of metal cups and a hip flask.*)

JESS. If I'm not inquisitive, why are you wearing a suit?

STORMY. What?

JESS. To a picnic. Why are you wearing the suit?

STORMY. What kind of a pass-remarkable question is that? Hey-hey-hey, answer this. . . why are *you* wearing a suit?

JESS. To show off that I'm hard up.

STORMY. Oh, yeah?

JESS. So tell us. Why are *you* wearing a –

RICHARD. Jess. . . easy.

JESS. Yeah. . . sorry.

STORMY (*pouring a drink*). Here, whet your appetite.

JESS. Thanks. Good on you.

STORMY. That'll soften your cough for you.

(JESS *gives him a hard look, but* STORMY *is oblivious and goes on pouring.*)

MICHAEL. What is it?

STORMY. Pewter.

MICHAEL. No, I mean the –

STORMY. Anniversary present, cost a mint. Try it.

MICHAEL. Cheers.

STORMY (*warning him, indicating the women*). Shhh...

JESS. Good stuff.

RICHARD. Need we ask how's business?

STORMY. Divil by the tail. You?

RICHARD. Surviving.

STORMY. These days, if you're cute, you go in for quantity. I have a new estate under way at Pine Valley. Eight units to the acre.

RICHARD. Bit on the small size.

STORMY. No, no, compact.

RICHARD. Sure.

STORMY. It's the modern concept: space elimination.

MYRA. Trina, look what she brought. Strawberries.

TRINA. Ooooh!

THE MEN. Ooooh!

JAN. There's no cream to go with them. Terry's on a cholesterol-free diet.

MYRA. Jan, I envy you.

JAN. The strawberries?

MYRA. Going to be a granny. (JAN *looks at her coldly*.) Now you're thrilled to bits.

LOU. Don't bet on it.

MYRA. While I have to wait a whole long year.

JESS. A year?

MYRA. Till Noreen is nine months married.

TRINA. Ah God, Myra, she's not a greyhound.

MYRA. How?

TRINA. I mean, it's a wedding. You're supposed to have a prayer book, not a stop watch and a starting gun.

MYRA (*beaming*). Go on. You're just an old jealous-boots because Jan and me are going to be grannies.

JAN. Myra, must you use that word?

MYRA. What word?

JAN. While we're handling food.

LOU. Oh, mum.

JAN. Well, I'm sorry – it's a horrid word, it belongs in a geriatrics ward. It's maudlin, it wears a cameo brooch and black taffeta. It – (STORMY *switches on his cassette player: a Beatles number: 'When I'm Sixty-four'*.) Do we need that noise?

STORMY. It's what we brought it for.

JAN. It's your toy, *you* brought it.

STORMY (*to the men*). Great power, what?

282

JAN. I said, turn it down.

STORMY (*doing so*). 'Scuse me for breathing.

RICHARD. They get moody.

STORMY. Yeah, yeah. (*To* JESS) Refill? (JESS *shakes his head.*)
Yes, you will. You look as if one more clean shirt 'ud do you.
(JESS *looks at him as if struck.*) I'm coddin'.

JESS. Sure you are. (*He turns away.*)

STORMY. Hey, take a joke.

RICHARD. What's up with you?

STORMY (*nudging* JESS). C'mon, have a jar.

RICHARD. Is it what Myra said?

STORMY. When?

RICHARD. She was going on at him a bit about . . . (*He touches his
chest.*)

STORMY. Get away. Well, with respect to Myra, Jess, she knows as
much about T.B. as my arse knows about snipe shooting.

RICHARD. You had a mild dose. You're over it.

JESS. I know. I know I am.

RICHARD. Cured.

JESS. Yes.

RICHARD. Then what's wrong?

JESS. I'm going to die. (*He tries to grin at them. The muscles of his
face twitch; tears come into his eyes.* STORMY *turns off the
cassette player.*) Sorry.

STORMY. Where'd you get that for a yarn?

JESS (*rubbing his eyes*). Hang on. (*He takes out a handkerchief, as
grubby as previously.* RICHARD *nudges* MICHAEL, *who moves
away.*) No one told me – I just . . .'Scuse me. (*He wipes his
nose and sniffs loudly.*)

RICHARD. Take your time.

MYRA (*to* JESS). Have you a cold?

JESS. No.

STORMY. If no one told you, how do you –

JESS. I can't . . . stay alive.

STORMY. Balls.

RICHARD. Are you ill?

JESS (*indifferently*). Dunno.

RICHARD. But you're dying!

JESS. Couple of years ago, Myra and I flew over to stay with her
sister in Bradford. Bit of a holiday. Myra thought flying was
great gas – five miles nearer to God. I was scarified, spent the
whole time trying to keep the damn thing air-borne. (*He clutches an imaginary arm-rest.*)

283

RICHARD. Me, too.

JESS. Yeah. Well, I can't any more. I can't keep it in the air. I've let go. Yous know me. Am I a begrudger? See fellas getting on in the world, best of luck. As long as there was a couple of jars, me mates, something nice tomorrow. And old Myra the same: happy with the kids and the boy friend.

STORMY. Who? (JESS *points at the sky*.)

JESS. But when I had to go into the san, that was it. I said: Jesus, can't I win once in my life? Not a war, not a battle; is one lousy skirmish too much to ask for? At night, I'd look out at the fir trees and wonder if they'd planted evergreens so's we wouldn't know when the summer was gone. I lay there and I thought: why couldn't it be that pair for a change? You and you. Only it never rains on them that has umbrellas. You know what's dangerous? Laugh at a man when he hits you. He takes your money: tell a joke; he takes your job: sing a song. And if you won't cry, sooner or later he'll bloody well kill you.

STORMY. Is that all that ails youl You sap, you.

JESS (*trying to sound matter-of-fact*). You can't win, let go.

STORMY. Bullshit. (*He offers cigarettes*.)

JESS. Gave them up. (MYRA, *who is talking to* TRINA, *laughs out loud.* JESS *looks at her, then takes a cigarette from* STORMY *and puts it in his breast pocket*.) (*Doing so*) Ah, feck. (*Meaning 'What the hell!'*)

RICHARD. Jess, you'll bury the lot of us. (JESS *shakes his head violently; tears well up again*.)

STORMY. You'd have something to complain about if you were Martin Hewitt. Playing golf on Friday, funeral tomorrow. And him only forty. . . (RICHARD *shoots him a look*.) No, nearer sixty. Still it's young.

TRINA (*calling*). Grub's up!

RICHARD (*to* JESS). Watch it.

JESS. I'm okay. Where's Myra?

RICHARD. Talking to Louise.

TRINA. But don't stir, we'll wait on yous hand and foot.

STORMY. Proper order.

JAN. Oh, no, we won't. Let them stretch themselves.

TRINA. Right. No waitresses, it's self-service.

RICHARD (*to* JESS). Come on.

JESS (*rubbing his eyes*). Wait.

LOU (*to* MYRA; *she is anxious to change the subject*). Myra, I really couldn't tell you whether he is or not. He didn't honour

284

me with his opinion. (*She goes to* MICHAEL *with a wine bottle and a corkscrew*) Open this for me, would you?

MICHAEL. Sure. Jess was crying buckets. Says he's going to die.

LOU. Well, let him. Open the bottle.

TRINA. Myra?

MYRA. All I said was, was Pearse excited about the baby?

STORMY. Pearse? (*Angrily*) That little –

JAN (*warning him*). Terry. . .

MYRA. What is it?

JAN. Nothing, let it lie.

STORMY. I'll pierce him.

JAN. Yes, dear, you'll huff and you'll puff and you'll blow his house down. (*Serving food*) Myra, that's Jess's. (*To* STORMY) Now, diddums, this is um's right hand and this is um's left hand. . .

RICHARD (*singing*). 'And the rowlocks between um's knees.' (*As* JESS *joins in*) 'And we'll all sing together. For as long as we damn well. . .'

TRINA. This is not a singing pub. (*She serves* RICHARD) Richard.
. .

RICHARD. Looks fantastic.

STORMY. Where's me garlic bread?

JAN. No bread for you. Nor cheese, nor hard-boiled eggs.

STORMY. Aw, Jasus.

MYRA (*coming to* JESS *with his food*). We saved the sandwiches. You can have them for your lunch tomorrow and – (*She stares at him.*)

JESS. And what?

MYRA. . . . and Tuesday.

JESS (*rubbing his eyes*). We were laughing that hard. (*Raising his voice*) I was telling them, in the san, I always knew when the kids were praying for me. The bed used to levitate.

MYRA (*reproachfully*). Jess.

JESS (*guffawing*). Spiritual streptomycin.

STORMY. Oh, a bad bugger.

TRINA. Now dive in, make a start.

MYRA. Trina, wait.

TRINA. What for?

MYRA. Grace.

JESS. Lovely girl, you'll like her.

MYRA. 'Bless us, oh Lord, and these Thy gifts which through Thy bounty we are about to receive, through Christ our Lord, Amen.'

285

TRINA. Amen. Thanks, Myra.

JAN. And from the Church of Ireland.

LOU (*to* MICHAEL). Now. You pour, I'll serve.

MICHAEL. Nothing wrong?

LOU. No.

RICHARD. This fresh air – I'm ravenous.

(TRINA *moves to sit with* RICHARD, *but* JAN *gets there first.*)

JAN. May I sit with you?

RICHARD (*not pleased*). Pleasure.

STORMY. It's a mixty, is it?

JESS (*quietly, to* MYRA). I want a word with Stormy.

MYRA. Well, have it.

JESS. Private, it's business.

MYRA. Then mind your suit.

TRINA. Here, Myra – old maids' corner.

(MYRA *and* TRINA *sit together.* JESS *sits beside* STORMY. MICHAEL *and* LOU *distribute the wine.*)

STORMY (*to* JESS). Look at this . . . starvation diet. Hey . . . swap.

JESS. What?

STORMY. Gimme your plate. Now keep between me and her.

TRINA. How is it?

STORMY. Smashing.

JAN. I made the garlic bread.

RICHARD. Delicious.

JAN. Try tasting it.

STORMY (*as* LOU *serves him with wine*). Attagirl.

LOU (*referring to his food*). Naughty.

STORMY (*a whisper*). Shut up!

LOU. Jess. . .

JESS. Blessings on you.

LOU (*as American air hostess*). Our pleasure, sir. Enjoy your flight with us.

(LOU *sits with* MICHAEL. RICHARD *samples the garlic bread.*)

JAN. Yes?

RICHARD. Mm!

(*A silence as everybody eats.* STORMY *wolfs his food.*)

JESS. You won't broadcast it? I mean, about just now.

STORMY. When? God, no.

RICHARD (*calling across*). How are you doing? (STORMY *gives him a glimpse of the garlic bread*) I wouldn't doubt you.

JAN (*sotto*). I suppose he's eating garlic bread.

RICHARD (*sotto*). Of course.

JAN (*meaning* STORMY). Fool.

LOU. Mum, it's super.

MICHAEL. Better than super.

JESS (*to* STORMY). Meaning to ask you. . .

STORMY. Ask.

JESS. Noreen's wedding. . .

STORMY. We'll be there.

JESS. No, the thing is . . .

STORMY. Get's another bit of bread. Discreetly.

(JESS *goes to the table for the bread.*)

JAN. Does Michael still live at home?

RICHARD. How does the saying go? A house is not a home.

JAN. You mean, more of a box number.

RICHARD. Right. Michael tries everything . . . bit of this, bit of that . . . get it all in.

JAN. Good!

RICHARD. Is it? He's my son, and I shouldn't say this. . .

JAN. But you're going to.

RICHARD. He reminds me of an American tourist.

JAN. Monster.

RICHARD. So how's *your* life? Keeping well?

JAN (*still smiling*). No. (RICHARD's *face darkens with ill-temper.*) If you don't want to know, don't ask.

RICHARD. My mistake.

JAN. Just . . . spare me your politeness. (*Eating, in her party voice*) Mm . . . it's not bad.

MYRA (*to* RICHARD). You're getting it.

RICHARD. Who is?

MYRA. You are. Hot and heavy . . . from Trina.

RICHARD. Never.

TRINA. Hold your tongue. (*To* MYRA) So his lordship waltzes in, calm as a millpond to say he's used the money my poor mother left me to take a lease on the old baby-linen shop. In my name!

MYRA. Not a word to you?

TRINA. Oh, a back-stabber.

MYRA (*to* RICHARD). Are your ears red?

TRINA. I said to him: 'Me, run a shop?'

RICHARD (*not looking at her*). Boutique.

TRINA. I couldn't sell choc-ices in Purgatory.

JESS (*to* STORMY). While they can't hear us. . .

STORMY. Me mouth's full, don't make me talk. Sit forward.

287

TRINA. I hadn't been in that place a week before I found out that the women in this town would wear flour sacks if you stuck 'Made in Italy' on them. Now I wouldn't be parted from the shop.

JAN (*as* RICHARD *opens his mouth to correct her*). Give up.

MYRA. You may thank Richard.

TRINA. Mm. (*To* RICHARD) Thanks.

STORMY (*to* RICHARD). Hey, you missed it at the Druids.

RICHARD. Did I?

STORMY. Monica Riordan threw a large vodka at Noreen Cooney. Said to her: 'That's for sending my husband home to me sobbing his eyes out.' Pandemonium.

RICHARD. Nasty.

STORMY. No, it was the August Bank Holiday. People feel that something special's called for.

JAN. Like throwing vodka?

STORMY. Better than sitting at home.

JAN. Eat your garlic bread. (*To* RICHARD) What if I threw this in your face? (*As he looks at her*) No, why waste it?

RICHARD. Don't get fraught.

JAN. Fraught? Do you know – (*She gets her voice under control and smiles for the benefit of the others*) ...What I've been through? Or care?

RICHARD. Not here.

JAN. All right, where? (*With self-anger*) I swore I wasn't going to behave badly. That's another of your accomplishments. There was a time I had pride.

RICHARD. You'll drop us both in it.

JAN. Have I – (*She stops.*)

RICHARD. What?

JAN. A successor yet?

RICHARD. Will you stop?

JAN (*looking around*). They're gossiping? Have I?

RICHARD. No.

JAN. Trina looks happy. Cat that swallowed the cream. (*As this gets no reaction*) I hate seeming a bore, but after six years it would be nice to be given a reason.

RICHARD. You got one.

JAN. That makes sense.

RICHARD (*about to move*). Excuse me.

JAN (*gripping his arm*). Don't go . . . I'll be good as gold.
  (MYRA *looks at them, curious.* RICHARD *raises his glass.*)

288

MYRA. All the best.

JAN. Please. . . ? They can't hear.

RICHARD. They can feel.

JESS (*to* STORMY). I need three hundred quid.

STORMY. You what?

JESS. For the wedding. Excuse abruptness. I hate borrowing. It's a girl's big day. Your Louise – now, she was fantastic, all them yards of lace and stuff. Thing is, you don't get many oohs and aahs ploughing up to the altar in a pink going-away suit. It's okay for some, but people like us are too poor not to spend money. Them that haven't it have to prove they have.

STORMY. Three hundred.

JESS. We saved a bit . . . Myra saved it. Then I got sick and it melted. I'm driving an untaxed car.

STORMY. That's bad.

JESS. I did me sums. I can pay you back half of it by April, guaranteed, and the other half this time next –

STORMY. You what?

JESS. I worked it out. I –

STORMY. How can you pay me back if your're going to die? (JESS *stares at him. Crowing*) Gave the game away, didn't you? You're a fake, a fraud. Own up.

JESS. Yeah.

STORMY. That shook you. Next time get up early in the day. Hey, how come you didn't ask him first? (*He nods towards* RICHARD) Your buttie.

JESS. He's not doing too well.

STORMY. Trina'd give it to him. She is.

JESS. He couldn't ask her.

STORMY. Why couldn't he?

JESS. Reasons.

STORMY (*eager for scandal*). Come on.

JESS. Because.

STORMY (*shrugs, offended but letting it pass*). Three hundred. Jess, you're a mate, so I'll do you a favour.

JESS. Thanks. I'm –

STORMY. Not a tosser. (JESS *half-smiles at him, not believing.*) Why? Because borrowing never helped anyone. They get out of the woods, they sit on their hunkers, relax, it happens again. Jess, I've been through that mill. You're a mess, you pull yourself out, and that's what builds character.

JESS. It's not character I'm asking for.

STORMY. You're an improvident sod. I lose sleep over you, you know that? I say: what'll be the end of him? A wife, six kids, and it's all come-day, go-day, God-send-Sunday. Man, shift your backside. Do what I do...move!

JESS. I can't; I'm shagged. Three lousy hundred.

STORMY. Jess, for your own good, no. You want to harm a man, lend him money.

JESS. Then harm me!

(STORMY *laughs aloud.*)

TRINA. There they go; dirty jokes.

MYRA. They never.

STORMY. He's a panic. Drop of the hard stuff, good for you. (*He pours a drink for* JESS.)

LOU (*to* MICHAEL, *almost choking on her wine*). Blizzard?

MICHAEL. It's a detergent.

LOU. I know it is . . . I use it. You work for –

MICHAEL. What's funny?

LOU (*still laughing*). Sorry. When they said you were a bio-chemist, I thought of, oh, I don't know, a cure for something.

MICHAEL. So it is . . . a cure for dirt.

LOU. Get off.

MICHAEL (*dogged*). It is a cure for –

(*She yelps with laughter.*)

JAN. Louise?

LOU. Make him stop.

MICHAEL. Just because I work for –

LOU. Don't say it.

MICHAEL. Blizzard? (*This starts her off again.*)

RICHARD. What's the joke? (LOU *makes a 'Don't ask' gesture.*) Share it.

JAN. Leave them. I'm just thankful she's laughing.

RICHARD. Louise?

JAN. Like her mother, she has a fondness for men who don't want her. (*As his face tightens*) Sorry. Pax.

RICHARD (*nodding towards* LOU). Problems?

MICHAEL. It's Irish-based, it gives employment, it makes life easier. What more do you want?

LOU (*mock-serious*). Quite right.

MICHAEL. And how much missionary work have you done lately?

LOU. Now that's not nice.

MICHAEL. Anyway, Blizzard is only this year's job.

LOU. Oh?

290

MICHAEL. I keep on the move. Next year, who knows?

LOU. Persil?

MICHAEL (*letting it pass*). The old man thinks I'm restless, says all I ever do is chop and change. Not so. I just like to stay off tramlines.

LOU (*non-commital*). Ah.

MICHAEL. Exactly. Look at them. (*His gesture embraces the others*.) There was a time they could go down any street they wanted, leave town, go to another country. Not now. Now they're on a tram all the way to the shed. Jesus, ten minutes ago, Jess was crying.

LOU. You said. Over what?

MICHAEL. It. The tramshed.

LOU. Oh, God.

MICHAEL. Yeah.

LOU. So you . . . what do you do?

MICHAEL. People and jobs, they're the killers. I stay clear.

LOU. Don't get caught? (*He makes a thumbs-up sign*.) And at the end of it, what have you got?

MICHAEL. Well, I'll find out, won't I?

LOU. It's incredible.

MICHAEL. Oh, yeah?

LOU. Six years later, and you're exactly the same.

MICHAEL (*taking it as a compliment*). Thanks.

(*She stares at him.*)

TRINA (*calling*). Jan. . .

JAN. Hello.

TRINA. Myra was telling me. . .

JAN. Ah-ha?

MYRA. Ronan, our second youngest, was nearly run over at the People's Park. They ought to put lights there, Jan, they ought to.

TRINA. And they drive like it was. . . Richard, where do cars race?

RICHARD. Brand's Hatch.

TRINA. Brand's Hatch.

MYRA. We thought if your committee got on to the Borough Council. . .

JAN. I gave up that nonsense years ago. But talk to Molly Bolger: she'll get them after it like wolves. (*To* RICHARD, *quietly*) I liked my committee work; I gave it up to make time for us. You were jealous then, even of that poor old Victorian lamp-post I wanted to save. You pounced on every minute I had as if it was

291

yours and you'd lost it. Once, I even invented a committee, for
the pleasure of having you wheedle and nag and bully me into
resigning from it.

RICHARD. You never.

JAN. Truly. Now you tell me to find an interest, to get out more.
I burned all those bridges, and you expect me to unburn them.
Richard, I am a person of value, and I will not be squandered.

RICHARD (*uneasy*). Please. . .

JAN. I don't have Louise anymore. There's no one. And I miss
you.

LOU (*to* MICHAEL). Well, honestly.

MICHAEL. Don't get huffy. All I asked was –

LOU. I know, I heard you.

MICHAEL. A drink.

LOU (*coldly*). You and me.

MICHAEL. Seeing as you're in town.

LOU. Ah, but tomorrow I won't be. Early start . . . the Cork tram.

MICHAEL. Pity.

LOU. Isn't it!

MICHAEL. You fancy yourself, you know that? This may come as
a rude shock, but once in a blue moon being asked to have a
drink means being asked to have a –

LOU. You were told, weren't you?

MICHAEL. Pardon?

LOU. Mum wouldn't tell. (*Indicating* STORMY) Was it Dad?

MICHAEL. Sorry, I don't –

LOU. Once a girl's been walked out on, she's supposed to be easy
meat, isn't she? The slice that's never missed off a cut load, is
that what they say?

MICHAEL (*impulsively taking her hand*). I didn't know.

LOU. Let go.

MICHAEL. I didn't.

LOU. I said, leave off. (*She pulls her hand free.*)

RICHARD (*to* JAN). We were a public joke. The whole town knew
about us.

JAN. They knew within a month.

RICHARD. And sooner or later –

JAN. Here it comes.

RICHARD. Trina would have found out.

JAN. I disagree.

RICHARD (*nodding towards* STORMY). So would he.

JAN. Oh, yes? We were watching this thing on television. Man and

woman in bed together. Husband comes home. Need you ask,
a comedy. So the man flies out of the window, hangs from a
ledge. I laughed. Not Terry, because now that he could see the
outside of the house, he was pricing it.

LOU (*to* MICHAEL). You a jazz buff? I met Pearse at this Dave
Brubeck Concert. Inside a week I was six pound lighter, and
that was the last of Labrador. I was so bloody smart. He had
a girl friend, but what chance did a country mouse have against
worldly-wise, sophisticated me? And there was an added attraction: I was a Protestant – the lure of the unknown. When I told
Mum that he'd asked to marry me, she smiled – you know
Mum – and said 'Marriage to one of us? How very liberated!'
He was that all right. He's back with her.

MICHAEL. The girl friend?

LOU. He said we'd married in haste – my God, he could turn a
phrase. And that he and she – here comes another one – had
been intended from the cradle up.

MICHAEL. Nice.

LOU. As for becoming a father, he's promised to do the right
thing. I think in Cork that means maintenance.

MICHAEL. And you're going back there?

LOU. Yes! He may not be married, but I am. I'm worth something,
and I'm not going to be thrown away.

MICHAEL. You want him back?

LOU. Errah, boy, he'll get sense. If he had any now, he'd be giving
thanks my dad hasn't killed him.

MICHAEL. What about his people? Whose side are they on?

LOU. Dunno, they're separated.

MICHAEL. Are they, now?

LOU. Years since.

MICHAEL. Well, that's it!

LOU. What is?

MICHAEL. The cause of it. Broken home. My God, it's textbook,
he hadn't a hope. Don't you *know* that? Well, compare . . . his
parents with ours. Ours are together, his aren't. He can't handle
his life, you can handle yours. *I* have no problems. At least, we
can thank them for that much.

JAN. If we'd been honest. . .

RICHARD. Sure.

JAN. We'd have told them.

RICHARD. And gone away.

JAN. Others have done it.

293

RICHARD. I can't.

JAN. Others have courage.

RICHARD. 'Away.' I don't know where 'away' is. And I find –
(*He stops.*)

JAN. Go on.

RICHARD. I find it a bit late in the day and more than a bit stupid
to swap one loneliness for a worse one.
(*Pause.* JAN *puts a hand over her mouth. He looks towards the
others in alarm.*)

JAN. You should know by now that I don't cry. I get sick
sometimes; I don't cry.

STORMY (*to* JESS). You're in the sulks.

JESS. Me?

STORMY. You're mad at me.

JESS. I'm brooding.

STORMY. Over what?

JESS. Money. If I don't get it somewhere Noreen can go to the altar in
her pelt, and the St Vincent de Paul can do the catering.

STORMY. You'll get it.

JESS. Not unless I print it.

STORMY. You'd persecute a saint, you know that? (*Taking out a cheque book.*) And I'm worse to give in to you. Can't even eat in peace.

JESS (*grabbing his wrist*). Thanks mate.

STORMY. Let go.

JESS. You'll get it back.

STORMY. I will not. Because I won't renege on my principles. No
lending money, never have done, never will. I'll give it to you.

JESS. You'll do what?

STORMY. A present, me to you, no messing. (*Finding his pen*) Ask
for it and it's yours.

JESS. *Ask*?

STORMY. Now is that fair do's or isn't it?

JESS (*getting angry*). Ask you for –

STORMY. No strings. Ask and ye shall rec –

JESS. Stick it.

STORMY. What?

JESS. Stick it where the monkey stuck the –

STORMY. Hey, now watch your tongue. I'm doing you a good –

JESS. Well, don't.

STORMY (*waving the cheque book*). Three hundred quid, do you
want it or – (JESS *walks away, towards where* TRINA *and*
MYRA *are sitting.*) – or don't you? Hey?

TRINA. Myra, you're being silly. Louise would be thrilled. Give it
to her.

JESS (*harshly*). Give? Give what?

MYRA. It's the little medal of the Blessed Virgin. To protect her.
(*To* TRINA) Jan and Stormy don't believe the way we do.

TRINA. What odds? It's the thought.

MYRA. I'd think bad if she took it to humour me.

TRINA. Louise? Never.

MYRA. I know full well I'm behind the times. If she made a joke
of it. . . (*Deciding*) Oh, no.

RICHARD. It takes so many years and you do so much harm before
you own up to it that in your whole life there is you and there
are strangers and there is no one else. There's a clock in the
room, and you invite people in for drinks, and hope the chat
and the laughing will drown out the noise of it. Well, it doesn't,
and after a while you realize that they're listening to it, too. You
wish they'd go home.

JAN. A worse loneliness, is that what you said I was?

RICHARD. Because it nearly worked.

TRINA (*to* MYRA). If you're all that afraid, let Jan give it to her.

MYRA. Would she?

TRINA. God. The commotion over a medal. Ask her.

(MYRA *comes down behind* RICHARD *and* JAN *and stands
waiting to interrupt.*)

JAN. Nearly is not so bad. (RICHARD *grins and shakes his head.*)
I'd settle for it.

RICHARD. You would!

JAN (*her voice falsely brisk, to conceal an underlying desperation*).
Look here, my lad, I'm not going to let you throw our six years
away. Tomorrow, I'll tell Liz Geraghty it's on again and get the
keys of her flat.

RICHARD. Don't do that.

JAN. Perhaps you'd prefer it if I took another man there and made
love to him in our bed? I thought of it. (*With a change of tone*)
Darling, no one will find out. We've been careful up to now,
we'll be careful in –

TRINA. Myra?

(JAN *looks around to see* MYRA *staring at her and*
RICHARD.)

RICHARD (*trying to sound casual*). Jan was just saying, she –

MYRA (*her voice hoarse*). God . . . forgive . . . you.

TRINA. Myra, what is it?

295

(*The others look around.* MYRA *is too distraught either to realize or care that they are listening.*)

MYRA. I never believed. I heard in the town. I said to people 'If you repeat those lies, that slander. . .'

STORMY. What's she on about?

MYRA. And, oh Jesus, it's true. As bad as the rest of them, as bad as the worst of them.

JESS (*alarmed, realizing*). Myra. . .

MYRA. Him that I thought . . . thought the world of. Like . . . animals.

RICHARD. We were talking...

MYRA. Liar. . . you liar.

JESS (*going to her*). Will you shut up?

MYRA. Carrying on these six years . . . him and her. I heard them.

JESS. You misheard.

RICHARD. Sure. All Jan and I were –

MYRA. In front of their own children. No shame in them. The worst . . . the worst sin.

JAN. You bloody fool.

MYRA. Deny it. To my face, deny that you're dirt. Deny it!

JAN. Well, seeing as it's true I don't propose to deny anything. (*A pause.*)

RICHARD. She. . .

STORMY. Seeing as it's what?

JAN. As it's true.

STORMY. Ah. As it's true. . . I see. I won't have this, I'm damned if I will. (*Violently*) Christ, woman, don't make bloody jokes when you can see she's upset. They were acting the goat, Myra, same as we all do.

JAN. Terry, what she said about Richard and –

STORMY. Now that will do! Myra takes things to heart. She's not like us, so don't jeer.

JAN. I'm not. . .

STORMY. Shut up!

TRINA (*laughing*). Myra . . . honestly.

(MYRA *looks about her at the faces.* MICHAEL *sniggers audibly.*)

RICHARD (*angrily*). Michael. . .

(MYRA *finds the religious medal still in her hand. She flings it at* JAN.)

MYRA. Pros...prostitute!

STORMY. Ah, now.

JESS (*grabbing* MYRA). Will you shut that evil stupid mouth of yours? Will you?

296

(MYRA *begins to cry.*)

TRINA. Jess, no. Myra, you made a mistake.

LOU. Of course you did.

(MYRA *shakes her head.* TRINA *puts an arm around her.*)

MICHAEL. Just your quiet, average Sunday.

RICHARD. I warned you.

JESS (*to* MYRA). What are you doing? Rehearsing for Noreen's wedding, is that it? (*To* RICHARD) Sorry mate. (RICHARD *makes a gesture: 'Forget it'.*)

STORMY. I blame that wine we had. If you've no head for drink. . .

RICHARD. Treacherous.

STORMY (*to* JAN). You all right?

JAN. Fine. Just a mistake.

JESS. I was on the beach once, at the White Rock. Heard one woman saying to another 'I've got a bigger pair than you have. Here, weigh them in your hands.' I near broke me neck whipping my head around. They were eating pears.

STORMY. That's how it happens.

JAN. Jess. . . (*handing him the medal*) It's Myra's.

STORMY. And I'll murder you for making it worse. Sneering at her.

JAN. Sorry. We said it because we knew Myra could overhear. Couldn't resist it. (*She looks directly at* MYRA, *letting her know that the lie is precisely that: a lie.*)

MICHAEL (*suddenly, hand extended*). Hey. . .

RICHARD. What?

MICHAEL. Spot of rain.

TRINA. I felt it.

STORMY (*looking at the sky*). It'll clear.

MICHAEL. I dunno.

JAN. So . . . shall we have our coffee or make a beeline?

TRINA (*making a face towards* MYRA). I could do with a cup.

STORMY. And me.

TRINA. Jan, have you a thermos?

JAN. Mm-hm. (*Going to help*) How is she?

TRINA. Leave her. (*With compassion for* JAN) Oh, love.

JAN. It's *all right*.

LOU (*to* JAN). Hi-ya, sexy.

JAN. You horror.

(JAN *and* TRINA *pour the coffee.* STORMY *lights a cigarette.* JESS *sits beside* MYRA.)

JESS. I never knew you were musical.

297

MYRA. I know what I saw.

JESS. What you thought you saw.

MYRA. You took their part.

JESS. Maybe you've forgotten what name you called her. You went bonkers. (MYRA *looks ahead sullenly*.) Myra, I've got enough troubles, there's vultures in our front garden. At least leave me my friends.

MYRA. Nice friends!

JESS. First thing tomorrow you'll ring up Jan –

MYRA. Ring up?

JESS. And apologise.

MYRA. Not to my dying day.

JESS. You may be talking of the immediate future. What's it to you what other people get up to? Are you their keeper?

MYRA (*tearful*). Go away.

JESS. I'm asking you – why?

MYRA (*looking towards* RICHARD). When you . . . you have a high regard for people, and he . . . and they disappoint you. . .

JESS (*understanding*). Sure, okay. Poor Myra. You're a fierce woman. The day you get to heaven, God'll take down the bunting.

    (STORMY *comes over to* RICHARD *and gives him a cigarette*.)

STORMY. Bloody funny world.

RICHARD. Isn't it.

STORMY. So what's the latest? Did Jan and you make it up? (RICHARD *freezes and stares at him*. STORMY *offers him a light*.) You've been giving us the go-by lately. She was peeved.

RICHARD. Pressure of business.

STORMY. If that's all it was.

RICHARD. What else?

STORMY. Good. It takes years to get used to people, be a pity to bugger it up. The time I was starting out in the trade, if a carpenter skimped the job I'd sack him there and then. Every house a model home. Then I learned to loosen up. Like with people. You give an inch, put up with what you might have killed a fellow for ten years ago. The main thing is to stick close. You're in the boat, so stay in it. The sea is cold. Yeah?

RICHARD. Right.

    (JESS *comes and stands between them, an arm over each shoulder*.)

JESS. You are a pair of thieves. So when's the next outing?

STORMY. Next Sunday?

RICHARD. Why not, while the weather lasts. But this place has had it.

STORMY. We can move further out, sure what else are wheels for? If Jemser here is still breathing.

JESS. If I'm not, I'll ignore the fact. Good lads, we shall rise again.

TRINA. Coffee's ready.

STORMY. But we'll have a jar on Wednesday, what?
    (*They go to collect their coffee.* TRINA *is pressing some on* MYRA, *who shakes her head.*)

TRINA. You will so, it's good for you. (*She gives both cups to* JESS.)

RICHARD. We thought, if it stays fine next Sunday...

MICHAEL. You've a hope.

RICHARD. We might make another day of it.

STORMY. Some place different.

JAN. Mm, why don't we?

JESS. Got it. The Vale of Clara.

STORMY. The very place.

JESS. Myra loves Clara, don't you? (*Cajoling her*) Of course you do . . . with the little church. What? (*She looks at him bitterly.*)

STORMY. Motion carried, it's a fixture.

LOU. Well, I'll be in Cork.

JAN. More fool you, then.

MICHAEL (*sotto*). Hear that? Stay in town.

JAN (*catching* RICHARD's *eye*). On second thoughts, I wonder should we. It's a nuisance, you buy all that food, and then the weather is –

STORMY. You're a wet blanket.

TRINA. She is not. (*Sympathetic*) Jan, she'll get over it. She *will*. (*Laughing*) God, trust Myra. You and Richard. . . as if at our age we hadn't better things to fill our heads with.

STORMY. V.A.T., P.A.Y.E. . . .

TRINA (*the businesswoman*). Don't talk to me. And if it rains itself, we can save the picnic and have lunch in that new restaurant where the Tara Castle Ballroom used to be. . . where I –

STORMY. Where you what?

TRINA. Made a show of myself once. (*As he looks puzzled*) Family secret. (*Briskly*) Now all finish up. So's we can pack.

STORMY. I'm done. (*He deliberately throws his paper cup on the ground.*)

JAN. Terry!

299

STORMY. It's a building site.

RICHARD. Lou, you're in a tearing hurry to leave us.

LOU. I'd better. I've had tickets these months past for a jazz concert at the Opera House.

MICHAEL. Do you mean you have a spare? (*He is aware of having
made a gaffe.*) Sorry, I didn't –

LOU. Don't be sorry. Yes, I may have a spare.

MICHAEL. Great. Thanks. Joplin isn't jazz, though; he's ragtime.

LOU. Same thing.

MICHAEL. It is not. Different entities.

LOU. One came first, didn't it? Joplin, Marshall, James Scott.

MICHAEL. But there's no connection. Sure, they have Afro-
American roots in common, but what else?

LOU. It's obvious.

MICHAEL. Not to me.

LOU. Well, hard luck.

STORMY. Hit him, why don't you?

LOU. It turns out we're jazz buffs.

MICHAEL. You aren't, if you confuse rags and cakewalks with –

STORMY. Jazz went out years ago.

MICHAEL. No, it –

JAN. It's come in again, darling. The past is fashionable.

STORMY. You're coddin'.

JAN. It's the in thing.

RICHARD. Any decade but this one.

STORMY (*to* LOU *and* MICHAEL). Well, God pity the pair of you.
No culture of your own, so yous have got to live in
Methuselah's time.

MICHAEL. Jazz is not archaic, it's –

STORMY. G 'long out of that. Why can't yous be up to date? God,
we may be old fogies, but at least we know what age we're living
in. Where's me player? (*He heads for the cassette player and
picks a cassette from the case.*)

JAN (*laughing*). I knew it. He'll inflict that thing on us if it kills
him.

STORMY. Got it. Now come into the present day and listen to this.
A bit of reverential hush. (*He switches the player on. They
listen. We hear McIntyre's 'Sentimental Journey'.*)

MICHAEL. He's kidding.

LOU. It's too much.

STORMY (*beaming*). What? What?

JAN (*laughing*). Oh, really.

(TRINA, *however, smiles and begins to hum to the music*.)

STORMY. Isn't that fantastic? 'To renew old memories . . . heaven.
. .' Here, Jan . . . come on, we'll show them. (*He pulls her to
him*.)

JAN. Show them what? Terry, no, I don't w – Oh, that disgusting
garlic bread . . . get away. Ugh.

STORMY. Be particular. Trina, then . . . come here to me, a bit of
the Fred and Ginger.

(*She is eager to dance. She looks at* RICHARD.)

RICHARD. Go ahead. I don't mind.

TRINA (*softly, even affectionately*). And I don't care. I haven't
cared this long while. (*She goes to* STORMY.)

STORMY (*to the young couple*). Now watch the feet. Watch the
feet! My God, this is magic.

(TRINA *dances with finesse:* STORMY *is making up for his lack
of expertise with a display of flashiness. It is dancing from the
jitterbug age. They swing apart, twist, come together*.)

MICHAEL. I can't look.

LOU (*laughing, weakly*). Don't mock the afflicted.

STORMY (*to the others*). Hey, don't leave it to us. Jess, get up.
Richard, show a bit of vitality.

JAN (*standing in front of* RICHARD). Well, they say if you can't
beat them. . .

RICHARD. Garlic bread.

(*She implores him with a look.* RICHARD *gets to his feet.*
MYRA *looks at him, unforgiving*.)

STORMY. There he goes . . . good lad? Now, Jess . . .

JESS. Myra, it'll make peace.

MYRA. I will not. (*Struggling*) I say I won't. And I'm not going
next Sunday either.

JESS (*between his teeth*). You'll do both. Don't shame us. . . Now
get up!

MYRA. You're not to force me.

JESS. I say you will.

STORMY. Begod, she's up. Myra, me sound woman.

JESS (*a comic patter*). I take my wife everywhere I go. It saves kissing her goodbye.

STORMY. ⎱
JESS.   ⎰ (*together*) Bah – boom!

MYRA. I don't want to.

(JESS *forces her to dance. He is a terrible dancer, and she is
unwilling; they slouch leadenly.* JAN, *uncaring, dances*

301

closer to RICHARD, *her arm about his neck.* MICHAEL *and*
LOU *watch, choking back their amusement.*)
STORMY. What about this then? (*An intricate step.*) My God, that
brought tears to me eyes. Good girl, good girl, keep it going.
(*He and* TRINA *sing the words. The music increases in volume.*
LOU *and* MICHAEL *now clap their hands in rhythm. The Lights
go down to black-out.*)

CURTAIN

A LIFE

IN MEMORIAM: JOHN T. MULLIGAN

CHARACTERS

DRUMM
DOLLY
MARY
MIBS
DESMOND
LAR
KEARNS
DOROTHY

A house and a park in a small town just south of Dublin.

This play was first produced at the Abbey Theatre, Dublin, for the Dublin Theatre Festival, on 4 October 1979, with the following cast:

DRUMM	Cyril Cusack
DOLLY	Daphne Carroll
MARY	Maureen Toal
MIBS	Dearbhla Molloy
DESMOND	Garrett Keogh
LAR	Stephen Brennan
KEARNS	Phillip O'Flynn
DOROTHY	Ingrid Craigie

A LIFE

ACT ONE

Darkness. Then Lights come up on a stone bandstand at stage centre. It is octagonal in shape, and although the roof is long gone the supporting pillars of curved Victorian iron remain. A short flight of stone steps leads down to stage level. The stage areas to left and right of the bandstand are in darkness.
DRUMM *is standing on the bandstand. He is wearing a fawn-coloured raincoat. He refreshes his memory by glancing at his notes, then puts them away. He addresses an unseen audience.*

DRUMM. To conclude. I have chosen to terminate today's walk in this park which is remarkable for its views of sea and mountains, such as may have inspired Bernard Shaw's observation that whereas Ireland's men are temporal, her hills are eternal. Any child familiar with the rudiments of geology could have told him otherwise, but then even Shaw was not immune to his countrymen's passion for inexactitude. These few acres have more than a scenic claim on our attention. This hillside is all that remains of what was called the Commons of Dalkey. Where the town — I speak in the Catholic sense: the Protestants call it a village — where it now stands there was once only gorseland and furze, moorland and wretched cabins. The coming of the railway in 1834 turned the wilderness into a place of habitation for the well-to-do, who were closely followed by tradespeople and members of the middle classes who knew their place and on that account lost no time in leaving it. The town evolved, grew and procreated, as our presence in its bears witness. Its population is four thousand, seven hundred, which figure can by simple division be broken down into nearly six hundred persons per public house. It was known to antiquity as the Town of the Seven Castles, of which the surviving two are vermin-infested, one being in ruins and the other the town hall. (*A thin smile, which disappears when there is no response to his joke.*) The climate is temperate, the birthrate relentless and the

305

mortal – (*He hesitates.*) . . . the mortality rate is consistent with
the national average. I see that some of you become restive. (*He
looks at his watch.*) And, coincidently, the licensing laws are
about to be in our favour. I thank you for your attention. The
next of the conducted walks so ingeniously entitled 'Dalkey
Discovered' will take place four weeks from today, on Sunday,
June 16th. Your guide will be Mrs Rachel Fogarty. Good day.

(*There is a thin spatter of applause, which suggests that his
audience has been a thin one. He watches them leave, then
takes a tube of Milk of Magnesia tablets from his pocket and
puts one in his mouth. He sits on the steps of the bandstand
and takes out a packet of Sweet Afton. With the cigarette
halfway to his lips, he sits absolutely still as if a realization
had suddenly come to him. A woman appears. She is his wife,*
DOLLY, *aged sixty.*)

DOLLY (*approaching*). Woo-ee! Dezzie!

(DRUMM*'s only reaction is to complete the business of lighting
his cigarette.*)

I came to meet you.

DRUMM (*not pleased*). Did you?

DOLLY. I climbed over the very tip-top and down the rocks. Amn't
I great? (*Catching her breath*) Whoo . . . It's so steep, I thought
to myself, God send I don't burst into a run and can't stop.

DRUMM. It would have enlivened my lecture.

DOLLY. I saw you from the top, talking sixteen to the dozen, only
I couldn't hear and I didn't want to come down and make you
nervous, so I waited. Was it a nice walk, what way did you go,
what did you say to them?

DRUMM. You are the only woman I know who can talk while
breathless.

DOLLY. I was dying to hear. Were they thrilled to bits?

DRUMM. They managed not to disintegrate. I spoke well. I think I
did. It's unimportant.

(DOLLY *has a natural gaiety, under which is a terror of his
displeasure. She seizes at any opportunity of staying in his
good graces.*)

DOLLY. Do you hear him! Where'd you walk them to?

DRUMM. To here.

DOLLY. You're mean. No, tell us.

DRUMM (*with a sigh, as if to say 'If I must'*). Along the Metals by
the old Atmospheric Railway, around the hill, along the Green
Road to the broken cross and from there to the old semaphore

station, which, thanks to my sense of smell, I kept them from entering. Then to Torca Cottage, and here by way of the Cat's Ladder and the Ramparts.

DOLLY. Such a distance.

DRUMM (*with satisfaction*). I think I may say that I lost one or two of them en route.

DOLLY. And you made a lovely speech.

DRUMM. Not a speech: I gave a talk.

DOLLY. And it's not everyone they ask. They're most particular. (*He looks at her coldly.*) And if they didn't ask you itself, a pity about them. What are they, only from the town.

DRUMM. Why did you come here?

DOLLY. To meet you.

DRUMM. I'm aware of that. I asked why.

DOLLY. I got tired of the four walls for company. (*Aware that he is looking at her*) The sun was splitting the trees out. You told me where you'd be finishing up, and I said why don't I give myself an outing and the pair of us can walk home.

DRUMM. So you went crawling through the gorse like a decrepit sheep.

(*She has no ready answer. Pause.*)

DOLLY. You put me in mind of an old statue.

DRUMM. What?

DOLLY. When I was coming down. You were sitting with the cigarette halfway to your mouth and not a jig out of you. No more life than an old statue.

DRUMM. I was admiring the view.

DOLLY. No, you weren't. Like a statue by that French artist.

DRUMM. Not artist. Sculptor.

DOLLY. Mm, by him . . . what's-his-name.

DRUMM (*deliberately*). Renoir.

DOLLY. Mm. (*A pause*) And I'm not a sheep, Dezzie.

DRUMM. Quite so.

DOLLY. Or decrepit, either.

DRUMM. To be sure.

DOLLY. I know it's only your way and you mean nothing by it, but other people don't know that, and it's not very –

DRUMM. Could we have done?

DOLLY. . . . very gentlemanly.

(*He looks at the view as if she were not there.*)

Are you not going to tell me what Ben said?

DRUMM. Who?

DOLLY. Ben Mulhall. I know you were in with him because I met Maddie Dowling in the chapel yard and she said she saw you coming out of his front gate.

DRUMM. So that's why.

DOLLY. Why what?

(*He does not answer: it is as if a reply would be beneath contempt.*)

I thought maybe he'd had news for you.

DRUMM (*affirmative*). Mm.

DOLLY. Had he?

DRUMM. We met in the street. I asked him if he had had the results of the X-rays. He took me into his surgery: I think that being in it reassures him that he's a doctor. He gave me one of those looks of his, redolent of the cemetery, and said that I should buy day returns from now on instead of season tickets.

DOLLY. Oh, Dezzie . . .

DRUMM (*annoyed*). He was being fatuous. Do you think he'd make jokes in the face of having his practice diminished by another patient? After he had used up his small reservoir of wit he condescended to get to the point. My own diagnosis was correct: I have a duodenal ulcer. He is to give me a diet sheet and a prescription, and he said that I am to watch myself. I told him that my name was Drumm, not Narcissus. (*As she looks at him blankly*) Of course it was lost on him, too.

DOLLY. You won't have to go into – I mean, to be –

DRUMM. Certainly not. Only a fool donates his body to science *before* death. Mulhall said that I am to drink milk instead of tea or coffee. Then senility overcame him and be began to babble about my giving up whiskey as well. An ulcer: one lives with it, but at least one lives.

(DOLLY *turns her head away and searches in her bag for a handkerchief.*)

Now what?

DOLLY. Nothing.

DRUMM. Not tears.

DOLLY. I'm grand.

DRUMM. Are you so disappointed?

DOLLY. Over what? (*Taking his meaning, reproachfully*) I'm relieved.

DRUMM. Oh, yes?

DOLLY. That's a terrible thing to –

DRUMM. Lower your voice.

DOLLY. Making out I was disapp—

DRUMM. This is a public place. You are incapable of recognizing a joke when you hear it.

DOLLY. It wasn't a –

(*He silences her with a look.*)

I was worried sick.

DRUMM. I didn't notice.

DOLLY. I wasn't going to let on to you, was I? But let's face it, Dezzie, we're not youngsters, and when you get to be our age –

DRUMM. Don't bracket our ages.

DOLLY. It's just the sort of thing that happens when you think at long last you're grand and clear and have the chance to enjoy life. Do you know what I said? I said: Ah no, God, not now, not when he'll be finished with the office in August and we can have our holiday and a rest and get the little car and –

(*She stops, dismayed that she has said more than she ought. Pause. He waits until she tries to disentangle herself.*)

I mean –

DRUMM. What little car?

DOLLY. If you owned up to it, you were as worried as I was.

DRUMM. You said a car.

DOLLY. When? (*As he draws in his breath; deprecatingly*) A small one.

DRUMM. Do you mean a motor car?

DOLLY. They're all the go.

DRUMM. All the . . . ?

(*She giggles nervously at the accidental pun.*)

DOLLY. Amn't I a panic.

DRUMM. What new foolishness is this?

DOLLY. We could afford it. You'll have your lump sum. (*Weakly*) It'd be nice.

DRUMM. How long has this been fermenting inside that brain of yours? A car. To be driven by whom, may I ask?

DOLLY. You could go for lessons.

DRUMM. You think so?

DOLLY. An ulcer wouldn't hinder you.

DRUMM. I daresay.

DOLLY. The Moroneys bought themselves one, and he gets blackouts.

DRUMM. And have you yet decided where we'll go in it, in this small car?

DOLLY. For . . . drives.

DRUMM (*without intonation*). Drives.

DOLLY. And we could visit people. Friends.

DRUMM. Such as whom?

DOLLY (*vaguely*). You know.

DRUMM. Friends, you said. Who?

DOLLY. New friends.

(*He decides that he has heard enough. He brushes down his coat and buttons it.*)

Don't be cross, Dezzie. I thought it'd be an interest for you.

DRUMM. I'm not at all cross, and it is of no interest either to me or for me. You take too much on yourself. Without consulting me, you sit weaving your little webs, letting your imagination run riot. And then, when I speak to you with the voice of reason, you come crashing to earth. You do yourself no kindness at all. Look here: don't you think there are enough fools and blackguards walking about on two legs without my having to contend with those in motor cars as well? Driving lessons, indeed.

DOLLY. If you don't want to learn, maybe I could.

DRUMM (*not unkindly*). Have sense. The entire population would take to the fields. (*He looks at his watch.*) A quarter to. Go, now: off home with you.

DOLLY. I thought the pair of us could –

DRUMM. . . . walk home. You said. I have a call to make.

DOLLY. Where?

(*He gives her one of his looks, as if she should know better by now than to pry.*)

I mean, I put the leg of lamb on for two o'clock. You won't be late?

DRUMM. Have I ever been late?

DOLLY. No, Dezzie.

DRUMM. No, never. Off you go, then.

DOLLY. Well, don't be –

(*She checks herself and sets off. He watches until she is out of sight, then goes towards the area at stage right, perhaps disappearing from view for a moment.*

Lights come up at stage right on the living room of a small red-bricked Edwardian house of the kind with a pocket-handkerchief garden in front. The room is neat and homely. It is newly decorated, and some of the furniture – perhaps the three-piece suite – is new as well. There is a television set and an electric fire with imitation logs.

MARY KEARNS *comes in. She is of an age with* DOLLY. *She is followed by* DRUMM.)

MARY. What is it they say? The dead arose and appeared to many. Come in.

DRUMM. If you're sure I'm welcome.

MARY. That's the last thing I'm sure of.

(*He stops in his tracks, affronted.*)

(*confused*) I dunno whether you are or not.

DRUMM. If you'd prefer I hadn't called . . .

MARY. I'll tell you that when I hear what brought you. (*Looking at him*) The same old face on you. A body daren't look crossways at you.

DRUMM. You're in an aggressive mood.

MARY. I'm surprised, do you mind?

DRUMM (*reasonably*). I daresay it would be surprising if you weren't. Perhaps this isn't convenient.

MARY. Ah, don't be such a dry stick.

DRUMM. I could call another time.

MARY. Aye, in another six years. Will you take that raincoat off you and sit. Wrapped up like an old mummy in the month of May.

DRUMM. A prudent man waits until June.

MARY. And one day you ought to go demented and buy yourself a new one. Give it me.

DRUMM (*removing his coat*). Is he in?

MARY. Is who in?

DRUMM. Your husband.

MARY. In or out, he has a name.

DRUMM. Yes. Is he here?

(*She snatches the coat and bunches up her fist in exasperation, shoving it up to his face.*)

MARY. I'll do it yet, you see if I don't. He's at the – (*Taking care to mention the name*) Lar is at Finnegan's, having his pint.

DRUMM (*smiling sceptically*). Pint, singular.

(*She does not deign to answer, but puts his coat away. We notice for the first time that she limps slightly.*)

Are you well?

MARY. The way you see me.

DRUMM. Fully recovered, I meant. The accident.

MARY. You're behind the times. I'm over that this long while.

DRUMM. I was concerned.

MARY. I know: I got your letter. I was surprised there wasn't a

311

'Mise, le meas' at the end of it. (*Regretting this*) And you sent
  Dolly to see me. It was nice of you.
DRUMM (*reasonably*). You'd been injured.
MARY. I do often say to Lar, I was such a good patient they put
  a barometer inside my leg for a present. It gives me the weather
  forecast.
DRUMM. The limp is hardly noticeable. Does it trouble you?
MARY. Only when people mention it.
DRUMM. You look very well indeed. Hardly a day older.
MARY. Since when? Yesterday?
DRUMM. I mean, since we –
MARY. You go past me every day in the town. I might as well be
  a midge in the air or a pane of glass a body'd look through. If
  you see me in time, you go across the street, and if you don't
  you put that face on you as if there was a dead dog in the road.
  Making a show of yourself and of me as well.
DRUMM. We weren't on speaking terms.
MARY. And don't I know it!
DRUMM. I am not a hypocrite. I will not affect a pretence of good-
  will simply for the benefit of every prying cornerboy and twit-
  ching lace curtain in the street.
MARY. A nod wouldn't have killed you.
DRUMM. You'd prefer me to be dishonest?
MARY. Be whatever you like. You're a bitter old pill, and you
  always will be.
DRUMM (*smiling tolerantly*). I have never yet met the member of
  your sex who didn't prefer common abuse to common sense.
MARY. Did you come in here to vex me?
DRUMM. No, I did not, and your point is well taken. Whatever bit-
  terness has been between us is in the past.
MARY (*ominously*). It's where?
DRUMM. I thought it was time we were friends again.
MARY. Is that what brung you?
DRUMM (*gently*). Brought me.
MARY. Brought you.
DRUMM. At our age, there aren't so many days left that one can
  afford to squander them in quarrels.
MARY. Life's too short.
DRUMM. Exactly.
MARY. That's the bee in your bonnet, is it? And so you walk in
  here, calm as you like after six years, expecting the welcome mat
  and to be offered rashers and eggs.

(*He makes no reply.*)
Do you want a cup of tea?

DRUMM. No, thank you.

MARY. There's a drop of whiskey.

DRUMM (*considering*). Ah. Well, in that case I won't give offence, as they say, with a refusal.

(*She goes to the sideboard.*)
The merest tincture. It'll sharpen the appetite. Dolly is doing us a leg of lamb.

MARY. How is she?

DRUMM. Unchanged.

MARY. This is a sudden notion of yours.

DRUMM. Pardon me?

MARY. To make up.

DRUMM. I had some news this morning to do with health. Good news. (*As she glances at him*) I wasn't ill, but there was the possibility. A cloud threatening the autumn day.

MARY. And it's gone now?

DRUMM. A passing shower.

MARY. So you feel full of yourself.

DRUMM. That, too, perhaps. But it brought it home to me that one's time is finite. If instead of cracking his execrable jokes Ben Mulhall had offered me that whiskey and if his eyes had avoided mine –

MARY. What was it that ailed you?

DRUMM. Tummy trouble. And if these antennae and these (*He gestures towards his eyes and ears.*) had detected a verdict of another kind, well, I would have lived to reg— (*He amends, smiling*) I would have regretted those six years.

MARY. Will you pour this? I never know how much. (*She gives him the bottle and a glass.*) Six years? Did you ever add up all the time we haven't been talking since I knew you? How many years out of the forty? You're an Irish summer of a man: sunny skies one day and rain the next. For a week or maybe a month you'd be the height of company: you'd make a cat laugh; next thing, there's a face on you like a plateful of mortal sins and you're off out that door as if there was a curtain rod stuck up you. You can get on with no one: a cup of cold water would disagree with you.

DRUMM. You say that, but in your heart you know that I am the most reasonable man in this town.

MARY. Drink your drink.

313

DRUMM. As well as being a person of principle.

MARY. Oh, I know that: no need to tell me. You won't be ten minutes in heaven before you're not talking to God. (*In wry despair*) I dunno what to do with you.

DRUMM (*raising his glass*). To both of us.

MARY. Until the next time.

DRUMM. No, no: I promise. I will never again allow you to provoke me.

(*He drinks. She opens her mouth to make an angry retort, then gives him up as hopeless.*)

An Irishman's claret: no finer drink.

MARY. You haven't noticed my room.

DRUMM. Haven't I? (*Looking about him*) Oh, yes.

MARY. We did it up with the compensation.

DRUMM. It has taste.

MARY. And got the few new bits of furniture.

DRUMM. I approve.

MARY. High time, says you.

DRUMM. I don't say. I felt always at home here.

MARY. It was too dark. The old people, them that's dead and gone, they went in for that: no sunlight, everything morose and dusty. I thought we'd get into the fashion.

DRUMM. You did.

MARY. We never set foot in here except for Christmas and funerals. That was the style in them days: one room for living in and another that was a museum for cracked cups. The Room, we called it. 'Who's that at the door?' 'Father Creedon.' 'Bring him into the Room.'

DRUMM (*smiling*). Yes.

MARY. I made a clearance. It's queer. The furniture was easy got rid of: out the door and that was that. But the smell of beeswax and the lavender bags my mother filled the house with: nothing'll budge that, it'll bury all of us. Still, we use the room now, by me song we do. And I had the kitchen done up as well. Do you remember how it was?

DRUMM. I know how it was.

MARY. See if you recognize it. Come on.

(*They start out of the room.*)

Do you remember the old range and the dresser and the one tap over the sink?

DRUMM (*humouring her*). Not all gone?

MARY (*pleased with herself*). You'll see. In you go.

(*During this, they cross into the area at the left, passing the foot of the steps as if walking across a hallway. As they enter this area lights come up. We are looking at the kitchen of forty years ago, with the dresser, the range and the cold-water earthenware sink as mentioned by* MARY.

At the kitchen table are MIBS *and* DESMOND, *who watches as she reads silently from a book, her lips moving. There are exercise books and pen and ink.*

DRUMM *looks at the young* MIBS *as* MARY *talks artlessly about the room as it is now.*)

What do you think of it? Mr Comerford put in the kitchen unit and the shelves, but they had a fierce job with the new sink and the hot-and-cold, and as for the washing machine, don't talk to me. Anyhow, with that done I thought I might as well be the divil for style and break the bank altogether, so I got the new table and chairs.

DRUMM (*only half paying attention, looking at* MIBS). You've done wonders.

MARY. At our age, what harm in a bit of comfort?

DRUMM. None.

MARY. If we don't spoil ourselves, no one else will. (*Prompting him*) So what do you think?

(DRUMM, *standing behind* MIBS, *touches her hair.*)

MIBS. Stop that.

DESMOND. Sorry.

MARY. Do you like it?

DRUMM. I'm sorry. It shines. What's that odious new word, that jargon they're so fond of? Functional. It functions.

MARY (*flatly*). I see.

DRUMM. I meant that the word was odious, not the room.

MARY (*coldly*). Yes, I know.

DRUMM. Once it was for living in, now you cook in it and wash clothes. It suits its purpose. Formica surfaces, a refrigerator, yellow cupboards –

MARY (*almost snapping*). They're primrose.

DRUMM. Are they? (*With false enthusiasm*) So they are.

MARY. I'm sure you're interested.

DRUMM. Mary, you must never ask a man to give you an opinion of a kitchem. Dolly now would be over the moon about it.

MARY. Dolly has taste. You left your drink. (*Still mildly affronted, she leads the way back to the living room.*)

DRUMM. It's become a new house. What it cost you, I –

315

MIBS (*pushing her book aside*). I can't make head or tail of it.
(DRUMM, *on the point of leaving, looks back at her.*)

DESMOND. It's simple.

MIBS. To them with brains.

DESMOND. Show me.
(DRUMM *follows* MARY *into the living room.*)

MIBS. This bit. (*Reading*) 'My friends, we will not go again . . .'

DESMOND. 'Or ape an ancient rage,
Or stretch the folly of our youth to be the shame of age.'

MIBS. What's it mean?

DESMOND. '—ape an ancient rage.' The writer – Chesterton –
what he's saying is that it's only natural for young people to be
wild and passionate. (*Almost blushing*) Angry, that is. And no
one minds foolishness, because it's too soon yet for them to be
wise.

MIBS. But *you* are.

DESMOND. No. I'm intelligent: there's a difference. But an elderly
person who behaves as if he were still young: that's . . . well,
it's not nice to see.

MIBS. That's what this means?

DESMOND. Mm.

MIBS. Pity he didn't say so, then. No it's me: I'm thick.

DESMOND. Never.

MIBS. Behind the door when the brains were handed out. Is that
why you don't see old people kissing and stuff?

DESMOND. Well, what Chesterton was –

MIBS. I mean, is it because they don't like to be seen doing it, or
because they're old and don't feel like doing it?

DESMOND (*embarrassed*). Well, a mixture, I'd say.

MIBS. Imagine being kissed by someone who's all wrinkled and
gubby. (*She thinks about it and shudders.*) Eeagh!

DESMOND (*picking up the book*). The next line –

MIBS. And anyway, kissing is one thing, but whether they want to
or not, they can't . . . you know.

DESMOND. What?

MIBS. Do anything. They're not able.
(*He conceals his discofiture by staring into the book.*)
At least the man isn't. The woman doesn't have to do a hand's
turn: she has it easy. (*She giggles.*) It's a tough old station for
fellows, isn't it? You start off in life by not being able to, and
you end up by not being able to. It's a panic. (*Noticing him*)
You're going red.

DESMOND. No such thing.

MIBS. Y'are so, you're on fire. (*Teasing him*) Answer this and
answer true: will you love me when I'm old and grey?

DESMOND. Yes. Yes, I will.

(*He replies so gravely and with such directness that it is her
turn to be taken off-balance.*)

MIBS (*deciding to make light of it*). Is that a fact?

DESMOND. I've said so.

MIBS. Honest to God, like? No, tell us.

(*He is silent, not knowing how to rise to her tone.*)

You'd want to watch out I might believe you. (*Affectionately*)
Chancer. You are: you're a fierce chancer, you know that?

DESMOND (*returning to his book*). We ought to get on with this.

(*He reads*) 'My friend, we will not go again or ape an ancient
rage . . .'

MIBS. Ah, quit it. My brains are in bits.

DESMOND. We're nearly done. Four more lines.

MIBS. Let me off them.

DESMOND. Two minutes.

MIBS. You will: you can't refuse me. (*She makes to put the book
to one side.*)

DESMOND. Don't do that.

MIBS. I'll give you a kiss.

DESMOND. No.

MIBS. What?

DESMOND. I said no.

MIBS. And that's the fellow that lets on he loves me.

DESMOND. I don't buy affection, thank you.

MIBS (*mimicking him*). 'I don't buy affection, thank you.' God,
talk about a dry old stick. Do you know what they call you in
the town? Do you know their nickname for you?

DESMOND. Because you can't have your own way –

MIBS. Mammy Cough-Bottle. It suits you.

DESMOND. 'Or stretch the folly of our youth to be the shame of
age . . .

But walk with clearer eyes and ears this path that wandereth.
And see undrugg'd in evening light the decent inn of death.'

MIBS. Mammy Cough-Bottle.

DESMOND. Chesterton saw death as a country inn.

MIBS. Did he.

DESMOND. A place of shelter.

MIBS. Wasn't he great.

DESMOND. He employs a metaphor.

317

MIBS. What night's her night off?

(*He slams the book down with just enough force to make her jump in spite of herself. A moment's pause.*)

Don't do a sulk.

DESMOND. You'll fail that exam.

MIBS. There's a blue moon out: we agree at last!

DESMOND. And you could pass it.

MIBS. No bother. Like winking.

DESMOND. You have a good mind. Fine, quick –

MIBS. And demented. You've driven me distracted. I get up in the morning and there's a looking glass in the door of the wardrobe, and I look in it and there's this person staring back at me. But it's not the person you see. God knows what *she* looks like.

DESMOND. You make difficulties.

MIBS. Yourself and bloody Chesterton: I'm unfortunate with the pair of yous.

DESMOND. He's easy.

MIBS. I'm sure. For them that had a schoolmaster for a da, yeah.

DESMOND. That has nothing to do with it.

MIBS. Not much, not half. He beat it into you. Lar Kearns told me.

DESMOND. That ignoramus.

MIBS. He says –

DESMOND (*jealous*). When did you see him?

MIBS. He says you were never let out after tea. You were kept in, and your da would take a cane and flay the legs off you. He says the roars of you –

DESMOND. He's a liar.

MIBS. The whole town knew it. Your da used to crease you.

DESMOND. I never roared: *that's* a lie.

MIBS. My da gave me the strap once.

DESMOND. When?

MIBS. I came home at all hours: missed the last tram and had to foot it out. I was sixteen. I walked in the door and he was weak from worrying. He asked if anyone had laid a finger on me, and when I told him no he murdered me.

DESMOND. My father . . . (*He hesitates.*)

MIBS. What?

DESMOND. It was in case the other boys might think I was his favourite. He wanted to show them how fair he was.

MIBS. Well?

318

DESMOND. So he'd pretend I was day-dreaming or whispering or copying answers. 'Drumm, get out here.'

MIBS (*fascinated*). Leave off.

DESMOND. And always on the legs, never the hands, because he wanted to be sure I could do homework.

MIBS. My da would have gone to the school.

DESMOND. I lacked that advantage.

(MIBS *gives a small giggle. She is listening intently.*)

He gave me extra subjects, you see. Three hours each evening, and he'd examine me next morning, before school. He wanted me to win scholarships. A teacher's son, he said, a boy with brains, ought to be ashamed to be paid for. If my work was poor, if it was slipshod, he'd take the cane out and lift my chin up with the tip of it. He'd say: 'I want you to know why I'm doing this. Let the others, the duds, the idlers, let them work in tramyards or on the roads or draw the dole. Let them live in public houses when they have money and on street corners when they have none. But not you, by Christ, no!' . . . excuse me. 'An education, that's what puts the world inside of you. And in time to come you'll cry salt tears of gratitude for this, for I'm the only man you'll ever call your master.' He used a thin cane, the sort we nicknamed a whistler. (*He smiles.*) I was the envy of the class because I was the first boy to be in long trousers. Do you know, he's dead these nine years.

MIBS. He was killed, wasn't he?

DESMOND. Mm.

MIBS. In the tunnel.

DESMOND. Yes.

MIBS. Were you sad?

DESMOND. The first thought I had was: no cane tomorrow.

MIBS (*insisting: sentimental*). Ah. And then you were sad.

DESMOND. I think I was. I was fifteen, and I wanted the moon and couldn't have it. I wanted my father alive and myself an orphan.

MIBS (*grinning*). Chancer.

DESMOND. Truly.

MIBS. Still, you got on, thanks to him.

DESMOND. How, got on?

MIBS. If he hadn't been so hard on you, you wouldn't be made for life today.

DESMOND (*amused*). Is that what I am?

MIBS. My da says so. He says the civil service is a bobby's job. He says you'll be a great catch.

319

DESMOND (*not displeased*). I'm sure.

MIBS. Some day.

DESMOND. He said that?

MIBS (*airily*). For someone.

DESMOND. Nonsense.

MIBS. Whoever she is. (*Then*) Of course, the way my da drops a hint, if it fell on your head it'd kill you.

DESMOND (*fishing*). What hint? What about?

MIBS (*mimicking again*). 'What hint? What about?' You're so innocent you'll skip Purgatory, won't you? Anyway, I'm not going to get married, not to anyone, and least of all to you, so you needn't ask me.

DESMOND. I won't.

MIBS. You bugger. No, you're too milk-and-watery for me: there's a nun inside of you.

DESMOND. A what?

MIBS. There is.

DESMOND (*apparently amused*). Really?

MIBS. Mm.

DESMOND. A nun.

MIBS. A Carmelite.

(*The fixed smile on his face begins to fall apart.*)
Well, it's time you were told.

DESMOND. I daresay it is. (*He makes a show of looking at his watch.*)
Good heavens, speaking of time –

MIBS. Now you're in a wax.

DESMOND. Not at all.

MIBS. You're raging.

DESMOND. Nothing of the sort. Only I think I ought to be –

MIBS. Take a joke.

DESMOND. I do: honestly.

MIBS. Then where are you going?

DESMOND. Home to the convent.

MIBS (*moving to intercept him*). Ah, you messer, come back. Yes, you will, do as you're bid. Now sit.

DESMOND. I have to go.

MIBS. Don't tell lies: sit. Now listen. Why do you pick on me to persecute? We're night and day, chalk and cheese: I'm not your sort. So why?

(*He looks dumbly at her.*)
What's the fatal attraction?

320

DESMOND. You're a . . .

MIBS. Go on.

DESMOND. . . . very fine type of person.

MIBS (*gently mocking*). Would you say?

DESMOND. Mind, I'm not a fool. The first time I saw you in the town I said to myself: she's human, she'll have faults like anyone else. And it's true. I mean, you fritter your time away on such rubbish. You moon over the latest crooner on the wireless and whatever the most slobbery song it. Your head is full of film stars with their divorces and carryings on. You have a mind like a mayfly. You don't read. That's one thing I can't understand: whenever I open a book it's the start of a journey. And you talk to cornerboys like Lar Kearns — do you know he goes into Larkin's? Well, it's no wonder you've picked up the habit of talking about people's . . . bodies and such. Honestly!

MIBS (*straight-faced*). But I'm a fine type of person.

DESMOND. Oh, yes.

MIBS. And the pair of us are a match, you'd say?

DESMOND. That's what I'm telling you.

(*She bunches up her fist and puts it to his chin as* MARY *did with* DRUMM *in the preceding scene.*)

MIBS. I'll do it yet. You see if I don't.

DESMOND. Do what?

MIBS. I'll — (*She is seized by an uncontrollable urge to laugh. She splutters and turns away from him.*) Oh, go home.

DESMOND. And that's another little fault of yours: you fly into moods for no reason.

MIBS. Will you buzz off?

DESMOND. Before I go —

MIBS. Goodbye.

DESMOND. Please. If you'll allow me, it'll make the whole evening seem worthwhile.

MIBS. Will it?

DESMOND. Let me.

MIBS. Well, don't take all night about it.

(*She closes her eyes and waits for the kiss.*
Instead, and without looking at her, he sits at the table and picks up the book of verse.)

DESMOND. The last two lines: one minute, I promise you.

MIBS (*outraged*). Oh, for God's sake.

DESMOND. 'For there is good news yet to hear and fine things to be seen,

Before we go to Paradise by way of – '
(*There are three loud knocks at the door opening on the back yard.*)

MIBS (*jumping*). What's that?

(*A low, eerie moaning is heard.*)

Oh, Sacred Heart, what is it?

(*The door opens slightly.*)

Go 'way. Desmond, save me, don't let it come in.

(LAR KEARNS *sticks his head in.*)

LAR. How are you, Mibs? I bet that shook you, what?

MIBS. It's you. (*Pleased to see him*) You bugger, you: I'm not worth me salt. (*To* DESMOND) It's Lar.

DESMOND (*coldly*). Is it?

LAR (*noticing him*). Ah, bejay, will you looka who's here.

(*As he crosses to greet* DESMOND, *lights dim on the kitchen and come up quickly on the living room, where* KEARNS *has entered and, in a kind of mirror image, is crossing to* DRUMM.)

KEARNS. It's the Cough Bottle himself. The dead arose and appeared, what?

MARY. That's what *I* said.

KEARNS. Me old flower, put it there.

(DRUMM *allows his hand to be shaken.*

KEARNS *is his contemporary: a feckless, good-humoured man, physically gone to seed.*)

Well, it's high time you came to see us. We missed you. Are you in form?

DRUMM. I'm told so.

KEARNS (*looking from one of them to the other*). And the hatchet's buried, what? The pipe of peace is lit, yes?

DRUMM (*querulously to* MARY). He takes me for a Mohican.

KEARNS. And the war-drums is silent. Drums . . . Drumm, that's a good one. Boom-boom. (*To* MARY) Did you offer him a jar?

MARY. Certainly I offered him a –

DRUMM. I don't want another one.

KEARNS. Yes, you do. Where's his glass?

DRUMM. My dear man, will you realize that there are people in the world who, unlike yourself, mean what they say?

KEARNS. Sure I know: you meet all sorts. (*He busies himself pouring drinks.*)

MARY (*signalling to* DRUMM). Take it, to please him. (*To* KEARNS) And don't you go pouring for yourself.

322

KEARNS. Only the one.

MARY. No.

KEARNS. So's the occasion won't go by unmarked.

MARY. I 'clare to God, if the cat died he'd drink to the repose of its soul.

KEARNS. Stop growling.

MARY. He's been in Finnegan's since half-twelve. Well, it won't be the first time his dinner had to be thrun out.

KEARNS (*handing* DRUMM *a drink*). You see what I put up with? It's the price of me for spoiling her.

MARY (*mock-anguish*). God forgive him.

KEARNS. I ought to have borrowed a page from your book. Dolly soon found out who the boss was. You used the whip from the first fence on, and now she's afraid to look crossways at you.

DRUMM. Is that meant to be funny?

KEARNS. That's where I slipped up: too much of a softy. Is it what?

DRUMM. That remark is untrue and impertinent. Dolly has never been afraid of me.

KEARNS (*grinning*). He's a terror.

DRUMM. Certainly not with cause. She's timid by nature, highly-strung, I grant you that. But to imply that I bully her —

MARY. Lar is joking.

DRUMM. Is he? I think not. And I'm sorry, but I do take exception. I despise tyrants, domestic or otherwise.

MARY. Sure we know. (*Glaring at* KEARNS) Trust you.

KEARNS. Trust me to what? Where's the harm in telling a man he wears the trousers? (*To* DRUMM) You're as prickly as bedamned: it's like talking to a gorse bush. Listen . . . good health. Delighted to see you. (*He swallows most of his own drink with evident enjoyment.*)

MARY. That's him. A glass in his hand and not a care in the world. You're talking to us again after six years and he's not even inquisitive enough to ask why.

KEARNS. What's there to ask? He's here and he's welcome. (*To* DRUMM) You'll stay and have a bite of dinner with us.

MARY. No, he will not. Dolly has his own ready for him.

KEARNS. Good oul' Dolly. How is she? Is she tip-top?

DRUMM. She went over the summit some time ago. (*Relenting.*) She's well.

KEARNS. And how's the pen-pushing?

DRUMM. If by that you mean work, I retire in August.

MARY. You never.

KEARNS. The oul' pension at long last, what?

MARY (*incredulous*). No, it's years away.

DRUMM. August 5th.

KEARNS. Not to mention the spondulicks into your fist.

DRUMM. It's called a gratuity.

KEARNS. Begod, but some fellows are rightly steeped, what? That's one of the disadvantages of being unemployed. There's no retirement age.

DRUMM (*ignoring him, to* MARY). Ten more weeks.

MARY. It's true, it's true. The minutes crawl; it's the years that run.

KEARNS. Answer me this, though.

(*He prods* DRUMM *with his finger and thrusts his face forward so that they are nose to nose.*)

Here's the question. Where does the time go?

DRUMM (*snapping*). What?

KEARNS. The time. Tell us.

DRUMM. Much of it goes in listening to banalities.

KEARNS. Oh, yeah?

DRUMM. Uttered by buffoons.

KEARNS. You're right: too bloody true. (*He reaches for the bottle.*)

MARY. So what'll you do?

DRUMM. Do?

MARY. With your time. I suppose you have it all cut and dried as usual.

DRUMM. I did my sums the other day. I discovered that I have been eight times around the world. Two hundred and ten thousand miles. Unfortunately, it was as a passenger on the Dalkey to Westland Row Train. Dolly says that now is our chance to visit Stella and her husband in Toronto.

MARY. You ought to.

DRUMM. She can go. I doubt if Canada and myself would see eye to eye.

KEARNS. Did it offend you?

DRUMM. Those who have been there tell me it wants for character. I get the impression of the great outdoors and next to nothing indoors.

MARY. You'll see Stella and the children.

DRUMM. She has four now.

MARY. I heard.

DRUMM. They were with us last summer. You may have seen the

boys in the town: they looked like pygmy lumberjacks. As for Stella, she's always been a rather colourless girl. Too docile: like her sister, like Una. Perhaps Canada and she were destined for each other. I've come to think of her as a kind of walking Ontario.

MARY (*reproachful*). Desmond.

DRUMM. No, I'll stay here.

MARY. You're not natural.

DRUMM. I beg to differ. I'm fond of both my children, but that fondness doesn't blind me to the fact that through some perverse biological quirk they favour their mother. I realized it in Una's case on the day of her confirmation. I am reliably told that when she was asked if she renounced the devil and his works and pomps, she blushed and said: 'I don't mind.' As for Stella, I ask her how she is; she tells me, and thereafter our conversation consists of a torrent of two words every half-hour. Hardly worth crossing the Atlantic for.

MARY. But you'll let Dolly go?

DRUMM. It'll be a holiday for her. And perhaps the change of air will blow some of the bees out of that bonnet of hers. She wants a motor car.

MARY. The style of her.

DRUMM. She gets worse with age.

MARY. How?

DRUMM. A car.

MARY. Buy it for her.

DRUMM. You're as bad as she is.

MARY. Don't be so mean.

DRUMM. It's a whim. She lives two hundred yards from a bus stop. She has no need of a car.

KEARNS. Ah, but there's places a bus can't take you.

DRUMM. What? (*As previously, this is almost a bark of hostility.*)

KEARNS. Halfway up Booterstown Avenue.

DRUMM. What about it?

KEARNS. You can't get there be the bus.

DRUMM. Well?

KEARNS. A motor car's your only man.

DRUMM. What have I to do with Booterstown Avenue?

KEARNS. You can get the Stillorgan bus that passes the top of it, or you can take a Number Eight or a Seven-A to the other end. But for any place in between the two you have to hoof it.

DRUMM. Hoof it where?

KEARNS. I'm telling you. Up Booterstown Avenue.

DRUMM. Are you mad?

KEARNS. To call on people.

DRUMM. I don't know anyone on Booterstown Avenue.

KEARNS. I'm not surprised.

(DRUMM *stares at him in fury, then turns to* MARY.)

DRUMM. Of course, what's behind this is, she wants to queen it in front of the neighbours . . .

KEARNS. *Don't* get her a car then! Walk her feet off to the knees.

DRUMM. . . . and thinks that I'm going to be her unpaid chauffeur.

KEARNS. We're getting a car.

DRUMM. *You* are?

KEARNS. I was thinking of a Vauxhall.

MARY (*smiling*). Don't mind him.

KEARNS. You won't laugh when I drive up in it. (*To* DRUMM) I'm putting in for a job as a rep. Car supplied.

MARY (*winking at* DRUMM). I'm sure you'll get it.

KEARNS. You wait.

MARY. At your age.

KEARNS. Me age is me trump card. An employer knows he can trust a man with snow on his thatch, a man that'll do a day's work and not go chasing bits of stuff. And I know the ins and outs of commodities. Didn't I travel for six months for Swinnertons' in kitchen implements?

DRUMM. You did? When?

MARY. He means the potato peelers.

KEARNS. A toppin' little gadget.

DRUMM. You hawked them, door to door.

KEARNS. I travelled, I was on the go. You're so hot with words: was I moving or wasn't I? I was my own worst enemy on that job. I could have swung the lead: instead, I saturated half the county. No one left to sell them to. Dolly bought one.

DRUMM. I know: it broke.

KEARNS. The time herself got the compensation, we coulda had a car then, only she wanted the house done up. I said to her: 'You're the one that got the going over: you spend the money.'

MARY. He did: it's true.

KEARNS. 'Buy whatever you like with it, even if it's a kept man.'

MARY. He said that, too.

KEARNS. I mean, fair's fair. She got a fierce old knock. 'Right,' says I, 'do the house up. I won't touch a ha'penny.'

DRUMM. I'm impressed.

326

MARY. He's not the worst of them.

DRUMM. I'm bound to say I wouldn't have given you that much credit. I apologize.

KEARNS. Ah, dry up.

DRUMM. No, no: I lack charity.

KEARNS. I won't forget that night in a hurry. I thought she was dead.

DRUMM. You saw the accident?

KEARNS. Did I see it!

MARY. It's over and done with.

KEARNS. Begod, I saw it.

MARY. Now that'll do.

KEARNS (*heartily*). Who do you think ran over her?

DRUMM. What?

KEARNS. You don't know?

MARY (*uneasily*). Desmond doesn't want to –

KEARNS. Give you a laugh. Sister of mine that lives the far side of Athboy, off in the bloody wilds – her second youngest is getting married, and of course guess who's invited. 'We'll go in style,' says I to your one here, 'or not at all.' So I get the lend of Joe Duggan's car: the Mini. Slip him a few quid: the job is right. Well, we have a good day of it: the Mass, the breakfast and the few harmless jars, and at the end of the story back we come: not a feather out of us. Grand. So I pull up outside Joe's house and your woman gets out to open the gate for me, so's I can reverse in, like.

MARY. I go behind the car –

KEARNS. Will you let me tell it.

MARY. It wasn't his fault.

(DRUMM *is motionless, waiting for* KEARNS *to finish*.)

KEARNS. The clutch pedal is so worn, me foot slips off it. Well, the car gives an almighty buck-jump backwards, and next thing she's pinned against the pillar of the gate.

MARY. Joe Duggan had no business lending that car to people.

KEARNS. Mercy of God she wasn't killed.

DRUMM. Yes, it was.

KEARNS. Still, it could happen to a bishop.

DRUMM. I'm sure: if he was drunk at the time.

KEARNS. Ah, now . . .

MARY. Lar wasn't –

DRUMM. You maim the woman for life, and then you have the gall, the impudence to put on airs because you magnanimously allow her to spend her own money as she chooses.

327

MARY. You weren't there. You don't know what happened.

DRUMM. I know this much: that if he were ever at a wedding and came home sober, there would be a prima facie case for an annulment. (*To* KEARNS) As long as I've known you you've been a millstone around her neck: soft, easy and worthless, an idler whose idea of hard work was having to stoop to pick up his dole money. I thought that trying to cripple her spirit would be enough for you, but apparently not: you wanted to break her body as well. I'm not surprised the boy left home.

(*A pause,* KEARNS *stares at* DRUMM, *then the moment passes. He laughs, shaking his head.*)

KEARNS. God, Dezzie, you're a queer harp. (*To* MARY) I'll go and give me hands a rub.

MARY. Are you all right?

KEARNS. Oh, a shocker. (*He goes out.*)

DRUMM. You see? No answer.

MARY. If you please, I want you to go.

DRUMM. You're upset. I'm not surprised.

MARY. You haven't changed and you never will. More fool me for thinking you could.

DRUMM. Are you saying you're vexed? With me?

MARY. I have a dinner to get.

DRUMM. Because I tell the truth?

MARY (*angrily*). You and your truth, I'm sick of yous. Take it home with you. Pour it over your leg of lamb. Bring it to bed with you and warm your feet on it.

DRUMM. Old age hasn't made you less contrary.

(*She faces away from, waiting for him to leave.*)

Very well. I'll leave you for a day or so.

MARY. I don't want you back here.

DRUMM. Nonsense. (*His smile disappears as he realizes that she means it.*) Or perhaps it isn't. (*Affronted*) As you wish.

(*He puts his coat on, watching as he does so for a sign that she may relent. Her face is tight with anger.*)

You know this is foolishness.

MARY. I won't have Lar talked to like that, by you or anyone.

DRUMM. I don't see the crime in saying what every inhabitant of this town over the age of reason knows to be true. He is weak, shiftless and irresponsible. It's hardly a secret.

MARY (*wearily*). Will you go away.

DRUMM. I really don't understand you. (*He goes to the door and stops.*) Would it change matters if –

328

MARY. No.

DRUMM. . . . if I were to tell you –

MARY. I said no.

DRUMM. I don't thank you for this. You force it upon me. If I'm forbidden the house it'll be on your conscience, and I'll not have that on mine. I don't thank you at all. Ben Mulhall gives me less than six months to live. Now am I to go?

(*The lights fade slowly. As if in counterpoint, music is heard: a vocal of* 'You Can't Stop me from Dreaming'.

The lights come up in the kitchen. LAR *is winding up a portable gramophone, while* DESMOND *is at the table resenting his presence.*)

LAR. It's real hi-di-hi stuff, wha'?

DESMOND. Pardon me?

LAR. Hi-de-hi, ho-de-ho, like.

DESMOND. I didn't know you were a linguist.

LAR. Yeah, Fred Astaire the second.

(MIBS *comes in. She has been getting ready to go for a walk.*)

MIBS. Who put that thing on?

DESMOND (*virtuously*). I didn't.

MIBS (*turning the gramophone off*). Lar Kearns, do you not know what day it is? If me ma and da walked in they'd skin me.

LAR. Wha'?

MIBS. Can you not be like Desmond and sit quiet till I've me coat on? Messer. (*She goes out.*)

LAR. Holy Thursdays is brutal.

DESMOND. Is they?

LAR. All the picture houses shut and no hops. Tomorrow's worse: it's Good Friday.

DESMOND. Never.

LAR. Oh, yeah: it's the day after.

(DESMOND *looks at him quizzically.*)

After Holy Thursday, like.

DESMOND. Ah.

LAR. Peculiar day, Good Friday: give you the hump. Me and the lads, we go down to the Lady's Well and play ponner for ha'pennies. It's sorta like stayin' out of the way till it's over. J'ever notice how if you say a curse on a Good Friday it doesn't sound right?

DESMOND. Amazing.

LAR. True as God. Try it.

DESMOND. I must.

LAR. You don't go to hops?

(DESMOND *shakes his head.*)
Y'ought to. It's how you get off your mark. I do always get up
for the slow waltz: you know: when there's only the coloured
lights goin' all over the place, like in the pictures when there's
a jail break. Last Sunday in Dun Laoghaire town hall, the
Missouri Waltz, I got a great old lie in. Massive.

DESMOND. I'm sure it was.

LAR. A nurse. I couldn't see her home on account of she was on
a bike, but I got a promise for Easter Monday. Don't tell Mibs.

DESMOND. Mary! Why not?

LAR. Spoil me chances.

DESMOND *looks at him with hostility.*)
No flies on Jembo. No names, no— Wha's up?

DESMOND. In your pocket.

LAR. Where?

DESMOND. Is that a pencil?

LAR. Yeah.

DESMOND. I thought it was. Where'd you find it?

LAR. I didn't find it. It's mine.

DESMOND. Yours? (*With an air of one solving a mystery*) Ah, I
see. You draw, do you?

LAR. No, it's for – (*He realizes that he is being insulted. Easily*) Ah,
that's good, that's quick, I like that. Sure I'm not a scholar, Dezzie: I never let on to be. (*He takes out the pencil.*) Do you know what
this is for? I help me cousin Mattie that has the fishin' boat: I count
the catch for him. That and tickin' off winners. Couldn't even write
a Christmas card to save me life. (*Still pleasantly*) Mind, if I could,
at least there's people I could send them to.

(MIBS *returns. She has her coat on.*)

MIBS. Maybe I ought to wait for them. Do you think?

LAR. What time did they go out at?

MIBS. Eight.

LAR. Sure doing the Seven Churches'll take till all hours. (*He
hands her the pencil.*) Here, write them a note.

(*She tears a page from one of the exercise books on the table.*)

MIBS. Desmond says he has to be off home.

LAR (*pleased*). Can you not come with us? Aw.

DESMOND. I don't *have* to be anywhere.

(LAR *signals to him not to stay.* DESMOND *pointedly ignores
him.*)
It's a good idea. A breath of fresh air. (*To* LAR, *as if not
taking his point*) Yes?

330

MIBS (*scribbling*). 'Gone . . . for . . . a stroll.'

DESMOND. Two 'l's.

MIBS. There, short and sweet. So where'll we go?

DESMOND (*a jibe at* LAR). Good heavens, need you ask? To a 'hop'.

MIBS. The very thing. Where . . . the Metropole? No, the Gresham for style, seeing as I have me fur coat on.

LAR. Why don't we?

MIBS. What?

LAR. Go to a hop. You think we can't? (*He snaps shut the catches on the portable gramophone and carries it towards the door.*) Come on . . . I'll show yous.

MIBS. Will you stop acting the –

(*He starts out, perhaps by way of the living room where* DRUMM *and* MARY *are, and where the lights now come up.*) Lar, you're not to take that out of the house. It's me ma's . . . she'll reef me.

LAR (*calling back*). Sorrento Park.

MIBS. No, bring it back. Lar!

(*She follows him out.*

DESMOND *picks up his coat and is unaware for the moment that she has gone.*)

DESMOND. I told you he was a cornerboy, but of course you knew better. Now you can –

(*He hurries out after her.*

During the following, lights come up on the bandstand. LAR *appears and sets up the gramophone on the balustrade. He takes a record out of the storage space in the lid, puts it on the turntable and begins to wind up the gramophone.*)

DRUMM. Nice news for a Sunday morning.

MARY. I think you're drawing the longbow.

DRUMM. Do I ever?

MARY. Ben Mulhall never said that to you.

DRUMM. He hummed and hawed, of course. I told him to waste his own time if he wished, but not mine, that I wanted none of his verbal placebos.

MARY (*insistent*). He never said it straight out.

DRUMM. I told him, I said to him: 'Look here, my friend, I was at the altar this morning, but one more word, one syllable of prevarication from you, and I shall unhesitatingly hurl myself into a state of mortal sin and you into eternity.' That changed his tune for him. (*He chuckles.*)

331

MARY. May God forgive you.

DRUMM. Eh?

MARY. What are you laughing at?

DRUMM (*a small bemused gesture*). I suppose at what I can.

MARY. Coming here to frighten a body. I don't believe any of it.

DRUMM. You will.

MARY. I know you too well. You're a cod.

DRUMM. More, I would say, of a mackerel.

(*She gives him an angry look.*)

The . . . um, specialist recommends what he calls an exploratory operation.

MARY. Well, then!

DRUMM. Impudence. I've been a civil servant for long enough to recognize as such the instincts of a customs official. I am not a suitcase to be stared into and ransacked.

MARY. If it cured you –

DRUMM. What I have, as Ben Mulhall admitted when I managed to hack down the bush he was beating about, is in here (*He touches his abdomen.*) and it's terminal. More jargon from America. I keep expecting to arrive at a celestial Dublin Airport.

(*In the bandstand.* LAR *mimes a compère speaking into a microphone.*)

LAR. And now, ladies and gentlemen, the last dance before the raffle will be a gents' Excuse-me.

DRUMM. It will go against me later, but if I could have just a drop more of . . .

(*He indicates his empty glass: it is as if he feared his composure might desert him.*

As MARY *goes to fetch the whiskey bottle,* MIBS *and* DESMOND *arrive at the bandstand.* LAR *starts the gramophone. The lighting is from a street lamp. It is an evening in early April:* MIBS *and* DESMOND *are warmly dressed;* LAR *wears a jacket and is tieless.*)

LAR (*to* MIBS). Now isn't there a hop? Come on.

MIBS. Turn it off.

LAR (*to* DESMOND). Hey, it's the tune, the one I told you. Do you remember?

DESMOND. No.

LAR. Yes, you do. The Miss –

MIBS. It's Holy Week. Do you want us to be read off the altar?

LAR. Who's to hear? They're all at the devotions. (*He dances on his own.*) All the Holy Marys. Hey . . .

(*This, as* DESMOND *gets to the gramophone and puts the brake on. A moan from the record as it slows down.*)
Feck off, that's not yours.
DESMOND. Is it yours?
(*A moment of confrontation.* DESMOND *is between* LAR *and the gramophone.* LAR *is too easy-going to want to fight.*)
LAR. Be a sport.
MIBS. Leave it off, or I'm going home. You loony, trying to get us a bad name.
LAR. It's all right for yous. Yous have coats, I'm freezin'.
(MIBS *sits on the steps.*
DESMOND *makes haste to sit beside her.*
LAR *blows on his hands and comes down to sit on the other side.*)
Dead losses the pair of you. Move over in the bed.
(MIBS *moves, obliging* DESMOND *to shift up also, so that he is almost off the edge of the steps.*
LAR *lights a cigarette.*
In the living room, MARY *pours water into* DRUMM*'s whiskey. He makea a sign when he has had enough.*)
MARY. He oughtn't to have told you.
DRUMM. Ben Mulhall?
MARY. He had no right.
DRUMM (*with some satisfaction*). In my case, I think he knew his man. But look here: not a word to Dolly.
MARY. Ah, now . . .
(*He puts a finger to his lips.*)
She'll have to know.
DRUMM. Not yet.
MARY. She's entitled.
DRUMM. I made up a story for her, days ago, just in case. A duodenal ulcer.
MARY. Desmond, why?
DRUMM. Peace of mind.
MARY. You're a nice man.
DRUMM. Not *her* peace of mind, for heaven's sake. My own.
MARY (*blankly*). I see.
DRUMM. I did it well. I even invented some cut-and-thrust between Mulhall and me, with myself putting a flea in his ear, just to make it convincing. I should have been a novelist.
MARY. It's wrong for me to know and not her.
DRUMM. You forced my hand. Anyway, you're an exceptional

woman: you have sense. Dolly is excitable and foolish: she'd make anyone's death a misery. Can't you see her? Beating a path between the chemist's and the church. And at home, the drugs and medicines set out in fearful symmetry like new ornaments. First, the cushions plumped; later on, the pillows. Sympathy and beef tea. She'll tell me hourly on the hour how vastly improved I look. She'll go about on tiptoe until my head splits. Her tenderness will saturate me like damp rot.

MARY. Nice talk. You don't know how well off you – (*She stops, remembering.*)

DRUMM. Don't I.

MARY. She's devoted to you.

DRUMM. Yes!

MARY. Thinks you're the be-all and the end-all.

DRUMM. I'm not disputing her affection, but I will not be at its mercy. Until I have to.

MARY. You don't deserve her.

DRUMM. The time I had pneumonia, she joked as if it were a head cold. Smiles and warm words, but the eyes of a child at the world's end. I don't want that again.

MARY (*understanding this*). I know.

DRUMM. You'll appreciate now why I won't go to Canada. I daren't. You know how I've always had a passion for language. The pleasure of minting a sentence that's my own: not borrowed or shopworn. Yet now I have to stoop to the banality of saying of a place that I wouldn't be seen dead in it.

(*He gives a fastidious shudder.*

MARY *looks at him, not knowing what to say.*)

In time, I suppose Dolly will send to Toronto for Stella and to Rathfarnham for Una. They'll have me helpless at – (*He breaks off.*) No . . . please.

MARY. What?

DRUMM. That's the look I don't want to see on Dolly's face.

MARY. Pity about you.

DRUMM. You're upset.

MARY. I can't come over it.

DRUMM. I agree. It's a damned imposition.

MARY (*rallying*). Well, I don't care what Ben Mulhall says, or what you say. If you turn your face to the wall, I won't.

DRUMM (*smiling*). What will you do? Pray?

MARY. Jeer away: no one minds you. I have a great leg of St Jude.

DRUMM. Ay, yes: hopeless cases.

MARY. He might surprise you.

DRUMM. Talk away to him: I can't hinder you. It's odd: I've been a Government employee for forty years; if he responds, it will be the first time I've used pull.

MARY. You cod, you.

DRUMM. In the Department, when a man retires there's a presenta- tion. The hat is passed. They give him a nest of tables or a set of Waterford. In August it'll be my turn, but I doubt if I'll put a strain on their pockets. I've indulged in unnatural practices with my subordinates, such as obliging them to do a day's work. But whatever it is, if it were only a fountain pen from Woolworth's, I mean to have it.

MARY. Sure won't you?

DRUMM. They won't be let off. I'll last that long. (*He looks at the ceiling.*) Our friend upstairs . . .

MARY. Do you mean Lar?

DRUMM. Will he come down?

MARY. What you said to him, he took it to heart. You mightn't think so, but he did: I know him.

DRUMM (*his thoughts elsewhere*). I'm sure.

MARY. Will I tell him you didn't mean it?

DRUMM. Mary . . .

MARY. Ah, I will.

DRUMM (*there is an intensity in his voice which stops her*). I need to know what I amount to. Debit or credit, that much I am ow- ed. If the account is to be closed, so be it: I demand an audit. Or show me the figures: I can add and subtract: I'll do my own books. A man has rights: if he is solvent, tell him. (*He realizes that* MARY *has not grasped his meaning. More calmly*) I have a most impressive title now: Keeper of Records. My enemies grow cunning. It takes a rare kind of peasant villainy to inflict injury and promotion with the same stroke of the pen. I have been a thorn in too many sides, and now I've been given a room to myself where I can antagonize the four walls and abuse the dust. In the strongroom there are files: so many, you could grow old counting them. Each one has a person's name and a number, and if I were God and breathed on them they'd become lives. I seem to have access to everyone's file but my own.

(*She has been watching him rather than listening; sensing rather than understanding.*)

Yes, you may tell him I didn't mean it: then I must go. And Dolly is not to be told.

DOROTHY'S VOICE. You can look as innocent as you like. I'm nobody's fool.

(MARY *goes out of the living room.*

In the bandstand area, DOROTHY *has appeared. She wears a
home-knitted Tam-o'-Shanter, with a woollen scarf and gloves
to match. She is carrying two library books.*)

You can swear black is white, but I know what I heard.

MIBS (*to* LAR). There, didn't I tell you? Me da'll find out and burst
me.

DOROTHY. What was it?

MIBS. It's our gramophone from home. He brung it.

DESMOND. Brought it.

MIBS. Do you know Desmond Drumm? And Lar . . . Laurence
Kearns.

LAR. Howayah.

MIBS. This is a friend of mine: Dorothy Dignam.

DESMOND. How d'you do?

(DOROTHY *is so flustered that she looks steadfastly away from
him.*)

DOROTHY (*breathlessly*). Hello, no, honest and truly, such a fright
I got, music in the pitch dark on a Holy Thursday, all
I could think of was the Agony in the Garden, I thought
I'd drop down dead, and then I said to myself, that's
the tune that goes "Way down in Missouri where you hear this
melody', a funny old ghost that'd be.

(*She gives a small, shrill laugh by way of providing a full
stop.*

DESMOND *looks at her stonily.*)

MIBS. You won't split on us?

DOROTHY. For what?

MIBS. Because –

LAR. No fear of her. Here, squeeze in. Dezzie's doin' gooseberry.

MIBS. Mm, sit with us.

DOROTHY. I said I'd be home after the library . . .

LAR. Where's your rush? Dezzie, good lad, be a gent.

DOROTHY (*looking at* DESMOND). If I'm disturbing anyone . . .

(MIBS *nudges* DESMOND, *who gets to his feet reluctantly to
give her his place.*)

MIBS. You aren't. For a minute . . . (*She pats the space beside her.*)

DOROTHY (*to* DESMOND, *shortly*). Thanks.

LAR. That's the dart: nothin' like an even number.

DOROTHY. I won't stay.

MIBS (*to* DESMOND). Dolly goes to the Tech in Dun Laoghaire.

DESMOND. Who does? Oh?

MIBS. She's blue-mouldy with brains . . . aren't you? She was the head of our class in the Loreto.

DOROTHY. Don't tell stories.

MIBS. You were.

DOROTHY. I was second.

MIBS. Well!

LAR. Begod, there's no doubt. Someone is well-matched, wha'?

DESMOND (*venomously*). And someone else isn't.

LAR. Steeped, so y'are.

MIBS. Desmond lives with his aunt on Nerano Road. I'm sure you know him to see.

DOROTHY (*lying*). I don't think so.

MIBS. He's around the corner. Yes, you do.

DESMOND (*suddenly amiable*). Why should she? I'm sure Dorothy doesn't walk about staring at people. You go to Dun Laoghaire Tech, do you?

DOROTHY. Yes.

DESMOND. Woodwork?

(*She makes to rise.* MIBS *holds her by the arm.*)

MIBS. Don't be so smart. Dolly does . . . what?

DOROTHY. It's called Commerce.

LAR. Hey, tell yous a joke. There's this fella and this mott, and they go out to Baldonnell . . . you know, to the –

MIBS (*indicating* DOROTHY). Now be careful.

LAR. No, it's clean. honest. They go out to the aerodrome, like. And they see this aeroplane landin' –

DOROTHY (*to* DESMOND). For your information, it's typing, short-hand, book-keeping and senior English.

LAR. Ah, Jasus, listen.

MIBS. Don't take the sacred name.

LAR. Sorry. They take this feckin' aeroplane –

MIBS. Lar!

LAR. They see this . . . oul' aeroplane comin' done. And your woman, the mott, she says to your man: 'Is that a mail plane?' And he says: 'No, them's the landin' wheels.'

(*There is silence for a moment. Then* MIBS *gives a snort and punches* LAR. *She averts her head so that* DOROTHY *cannot see her laugh.*)

DESMOND. Oh, for God's sake.

LAR. Good, wha'?

DESMOND. Yes, for a street corner I suppose it's –

DOROTHY. Excuse me, do you mind? (*To* LAR) And then what?

LAR. Hoh?

DOROTHY. After the landing wheels.

LAR. No, you don't get it. Your man, the fella . . . he thought that
she thought the wheels was –
(*In panic and to create a diversion,* DESMOND *snatches the
library books from* DOROTHY.)

DESMOND. These look interesting. What are they?

DOROTHY. Well, honestly.

LAR. . . . that she thought they were –
(MIBS *puts a hand over his mouth.*)

DOROTHY. Such manners.

DESMOND. This one's a waste of time: trash; but this isn't bad.
You'll enjoy it.

DOROTHY (*coldly*). You don't say.

DESMOND. It's not one of his best, mind. Have you read 'Goodbye
to All That'?

MIBS (*suddenly*). Dolly Drumm.

DESMOND. What?

MIBS. I just remembered. It's a sort of game Dolly used to play.

DOROTHY. Mary, you're not to.

MIBS. When we were at school, like. Honestly. Whenever she'd
meet a fellow, anyone, she'd put her name along with his.

DOROTHY. No, you're mean.

MIBS. To see how it would sound.

DOROTHY. It was for a joke.

MIBS. Trying it out, like.

DOROTHY. I was not.

MIBS. Dolly Drumm. God, that's the worst yet. Brutal.
(DOROTHY *looks at the ground in embarrassment.* DESMOND *is
aloof, unamused.*
LAR, *restless, goes into the bandstand.*)

LAR (*laughing, to* DESMOND). That's your hash cooked for you.

DOROTHY (*without looking up; a whisper*). Stop it.

LAR. Hey . . .
(*As they look around, he begins to sing, conducting as he does
so.*)
'Goodbye Dolly, I must leave you,
Goodbye, Dolly, I must go . . .'
(MIBS *at once joins in, motioning to him to keep his voice
down.* DRUMM, *in the living room, looks around, as if*

338

suspecting mockery. After a few lines, DOROTHY, *too, joins in, happy that the joke is over. Towards the end,* DRUMM *begins to beat the time with his finger and hums the tune audibly.*

Then MIBS *overrides the others.*)

MIBS (*loudly*). '. . . Goodbye, Dolly . . . Drumm!'

(*She laughs and hugs* DOROTHY, *whose feelings are again hurt.* DRUMM *and* DESMOND *are both looking at her resentfully.*

Her laughter as it tails off overlaps the entrance of KEARNS *and* MARY.)

I'm a horror.

MARY (*indicating* DRUMM). There he is now.

KEARNS. Dezzie, are you off? Sure put it there.

DRUMM. I was rude to you. It was uncalled-for.

KEARNS. What rude? When?

DRUMM. Mind, I hold to the substance of what I said, but this is your house and I was unmannerly.

KEARNS. Will you go 'long outa that. You weren't.

DRUMM. I insulted you.

KEARNS. Not at all.

DRUMM. Are you stupid? I say I did.

MARY. Now, Desmond.

DRUMM. And I ought not to have mentioned the lad.

KEARNS. Who?

DRUMM. The boy. Young Sean.

KEARNS (*flatly*). Sure you didn't.

(DRUMM *turns away in exasperation.*)

MARY. Now that will do. After tea, Desmond and Dolly will be coming over for an hour or so. (*To* DESMOND) Yes, you will.

KEARNS. And why the hell wouldn't they?

DRUMM. I'd like that. Thank you.

KEARNS. All together again like Brown's cows, wha'? Sure, Dezzie, do you know what I'm goin' to tell you? In this town . . . look at all the great characters we had. And you never seen such a clearance. They're all gone, except for the pair of us. You and me: that's as true as I'm standin'. Gone with the poor oul' trams. Sonny Doyle and Darley the landlord, and your own da in his time, God be good to him . . .

MARY. Will you let the man go to his dinner?

KEARNS. . . . an', an' Fanny Cash, an' Slippers we thought was the German spy. (*He clamps an affectionate hand on* DRUMM's

339

shoulder, his face at too-close range.) Meself an' yourself, the last of the good stuff. Sure they'll never bate the Irish out of Ireland.

DRUMM (*freeing himself*). Who else would have us? (*He puts on his raincoat. To* MARY) About Dolly. I'll give her this much: she's loyal. Our long silence, yours and mine: she had no part in it. So if she stopped coming here –

KEARNS (*amused*). If she did what?

MARY (*a warning*). Hold your tongue.

DRUMM. . . . That was my doing, not hers. You mustn't be cross with her.

MARY. With Dolly? Ah, get sense.
    (*She sees him to the door.*)

DRUMM. Do you remember once, when you thought of taking a secretarial course?

MARY. When *you* thought.

DRUMM. I tried to teach you a poem.

MARY. And I'm sure I learnt it!

DRUMM. 'My friends, we will not go again or ape an ancient rage,
    Or stretch the folly of our youth to be the shame of age.' No?

MARY. What about it?

DRUMM. 'But walk with clearer eyes and ears the path that wandereth,
    And see undrugg'd in evening light the decent inn of death.'
    (*Gently*) It isn't a decent inn, Mary. When you get up close, it's a kip.
    (*He goes out.*
    If possible, he should remain in sight; at any rate, there should be not impression given of an 'exit'.
    In the bandstand, LAR *is going through the other records in the lid of the gramophone. Stealthily, he puts one on.*
    DESMOND *is standing, perhaps still looking at one of the books.*
    MIBS *and* DOROTHY *are still seated together.*
    DRUMM *is seen walking to the rear of the bandstand.*)

KEARNS (*picking up his Sunday paper*). Sure poor oul' Dezzie.

DOROTHY (*to* DESMOND). I did see you in the town.

DESMOND. Pardon me.

KEARNS. I always had a great leg of him.

DOROTHY. Mary knows I did. And I knew your name and where you lived and that you were in the civil service.

DESMOND (*indifferent*). Really.

340

DOROTHY. I don't know why I pretended I didn't, because I was brought up to be straight with people. So I apologize for telling lies, and if I can please have my books back I'll go home.

MIBS. Stay.

DOROTHY. No, Mary. I think I've been disappointed enough in people for one night. If you don't mind . . .

(*She holds out her hands, waiting for* DESMOND *to return the books.*

He is about to do so when there is a blare of music from the gramophone.

It is a dance tune of the late 1930s.)

MIBS. Lar Kearns, you wretch. You turn that off.

LAR. You do it.

MIBS. Watch me.

(*She goes into the bandstand.* LAR *is between her and the gramophone. He grabs her, forcing her to dance.*)

You messer, will you . . . will you let me go. Lar, you'll get me into trouble.

LAR. I know, but we'll have a dance first.

DESMOND. Kearns, you stop that.

(MIBS, *yielding, begins to dance with* LAR. *Encouraged, he holds her close.* DESMOND *looks on, consumed with jealousy.*)

LAR. That's the girl.

MIBS. I'm going to be murdered.

LAR. Hey, Cough Bottle, how about this for a lie-in, wha'?

DESMOND. Kearns! (*He goes into the bandstand and makes for the gramophone.*)

MIBS (*laughing*). God, if someone sees us . . .

(DESMOND *stops the gramophone.*

DRUMM *is now visible at the far side of the bandstand.*)

LAR. Ah, will you put it back on.

DESMOND. You were told to stop.

LAR. Quit actin' the maggot. Fair do's now: give Dolly a dance, come on. (*He takes a step forward.*)

DESMOND. I warned you. (*He takes the record from the turntable.*)

LAR. Sure, you did.

DESMOND. I mean it.

LAR. Look, don't be such a –

(DESMOND *deliberately smashes the record.*

MIBS *screams.*

For a moment, DESMOND *is appalled by his own action,*

341

then, as LAR *moves forward, he attempts to take the other records from the lid.*

LAR *grabs him and throws him easily to one side.*)

DESMOND. You guttersnipe.

(*He rushes at* LAR, *who holds him off effortlessly.*

DESMOND *strikes out at him, but every intended blow falls short.*)

LAR. Easy, now. What the hell is the –

DESMOND (*flailing*). Damn cornerboy . . . you leave her alone . . . you lout, you blackguard, I'll kill you.

(LAR *grins at the ease with which he keeps him at bay.* DESMOND *is close to tears.*)

DOROTHY. Mary, Stop them.

MIBS. Yes, Desmond . . . Lar, will you stop it.

(DRUMM *enters the bandstand. He shoulders his way between* DESMOND *and* LAR, *causing them to fall apart. He looks at them, his eyes filled with his own pain and anger.*)

DRUMM. Be damned to the lot of you.

(*He goes off. They stare after him.*)

CURTAIN

ACT TWO

DESMOND *is in the bandstand, alone. He consults his notes, then puts them away as* DRUMM *did at the start of Act One. As an orator, he lacks assurance; this is merely a rehearsal, but his voice quavers from nerves.*

DESMOND. To conclude. As from December next this country shall at . . . or is it 'will'? . . . *will* at last cease to be merely a Free State and instead take its place as a free land. In place of − (*To himself*) You're rushing it: wait for applause. In place of a Governor-General, we will have a . . . no, blast it: we shall, *shall* have a President. My respectable . . . (*Almost moaning*) respect*ed* opponents have said . . . (*Under his breath*) God, make them say it! . . . that now is our opportunity to cut ourselves finally free of all that is English.

(DOROTHY *enters the bandstand behind him and listens, unnoticed.*)

Mr Chairman, I cannot understand people who hold grudges, who sulk, who cling to old wrongs and injuries. If it is in their nature, it is not in mine. I say that we should retain all that is best of the old to take with us into the new Golden Age, into the − and those of you who have been to the Picture House in Dun Laoghaire this week will grasp my meaning − into the beckoning Shangri La of which Mr De Valera is the two-hundred-year-old High Lama.

(*He laughs, pleased at his own wit.*)

DOROTHY. They'll boo you for that bit.

DESMOND (*embarrassed*). Good evening. I was −

DOROTHY. . . . Practising. I heard.

DESMOND. There's to be a −

DOROTHY. . . . Debate, at the Harold Boys' School. I know.

DESMOND (*annoyed*). Excuse me, but do you happen to live here?

DOROTHY. Pardon me?

DESMOND. I mean *here*. In the bushes somewhere or under a flat rock. (*As she stares at him*) I wondered.

343

DOROTHY. Honestly and truly, for a young man your age you're the most dreadful crosspatch.

DESMOND (*dismissive*). Amn't I.

DOROTHY. And for your information, the reason I'm here – and excuse me for mentioning that people talking to themselves is the first sign of madness – what brought me is to say that Mary can't go with you.

DESMOND. Do you mean to the debate?

DOROTHY. She said not to wait for her and all the best.

DESMOND. Why? It was –

(*He breaks off as* DRUMM *and* DOLLY *appear. They cross towards the living-room area.* DRUMM *notices* DESMOND *and* DOROTHY, *who wait until he and* DOLLY *have passed.*)

DOLLY (*lagging behind, breathless*). She spent a fortune on having the house done up, paid out every penny she got from the accident. Did she show you her kitchen? The cupboards and the new washing machine and the –

(DRUMM *stops suddenly so that she all but collides with him.*)

DRUMM. How do you know?

DOLLY. What? (*A small, nervous laugh*) I heard in the town.

(DRUMM *continues off, letting her pass him.*)

DESMOND. Why can't she?

DOROTHY. What?

DESMOND. Come with me.

DOROTHY (*the same nervous mannerism as* DOLLY'*s*). A toothache.

DESMOND. Since when?

DOROTHY (*embellishing*). I think it must be an abscess. She tried oil of cloves, and now her father is taking her to Mr Corbet.

DESMOND. Who?

DOROTHY. To have it pulled.

DESMOND (*dismayed*). But I wanted her to . . . (*He leaves the sentence unfinished. He will not show himself as vulnerable in front of her.*)

DOROTHY. He pulled one of mine once. See? (*She draws back the corner of her mouth to show him.*)

DESMOND. Damn.

DOROTHY (*pointing*). Arrh?

DESMOND. Yes.

DOROTHY. Her father is dragging her there. I know she'd miles rather go and listen to you and suffer.

344

(*He looks at her as if suspecting a gibe. Her face is ingenuous.*)

Really, she's as cross as two sticks. I mean, who wouldn't be? She said to me: 'He'll be there, standing his ground against T.D.s and professors out of colleges and such. The whole town will see him except me.'

DESMOND. She won't miss much.

DOROTHY. Do you hear him! Anyway, she said all the best.

DESMOND. It's my first time, you know.

DOROTHY. Go on. After this, you won't talk to us.

DESMOND. Far too grand, yes.

DOROTHY. You might be. Wait till you see tomorrow's papers: you'll be a stone's throw from famous. Do you know what my father says? 'Young Desmond Drumm? . . . oh, he's a born genius.'

DESMOND. Yes, I'm much liked by fathers.

DOROTHY. From this out, there'll be no stopping you. And Mary is going to be very sorry, you'll see. (*As he looks at her*) I mean, even sorrier.

DESMOND. Was that a story?

DOROTHY. What?

DESMOND. About a toothache.

DOROTHY. No!

DESMOND. Because –

DOROTHY. Excuse me, I'm not in the custom of telling –

DESMOND. Because if she'd prefer to go some place less boring . . . I mean she's free to, she needn't lie about it. I'm not her keeper. God forbid. (*Unable to keep the question back*) I suppose she went out with him.

DOROTHY. Who?

DESMOND. 'Who'!

DOROTHY. Do you mean Lar Kearns? You're wrong.

DESMOND. I'm sure.

DOROTHY. Well, you are wrong. Because he's going to the debate.

DESMOND (*appalled*). He's what?

DOROTHY. With a crowd from the town. To cheer you.

DESMOND. Oh, my God.

DOROTHY. Isn't it nice of him? So there.

DESMOND. What time is it? (*He pulls out his notes, sits on the balustrade and pores over them in an agony of stage-fright.*)

DOROTHY. I thought I might go as well.

(*He is memorizing, eyes closed, lips moving.*)

345

If nobody minded.

KEARNS (*to* DOLLY). Sure you're welcome.

(DRUMM *and* DOLLY *have appeared in the living room, ushered in by* MARY. *It is very much a Sunday evening occasion: sandwiches and a cake are on the sideboard. In the bandstand,* DOROTHY *lingers, watching* DESMOND.)

DOLLY. Hello, Lar. How are you?

KEARNS. Gettin' younger, the same as yourself. But sure you've been giving us the go-by for so long I wouldn't know a bit of you. Donkey's years, wha'? (*He gives her an overdone wink of complicity.*)

DOLLY (*nervously*). Oh, now.

MARY (*a warning*). Will you take Desmond's coat off him and not leave the man standing.

KEARNS. Who's this? Another stranger, begod. Haven't clapped eyes on him since dunno when.

DRUMM. Good evening.

KEARNS. Ha-ha, quick as a flash. Give us that.

(*He takes* DRUMM's *coat. From* MARY *and* DOLLY *there is a fusillade of small talk.*

DRUMM, *who loathes whatever he considers banal, looks on in disgusted fascination.*)

MARY. Isn't the weather glorious?

DOLLY. Beautiful.

MARY. I'm sure the crowds of the world are out.

DOLLY. The town is black.

MARY. Such a day. I did half me wash.

DOLLY. Go 'way.

MARY. And hung it up. Dry in no time.

DOLLY. Aren't you great.

MARY. 'It's a Sunday,' I said. 'It's a sin. I don't care.'

DOLLY. These days, no one minds.

MARY. But if it was twenty years ago . . .

DOLLY. Oh, then! Oh, yes!

MARY. One stocking on a line on a Sunday . . .

DOLLY. Don't I know.

MARY. And Father Creedon 'ud be at that door.

DOLLY. Giving out to you.

MARY. He was a terror.

DOLLY (*fondly*). Ah, Father Creedon.

DRUMM (*who can stand no more*). Oh, good God.

DOLLY. No, it's great drying weather. (*To* DRUMM) What, pet?

346

DRUMM. Will you have done with this damned table-tennis and look at your surroundings?

DOLLY. Where? (*She looks about her vaguely. It has slipped her mind that she is supposed not to have seen the room lately.*)

MARY (*prompting*). At me new room.

DOLLY. What? (*Then*) Oh. Oh, it's beautiful. Look at it, Dezzie, it's exquisite.

DRUMM. Really.

DOLLY (*babbling*). I wouldn't know it. That's new and that's new and the wallpaper is –

MARY. Before we sit, come and look at my kitchen. Lar, give Desmond whatever he's having. Be useful.

(*She urges* DOLLY *out of the room. As they cross towards the kitchen,* MARY *begins to laugh helplessly.*)

DRUMM. That woman becomes more of a fool each day.

(DOLLY, *although she has been shaken by her narrow escape, catches* MARY's *mood and laughs, too.*

DRUMM *turns his head suspiciously.*

As MARY *switches on the kitchen light, we see that* MIBS *is at the table, weeping. She dabs at her eyes with a handkerchief.* MARY *sits near her and wipes her own eyes.*)

DOLLY. It's not comical; it isn't.

MARY. You aren't safe to be let out on your own.

DOLLY. When he came home and said you'd invited us, I thought: I must remember now to act surprised at the house and go 'ooh' and 'ah' and all the rest of it. And it went clear out of my head.

MARY (*laughing again*). 'That's new', says you, 'and that's new and that's new . . .'

DOLLY. Stop it, I got a fright.

MARY. If he could see you having your Friday cup of coffee.

DOLLY (*frightened*). Will you hush.

(KEARNS *has produced an unopened half bottle of whiskey and a six-pack of stout.*)

KEARNS. I have me orders from the Commandant: no hard stuff. So you get dug into this. (*He opens the whiskey.*)

DRUMM (*testily*). A cup of tea would have sufficed.

KEARNS. You'll get that as well. No one goes out of here sayin' they weren't asked if they had a mouth on them.

DRUMM. You're an ostentatious man.

KEARNS (*proudly*). I am, begod.

DRUMM (*half to himself*). And a hopeless one.

KEARNS. No, I prefer the drop of stout. The occasional ball of

347

malt is harmless, but at my age, when there's a bit of mileage on the oul' clock, a man ought to go easy.

DRUMM. What about *my* age?

KEARNS. You're different, Dezzie. You have acid in you. 'S a fact: it's in the canals, I studied it. You could drink Jameson's distillery dry, and you might get half shot; but the element in the whiskey that does damage to the human liver would be nullified by the acid your system is glutted with.

DRUMM. Balderdash.

KEARNS. Laugh, I don't mind. You wouldn't be the first one to make a mock of science. The body doesn't manufacture acid for a hobby, you know.

DRUMM (*calling*). Dolly . . .

(DOLLY, *who does not hear, is in the kitchen talking with* MARY.)

KEARNS. Still, a man's a right to mind himself. Did you hear that poor oul' Nick Tynan was brought to the chapel yesterday?

DRUMM. Who?

KEARNS. Out of Begnet's Villas. You knew him.

DRUMM. Yes. His boy, his foster-son, was with me for a time: in my Section, that is.

KEARNS. A great oul' warrior.

DRUMM (*aggressive*). A what?

KEARNS. A character. There'll be a big turn-out at that funeral.

DRUMM. I'm sure.

KEARNS. The chapel was packed.

DRUMM. I'd expect no less. He worked hard and lived decently, and by now he'll have given his mind back to the Almighty in the same unused condition as he received it. Yes, I knew him. A man of no malice and less merit. Lord have mercy.

KEARNS. All the same, Dezzie, he was a –

DRUMM. A character, yes. It's a word used to describe any ignoramus or bigot over sixty. You'll have a most impressive funeral yourself one of these days.

KEARNS (*pleased*). Who, me?

DRUMM. Given the existing criteria for large attendances, I've no doubt of it. Mass cards and floral tributes. Your coffin will be invisible under the wreaths of intertwined platitudes.

KEARNS (*he looks at* DRUMM *for a moment; then, almost blushing*). How much do you want to borra?

DRUMM. Mine, I think, will be a more modest affair. The chief mourners are likely to be a small weeping group of unsplit infinitives.

KEARNS. Not at all. Aren't you one of our own?

DRUMM. Am I? (*He drops the subject, almost with contempt.*) Tynan's son, the boy he adopted: I took a special interest in him.

KEARNS. A brainy lad.

DRUMM. Dangerously fond of saying 'yes'. He needed starch in his backbone. I watched over him, took no nonsense, told him that as long as he worked for me he would pull his socks up. In the end, of course, he was a disappointment.

(KEARNS *makes to top up his drink.*)

(*Covering his glass*) Leave it. I wondered afterwards why I'd bothered with him. I'm not a masochist. I don't ask to have kindnesses flung back at me, or for that matter to become an office joke. 'I hear that Drumm has been let down again.' How stupidly we deceive ourselves. It was because of Sean.

(KEARNS'*s watery eyes become uneasy. He makes a lumbering attempt to avoid the subject.*)

KEARNS. I hear young Tynan is over for the —

DRUMM. He left here just about then. I suppose I missed him and made a friend of the other boy.

KEARNS. . . . for his da's funeral.

DRUMM. Do you hear from him? From Sean.

KEARNS. Herself does.

DRUMM. Don't you?

KEARNS. Sure he knows I read the letters. Christmas and Easter . . . he never starves us for news.

DRUMM. Is he well?

KEARNS. Tip-top, he says himself. He's teachin', you know, in a school in . . . uh, it's near London. Can't get me tongue around the name. Slow, is that it?

DRUMM. Do you mean Slough?

KEARNS. Slough! You done that for him . . . got him interested in books an' stuff. (*Grinning*) A bloody schoolteacher, wha'?

DRUMM. Bravo.

KEARNS. Was he married when you were here last?

DRUMM. Newly married, yes.

KEARNS. Him and her, there was what you might call a separation. I dunno the ins and outs of it. Sure over there is not like here. It's all choppin' and changin': everything on again, off again, like a vest in the autumn.

DRUMM. He had no right to go, not as he did.

KEARNS. Ah, well.

DRUMM. Ah, well what?

KEARNS. That's the way o' the world.

DRUMM. Will you stop mouthing banalities? He had a life here: his people. I'd have thought better of him: it showed a want of feeling.

KEARNS. Sean and me never hit it off. Chalk an' cheese.

DRUMM (*reluctant to seem to care*). Does he ask for me?

KEARNS. Hoh?

DRUMM. In his letters.

KEARNS. Oh, I'm sure he does.

DRUMM. Well, does he or doesn't he?

KEARNS. Yis. Oh, catch him forgettin'. 'How's . . . uh, Uncle Dezzie?'

(DRUMM *glares at him, not convinced*.)

There was a time I thought of makin' the trip, droppin' in to see him. But sure my travellin' days is over.

DRUMM. Your what? My dear man, I've been further around a chamber pot in search of the handle than you've travelled in your entire life.

(DRUMM *hears* DOLLY *and* MARY *moving back from the kitchen*.)

DOLLY. . . . He was great. He told them all about the Cat's Ladder and where Shaw lived and Sorrento Park and I don't know what else.

MARY. This morning, you say? How well he kept it to himself.

(*As they leave the kitchen,* MARY *shuts the door behind them.* MIBS *runs to it and speaks through it*.)

MIBS. Daddy? Can I come out? Can I please come out and talk to you and Mammy?

(*Getting no answer, she returns and sits at the table.* DOLLY *and* MARY *enter the living room*.)

MARY. I hear you've been speechifyin'.

KEARNS. Who?

MARY. Walking the legs off half the town and telling them what happened in old God's time.

DRUMM. There were two dozen people, and it wasn't a speech: it was a . . . talk.

DOLLY. Don't mind him: he was great.

DRUMM. You weren't there.

DOLLY. I saw you.

DRUMM. Now she reads lips.

DOLLY. Everyone's talking about it.

DRUMM. Who is? Name one.

MARY. That'll do. Behave yourself.

KEARNS. I remember Dezzie one time makin' a toppin' speech. Below in the Harold Boys', and that wasn't today nor yesterday.

DOLLY. Don't I know? I was there.

KEARNS. You were in me boot. You were at home in your pram. (*A shrill laugh from* DOLLY.

In the bandstand, DESMOND *rises, ready to face his ordeal.*
MARY, *who has brought a teapot with her from the kitchen, sets about distributing the cake-plates.*)

MARY. And I was in me go-car. Shift your feet. Dolly, will you sit?

DOLLY. Do you hear him, Dezzie? In my pram!

KEARNS. It was so packed, we were sittin' on the window-sills. I don't forget that night.

DOROTHY. Is it the time?

DESMOND *nods. Panic has set in.*)

Well, all the very best.

DESMOND (*dry-mouthed*). Thank you.

DOROTHY. You've no call to be nervous. Just don't think what a great night it is for you. Pretend it isn't.

DESMOND. Mm.

DOROTHY. And I know it's none of my business, but honestly and truly I'd leave out that bit about Mr De Valera, because it's only trying to be smart.

(DESMOND, *too nervous to heed her, begins to move off.*)

Do you want me to walk with you? If you'd sooner go by yourself, it's a free country. One thing I was taught and I've always kept to is, never go where you're not –

(*She realizes that he is moving out of earshot. She follows him off: a walk that longs to be a run.*

Through this, MARY *has been pouring tea and now offers milk and sugar.*)

KEARNS. Boys, oh boys, you gev them a great talk that night.

DRUMM. Did I?

KEARNS. You damn well did. I can still hear them clappin' and cheerin' you.

DRUMM. You heard more than I did.

MARY. Excuse me. Two spoons for you, Dolly?

DOLLY. Thanks.

DRUMM. You have a good memory.

MARY. How? (*A small embarrassed laugh*) Like an elephant. And for yourself it's . . .

DRUMM (*He waits a moment, calling the bluff; then*). None.

MARY (*affecting to remember*). None.

KEARNS. Acid!

DOLLY. Dezzie says he might write a book now. About the town.

KEARNS. A book?

MARY. You'd never.

DRUMM. Dolly takes the . . . whim for the deed. I said that *some one* should –

KEARNS. No better man. Y'ought to put me in it.

DOLLY. No, it's about the olden times. History. Dezzie knows every stick and stone in the town, don't you, pet? And he has all the bits out of the papers and the old maps, albums of them in the loft, and the reams of stuff his father left.

DRUMM (*to* MARY *and* KEARNS). Fuel for a bonfire.

DOLLY (*smiling*). Oh, I'm sure.

DRUMM. There are as many books in the world as there are fools. I don't intend to augment the ranks of either.

DOLLY. But you must do it.

DRUMM. Must?

DOLLY. You said you would.

DRUMM. It was a daydream.

DOLLY. Well, I don't see why you won't. You have all the time you want now.

(*A pause.* MARY *fetches the sandwiches and the cake.* DOLLY *looks at* DRUMM, *waiting for his response.*)

The first proper history, you said. You were over the moon: yes, you were. It was all you ever talked of. (*Bitterly*) It's only because you know how pleased I'd be. A book with your name on it. If I said it was foolish or a waste of time, then you'd write it to spite me.

MARY (*offering the food*). Dolly . . .

DOLLY. Wouldn't you? (*To* MARY, *attempting to act the role of the guest*) Oh, now, such trouble, aren't you awful?

MARY. What trouble? A bit of sweet cake. Desmond . . .

(DRUMM *takes a sandwich.*)

KEARNS. Eat away. When we haven't it, we'll do without. Do you know, Dezzie, the mornin' after that evenin' the talk in the town was that you might end up runnin' the country.

DRUMM. Running from it, I think.

KEARNS. No, 'clare to God: the whole shebang. Dolly, was he great or was he not?

352

DOLLY (*still hurt*). I dunno.

DRUMM. I do.

KEARNS. You were massive. I remember.

DRUMM. Through a Guinness glass darkly.

KEARNS. Wha'?

DRUMM. Delude yourself by all means: not me. Oh yes, you were there, perched on a window-sill, and by the door I saw the gentlemen of leisure who haunted the betting shop and Gilbey's corner. And when my turn came to speak, there was what disguised itself as a cheer. I imagine it was the kind of noise the Romans made when the first Christian entered the arena. I heard you shouting: 'Good old . . . Mammy Cough-Bottle.'

KEARNS. For a joke.

DRUMM (*sincerely*). I know it was. I cleared my throat, and at once half the room turned consumptive. I began to speak. Someone yelled: 'Can't hear you.' That was the signal for a barrage of meaningless, inane catch-phrases: the sort that are thrown as boys throw stones at a broken wall, to see which one brings it down. Did my mother know I was out? Who swallowed the dictionary? Did I wash my neck lately? Would I work for a farmer?

KEARNS. Not at all: you're dreamin'.

DRUMM. It was like a dream at the time: a bad one. My nerve went. I gabbled. I heard my voice become shrill, like a girl's. Whenever I used a word with more than two syllables, they hooted. I skipped to the end, I fled to it . . . to a facetious – I suppose a juvenile – quip about De Valera. They applauded that.

KEARNS. Amn't I sayin'?

DRUMM. Yes, they clapped: slowly. May I? (*He offers his cup for more tea.*) Our chairman was the then parish priest. When he obtained order, he said: 'And now that we've all had our bit of fun . . .'

KEARNS (*laughing, meaning* DRUMM). A fierce man for drawin' the longbow.

MARY. Desmond, will you get sense? Any place you go, you'll find a pack o' jeers. More fool you to mind them.

DRUMM. Once it was over and I'd sat down, I didn't mind them in the least. I even saw the humour ot it.

(DESMOND *runs on, in flight from the humiliation of his speech. He stops by the bandstand. He is shaking. In a wave of nausea he grasps one of the iron pillars and begins to retch.*)

353

I was calm, quite unperturbed. You see, I understood. It was a punishment. I had broken the eleventh commandment. I had tried to be different, to be the clever boy, the . . . (*A look at* DOLLY) born genius. Well, they were not impressed.

DOLLY (*suddenly*). I cried.

DRUMM. What?

DOLLY. That evening.

DOROTHY (*calling, off*). Desmond . . .

DRUMM. Did you? I was amused. I had discovered for the first time that being clever was like having a disfigured hand – to be tolerated as long as you kept it decently hidden.

DOROTHY (*off*). Desmond, is that you?

(DESMOND *runs quickly towards the kitchen area.*
DOROTHY *appears and follows him.*)

DRUMM. I actually believed that if I spoke well and carried the argument they would admire me. I wanted it. I longed to be . . . (*He looks at* KEARNS.) one of our own. Dear God, what a contemptible ambition: to please the implacable. Well, I never gave them a second chance: I had that small triumph. (*He smiles at* MARY.) Your tea is as good as it ever was.

(DESMOND *comes into the kitchen.* MIBS *looks at him sullenly.*)

MIBS. Who let *you* in?

DESMOND. Your father. He said . . . well, he seems to be in a bad humour.

MIBS (*toneless*). That so?

DESMOND. Grumpy, I thought. You'd think he was the one with the toothache. (*He gets no answering smile.*) That friend of yours – Dolly Dignam – gave me your message. I was sorry you couldn't come.

MIBS. When? Oh, to the thingummy.

DESMOND. It was too crowded: I doubt if you'd have enjoyed it. And there was a rough element: it wasn't quite the occasion they'd hoped for.

MIBS. How was your speech?

DESMOND. Well, I clowned, so they laughed a lot. I mean, if they weren't going to take it seriously, why should I? The history professor from Trinity, he got a rough time of it. Still, for the experience –

MIBS. I'm in awful bloody trouble.

DESMOND. . . . I daresay it was worth it.

MIBS. I said, I'm in –

354

DESMOND. I know: I heard you. What kind of trouble?

MIBS. Don't ask me.

DESMOND. Is it . . . pyorrhoea?

MIBS. No, it's – Is it what?

DESMOND. She said your father was taking you to the dentist.

MIBS. It was to Father Creedon. (*As he stares at her*) Are you thick? He took me to see old Credo on account of a letter Lar Kearns writ me.

DESMOND. Wrote you. (*Almost laughing*) Lar Kearns?

MIBS. The first letter he ever writ in his flamin' life, and he sends it to me and me da opens it.

DESMOND. It must have been . . . worth reading.

MIBS. You shoulda heard old Credo. (*A florid, booming voice*) 'Oh, yas, yas, this is what happens in the house that neglects that grand and glorious Irish custom of the family rosary.' Me da was buckin'.

DESMOND. I don't see why.

MIBS (*sourly*). Do you not!

DESMOND. If Kearns's level of prose is anything like his level of conversation, I can imagine the kind of letter it was. That isn't your fault.

MIBS (*not answering*). Do you want tea?

DRUMM. If you're making it.

MIBS. Might as well. I'm to stay here till I'm called. Put the cups out. (*She sets about making tea.*)

DRUMM. Why'd your father open the letter?

MIBS. Because I never get any. 'Specially ones with 'S.W.A.L.K.' on one side and 'S.A.G.' on the other. The rotten messer didn't even seal it: he tucked the flap in and put a ha'penny stamp on it.

DESMOND. What did it say?

MIBS. Stuff.

DESMOND. Such as?

MIBS. Things.

DESMOND. Keep it a secret, then.

MIBS. Such a fuss. I went out with a girl I know to Killiney. There was a hop on in the White Cottage, that place on the strand. Lar was at it. He asked me up and bought me a cornet, and at the interval we got two pass-outs and went up on the bank of the railway.

DESMOND. You and he.

MIBS. God, don't you start.

355

DESMOND. Well?

MIBS. Well nothing. Mind your own business. Anyway, this morning this letter comes. Writ with a pencil, smelling of mackerel, and all slushy and romantic. (*With an embarrassed laugh*) Saying he loved me. I mean, Lar Kearns: would you credit it?

(DESMOND *is silent.*)

And God, doesn't he put in the lot about him and me on the bank of the railway. You'd think I wasn't there and had to be told: it was like the Grand National on the wireless. He even went and put in extra bits: he must have got them out of some book. When I think of me da reading it: all about me creamy breasts. Two 'e's' in 'creamy' and 'b-r-e-s-t', 'breasts'.

DESMOND. Father Creedon must have enjoyed it.

MIBS. Desmond, he was awful, he ate me. I mean, you'd think we'd done something desperate.

DESMOND. I wouldn't know: I wasn't there.

(*The thought of* DESMOND *being present causes her to giggle.*) Not that I'd want to be.

MIBS (*on the defensive*). We had a coort.

DESMOND. Is that what it's called?

MIBS. Well, blast your nerve.

DESMOND (*feigning amusement*). A coort!

MIBS. A bit of messin'. I didn't go all the way with him.

DESMOND. Ah-ha.

MIBS. No, I did not.

DESMOND. Wasn't it dark enough?

MIBS. If you want to know, I nearly did. It was the closest I ever came. Only I wouldn't let him. I wouldn't let anyone.

(*He is unmollified.*

She glares at him, fetches the tea-tray and slams it down.)

MIBS. Because I haven't the nerve. Here.

DESMOND. I don't want your tea.

MIBS. It's bloody made. (*She sloshes tea into his cup.*) Me da went down to the harbour to see him . . . to see Lar, I mean, and give out to him, (*She puts one spoonful of sugar into his cup.*) How many?

DESMOND. None.

MIBS. Don't stir it. He says he wants to marry me. (*This is what she has been leading up to. She affects to give her attention to putting milk and sugar into her own tea.*) I dunno how he came

out with it. I bet you me da waved the letter at him and began
rantin' and ravin'. And of course you know Lar. If you said
you were starvin' he'd tell you seaweed was bread and butter.
Whatever he thinks you want to hear, that's what he'll say to
you, so I suppose he told me da he'd marry me.

DESMOND. In the letter he said he loved you.

MIBS (*derisive*). E-eh.

DESMOND. Well, didn't he?

MIBS. Yeah, because he got a red-hot coort . . . don't mind him.
So now what am I to do?

DESMOND. Marry him.

MIBS. Ah, for God's sake.

DESMOND. Why not?

MIBS. Old jealous-boots.

DESMOND. Who?

MIBS. He hasn't even a proper job. Give over.

DESMOND. Jobs aren't important. I think you should marry him
because I think you're his sort.

MIBS. Yeah, the perfect – (*Her smile dies away as the insult goes
home.*)

DESMOND. And you won't need a railway bank then, will you, or
to be afraid of going all the way with him.

MIBS. Ah, Desmond –

DRUMM. No, you could do worse. I doubt if you'll do better. And
you'll be much more your own self at his level than at . . .
anyone else's.
(*She realizes that he is determined to tear down their rela
tionship past all chance of repair.*)

MIBS. Sure. Go on, now: go home.

DESMOND. Mm, it's all hours. I'm sure you'll have a happy life.
You'll make a nice home for him, perhaps in one of those cottages in the Alley Lane. He needs someone like you: you can
help him count his dole money.

MIBS (*waiting for him to go*). Yeah, thanks.

DESMOND. Because –

MIBS. I said, go. You done what you wanted: you said what can't
be took back.

DESMOND. Taken back. (*He is unable to leave ill enough alone. He
wants to draw blood, needs to be certain that her hurt equals
his own.*) I'm very stupid. I mistook you for someone with self-
respect. It was my fault. I thought that at least your ambitions
went higher than Lar Kearns.

MIBS. Do you mean you?

DESMOND. I was wrong.

MIBS. Yes . . . you do. Well at least Lar is a bit of gas. I can laugh
with him. He's glad of me the way I am. I don't need to have
a scaffolding put around me brain before I'm fit to be seen with
him. He can give a body a coort and a kiss, and they know it's
a person, not bones and cold skin. You think you're so great.
Just because you get up and make a speech and they slap you
on the back and cheer you, you act like you were someone.
Well, you're not. They laugh at you. You have a smell of
yourself and you're no one. Honestly, you're not all there, you
know that? The whole town knows about the Drumms. Ask
them. Go and ask. You're as cracked as your oul' fella was. I'm
not surprised he went and — (*She breaks off.*)

DESMOND. That he what?

MIBS. Go on home.

DESMOND. Yes.

(*As he turns to go, the lights fade in the kitchen and come up
in the living room.* DRUMM *is in genial mood.*)

DRUMM. It was in that field across from what they called the rabbit
wood.

MARY. The back meadow.

DOLLY. There are bungalows now.

MARY. Oh, but then it was the meadow.

DOLLY. Oh, then!

DRUMM. We were walking, the four of us.

KEARNS. Was I there?

DRUMM. My dear man, was Hamlet in Denmark? This, mind you,
was in the far-off days when young people wore shabby clothes
from poverty rather than affectation. There were still fields to
walk in: it was before the country became one vast builder's
yard.

MARY. Tell the story.

DRUMM. There were the four of us . . .

DOLLY. The times we had.

DRUMM. And on the path alongside the wood we found a baby
bird.

MARY. He's romancin'.

DRUMM. It had fallen from its nest. And he (*indicating* KEARNS)
picked it up.

KEARNS. God bless your memory.

DRUMM. And there in a hedgerow he saw a nest filled with baby birds. So he took this . . . foundling and very tenderly put it in with them.

DOLLY. Ah.

MARY. Well, I'll say this much for him: that's Lar. Now that's him to a 't'.

KEARNS. Yis, that'd be me.

DRUMM (*to* MARY). I agree with you. It sums him up. Because I went back a week later, and all the other birds had gone. (*To* KEARNS) But yours was still there. Plump and thriving, and no wonder. It was a cuckoo.

MARY. No.

DOLLY. Lar, you didn't.

KEARNS. He's drunk: don't mind him.

MARY. A cuckoo. Oh, that's him, that's the price of him.
   (DRUMM *laughs*. DOLLY *joins in*.)

DRUMM. That man . . . put a predator into a –

KEARNS. Yis, more power. Laugh away, make me out a gobshite.

MARY (*reprimanding him*). Lar.

KEARNS. Take his part, why don't you?

DRUMM. It did happen.

KEARNS. When?

DRUMM. That Sunday.

KEARNS (*suddenly violent*). In me hump it happened.

MARY. Now, boys, boys . . .

KEARNS. You think I wouldn't recognize a coo-coo? With my experience? Who was it owned Mary Mine?

DRUMM (*mystified, look at* MARY). Mary M—

MARY. Not me: his pigeon.

KEARNS. Dezzie, we're all goin' downhill. 'S a fact. And in your case the cells of the brain is handin' in its cards.

DRUMM. Drivel.

KEARNS. Take this evenin'. What did happen, you can't remember, and what didn't happen you have off be heart.

MARY. Can't you take a joke?

DRUMM (*to* MARY). You miss the point.

MARY. No matter: leave it. Dolly, more tea . . .

DRUMM. This afternoon, I took it into my head to go over some old accounts. (*The remark is intended for* MARY.) A few figures to be totted up, interest paid, a balance struck.

MARY. Doing sums in this weather.

DRUMM. I sat in the garden. I dragged the deckchair around with me, to keep out of the shadow.

359

DOLLY. It's still the month of May. Out of the sun it's bitter.
(DRUMM *looks at her.*)
Sorry, love.

KEARNS. The news first, Dolly, then the weather.
(*He laughs.* DOLLY, *smiling, put a finger to her lips.*)
Ah, God. Say what you like. I'm a great character.

MARY (*to* DRUMM, *prompting*). And then what?

DRUMM. It's no matter.

MARY. Yes, it is. You thought of that day and the four of us.

DRUMM. That unimportant walk we had. From forty years ago:
why? What value had it? So I went back to my accounts, and
I remembered another time: when a priest came to my aunt's
house. I'd been sent to live with her: it was the day of the in-
quest. He told me to be a brave boy and never turn from God,
and he asked a strange question. Had my father written me a
letter? I said no: never. I had lived with him in the master's
house: why should he write to me! That priest with the pink
hand that shook mine: today I remembered him and understood
what he'd been after. It was for evidence of suicide . . . the
business of burial in consecrated ground.

KEARNS. Suicide? Who?

MARY. Priest and all, the cheek of him.

DOLLY. Aren't people dreadful?

DRUMM. Why?

MARY. Why? Being killed like your father was is one thing, but to
take the poor man's character . . .

DRUMM. How?

KEARNS. I remember him: a decent skin. He taught me.

DRUMM. Now *that's* taking his character. (*To* MARY) And if the
poor man, as you call him, did die by accident, it was by the
same law of probability as being run down by the Dun
Laoghaire mailboat halfway up the Volga.

MARY. Desmond, you have no nature in you.

DOLLY. Honestly and truly, some people have nothing better to do
than spread stories.

KEARNS. It was a mishap. He was short-cuttin' it through the
tunnel.

DRUMM. That was the coroner's finding.

KEARNS. Down the bank at the Ramparts, through the dark along
the railway line and up the bank again. I done it meself.

DRUMM. Boys do it, yes.

KEARNS. Oh, a dangerous pastime.

DRUMM. At school I was informed with some glee that he had put his head on the track.

MARY. You're not to say that.

DRUMM. The town says it.

MARY. When? I never heard it.

KEARNS. No, nor I.

DRUMM (*to* MARY). I thought you did.

(*Almost certainly*, MARY *has forgotten their old quarrel, but she senses an accusation.*)

MARY. You were wrong, then. And your song and dance about it has Dolly upset.

DRUMM (*to* DOLLY). Are you? Why?

DOLLY. It was the thought of a soul going to hell.

DRUMM. My father?

DOLLY. It's what the Church says. A mortal sin.

DRUMM. I know what the Church says. That the creator of heaven and earth is a bungler who burns his mistakes. Tommy-rot. God made him, let God put up with him. A least He knew him: I never did. Whatever was breakable in him, he kept under lock and key, away from vandals. Sooner a shuttered house than a plundered one. You were welcome to what was left, what passed for all there was of him . . . the bones and cold skin. If he ever tried to speak to me, or to anyone, it was in that tunnel. And damn them: they called it an accident, so he said nothing. (*To* MARY) I'd say that was taking his character.

(*A pause. He looks at his watch, then, with a social smile*) Well, now.

DOLLY (*taking her cue*). It was gorgeous.

MARY. Where are you harin' off to?

KEARNS. They're not goin'. (*To* DRUMM) Will you sit?

DRUMM. Tomorrow is Monday. I'm not on a perpetual holiday, like some. (*Not unkindly*) Do you know, this man's continued survival without ever lifting a finger makes the mystery of the Holy Trinity look like a card trick.

DOLLY (*laughing*). Poor Lar.

KEARNS. You'll have a tincture.

DRUMM. I will not.

KEARNS. To see yous up the hill. I've two jars left for meself, and if yous go home on me she'll have them locked up before you're on Sorrento Road. You will.

MARY. Humour him.

DRUMM. One, and that's all. (*To* DOLLY) Yes?

DOLLY. I'm enjoying myself. And you are, too: don't pretend. Dezzie got great news this morning.

KEARNS. That a fact?

DRUMM (*muted*). Dolly . . .

DOLLY (*winking at* MARY). It's a secret.

KEARNS (*getting the drinks*). Ah, but Dezzie, the changes in this town. If your da, God be good to him, cem back again, he wouldn't know a bit of it.

DRUMM. I'm sure.

KEARNS. He would not. If you told him the oul' steam trains was gone, he wouldn't believe you.

(*They stare at him. He realizes his gaffe and makes a bumbling attempt to cover up.*)

An' . . . the poor oul' trams, wha'? Yis. An' . . . an' the fizz-bags the chiselurs could buy for a ha'penny. An' did j'ever go out in the Sound and look at the nuns on the rocks below the Loreto, with the striped bathin' togs down to their ankles?

DRUMM. You've drained life's cup to the full, haven't you?

MARY (*smiling*). Trust him! (*To* KEARNS, *privately, she presents a bunched fist for his indiscretion about the trains.*)

KEARNS. Yis. An' do you 'member Cussin's shop? With the yoke for slicin' the rashers. I'd stand for hours and look at that thing goin' round. It was better than the pictures.

MARY. Give the man his drink.

KEARNS. True as God. Zz . . . zzz . . .

DOLLY. Did it have a happy ending?

(*She almost blushes at her own daring.* DRUMM *is surprised, almost admiring.*)

DRUMM. Well, now.

KEARNS. Did it have what?

MARY. Was Laurel and Hardy in it?

(*There is a faint yelp from* DOLLY. KEARNS *ignores her.*)

KEARNS. And, Dezzie, I'll tell you what else I remember. Girls, will yous listen. A bit o' shush. No, this is as true as God. (*Impressively*) An' it was the best thing that ever happened to me.

(DOLLY *mutters inaudibly.*)

DRUMM. I can't hear you.

DOLLY. 'Gone with the Wind' was on the bacon slicer.

(*Her laughter goes out of control.* MARY *joins in.*)

DRUMM. Dear God.

MARY. Desmond, will you stop her?

362

DRUMM. Dolly, that will do. I said, it's quite enough. (*His voice trembles. He leans his head on one hand.*)

KEARNS (*still trying*). No, as true as you're sitting. In the whole o' me life, the best thing that ever – Well, if yous are all goin' to make a shaggin' he-haw of it –

MARY. We're listening.

(*A whimper from* DOLLY. DRUMM *nudges her and, unwilling to trust himself to speak, signals to* KEARNS *to continue.*)

KEARNS. There was nothing like it before nor since.

MARY. This'll be good.

DRUMM. You might get a compliment.

MARY. Not before it's time.

KEARNS. I'll tell yous . . .

MARY. Do.

KEARNS. It was the day Workman won the National.

MARY. Thanks very much.

DOLLY (*a handkerchief to her mouth*). Mmm . . .

KEARNS. Yous can laugh. It was the time herself and me were as poor as Job's ass. Nothin' comin' in only the few shillin's assistance, and your one here expectin'. Weren't you? You were expectin' Sean.

MARY (*a hint of reserve*). I might have been.

KEARNS. No one remembers nothin' tonight. Yes, you were, and your da was six months dead, so he couldn't help us. Yis, hard times. Herself had a path worn between here and the pawn office. Everythin' you could wrap up in a parcel, so's it wouldn't shame you. The watch her da left her. thirty years on the trams. An' there was this sweepstake up in Larkin's-that-was, a draw on the National. I won a couple o' bob that day playin' pitch-an'-toss, so I said to meself: 'I'll risk the lot.' An' didn't I draw a horse, and wasn't it Workman.

DRUMM. Highly appropriate.

KEARNS. You're right. Well, I wasn't worth me salt till the day o' the –

(DOLLY, *as a result of* DRUMM*'s remark, holds back another fit of laughter and gets to her feet.*)

MARY. Dolly, are you all right?

DOLLY. Grand. I'll just use your upstairs. Excuse me.

DRUMM (*mischievously, as she passes*). Disgraceful woman.

(*She slaps at his shoulder and hurries out. In the passageway, she releases her laughter in one gasp. She leans against the wall, recovering. During what follows, she goes out of sight: presumably upstairs.*)

363

KEARNS. It must be Dolly's night for laughin'. Yis, now where was I . . . ?

DRUMM. Presumably the horse won.

KEARNS. Dezzie, it walked it. Fifty quid put into me fist, and I mean fifty quid then, not now. We were landed.

DRUMM. I'd say so.

KEARNS. Steeped. We were in the clear. Everythin' back from the pawn – may I drop down dead, I had to borry a handcart – and the pram and the stuff for the baby bought and paid for. Dezzie . . .

DRUMM. What?

KEARNS. It was the hand o' God.

DRUMM. Was it?

KEARNS. I said to meself the day the lad was born: 'He didn't see us stuck, and I'll never doubt Him be worryin' again.'

DRUMM. A promise you kept.

KEARNS. I never reneged.

DRUMM. God will provide.

KEARNS. Leave it to Him.

DRUMM. And He watches over you?

MARY. Over all of us.

KEARNS. Them that has faith in Him.

DRUMM. Ah, yes. Don't dig the garden: pray for an earthquake.

KEARNS. Jeer away.

DRUMM. Faith? If either of us, you or I, had a scrap of it, we'd be in a monastery living on black bread and doing atonement. What we have is hope. We call it faith.

KEARNS. Rubbidge.

DRUMM. Mind, I'll concede that as a race we have more to believe in than others. Christians elsewhere worship three Divine Persons: God the Father, God the Son and God the Holy Ghost. We have added a fourth one. God the Jockey.

KEARNS. You won't act the hard root when your time comes.

MARY. Now, Lar . . .

KEARNS. Then what'll you do?

DRUMM. Envy you your certainty.

KEARNS (*crowing*). Ah! You've had it too soft, Dezzie. No goin' short, nothin' to pray for. A grand cushy job with a collar an' tie on it, an' a pension in the wind-up.

MARY. Don't row with the man.

KEARNS. What rowin'? Sure more power to him. I'm only sayin' that poor people like ourselves, them that has it hard, we're more in with God, like, than the rest of them.

364

DRUMM. He's one of your own.

KEARNS (*delighted*). Now you have it. (*Grabbing* DRUMM's *glass*) Gimme that.

DRUMM. I won't.

KEARNS (*masterful*). I say you will.

DRUMM. A cushy job, you called it. Perhaps it is. But a man who carves penny whistles at least knows his own worth: I don't know mine. I spend a third of my life in a hot-house of intrigue and skulduggery which would make the court of the Borgias seem like a whist drive, and I do work of doubtful value for a government of doubtful morality. Cogito ergo sum. I am a cog, therefore I am.

KEARNS. Still, isn't it money for jam?

DRUMM. Quite.

KEARNS. And you're on the home stretch now, with the pension at the winnin' post.

DRUMM. If God doesn't get there first.

KEARNS. Not forgettin' the lump sum.

DRUMM. True.

KEARNS. Paid for, don't forget, by yours truly.

MARY. By who?

KEARNS. Income tax. I don't begrudge it to you. Only it's time you stopped takin' life so serious. Y'ought to pop off some place: folly the sun. An' give Dolly a bit of a break. That's a great girl.

MARY. He's right there.

KEARNS. A topper.

DRUMM. Yes.

KEARNS. 'Yes,' says he. Say it an' mean it.

DRUMM. You seem to think at this late stage in her life she needs references.

KEARNS. I'm sayin' you got the right girl, the same as meself did. Only you were slow in findin' out, on account of you had a soft spot for this one.

MARY. Now no blatherin'.

KEARNS. I don't miss much.

MARY (*embarrassed*). I'll guzzle him.

KEARNS. What harm's in sayin' it? We're all past that sort o' jack-actin', wha'? The blood is gone cool.

MARY. In a minute it won't be the only thing.

KEARNS. No, own up to it, I wiped your eye. And sign's on it you got Dolly and she's a credit to you.

DRUMM. I'm sure.

KEARNS. *Be* sure.

DRUMM (*becoming nettled*). Yes, now could we have done?

KEARNS. A smasher, so she is.

DRUMM. My dear man, don't tell me about it: tell Dolly.

KEARNS. I did tell her.

DRUMM. Well, then.

KEARNS. Many's the time.

DRUMM. Well done.

KEARNS. More times than you told her.

DRUMM. No doubt.

KEARNS. In this room you're sittin' in.

MARY (*anxiously*). Lar . . .

KEARNS. Last Friday.

> (*A pause.* DRUMM *is quite still.*)
> No. No, it was the time I met her up the town. Yis, that was when I told her.
> (DRUMM *looks at him with contempt.*)

MARY. That tongue of yours: it ought to be cut out of you.

KEARNS. Wha's up?

MARY. You'd talk if it killed you. A mouth. A mouth, that's what you are, no good for an'thin' else.

KEARNS. I met her up the town –

MARY. Shut that gob of yours. Shut it. (*To* DRUMM) She came in for a cup of coffee. She'd do her shoppin' and buy the few things for the week, and she'd come in and I'd put the kettle on. No harm in that.

> (DRUMM *is silent.*)
> Ten minutes the one day in the week. She has her neighbours: who else has she? Do you expect her to live like a statue? I said to her: 'Tell him, why can't you?' She said: 'I'm afraid to.'
> (DRUMM *does not react. A faint cough as* DOLLY *comes into view outside.*)
> (*Hearing her*) Now let it lie. You will.
> (DOLLY *comes in.*)

DOLLY. Honestly and truly, I'm weak from laughing. Look at me: I'm a sight for the crows.

> (DRUMM *looks towards her.*)
> You're very quiet. Is something up? (*Touching her hair*) Is it me?
> (*The lights cross-fade with those in the kitchen.*
> DESMOND *is standing facing* MIBS *and* LAR. *He is holding a package.* LAR *is wearing a new off-the-peg blue serge suit.*)

366

DESMOND. I'm sorry. I came to leave a message. Your father said
I was to come in.

LAR. Cough Bottle, the hard man: I wouldn't know a bit of you. Hey,
c'm'ere an' tell us. (*Modelling the suit*) Is this the berries or isn't it?

DESMOND. Pardon me?

LAR. The suit. I was tryin' it on for Mibs.

DESMOND. Very smart.

LAR. You're supposed to say 'Well wear'.

DESMOND. Well wear.

LAR. Might as well go to me doom in style, wha'? Fifty-two an' a
tanner . . . five bob a week.

MIBS. Don't tell everyone our business. (*To* DESMOND, *coldly*) Did
you want something?

DESMOND. I was at the Sodality Mass yesterday. I heard the banns
being read out . . .

MIBS (*flatly*). Did you?

DESMOND. It was the first I knew of it.

LAR (*revelling in his moment*). Wasn't it lovely? . . . makin' a
show of a man, readin' his name out from altar. Dezzie, she
landed me. Talk about a conger-eel: you never seen the fight I
put up, an' just when I was away an' clear with the hook in me
mouth, she stuck the gaff into me.

MIBS. Dry up.

LAR. The banns called, the new suit bought and the chapel booked. Here, look at the Made-in-Shanghai. (*Taking hold of*
MIBS'*s left hand*) Show him.

(*She pulls her hand away.*)

The diamond cem out of a watch.

DESMOND. Anyway, I thought I'd offer my congratulations.

MIBS. Thanks.

LAR. Me oul' comrade, put it there.

DESMOND (*offering the package*). This isn't very much. Just to . . .
mark the occasion.

LAR. Ah, for the love-a! (*Feeling the shape*) It's a book.

DESMOND. Nearly as bad. But with every good wish.

LAR. Can we open it?

DESMOND. Well, it's not for Christmas. (*Less abrasively*) Of
course. (*To* MIBS) When is the . . . uh?

MIBS. The 2nd.

DESMOND. Ah.

LAR. Did you hear tell her da put me to work? 'S a fact.
He found me a spiffin' job. I'm in it for life.

DESMOND. Oh, yes?

LAR. I'm on the trams.

DESMOND. Good for you. As a conductor?

LAR (*shaking his head*). I'm above in the yard. Not so much on them as under them. Sure isn't it a start? Hold on: I have it. (*He has undone the wrapping and finds an attractively-framed Van Gogh print. It is a still-life: 'Yellow Chair with Pipe'. We have already seen this reproduction: it is hanging in the living room.*)

(*To* MIBS) It's a pitcher.

DESMOND. Not the original, I'm afraid. It's by Van Gogh, a Dutch artist. I've always been fond of it.

LAR. Mibs, have a dekko.

(*She moves reluctantly to inspect it.*)

DESMOND. Wherever it is you'll be living, I thought you might find a place for it.

LAR. Mibs's oul' lad: he says we can bunk here.

DESMOND. I see.

LAR. Until we find a place. Dezzie, about the weddin'. The spondulicks is a bit short, so there'll only be her parents an' me ma, an' Harry Young, that's standin' up for me.

DESMOND. I understand.

LAR. I mean, don't expect a card in the post with gold writin' on it. You have me?

DESMOND (*heartily*). Yes!

LAR. You're sure now?

MIBS (*suddenly*). It's only an old chair.

DESMOND. That's all.

MIBS. A bit of wood standing there: it's nothing. And yet it's like as if whoever done it . . . put himself inside of it. (*She smiles at* DESMOND, *delighted by her discovery*.)

LAR. Give us a gawk. Hey, it's crooked. I wouldn't sit on that yoke. (*Remembering his manners*) It's nice an' bright, but. Great in a room.

(*It is the difference between the two reactions that provokes* DESMOND *into the following*.)

DESMOND. Mary, if I might talk to you . . .

MIBS. Talk away.

DESMOND. No . . . uh . . . (*He indicates* LAR.)

MIBS. If you mean where he can't hear us, no, you can't.

DESMOND (*to* LAR). You don't mind.

MIBS. Yes, he does. (*To* LAR) Stay where you are. (*To* DESMOND)

I know what you want to say, and I'll save you the trouble.
'Marry Lar,' you told me, 'you're his sort.' And you were right.
DESMOND. No.
LAR. Decent man. Won't forget it to you.
MIBS. Yes, you were. You used to say to me: 'Think for yourself.'
Many's a time you said it. 'Put this on one side and that on the
other and look at them.' And it's what I done. (*Amending*)
What I did. And I knew that with Lar there'd be a bit of me
left over. Not with you: you'd want the lot. The bit of me that's
not yours at all: that likes to go to a do or a hop and sing songs
on the road home. Or talk too loud and say 'Shag it' and be
what you call common. You'd take it all: there'd be nothing left
for Lar, not even the bit of harmless likin'. You don't know
where halfway is. Lar does: he's glad of what you can give him.
He won't begrudge you the bit of me that's yours. (*With a grin*)
Even though you'll turn your nose up at it.
(*A pause.* LAR *has been listening with an amiable, uncom-
prehending smile.* DESMOND, *knowing his cause is lost, wants
to back out with at least his pride intact.*)
DESMOND. I don't take leavings.
MIBS. Hard lines, then.
DESMOND. Yes . . . well, you know best. (*Formally*) I'm obliged to
you for the courtesy of a –
MIBS. Oh, balls.
DESMOND (*ignoring this*). And forgive the intrusion. I wanted to
wish you both all . . . (*Unable to resist the inflection*) possible
happiness.
LAR. Look, sit down.
MIBS. Let him alone.
LAR. Well, listen . . . you're to drop in on us, do you hear? No
makin' strange.
MIBS. And thanks for the picture.
DESMOND. Oh . . . there's a card with it. The very best, then.
MIBS. Yeah. 'Bye, now.
(*He goes.* LAR *follows him to the door.*)
LAR (*calling*). Now if you don't drop in you'll be back o' the neck:
I mean it. Hey . . . and don't pick up any good things.
(*He comes back into the room.* MIBS *is searching the wrap-
ping paper and finds a greeting card.*)
I think the Cough Bottle's gettin' a bit queer in himself, do you
not? Too much oul' readin' an' stuff. (*He looks at the picture.*)
Hey, was I polite to him?

369

MIBS. You were great. Change out of that suit.

LAR. 'Cause I wouldn't like to hurt his feelin's. Whoever sold him that yoke rooked him.

(MIBS *is reading, half-audibly.*)

What's on it?

MIBS. 'For there is good news yet to hear and fine things to be seen, Before we go to Paradise by way of Ken . . . sal Green.'

LAR. Wha's it mean?

MIBS. Nothing. It doesn't mean anything. Except that he'd make me finish that bloody lesson if it killed him.

(*The lights cross-fade with those in the living area.*

DOLLY *is tense and silent.* MARY *is trying to keep up the pretence that the evening is on the same relaxed level as previously.*)

MARY (*referring to* KEARNS). One day he was off out mowin' her grass, and the next he was puttin' a washer on her tap, and the day after that her drains needed mendin' . . .

KEARNS (*protesting*). Now you're makin' a yarn of it.

MARY. 'A poor widow,' says me man here, 'with no one to do her a hand's turn.' Oh aye, I thought to myself that's how it starts. Josie Murnaghan on the Barrack Road . . . Josie McDonald that was. (*To* DOLLY) You know her.

(DOLLY *shakes her head.*)

Ah, you do. Well, 'clare to God, I was at the state where I was examinin' his coat for hairs.

KEARNS. Yis, at my age.

MARY. The older they are, the worse they are. Next thing, he says her wall needs whitewashin'. 'It's a big job,' says he. 'I know,' says I, 'I've seen her.' And then, doesn't this woman, a total stranger, come to the door, and a little boy with her, and he roarin'. Him . . . (*Meaning* KEARNS) it turns out he's after burstin' the child's chestnut. He was never next or near Josie Murnaghan: he was off playin' . . . (*To* KEARNS) What?

KEARNS. Conkers.

MARY. Conkers . . . with the little chiselurs off the road.

DOLLY (*faintly; a glance at* DRUMM). Goodness.

MARY. When he ought to be sayin' his prayers.

DOLLY. Oh, now.

MARY. A right go-be-the-wall. But sure there wasn't a family yet where there weren't secrets.

KEARNS. She thought I was –

MARY (*silencing him; to* DRUMM). Do you hear me?

DRUMM. Perfectly.

MARY. So will you come out of your sulks.

DRUMM (*not harshly*). Now don't interfere.

MARY. You can blame it on me. I met her in McLoughlin's one day, and I said: 'Come back to the house.' She didn't want to. I made her.

DRUMM. At gunpoint.

MARY. What?

DRUMM. You abducted her.

MARY. No, I didn't need to. But Desmond, don't go gettin' sarky with me, not in here. This is my house you're sittin' in.

DRUMM. That can be rectified.

MARY. It can, yes, and off you go again. But for how long this time?

(*It is a reminder. He looks at her resentfully.*)

MARY. That'd suit you. You could spend the rest of your life with your feelings hurt: being cool with one half o' the world and not talking to the other half.

DOLLY (*not wanting a scene*). Don't . . .

KEARNS. I think we ought to be all grand and sociable and as happy as Larry. I wasn't christened be accident, you know.

MARY. Have sense. What did she do on you? Nothin'.

DRUMM. Whatever Dolly did or did not do, I don't wish to discuss it outside my own home.

KEARNS. Proper order.

MARY. You hold your tongue. (*To* DRUMM) Too true you don't. Because you know I'm well able for you and she isn't. She walks on tippy-toes around you. When you come home like a divil because someone has got on the wrong side of you, she has to put up with it. I don't.

DRUMM. I agree. And you won't have to. Dolly . . .

MARY. No. You'll go out of here when you tell that woman she done nothing wrong. Ah, Desmond: all this because she was still talking to me when you were black out with us.

DRUMM (*indignantly*). No.

MARY. What, then?

DRUMM. Nothing of the sort. Dolly is free to make friends. Or to lose them, or keep them: it's her choice. I don't ask her to live in my pocket. I don't want it.

MARY. Then for the love an' honour –

DRUMM. Because of the deception. How do you think it feels to know that one has been listening to the same lie for five years?

371

DOLLY (*timidly; helpfully*). Six.

(*He looks at her as if suspecting an attempt at humour. Then*)

DRUMM. Six.

MARY. I know, yes. And all the harm it did you!

DRUMM. It was behind my back. You knew and he knew. Probably half the town did as well.

MARY. Now we have it.

DRUMM. And laughed at me for a fool.

MARY. Oh, aye: the town. What'll the town say?

DRUMM. I don't give a damn what it says, but I will not stand arraigned before a judge and jury of gossip-mongers and idlers. They've had their day.

MARY. You told us. They made a mock of you because you were out of step with them, so you got your own back. You stopped walking. You were going to do the divil an' all: yes, you were, but no: you might get laughed at. You let on they're not worth passing the time of day with, but they rule you.

DOLLY. Mary, they do not.

DRUMM. Thank you, I can defend myself.

MARY. It's true, they bett you.

DRUMM. Beat me.

MARY. However you say it.

DRUMM. I do fear them, yes. I fear the . . . good nature of their malice. But if I failed to accomplish the devil and all, as you call it, it wasn't because of the town: the town had nothing to do with it. It was because the devil and all wasn't in me. But I'll tell you what is. I've never lied to a man or about him, and I've never smiled into the face of a blackguard or been called an idler or a licker of boots or a hanger-on. I don't call that a total defeat. And if it makes you happy, the reason I was angry with Dolly is that I can no longer afford to be angry with her. I consider that . . . an impertinence.

(MARY*'s smile is hard as she turns to* DOLLY. *Inside her, probably to her own surprise, an old wound has been re-opened.*)

MARY (*to* DOLLY). There, now. Isn't he good to you?

KEARNS. That's the dart: forgive an' forget. Sure who could be cross with Dolly? And Dezzie is not the worst o' them either.

MARY. Oh, he's a great man.

(DRUMM *catches the note of hostility. He looks at her, puzzled.*)

DOLLY. I'm glad Dezzie found out.

KEARNS. A fuss over nothin'.

DOLLY. Because I hate anything that's hole-and-corner. (*To* MARY) I do, I told you.

DRUMM. It's over and done with.

MARY (*to* DOLLY). It is. Everything except the absolution and the three Hail Marys.

DRUMM (*to* DOLLY). We must go. (*To* MARY) You're in fighting mood.

MARY. Am I?

KEARNS (*to* MARY). But be the holy, you're a fierce woman. Goin' for him bald-headed, wha'?

DRUMM. Mary herself says it: she's well able for me. (*To* DOLLY) Had you a coat?

KEARNS. Still, there's one thing that's askin' for a puck in the gob, an' that's to go interferin' between a man an' a wife. I thought he was goin' to draw out at you.

DRUMM. It was close. If today hadn't been Sunday . . . !

(DOLLY *laughs*.)

KEARNS (*to* MARY). There was a narra escape for you.

MARY. He interfered between *us*.

(*The suddenness of the accusation takes* DRUMM *off guard*.)

KEARNS (*unheeding*). Oh, a comical card.

DRUMM. Do you mean me?

MARY. So exchange is no robbery.

DRUMM. Interfered between you? I never did.

KEARNS. Between *us*? Begod, he'd have his work cut out for him, so he would. What are you carryin' on about?

DRUMM. How did I? Well?

(*She retreats from the edge. He manner becomes sullen, evasive*.)

MARY. Coming in here, telling us how great you are. Never told a lie in your life, never kow-towed to no one, never done nothin'. A saint, so you are. And poor oul' Dolly, the row there was over a mangy cup of coffee in her hand the one day in the week.

DRUMM. I thought that was settled.

KEARNS. Don't mind her.

DRUMM. You said I interfered between the two of you.

KEARNS. Not at all. She's romancin'.

DRUMM. I'm asking her what she meant.

MARY. Nothing.

DOLLY. Dezzie, leave it. She's upset.

DRUMM (*gently*). Mary? Are you going to tell me?

(*She shakes her head.*)
No need, then. Are we friends?

MARY (*almost in despair*). Yes.

KEARNS. Certainly we're friends. Who the hell says different?

DRUMM. That's what matters. We'll see you soon.
(*He has taken* MARY*'s hand. She keeps a grip on his when he makes to leave.*)

MARY. This morning . . . you said about what you were owed. I've no head for words . . . credit and something.

DRUMM. Debit and credit.

MARY. To add up with.

DRUMM. To add and subtract.

MARY. I thought all day about it. At first I said No, then I said: 'It's what's due to him.' And that's why. Not to harm you . . . I wouldn't, but you have the right. (*A pause*) You were good to Sean. No one could have –

KEARNS (*in alarm*). Eh . . . eh . . .

MARY. . . . could have done more for him. You paid for him at the Christian Brothers, you taught him, made a scholar of him . . .

KEARNS (*blustering*). Now I'm the boss here, and I say No.

MARY. You took him for walks with you. Yourself and Dolly and the girls, yous brung him with yous that time for a holiday. The day of his confirmation, it was you put the suit on his back. And we let you. We never stood between you and him, because it was take what you gev him or go without. Now I'm not sayin' you meant to do it –

KEARNS. I'm tellin' you you're not to.

MARY. I'm not sayin' that. But you turned him against Lar.

KEARNS (*muttering to* DRUMM *and* DOLLY). Get out, get out.

DRUMM. I turned him against . . .?

MARY. Maybe without meaning to.

DRUMM. No, it's untrue. I never did.

KEARNS. Sure certainly it's –

DRUMM. Meaning to or not meaning to . . . I reject it.

MARY. His father was no good. He never did a tap of work. He was ignorant, he was useless. He smelt of porter.

KEARNS (*weakly*). I told you. The lad an' me . . . ile an' water.

DRUMM. I never uttered one word . . .

MARY. No, I'll give you that. But you schooled him well. He seen you look at Lar and heard you talk to him, throwing a word to him the way you'd throw a bone to a dog. Sean couldn't stand to be in the same room as him. Do you wonder he got the idea into his head?

374

KEARNS. Now that will do.

DRUMM. Idea?

MARY. He said it to us. It was the evening he had the row with Lar and went off to England. It's why you've heard the last of him, because you have . . . you may bank on that. It was the exam he passed that summer and the great marks he got. I think that was what started him wondering . . . wondering where he got his brains from.

(DRUMM *and* MARY *look at each other.*)

KEARNS. Dezzie, listen . . .

MARY. Be quiet, now.

KEARNS. A bee in his bonnet.

MARY. Now you can do your adding up. Desmond, it wasn't to harm you.

DRUMM (*dazed*). Very well: he was your son, I meddled, I took too much on myself; but it was to find him a place in the world, away from street corners. But to put that idea in his head, to work that kind of mischief . . . no.

DOLLY. Dezzie wouldn't, Mary. It's not in him.

KEARNS. Sure don't we know, aren't we sayin'? Me oul' comrade, wha'?

DRUMM (*to* KEARNS). And you. You've known why the boy went, and all these years you've let me be a guest in this house?

KEARNS. Why wouldn't I? Aren't we pals, tried an' true, the last of the oul' stock. Put it there!

DRUMM (*it is the nearest he has come to liking* KEARNS). You really are an impossible man.

KEARNS. An' in the heel o' the hunt wasn't it tit for tat? I took your one here offa you. So you took the lad, and aren't we even?

(DRUMM *looks at him in shock. It is as if a blow had been struck.*)

Listen, you'll have a jar. There's a drop still in the –

(DRUMM *turns and goes out.* DOLLY *starts after him, see his raincoat, picks it up and follows him.*

The lights dim on the living room and come up on the bandstand. DESMOND, MIBS, LAR *and* DOROTHY *are there. They watch as* DRUMM *comes into view. He stops, as if from exhaustion.*)

LAR. We'll scram off outa here to some place else. Are yous on?

DOROTHY. I know . . . we'll go to the White Rock.

MIBS. That'll take us till all hours. I have a tea to get ready.

375

LAR. Tell yous what. We'll go up Higgins's Hill and round be the Back Meadow. I'll show yous a bird's nest. Hey, Cough Bottle . . . mind the missus for me.

(LAR *takes* DOROTHY *by the hand.* MIBS *follows.*
DESMOND *looks at* DRUMM *and is the last to go.* DOLLY *appears.*)

DOLLY. Honestly and truly, going off without your coat. You're asking for it. Are you all right?

DRUMM. I walked too fast. Give me a moment.

DOLLY. Put this on.

DRUMM. Yes.

DOLLY. I mean now. (*She helps him into his coat.*) What Mary said, you're never taking it to heart? Such a thing for her to come out with.

DRUMM. Wasn't it!

DOLLY. And poor Lar . . . you'd pity him.

DRUMM. One day . . .

DOLLY. What, love?

DRUMM. I'll take a microscope and an axe. With the microscope I'll discover where his brain is, and then I'll sink the axe into it.

DOLLY. Will you stop . . . no one minds you.

DRUMM. I know.

DOLLY. I think Mary has a jealous streak in her. The way she's forever trying to make out that you and she are so great. It's to show off in front of me.

DRUMM. Dolly . . .

DOLLY. I mean, she missed her chance. You were the brainiest boy in the town, and now it's too late. Lord knows I'm fond of her, but it's her own fault. (*She sees that* DRUMM *is glaring at her.*) I'm listening, pet.

DRUMM. I've achieved nothing.

DOLLY. How?

DRUMM. Three hundred days a year for forty years . . . I've spent twelve thousand days doing work I despise. Instead of friends, I've had standards, and woe betide those who failed to come up to them. Well, *I* failed. My contempt for the town, for the wink and the easy nod and the easier grin . . . it was cowardice; Mary was right. What I called principles was vanity. What I called friendship was malice.

DOLLY. Will you go 'way. This is because Mary upset you.

DRUMM. Not much to boast of at the end of the day.

DOLLY. The end, how are you.

DRUMM. Well, is it?

DOLLY. You're in the glooms: I'm not going to answer you. And if it were true itself . . .

DRUMM. Well?

DOLLY. And it isn't, not a blessed word of it. You have me as bad as yourself.

DRUMM. Go on. If it were true itself . . .

DOLLY. I was going to say, if it was, it needn't be from now on. I mean, Dezzie, are we alive or aren't we? (*Pause*) Now don't stand here: come home. Look at the way the evenings are getting a stretch: there's still light in the sky.

DRUMM. I have a question.

DOLLY (*smiling*). More silliness.

DRUMM. Supposing I were to offer you a choice between buying a motor car –

DOLLY (*excited*). Dezzie!

DRUMM. Be quiet. Between that and my writing a book about this place. Which would you choose?

DOLLY (*after a pause*). The motor car.

DRUMM (*a little sadly*). Of course you would.

DOLLY. Because . . . whatever I want, you do the opposite.

DRUMM. You are a most aggravating woman: you get more foolish every day. Go . . . be off home with you. Make a start.

(*They set off.* DRUMM *holds out a hand, looking up, then opens his umbrella, a pall over his head, and goes off slowly.*)

CURTAIN

377

KILL

CHARACTERS

WADE
THERESE FITZACKERLY
TONY SLEEHAUN
NESSA SLEEHAUN
MORT MONGAN
FATHER BISHOP
ISEULT MULLARKEY
MRS WADE
JUDGE LAWLESS
MADGE LAWLESS

Seventy minutes' drive from town, if you happen to know the short cut via the bog road. This October evening.

ACT I
Aperitifs

ACT II
Liqueurs

At first encounter, *Kill* might appear to be a straightforward black comedy, swinging at times into farce. If, however, one recognises the setting – a deconsecrated church – as a metaphor for a newly-laicised Southern Ireland, then an entire sub-level comes into view. The besieged and much-disputed 'alms house' is clearly Northern Ireland, and the hooligan, MORT MONGAN, is a rampaging microcosm of the Provisional I.R.A. On this level, the play is a lampooning – more accurately a harpooning – of Irish attitudes towards the North: the vocal outrage counterpointed with the unspoken indifference or partisanship on the side of the terrorists. Each character represents a facet of power: the law, the Church, business, the arts and, in the person of WADE, political power. It is emphasised, however, that *Kill* is a comedy, not a tract.

KILL

ACT ONE

*The setting is the converted interior of what was once a small
country church and now serves as an impressive drawing room. At
the right, from the audience's viewpoint, there is a raised marble
platform where the altar once was; now it is the dais for a throne-
like chair draped in imperial purple. This is backed by a reredos
behind which is a door. At the rear, there is an organ loft, reached
by way of an oak door and staircase beyond. Further towards the
left is a stained-glass window. Upstage, in the left wall, is the main
entrance door. Downstage, an ornamental gate leads into a recess
which was once the baptismal area and overnight mortuary. The
room is comfortably furnished, but a closer look suggests that
several items need attention: a rug is threadbare; the throne has a
book under one leg; the upholstery of a sofa seems to have shifted
towards one end; the door of a cabinet hangs askew on one hinge.*

It is a stormy October evening.

*Before rise of curtain, we hear organ music: Bach's Toccata and
Fugue.*

Curtain up.

*WADE, wearing an expensive silk dressing gown, is seated at the
organ keyboard, his shoulders heaving with the effort of applying
himself to the keys and pulling out various stops. The music ends.
His frame slumps from the effort of the recital. He sets off down
the stairs and emerges into the living room. As he does so, organ
music starts up again. He switches off the record player which is,
and has been, its source. He mounts the dais and adopts a brooding
Napoleonic attitude on the throne, on which a small key light is
trained. He is of less than average height – perhaps there is a
shortness in the legs – but possesses an imposing brow, which he
strokes moodily.*

*A heavy knocking at the outer door disturbs his idyll. He scowls
at the imminent intrusion. THERESE appears in the mortuary
recess and enters the living room. She is in her 30s, efficient, attractive, superbly groomed. She looks towards him, awaiting his
instructions.*

WADE. What time was on the invitations?

THERESE. Seven-thirty.

WADE. What time *is* it?

THERESE (*without checking her watch*). Seven-forty-seven.

WADE. They're years early. Barbarians.

THERESE. Of course. (*A smile*) How troublesome if they weren't.
(*He smiles faintly in return: she has a point. He rises,
indicates with a crook of the finger that she should admit the
guests and goes out by the door behind the reredos. She
switches on a lamp, give an appraising glance at the room,
then partly pulls aside the curtains which mask the main door
and serve as a draught-excluder.* TONY SLEEHAUN *appears.*)
Hello, welcome. You found us, how clever.
(SLEEHAUN *is forty, chubby and of provincial origins. He has
a practised smoothness. If he were pressed to describe himself
in one word, he would have a struggle not to say 'charming'.*)

SLEEHAUN. Hello, I'm Tony Sleehaun. A thrill to see you. Mrs
Wade, is it?

THERESE. I wish I were, don't we all? I'm Therese Fitzackerly . . .
Mr Wade's p.a.

SLEEHAUN. Delighted.

THERESE. Isn't Mrs Sleehaun with you?

SLEEHAUN. Yes, she —
(*He becomes aware that someone is caught in the folds of the
curtain and struggling to find a way out.*)
Nessa? She's in here somewhere. Don't thresh, darling, you'll
make it w— Will you wait? Got her.
(*He manages to extricate his wife,* NESSA. *She is not the kind
of lady who shines on glittering occasions. She is gauche,
because shy, and her dress sense is delinquent. Her hair is in
disarray.*)
(*Jovially*) That's the girl . . . long threatening comes at last. My
wife, Nessa . . . Miss —

THERESE. Mrs. Mrs Fitzackerly. Welcome to Kill House.

NESSA. I got all caught up in your —

THERESE. They're a nuisance, but they keep out the elements. May I
take your things? (*As they discard their coats*) What a
wretched evening. Was the drive down awful?

SLEEHAUN. I have a Merc.

THERESE. Ah.

SLEEHAUN (*Spanish intonation*). No prob-lem!

NESSA (*in mild dismay*). Tony, I think we're the first.

SLEEHAUN. We're not?

THERESE.Somebody must be . . . well *done*! I'm afraid that Mrs
Wade's health hasn't been good for some time, so I'm her
locum for the evening. So . . . (*to* NESSA) perhaps you'd care
to freshen up?

NESSA. Thank you. My hair is all —
(*She remembers that she is holding a brown paper bag con-
taining a small box.*)
A few sweets.

THERESE. Aren't you kind, he will be pleased. (*To* SLEEHAUN)
Won't be a jiffy. (*To* NESSA) This way.
(*She takes the coats and leads the way.*)
Years ago, when it was a church, this used to be the mortuary.
NESSA *falters slightly, looks back at* SLEEHAUN *and precedes*
THERESE *out D.L. Left alone,* SLEEHAUN *takes in his sur-
roundings. He is pleased. If he were a Moslem, this could be
Mecca. He slams a fist into his hand and laughs to himself.*)

SLEEHAUN. Begod, what?
(*He sees the throne, advances towards it and stands in awe.*
THERESE *returns and watches him for a moment.*)

THERESE. That's his. He likes to sit unobtrusively to one side and
not be the centre of everything. Now . . . you'd like a drink, I'm
sure.

SLEEHAUN. A g. and t., go raibh maith agat. (*'Guh rev mawh
agut' — 'Thank you'*)

THERESE. He's a great observer.

SLEEHAUN. He's a great man.

THERESE (*simply, sincerely*). He likes to think so.
(*She goes to an alcove where there is a halo-ed statue on a
plinth. She spins the statue around, revealing it to be hollow,
the interior serving as a drinks cabinet.*)

SLEEHAUN. Have you been with him long?

THERESE. Since he first acquired the . . . (*indicating their surroundings*) leasehold. Going on five years. Ice and lemon?

SLEEHAUN. Ta. Fitzackerly . . . that's an uncommon name.

THERESE. It was a wedding present.

SLEEHAUN. Ah-ha. Your husband, is he here?

THERESE. Neither here nor there, as the saying goes. Do you happen
to know what Mrs Sleehaun's preference would be?
(*He passes behind her as she is occupied with the drinks. He
clamps his hand around her buttock.*)

SLEEHAUN. Something soft.

383

(*He moves on. She remains still for a moment, then looks at him and decides that it has not happened.*)
She's a great girl, Nessa is: true blue. We're reputed, you know, to be the most devoted couple in big business, which is no mean achievement, considering that my rise was so meteoric.
(*She detaches the metal halo from the statue, puts the drink on it and approaches him.*)
There was a profile of me in 'Business and Finance', aptly entitled 'Sleehaun Ascendant'. Did you see it?

THERESE. We have it on file.

SLEEHAUN (*pleased*). Get away. Still, dynamic and all as I am, I never thought this day would dawn. (*As he takes his drink*) How's the organ? Does it work?

THERESE. The . . . ? Yes, perfectly.

SLEEHAUN. . . . Once you pump it.

THERESE. As it happens, it's electric.

SLEEHAUN. Modern times, what?
(NESSA *returns. He drinks.*)
G'luck to you.

THERESE. Mrs Sleehaun . . . do come in. And please, both of you, be comfortable. Your husband has very primly instructed me to offer you something unexciting.

NESSA. If it's no trouble.
(*She sits on the settee and starts up again.*)

THERESE.Do move further down . . . it's the upholstery: the man never turned up. So much needs to be done, but my employer believes that efficiency carried to extremes is a form of laziness. He feels that we should preserve our energies for contemplation . . . of the way ahead, you know. He has a saying. Whenever he comes across imperfection . . . a train that's late, perhaps, or a wasp in the soup, or bad teeth, or a stopped-up sink —

NESSA. The cistern in your bathroom doesn't —

THERESE. . . . Then he smiles that charming smile of his and says: 'It'll do.'

SLEEHAUN (*admiringly*). Good God.

THERESE. There's really no end to him.

SLEEHAUN. Bernard Shaw, go home.

THERESE. Indeed.

SLEEHAUN. Shakespeare, go with him. (*He shakes his head in wonderment.*)

NESSA. We're still the first.

SLEEHAUN. What?

384

NESSA. We're the only ones. I don't know what Mrs Fitzackerly —
SLEEHAUN (*correcting her*). Therese.
THERESE (*same tone*). Mrs Fitzackerly.
NESSA. . . . will think of us. (*To* THERESE) We left early in case we
    got lost, only we didn't. And to be sure certain, we stopped to
    ask at the little house by the iron gates.
THERESE. You stopped where?
SLEEHAUN. There was a light on, but nobody answered.
THERESE. Nobody ever does. That would be what was once the
    alms house. The trustees for the estate have served them with
    notice to quit. A waste of time . . . they've barricaded
    themselves in.
SLEEHAUN. Are they squatters?
THERESE. No better than. (*Then*) You will forgive me if I look in
    at the kitchen? The woman who comes to us from the village
    is inclined to over-boil the mutton.
SLEEHAUN. When is himself likely to do us the —
THERESE. He's not far away. His private apartments are in the old
    presbytery. (*Indicating off*) There's a connecting pergola
    behind the reredos.
    (*She goes off, D.L.*)
NESSA. What did she say?
SLEEHAUN. I think it's an impediment.
NESSA. I mean about giving us mutton.
    (*He shrugs, indifferent.*)
    Boiled. You'd think they'd do us a rack of lamb.
SLEEHAUN. Don't start.
NESSA. Or a nice leg.
SLEEHAUN. You have lamb on the brain.
NESSA. I can't eat mutton.
SLEEHAUN. You don't try.
NESSA. I do, and it won't stay down, it comes back up. Just think-
    ing of the gristly bits makes my eyes go all —
    (*Her gorge rises. She fumbles for her handkerchief.*)
SLEEHAUN. Your trouble is, a sophisticated life-style has you
    spoilt. In our house, we were reared on mutton, all eight of us.
NESSA. You told me.
SLEEHAUN. And you ate it or went without. Fat or gristle, you
    were glad of it. Get it down you . . . lovely.
    (*Her shoulders heave.*)
    Ah, but the treat of the week was on Saturdays. Every Saturday
    —

NESSA (*who has heard it before*). Don't.

SLEEHAUN. That was the evening when the ma, God love her, would do us a sheep's head. We'd be at it like savages. (*She makes a guttural noise.*) Oh, you may well lick your lips. None of your medium-rare codology in them days. Off to school on a Monday with a feed of bread-and-dripping inside you. (*Nostalgically*) Mutton fat.

NESSA (*feebly*). Stop.

SLEEHAUN. No, no, love . . . a snob, standing where I am, might forget the old days: I don't. The hard road behind us and easy street in front. Listen to me. (*Pointing off*) That man . . . a crook —

NESSA (*incredulous*). No . . .

SLEEHAUN. . . . a crook of his finger or the wink of an eye: that's all it takes. Powerful? . . . he's bigger than God. I mean, *he* doesn't consort with nonentities. And once he gives you the beck, you're elected, you're in.

NESSA. Are you?

SLEEHAUN. Will you wake up, girl? Look where we are.

NESSA. I know where. Still getting mutton.

SLEEHAUN. Well, thanks. Thank you, Nessa, for being so happy for me. (*A pause. He sulks. Then, for* NESSA, *an outburst.*)

NESSA. I hate going to places where I feel stupid.

SLEEHAUN. You mean here?

NESSA. I mean to where people talk to a body as if her straps were showing. (*Nodding towards D.L.*) Like she did. And when I look, they always are.

SLEEHAUN. For God's sake.

NESSA. Or else they're like that man at the Chamber of Commerce dinner that made free with me. (*This is different.* SLEEHAUN's *face darkens.*)

SLEEHAUN. I took exception to that. Lucky for him we were having our trifle. Ten minutes earlier I'd have taken the steak-knife and I'd have —

NESSA. Ah, don't.

SLEEHAUN. They'd better not try it, not with my wife, I don't care who they are. Pack of whoormasters, degenerates . . . dirty, filthy animals.

NESSA. I'm sorry I mentioned it.

SLEEHAUN. If one of them so much as lays a finger, I'll — (*He picks up a cushion and in his rage tears it nearly asunder.*)

I'll gut him. I'll sink my nails into his gizzard and tear the tripes from his rotten carcass. I'll —

NESSA. You're putting yourself in a passion. All I meant was, I can't abide the sort of man who's a — What's the word?

SLEEHAUN. A groper. (*Panting, his rage spent*) I need a refill. (*He thrusts the cushion into her hands and goes to the bar. A snowfall of feathers drifts to the floor.*)

NESSA. It's not manners.

SLEEHAUN. I don't care, I feel weak. Anyway, if she's not here to serve us, we'll — What are you at?

NESSA. How? (*Noticing the feathers*) Oh, my God.

SLEEHAUN. The good cushion. Honestly, Nessa.

NESSA. And the carpet . . . what'll we do?

SLEEHAUN. Really, love, it's a bit much.

(NESSA *goes on her knees, frantically picking up bits of down and pushing them back into the cushion.* SLEEHAUN *tops up his drink, facing away from the room. He examines a piece of glassware.*)

Hey, have a gawk . . . best Waterford. Look.

NESSA. Yes . . . in a minute.

SLEEHAUN. And Glenmorangie.

NESSA. If she comes in on us, we're destroyed.

SLEEHAUN. Yes, well get a move on.

NESSA. You oughtn't to fly into such tempers. The doctor told you —

SLEEHAUN. Yeah, yeah.

(*She breaks off as* MORT MONGAN *comes from behind the reredos. He wears a tattered gabardine raincoat tied with string; his face is smeared with black and partly hidden by a balaclava. He carries several sticks of gelignite taped together and with a fuse protruding. He is surprised to see* SLEEHAUN *and* NESSA, *who is still on her knees. He looks at her menacingly and edges his way across the room, always facing her.*)

SLEEHAUN. Everything the very best. Easy knowing we're in the presence of quality, what?

(NESSA *opens her mouth, but no sound is heard.* MONGAN *holds a cigarette lighter close to the fuse and flicks it on: it is a threat directed at her.*)

Now . . . ice. Where do they keep the — Got it.

(*As* SLEEHAUN *turns, drink in hand,* MONGAN *has crossed to L. The flame of the lighter goes out, and he disappears silently, D.L.*)

I oughtn't get aggravated. It takes too much out of me. (*A breath of relief*) Whooh. How goes the work?
(*She points after the departed* MONGAN *and at last finds her voice: a thin wail that is almost rhythmical.*)

NESSA. Eeeeeeeeeee.

SLEEHAUN. Ha-ha. (*Joining in, as he think*) 'Oh, the moonlight's fair tonight along the Wabash . . . From the fields there comes the scent of new-mown hay . . .'

NESSA. Tony, there was a man.

SLEEHAUN (*hard*). A what?

NESSA. I'm telling you . . . he came between us. A *man*.

SLEEHAUN. Kneeling to me won't help you. I want his name.

NESSA. A terrible person, with a black face.

SLEEHAUN. With a — (*He staggers back, clutching his mouth in revulsion*).

NESSA. And oh, Tony, what he had in his hand!
(*He stares at her, then gives vent to a cry that is more animal than human.*)
What is it?
(*He looks about wildly and finds himself another cushion.*)
Ah no, love, I'm still clearing up from the — (*As he picks one up*:) We'll have nothing left to sit on.
(THERESE *returns from D.L.*)

THERESE. Profuse apologies. What a way to treat guests, but if I take my eye off that woman for an —
(*She breaks off at the sight of* NESSA *getting to her feet.*)
Lost something?

NESSA. Mrs Fitzackerly, did *you* see him? He went through there.

THERESE. Pardon me?

NESSA. That awful man . . . just now.

SLEEHAUN. Wait a sec, do you mean —

NESSA. You can't have missed him.

THERESE. Nor did I. That was Mongan, my employer's valet. So fastidious. We always say he makes Jeeves seem like a casual labourer.

NESSA. No, no . . . his face was black.

THERESE. Tanned, you mean. He's a sun-lamp fanatic.

NESSA. But he was holding what looked like . . . sticks of dynamite.

SLEEHAUN (*relieved*). Is *that* all?

THERESE. Oh, dear. (*Smiling*) He was carrying candles. Out here, our electricity often fails, so we take precautions.

388

NESSA. But —

(*A knocking at the outer door.*)

THERESE. Here's company for you at long last. Excuse me?

(*She goes towards the door.*)

NESSA (*to* SLEEHAUN). He didn't look one bit like a what-she-said-he-was. The clothes were falling off him.

SLEEHAUN. So what? An Irish valet has less codology about him than an English one.

(THERESE *admits the guests. They are: a genially impressive gentleman of fifty-five or so wearing a black overcoat, and a lady in her early thirties. She is striking in appearance: raven-haired and pale, luminous skin. She wears a long evening cloak fastened with a Tara brooch.*)

THERESE. Hello, hurry in . . . lovely to see you. Did you drive down together?

BISHOP. Our good host suggested that I give myself the pleasure of Miss Mullarkey's company.

ISEULT. He had no choice. Sure I don't drive.

NESSA (*in a whisper. Tony, it's Iseult Mullarkey.*

SLEEHAUN. Who?

(ISEULT, *who has a built-in adulation-detector, flashes a smile designed to do them for the moment.* NESSA *smiles back and makes a tiny worshipful noise.*)

THERESE. How brave of you to travel. Need one ask if it's still raining?

ISEULT. In torrents.

BISHOP. Pceing down.

THERESE. How depressing. May I take your things?

SLEEHAUN (*a whisper*). What does she do?

NESSA. She . . . (*She mouths the rest*).

SLEEHAUN. What?

(NESSA *crouches slightly with her back to the visitors and makes a sawing motion across her thighs.*)

Good God.

THERESE (*assisting* ISEULT). You can plan nothing ahead of time. Our climate is simply disgusting.

BISHOP. That's the word for it. Feckin' disgusting.

(*He removes his overcoat, revealing the attire of a priest.*)

Climate, how are you . . . bloody brutal.

NESSA (*staring*). Tony . . .

BISHOP. By the by, I told my driver that if he went round to the kitchen there'd be a cup of tea for him.

THERESE. I think we can do better than that. There's mutton.

BISHOP. Grand. (*Jovially*) So long as you don't give him what we're having, what?

(THERESE *blinks at this.* ISEULT *gives her the cloak and takes a step forward; The tips of her fingers are together prayerfully as she takes in her surroundings. Her full-length evening ensemble is classically Irish: only a wolfhound is lacking.*)

THERESE. Miss Mullarkey?

ISEULT. Don't mind me. I'm wide-eyed and childlike with awe and amazement. It's so spiritual.

THERESE. Isn't it? Before I put your things away, come and meet the Sleehauns.

BISHOP. I'm dying to.

(*He starts forward and unthinkingly is genuflecting before where the altar was when he catches himself in mid-dip.*) Dear God, I do it every time. (*To the* SLEEHAUNS) How are you?

THERESE. May I introduce Mr and Mrs Sleehaun? Bishop —

BISHOP. Father.

THERESE. I get so muddled. . . . Father Bishop.

BISHOP. Delighted.

SLEEHAUN (*shaking hands*). Tony Sleehaun . . . it's a thrill.

THERESE (*drawing* ISEULT *over*). And in this lady's case, I think introductions are hardly necessary.

ISEULT (*slapping her wrist gently*). That's bold. You'll make them die of shyness.

NESSA. I'm a great fan of Miss Mullarkey's. We both are.

SLEEHAUN (*coerced*). Yeah.

(THERESE *bears the coats off, D.L.*)

ISEULT. Bless you. (*To* BISHOP) Aren't people gorgeous? I can go nowhere.

NESSA. I went to your concert all on my own. I cried.

BISHOP (*happily*). There, now.

NESSA. I'm sorry. You must be sick and tired of everyone telling you.

ISEULT (*embracing her*). You goose, what silliness . . . I'm no such thing. The way I look at it . . . what's your name, love?

NESSA. Nessa.

SLEEHAUN (*unasked*). Tony.

ISEULT. . . . Nessa, is that my artistry is a precious gift from God, and when you praise me you praise Him. So 'twould be a class of a sin for me to stop you: 'twould be belittling him. You praise away.

390

BISHOP. You're a credit to us.

ISEULT. No, no: God is. (*With a smile and a steeliness of eye*) *You* weren't at the concert, Mr Sleehaun?

SLEEHAUN. Uh . . .

NESSA. He works till all hours.

BISHOP. You'd be in business, then?

SLEEHAUN. In development.

NESSA (*overlapping*). Demolition.

SLEEHAUN. Same thing.

ISEULT (*with relentless humility*). I think this gentleman hasn't a notion who I am.

SLEEHAUN. Me?

ISEULT. Or what it is I do.

BISHOP. He'd want to be deaf and blind not to . . . (*to* SLEEHAUN) wouldn't you?

(ISEULT *looks implacably at* SLEEHAUN. *He summons up a grin, crouches, and attempts to reproduce* NESSA'*s sawing motion of a minute earlier. It is not the sort of performance that augurs a long run.* ISEULT *crosses herself and turns away.*)

BISHOP (*covering*). Ah, an exquisite instrument. And do you know, with our host in absentia I think we might help ourselves to a jorum. I feel the need.

NESSA. Tony, you do it.

SLEEHAUN. Certainly . . . no prob-lem. Miss Mullarkey . . .?

ISEULT. Water.

BISHOP. And brandy for the parson. Seeing as how the weather is oo effing dreadful. (*To* NESSA) You'll notice I use bad language. I believe, you see, that the Church, to be truly ecumenical, ought to speak with the voice of the people. It's a shagging nuisance, but I do it. This is your first visit to Kill House, Mrs Sleehaun?

NESSA. Yes, it is. We —

ISEULT. Do you believe in ecumenism, Father? (*Her tone implies that she does not*).

BISHOP. I believe in the Divine Paradox, Miss Mullarkey; i.e., that all things are and should be equal, but that God knows His own. (*Returning to* NESSA) There's been a church on this site since the year dot. But in recent times, what with emigration and the drift to the towns, there weren't enough parishioners to feed a priest and a curate. So they shut up shop, removed the altar and deconsecrated the rest of it.

391

ISEULT. The tragedy of our race.

BISHOP (*nodding*). It's a whooring shame. The entire shooting match went to a board of trustees: lands, church and presbytery. It was they hit on the idea of leasing it out to an approved tenant: all except the little alms house by the north gate . . . there's some wrangle there over the title.
(*He crosses to* SLEEHAUN *and takes his brandy.*)
God bless you.

SLEEHAUN. How long does the lease run?

BISHOP. Five years.

SLEEHAUN (*surprised*). Oh?
(*He turns to give* ISEULT *her glass of water. She drifts through the door leading to the organ loft.*)

BISHOP. The tenant is held responsible for upkeep, restoration and improvements. A short-term lease enables the trustees to get rid of him if he makes a balls of it.

SLEEHAUN. I see.
(*He makes to follow* ISEULT, *but turns back.*)
Father, I do know what instrument Miss Mullarkey plays. I just can't pronounce it.

BISHOP. Get away.

NESSA. Tony, it's the —

SLEEHAUN (*disarmingly*). Tell you the truth, I'm not even sure how it's spelt.

BISHOP. *I* usually spell it 's-a-w'.

SLEEHAUN. Ah.
(*A pause. Then he grins and raises a finger in the manner of one on whom there are no flies. He disappears towards the organ loft.*)

BISHOP. Charming man. I take it he was a Christian Brothers boy.
(THERESE *returns.*)

THERESE. Hello. Helping yourselves, are you? Good.
(NESSA *approaches the* BISHOP *with timid daring.*)

BISHOP. We're tip-top, and Miss Mullarkey is above our heads as usual. (*He turns to* NESSA.) My child . . .?

NESSA. I saw you doing Confirmations.

BISHOP. You what?

NESSA. On the TV. And you gave out about people robbing banks and killing policemen. You're the Bishop of —

BISHOP. Ah, shag. (*In mock dismay.*) Mrs Fitzackerly, our secret is out. I'm exposed.

NESSA. The minute your grace walked in, I —

BISHOP (*silencing her*). Shup! Child, listen. (*He takes her arm*)

392

Every outing I go on is ruined. People bow and scrape to me.
They bend the knee and make a fuss, instead of just effing and
blinding like they do at home. I like to enjoy myself. So when
I'm invited out, I employ the stratagem of dressing up as you
see me . . . as a civilian. Have you me?

THERESE (*to* NESSA). You won't spoil his evening, will you?

BISHOP. This one? Nary a fear of it.

NESSA. You can trust me . . . (*coyly*) Father.

BISHOP. That's the girl. I'm off duty, so treat me as the lowliest of
the low.

NESSA. I will.

BISHOP. Grand.

(*He thrusts his ring at her. She kisses it.*)

Oh, but I'm a wicked divil, a scoundrel. Do you know,
whenever somebody bores me, I let on I'm deaf.

NESSA. You don't!

BISHOP (*cupping his ear*). Pardon? (*He laughs: it is his little joke.*)

THERESE. Does Miss Mullarkey know?

BISHOP. She believes what you tell her. A jewel among women . . .
they say she's an hourly communicant.

(*In the organ loft,* ISEULT *is conversing with* SLEEHAUN. *The
following, intended at first for his ears, ends as for the benefit
of all.*)

ISEULT. 'Twas early of a Christmas morn. A small, bright-eyed
slender child tippy-toed shyly into her parish church, and there
she saw the manger, with the Infant lying on a bed of straw, and
the kneeling figures and the cows and sheep. Tears of wonderment ran down her freckles that were to clear up later. She said:
'Oh, I wish I could give the Infant a present for Christmas!'

(NESSA, *the* BISHOP *and* THERESE *are by now looking up at
her.*)

At that moment, her eyes fell upon a saw that the workman who
made the crib had left behind him. As if in answer to a heavenly
bidding, she took the elastic from her stocking. She put the saw
between her knees and drew the little garter across it. There was
a strange, sweet music. The candles flickered in the frosty air,
and people came to listen. And among them was the drunkard
of the town. When he saw her, he put his hands over his eyes
and said: 'I swear I'll never touch another drop.' Nor did
he.

(*A pause, broken by* NESSA's *sobbing.*)

SLEEHAUN. You must have fine strong thighs.

393

ISEULT. Thanks be to God, they're like iron. (*Raising a knee*) Don't take my word.

SLEEHAUN (*feeling*). Granite, granite.

THERESE. Mrs Sleehaun is distressed.

BISHOP. Ah, you creature.

NESSA. I'm awful. I was the same the night of the concert, when she sang her 'Lament for a Sick Mother'. (*She finds her handkerchief.*)

BISHOP. That's it . . . blow away.

(As NESSA *does so,* SLEEHAUN *accidentally causes the organ to emit a bass note. The* BISHOP *starts and looks up.*)

BISHOP. What the friggin' hell was —

SLEEHAUN (*calling down*). Sorry. Didn't know it was loaded.

(NESSA *is staring at her handkerchief.*)

THERESE (*reassuring her*). It was the organ. Someone must have left it switched on. I'll just run up and —

(*She is taken aback to see* MRS WADE, *who enters from behind the reredos. She is fine-boned, her looks fading. An Anglo-Irish accent. Her dress is expensive, but old: there is a suggestion, even, of other times.*)

(*Not pleased*). Mrs Wade . . .

MRS WADE (*to* THERESE, *vivaciously*). How do you do? So kind of you to have come.

THERESE (*reminding her*). I'm Mrs Fitzackerly, Mrs Wade.

MRS WADE. And as pretty as your name.

(*The perfect hostess, she goes smiling towards the* BISHOP *and* NESSA.)

THERESE. Let me introduce your guests. (*Bowing to fate*) As a lovely surprise, our hostess has joined us after all. (*To* MRS WADE) I don't think you've met the Father.

MRS WADE. Really? So much for celibacy, how do you do?

THERESE. And Mrs Sleehaun.

MRS WADE. Charming.

NESSA (*almost a whisper*). Pleased to meet you.

MRS WADE. How lovely you could be with us. But isn't there a Mr . . . Sleehaun?

NESSA (*indicating*). He's up there.

MRS WADE (*tragically*). Oh, my dear. And so young.

THERESE. She means, in the organ loft.

NESSA (*beckoning*). Tony . . .

(MRS WADE *looks up – and up – to the point where she slowly teeters backwards and is caught by the* BISHOP. SLEEHAUN *and* ISEULT *start down.*)

394

BISHOP. Oops.

MRS WADE (*in surprise*). I'm light-headed.

THERESE. Whatever possessed her? He'll be furious.

BISHOP (*assisting* MRS WADE). What you need is a little sit-down. Here we go.

MRS WADE. I dressed too quickly.

BISHOP. To be sure. (*Seating her*) There, now . . . right as rain.

MRS WADE (*grasping his arm*). Rain. Oh, the weather.

BISHOP. It's a bugger.

MRS WADE. I can endure the winters. Woolies on and bracing walks, dead leaves and the cry of rooks. But I often think I shall never survive another summer. I was brought up as were all young women of my class, to believe in seasons. Madness.

NESSA. Excuse me. This is my husband . . . (*to* SLEEHAUN) it's Mrs Wade.

SLEEHAUN. Privileged. A climax in my life.

MRS WADE (*looking from him to* NESSA). You re-married? How very brave.

THERESE. And I'm sure you recognise Miss Mullarkey.

ISEULT. Oh, now.

MRS WADE. I shall in future, how do you do? Yes, the privations of summer. By October, I'm at death's door.

THERESE. She should be in bed.

MRS WADE. I was. I was good, I took my pills, then — Might I have a glass of sherry?

SLEEHAUN. On the way. (*He attends to it.*)

THERESE (*too late*). No . . .

MRS WADE. I was dozing off. The shots awakened me.

BISHOP. Shots?

MRS WADE. Mm. People shooting.

THERESE. I'm sure you're mistaken.

MRS WADE. Out there. Shots and cries of anger.

ISEULT. Music critics!

BISHOP. What?

(ISEULT *shakes her head, dismissing the idea.*)

THERESE (*quietly, to the* BISHOP). I think we've been having a bad dream.

BISHOP (*buying it*). Ah!

MRS WADE. My parents, and theirs before them, used to shoot over these lands. Generations of us. A wilderness when we came, a park when we left. (SLEEHAUN *arrives with the sherry*). What a charming man . . . I am spoilt. Sit by me.

SLEEHAUN. Your family went away, then?

MRS WADE. They and the shooting became poor together.

SLEEHAUN. Pity.

> (*He is looking at* NESSA. *She fumbles in her bag as she approaches* ISEULT.)

MRS WADE. You know, I don't wish to dishearten you, but you must accept that deep down she'll always love the other one best.

SLEEHAUN (*baffled*). Aha.

NESSA (*to* ISEULT, *producing a slip of paper*). All I have is the bill for the milk. If you wouldn't mind . . . I think I've a biro.

ISEULT. You'll turn my head.

SLEEHAUN. Excuse me. Love *which* other one best?

MRS WADE. The one before you. She told me.

> (*He stares at* NESSA. THE BISHOP *and* THERESE *are apart from the others.*)

BISHOP. It would be a complaint of the nerves, then?

THERESE. Of a kind. Opinions differ, but my own belief is, she's a victim of shock.

BISHOP. A private tragedy?

THERESE. An excess of happiness.

> (*The* BISHOP *expresses polite surprise.*)

Her people were not our sort – yours and mine. They had position and acquired one or two titles along the way. Her life was one of privilege. She had pedigree and refinement, and she was considered a beauty some years ago. Then she met Mr Wade. I'm not a doctor, but if you ask me, her mind was unable to cope with the shock of marrying above her station.

> (ISEULT *hands the inscribed piece of paper to* NESSA.)

NESSA. Ah, thanks. (*Reading*) 'Yours, with humility and . . . in a basement . . .'

ISEULT. It's one word, dear.

NESSA. I love it. Tony, look what Miss —

> (*She sees that he is glaring at her murderously.*)

What is it?

MRS WADE. It was sad that the local people never made my family feel welcome. We did what we could. We even bequeathed them one of our treasures. It did wonders for their self-reliance.

SLEEHAUN. Oh, yes?

MRS WADE. They have it to this day.

SLEEHAUN. What was that, then?

MRS WADE. A grievance.

(*She thrusts her empty glass at him. As he rises to refill it,* WADE *comes in. It is a hurried, purposeful entrance. He at once does the round of his guests with great speed, urgency and sincerity.*)

WADE (*swooping on* ISEULT). Miss Mullarkey, you're welcome here. These hallowed walls have thrilled many a time and oft to the glorious music of your saw . . . melodies which not only soothe the soul and raise the spirit, but are part of our heritage and will continue to be so in the great days ahead when we reclaim what is rightfully ours.

ISEULT. All I am is God's —

(*He has already left her for* NESSA, *with* THERESE *in close attendance.*)

WADE. And you would be —

THERESE. Mrs Sleehaun.

WADE (*almost overlapping*). . . . Mrs Sleehaun, I know that, who does not? Céad míle failte. Your comeliness and fresh wholesome charm have gone before you. We in Kill House have our own standards of what is beautiful. We are not taken in by the cheap, the gimcrack and the foreign, and you are a shining adornment to our home.

(*He leaves her, open-mouthed, and descends on the* BISHOP.)

WADE (*about to kiss the episcopal ring*). Your Grace —

THERESE (*prompting*). Father Bishop.

WADE (*shaking hands instead*). Your graceful presence here overwhelms us. I'm aware, as who is not, of your inspired and inspiring shepherding of your flock. Especially, I applaud your fearless and unwavering condemnation of the evil men whose crimes threaten the fabric of our community. This is an evening I have prayed for.

(*He departs, now bearing down on* SLEEHAUN, *who is on his feet and standing apart from* MRS WADE.)

BISHOP (*stunned*). Well, shag me.

THERESE. And Mr Sleehaun.

WADE. Ah? (*He seizes* SLEEHAUN *by the shoulders and gives him a point-blank scrutiny*). What can I say?

SLEEHAUN. Oh, now.

WADE. What . . . can . . . I . . . say?

(*Pause. His stare is unwavering.*)

SLEEHAUN (*overcome*). Well, I dunno, I —

(WADE *grabs him, mafioso-style, by the skin of his cheek-*

bones, squeezes, releases him and abruptly heads for his chair.)

MRS WADE (*from behind* SLEEHAUN). He didn't say very much, did he?

(*The sound of her voice brings* WADE *up short.*)

THERESE. Mrs Wade joined us.

WADE (*without turning*). Apparently.

THERESE. She seems to have had a nightmare. She thought she heard shooting.

WADE. And she joined us.

THERESE. Perhaps you could persuade her to —

WADE. Later, not now. See to the guests, will you?

(*He takes his seat on the dais and surveys the company. During this,* THERESE *serves him with a drink and replenishes empty glasses.*)

MRS WADE (*to* SLEEHAUN, *looking at* WADE.) It's really annoying. I do know his face, but from where?

(*A moment's uneasy pause. The guests wait, focussing their attention on the host.*)

WADE. Did you have a good journey?

(SLEEHAUN, NESSA, ISEULT *and the* BISHOP *all reply at once, speaking eagerly in unison.*)

SLEEHAUN. Well, it's a filthy night and we left at rush hour, but even so, I knew the short cut out by Sallins and luckily I have a Merc.

NESSA. Tony thought we'd lose our way, only we didn't, and what with leaving so early and the speed he drives at, we were here the first, we're awful.

ISEULT. I never mind travelling. There's so little privacy in my life that I always use the weeny bits of time I have to meditate.

BISHOP. I just gave the driver his instructions and that was it. A great motor car, it could take you for three hundred miles and not so much as a sore arse.

(*All finish in a dead head, except the* BISHOP, *whose last few words trail the field.*)

WADE. Yes. (*To* THERESE) I take it that Judge Lawless hasn't yet honoured us?

BISHOP. Is *he* coming?

THERESE. Probably he was detained.

WADE. Possibly he wants for manners.

BISHOP. The law's delay, what? The insolence of office.

WADE (*approving*). That's good. *That* should be written down.

(*His mood restored*) Well, Miss Mullarkey, have you brought your magical saw?

ISEULT (*pleased*). You oughtn't to mock.

NESSA. Oh, say you have.

ISEULT. I never tell lies: I do always carry it with me, but not to play. 'Tis out of habit . . . for protection.

NESSA. Ah, but to please us.

BISHOP (*deferring to* WADE). A command performance.

WADE. No, no. Miss Mullarkey is a guest.

ISEULT. Go on: I know you'll force me. I forgot to bring it in . . . I was so awed and overwhelmed. Like on one Christmas morn, when a small, bright-eyed, slender child tippy-toed into a church and saw the manger, with the Infant lying on its bed of —

BISHOP (*terminating the re-run*). That's how it is. You may often visit Kill House, but your first glimpse of it is like your first sick call: unforgettable.

WADE. You've been a guest here?

BISHOP. During your predecessor's time, yes.

WADE. That ruffian.

BISHOP. Would you say?

WADE. A blackguard who betrayed his trust. A rogue who brought this place to rack and ruin and left me to clear up after him. A legacy of decay and mismanagement, a litany of neglect and knavery. If Kill House is today restored to its former magnificence, it is not because he lifted one finger.

(*To make his point, he raises a hand and takes with it the arm of the chair.*)

I blame the trustees. They were gullible, they believed his promises. Blind, credulous fools.

(*His hand drops, an eloquent comment on human folly. The chair-arm is incidentally restored to its socket.*)

SLEEHAUN. They must be madmen.

BISHOP. Shitehawks.

SLEEHAUN. Still, the right man is in now.

WADE. And will stay in.

BISHOP. Praise be. At least until the lease exp—

WADE. Permanently.

BISHOP (*intimidated*). That's . . . good news.

THERESE. Aprés nous le déluge.

WADE. Oui. (*Reverting to his theme*) That man's worse crime was not his laziness and crass dishonesty, nor even his inexplicable dislike of me . . . God knows I live and let live, great men don't grow on trees. (*Pointing off*) But that hovel, that alms house, that abode of rabblement . . . I say that its continued existence out there is an abomination, a boil for the lancing. Did *he* lance it? He looked upon it, he smiled (*a gay laugh*) and he turned his back.

BISHOP (*uneasily*). I daresay once the title is put right —

WADE. Title? (*With elaborate malice.*) Sorry, slightly deaf . . . that word again?

BISHOP. I mean, they say there's a question of —

WADE. A question of! Father, if you weren't a blessed innocent, a near saint, you would know that wise men have answers; it's the fools who ask questions.

SLEEHAUN (*admiringly, almost to himself*). Is that a fact?

WADE. My dear wife's family had hearts of gold. When they at last packed their belongings and took themselves out of here, they made, if you please, a gift of the alms house to their footman. Six rooms with septic tank . . . (*In an improbably effete accent*:) 'Oww, do take it, we insist, our pleasure, pip-pip, Ai say.' They gave that flunky what wasn't theirs to give – my property, or as good as – to make a slum of it and spawn a litter of mongrels like himself. And you talk to me of title.

BISHOP. My apologies, I have been gravely misinformed. Feck.

NESSA. It's scandalous. And who's in there now?

WADE. Mrs Sleehaun, if I were to describe them it would spoil your dinner. Half of them don't even go to Mass.

ISEULT. Oh, my God.

WADE. And that is my sworn destiny: to be the one who at last achieves the return of the alms house to Kill. I take that pledge. (*He sips from his glass.*)

BISHOP. And you'll do it, God reward you.

WADE. What's more, I'll live to see the day when, to my acute embarrassment, they put up a plaque with my name on it.

ISEULT. They will. I can picture it now.

WADE. I have it in the house . . . I'll show you.

THERESE (*indicating her watch*). By the way . . .

WADE. Of course. Enough of this airy chit-chat. Mrs Fitz . . .
(*With a gesture, he indicates that* THERESE *now has the floor.*)

THERESE. And now we have a treat in store which I know will delight everyone . . .

ISEULT (*on the move*). I'll get the saw.

THERESE. Not that, Miss Mullarkey: we'll save the best wine for last. (*To the group*) Mr Wade would never suffer his guests to

400

leave Kill without the opportunity of seeing a few of its antiquities. Most of them are housed in the presbytery, so when
you've quite finished your drinks I'll lead the way.

WADE. No rush.

(*He holds his glass out to* THERESE, *who goes for a refill.*
NESSA *sits near a glowering* SLEEHAUN. MRS WADE *is perhaps
between them.*)

NESSA. You're very quiet.

SLEEHAUN (*grimly*). There'll be noise soon enough.

NESSA. Why?

SLEEHAUN. When I find out his name.

NESSA. Whose name?

SLEEHAUN. You know whose. The whoormaster before me.

MRS WADE. Oh, are you one, too? (*To* NESSA) You aren't having
much luck, are you?

NESSA. What are you giving out to me for? What whoormaster?

SLEEHAUN (*side of mouth*). Don't make a show of us. I'll talk to
you at home.

(NESSA *mutters inaudibly.*)

And less of your bad language. You're not a priest.

(*They remain seated, he moodily,* NESSA *aggrieved. The*
BISHOP *ambles over to* WADE.)

BISHOP. So what have you in store for us? Flint arrowheads?

WADE. My period is Early Christian. You'll be interested in one
item: St. Patrick's crozier.

BISHOP. That's a rarity.

WADE. A tinker discovered it, and I bought it from him for a song.
Naturally, I was sceptical at first, but its authenticity was
vouched for by an eminent veterinarian.

BISHOP. Do you mean a vet?

WADE. There were traces of snake venom.

BISHOP (*a trifle wildly*). Yes, that's this land of ours: rich in past
and present. And the Church, too. In the old days the priest
would shower down brimstone from the pulpit: he was judge,
jury and hangman. Now we move with the times. We win them
by love, the Christian message. Mind, the laws of the Church
stay, the Ten Commandments, no change there. A sin is still
a —

(THERESE *comes over with* WADE's *drink.*)

THERESE. Excuse me, Father. (*To* WADE) Will you be requiring to
sleep with me tonight?

WADE. I'm not sure. I have my eye on Miss Mullarkey.

THERESE. It's no matter: I just thought I might wash my hair.
(*She smiles at the* BISHOP *and goes away.*)

WADE. Sorry.

BISHOP (*as before; only his words suggest that his mind is elsewhere*). . . . A sin is still a sin, a kiss is still a kiss, but a bit of forbearance, give and take, bib and tuck, tooth and nail . . .
(*A knocking at the outer door.*)

THERESE. Thank heaven for that . . . they got here.

BISHOP (*winding down*). . . . early and often, tit for tat, Crosse and Blackwell . . .

WADE. Excuse me.

BISHOP (*becoming inaudible*). . . . jelly and custard, chalk and cheese . . .
(WADE *goes to welcome the newcomers as* THERESE *admits them.* JUDGE LAWLESS *is holding a dispatch case over his head to keep the rain off. He has learned to look and speak as befits a distinguished member of the judiciary; the wrappings are, however, brighter than the contents.* MRS LAWLESS (MADGE) *is nearing fifty, bulky in build, plain of face and manner. She has a suspicious nature: to her, charm and the social graces are as whitewash on a sepulchre of particularly ill repute. Her coat is draped over her head. At the moment, her temper is foul, especially as she is confronted by her natural enemy:* WADE.)

WADE (*a sunburst of charm*). Come in . . . fortune smiles, our evening is complete. Judge Lawless . . . an honour as always. I take it your journey was a smooth one?

JUDGE. Well, in point of fact —
(WADE *turns to* MADGE, *who is regarding him balefully.*)

WADE. But where is *Mrs* Lawless? Surely this creature cannot be — (*A start of surprise.*) It is! What sorcery is this? We mortals are slaves to time's ravages . . . she laughs at them.

MADGE (*sourly*). Good evening.

WADE. And that peerless wind-and-rain complexion. How does she do it?

MADGE. If you must know, by walking half a mile in wind and rain.

WADE. No!

JUDGE. I'm afraid the verdict is that we've had a mishap.

MADGE (*looking at* WADE). Through negligence.

WADE. Don't blame yourself, I never do. What matters is, you've come to us, you're here, and as the poet says, journeys end in — (*he snaps his fingers at* THERESE *for a prompt.*)

THERESE. Drop it.

WADE. Drop it. (*He propels them both forward*). Come and meet our little galaxy. (*Announcing*) Judge Lawless is chairman of our board of trustees. From the performing arts . . . Miss Iseult Mullarkey.

JUDGE. Of course. May I declare myself a most ardent admirer?

ISEULT (*quietly, extending a hand*). Stop.

(MADGE *is not a shaker of hands; she nods and says 'How d'you do?'*)

WADE. And, from the world of prayer, our distinguished churchman . . . Father Bishop.

JUDGE. Father . . .

BISHOP. I know his worship well by repute. Mrs Lawless . . . delighted.

WADE. And here, our lovely representative of home and hearth . . . Mrs Sleehaun.

JUDGE. How do you do?

MADGE. 'Evening.

NESSA. Terrible weather.

WADE. And finally, flushed from his triumphs in the market-place . . . *Mr* Sleehaun.

SLEEHAUN (*waggishly*). Can you fix a summons?

JUDGE (*blankly*). Pardon me?

(*In* MADGE*'s brain a faint and dissonant chord is struck.*)

MADGE. Excuse me, don't I know this gentleman?

SLEEHAUN. Me? Sorry, I don't think so. Business training, you know: I've an infallible memory for — (*He remembers her, and his memory, too, is less than blissful*). No. No, sincerely not. No way.

MADGE. I think we've met.

SLEEHAUN. Couldn't have. (*Gibbering*) I did meet a woman like you once, dead spit, a Mrs Lucey, couldn't have been you, she died. So maybe you're confusing yourself with —

MADGE (*a cry*). It is!

SLEEHAUN. No!

(*He starts back in fear as she seems to come at him. Her cry, however, is because she has caught sight of* MRS WADE.)

MADGE (*with warmth*). Mrs Wade . . . you're up and about. How are you? Are you well in yourself? (*Reminding her*) Madge Lawless. (*To the* JUDGE) Pronnsias, it's Mrs Wade.

MRS WADE. A kind voice is so rare . . . how do you do?

403

(WADE *is impatient and resentful of any acknowledgment of* MRS WADE*'s presence in the room.*)

MADGE. But we had no idea you'd be here. It's gorgeous to see you.

WADE. My wife has been allowed to join us for a few minutes. She mustn't become over-tired.

MRS WADE. You should tell her to sit down more.

WADE. Besides, now that you've met everyone, Mrs Fitzackerly is anxious to begin our conducted tour.

THERESE (*taking the hint*). To show off our treasures.

MADGE. Thank you, I've walked far enough for one day. (*To* MRS WADE) I'll just go and tidy myself, then we can have a chat.

THERESE. It's —

MADGE. I know the way. (*Starting out, quietly to the* JUDGE) Stay here, and be careful.

(*She goes out, D.L.* THERESE *gives* WADE *a shrug of helplessness, then turns to the others.*)

THERESE. Shall we make a start, then?

BISHOP. Lead on. I can't wait to see this crozier.

THERESE. It's priceless, of course. Mr Wade believes that the previous owner was terrified of thieves. Otherwise, why would he have had it engraved with 'Made in Taiwan'?

(*She ushers them off through the door behind the reredos:* SLEEHAUN, NESSA, ISEULT *and the* BISHOP.*The* JUDGE *removes his overcoat.*)

WADE. Peace at last. (*Going towards the bar*). A mishap, you said. Never mind: what can I offer you?

(*The* JUDGE*, his coat half off, freezes as if instantly petrified. He stares agonisedly at* WADE.)

Now, there's Irish, Scotch, gin, vodka, bourbon, rye, brandy, liqueurs, Dubonnet, Martini and Madeira. What would you like?

JUDGE (*a strangulated noise*). Urrghh.

WADE. I don't think we have any. I know . . . why not a glass of sherry? (*He looks around for the first time*). Judge?

(*The* JUDGE *nods violently as if shaking off an affliction.*)

JUDGE (*hoarsely*). Yes . . . sherry.

WADE. The old trouble again?

JUDGE. This wretched infirmity . . . a form of paralysis. It comes on me whenever I'm obliged to make a decision. Thank you . . . a glass of sherry, since you've been kind enough to choose.

WADE. Good. Sweet or dry?

404

JUDGE. Urrghh.

WADE. Let's try medium.

JUDGE (*recovering*). I'm in your debt. It gets worse every year. It's agony having to hear evidence. Only for my dear life's companion, Madge, sitting in the well of the court every day and doing either this (*thumb up*) or this (*thumb down*) I really might lose faith in myself as a judge. Forgive me.

WADE. Nonsense. I, too, have lived with affliction.

JUDGE (*looking at* MRS WADE). Of course. Dare one hope for an improvement?

WADE. Oh, yes. What she's suffering from now is medication. The very essence of today's wonder drugs is that they relieve one illness by replacing it with another. So for all we know, she may be in perfect health.

JUDGE. How splendid.

WADE. Isn't it? And I'm prepared to perish in the attempt to find another drug to cure the present one. But enough of me. Your own good lady . . . no fatal ailment, bravely borne?

JUDGE. Heavens, no.

WADE (*stoically*). Ah, well.

(*The* JUDGE *takes a sip of his sherry and sets the glass down on a side-table by which* MRS WADE *is sitting.*)

A private word. Now and again I get the impression – and I know it's nonsense – that Mrs Lawless is less than my devoted admirer.

JUDGE. Who, Madge?

WADE. I tell myself it's timidity, that she worships from afar, and yet I detect a non-magnetism: she isn't *drawn*. Could she, do you think – and this is madness – could she in any way not rejoice at my being here?

JUDGE. Here?

WADE. In Kill.

JUDGE. The trustees, you see —

WADE. Exactly. I was appointed by acclamation. There were fifteen of them.

JUDGE. Eighteen of whom voted.

WADE. Which I call unanimous.

(*The* JUDGE, *ill at ease, reaches for his glass and finds it empty.* MRS WADE *has a small, happy smile on her face.*)

No, how could she not be ecstatic? Especially as this year we shall outdo ourselves. (*A sharklike grin.*) Yes?

JUDGE (*nervously*) Oh, now: sub judice.

WADE (*a reassuring arm around the* JUDGE*'s shoulder*). Judge, all
I ask is that you will preside, as always, without fear of favour,
steely of purpose, eagle-eyed, staunch of sinew and, above all
else, incorruptible.

JUDGE. Oh, I can manage that.

WADE. Great. Question is . . .

JUDGE. Ah-ha?

WADE. Incorruptible on whose side?

(*The* JUDGE *looks at him.*)

Idle curiosity, don't be shy, would I break a confidence? We're
alone, pronounce judgment. On whose side?

JUDGE (*the old trouble*). Urrghh.

WADE (*in disgust*). Oh, my God.

(MADGE *returns.*)

MADGE (*to the* JUDGE). The scuff marks on my shoes are there for
good. What's more, I don't know how you propose to get us
home tonight. (*Seeing and diagnosing his trouble*) And
whatever you were asked, the answer is 'no'.

WADE. What signifies this blaze of light? (*Affecting to notice her*)
She is with us . . . oh, bliss. Dear lady, a tincture?

MADGE. Not now, thank you.

JUDGE (*extending his empty glass*). If it's no bother . . .

MADGE. You've already gulped one down you: that's enough. (*To*
WADE) We've no car to go home in. We ran into a pothole and
could have been killed.

WADE. I'm appalled.

MADGE. The front wheels are . . . (*demonstrating*) that way.

WADE. County Council heads will roll for this.

MADGE. Heads my foot. I'm talking about your private road . . .
out there. We had to tramp the length of it, and it's a mud-bath.
Worse than the trenches in World War One.

WADE (*under his breath*). You remember them, do you?

MADGE. Pronnsias, get the briefcase.

WADE. I charmingly protest. A time and place, surely. This is an
evening for revelry, for wine, women and saw.

MADGE. Mrs Wade, excuse me. (*Turning to* WADE) We declined
your invitation; you insisted. Now that we're here, it's to tell
you that my husband will not support your attempts to stay on
in Kill.

WADE (*smiling*). My attempts?

MADGE. Not so long as I have a thumb on my hand. He may be
a soft man, but he's an honest one.

JUDGE. Madge, I protest.

MADGE (*referring to the briefcase*). Give me what's in it.

JUDGE. On the bench, I'm noted for my severity. (*Almost smirk-ing*) In fact, I happen to know that behind my back they call me the Hanging Judge?

MADGE. You oul' fool, that's because you give out suspended sentences.

(*She relieves him of the papers he has taken from the dispatch case.*)

According to the terms of the lease —

WADE. Excuse me . . .

MADGE (*dogged*). . . . you as tenant are responsible for care and maintenance of the estate —

WADE. If you'll permit . . .

MADGE. . . . for which you receive a monetary grant from the restoration fund.

WADE. Judge, enlighten me. Why is it that in the presence of this enchantress I forget home and loved ones – everything, in fact, except that she is *not* one of the trustees?

MADGE. Thank you, I've no need to be: I have a good husband who can be trusted to do as I see right. This is a copy of the surveyor's report. There's dry rot in the rafters and death watch beetle in the walls. From his description of the roof, if it was a horse I'd shoot it. (*She thrusts the paper at him.*) And not one penny spent by you on repairs.

WADE. A farrago of lies.

MADGE. Read it.

WADE. I see a certain signature. This man, this surveyor, I know him. A notorious homosexual.

MADGE (*impatiently*). Oh, for —

WADE. And his wife is no better. I was at school with him: he fail-ed his maths, couldn't add. It all comes back: a pimple-squeezer, a wetter of beds and a player of foreign games, who was expelled for indecently assaulting the woman who brought the milk.

MADGE. Just now you called him a —

WADE. She was a pervert. Yes, I knew him: for God's sake, how many Michael Murphys are there? A slimy, skulking toad who has it in for me because at school I was always the clean-limbed one. A man whose sister became a Carmelite to keep her mouth shut. A rogue whose career as a bogus chartered surveyor has been a miasma of fraud, wrong measurements and back-

stabbing, spoken and unspeakable. Are you surprised that he's
fleeing the country?

MADGE. Since when?

WADE. Believe me, he will.

(*He crumples the paper and, drained by emotional exhaustion,
addresses the* JUDGE.)

Sad times, when an honest man must answer calumnies. I rest
my case.

JUDGE (*a conditioned reflex*). Thank you. There has been far too
much of this sort of thing going on of late . . .

MADGE (*sharply*). Pronnsias.

JUDGE. Probation Act, and in future I shall not be so . . . (*Coming
to*) Pardon?

(MADGE, *holding her ground, goes briskly through the other
papers, citing one item from each.*)

MADGE. Shelter belt of trees: cut down and sold. Livestock . . . fifty sheep: missing, believed dead. Crops: unharvested. Trout
stream and lake: polluted from overloaded sewage pipe following party on election night. Outbuildings . . .

WADE (*suavely*). Might I just see those signatures?

(*She yields all the papers except a last one.*)

What a Worrying Winnie she is, fretting that pretty head on my
account. She does care, after all. (*He looks at the signatures.*)

MADGE. I have here the auditor's report. It says —

WADE (*a discovery*). Wait! I know this man. A flagrant nose-
picker and an agnostic.

MRS WADE.It alleges that you've been cooking the books . . .

WADE. A begrudger with his knife in me . . .

MADGE. . . . That you've been boiling, roasting, steaming and
stewing 'em. Accounts falsified, moneys converted, receipts
forged. (*To the* JUDGE) Fraud is a crime, isn't it?

JUDGE. Are you a professional man? Law, accountancy?

WADE. No.

JUDGE. Then it's a crime.

MADGE. You've squandered the restoration fund, bribing trustees
to extend your lease. The village is rich on your promises. You
give them pennies and pledge pounds. On every wall there's a
poster. 'W.W.W. – Wages Without Work'.

WADE. I follow the Christian ethic. He rewarded His followers.

MADGE. Not with bribes.

WADE. Ever hear of Heaven?

MADGE. Why do you do it? What for? At the rate you're going, there'll soon be nothing left here for you to be tenant of.

WADE (*musing*). The Last Lord of Kill . . . I like it! But what a worldly creature you are. Dry rot, a strayed sheep or two, pot-holes, account books: are these your poetry? Who cares? Give a barefoot man a dream, I always say: let him aspire to greatness; then he won't pester you for shoes.

MADGE. What greatness? Not that alms house.

WADE. I ask for so little. It's my only territorial demand.

MADGE. But nobody wants it.

WADE. Wash your mouth out: everyone wants it. When I talk of it in the village, they listen spellbound. They weep, they cheer, they follow me in the street. The hems of my garments are in flitters.

MADGE. Of course they follow you: it's less strenuous than working. And if you get the place —

WADE. *When* I get it.

MADGE. What then?

WADE. Nothing. I hate the sight of it. The present occupants can stay in it and rot, provided they behave themselves, pay their rent and do as I tell them. I'm a peaceful man, no violence, but it's ours and I meant to have it. I want it, I want it, I want it, I want it, I want it. (*His voice has become a shriek.* MADGE *and the* JUDGE *stare at him.*)

MRS WADE. He invites such noisy people.

MADGE (*shaken*). I think I'll have a drink now. (*As* WADE *makes to move*) I'll do my own. (*To the* JUDGE, *as he extends his glass*) No.
(*She moves upstage and, through the following, pours herself a whiskey, neat.*)
Such caterwauling. The joke is, all you'll get in the end is a burnt-out ruin. Mort Mongan will see to it.

WADE. Who?

MADGE. He's set fire to the alms house twice in the past month.

WADE. Mongan? Never heard of him.

MADGE. That's odd, considering it was your speechifying that drove him off his head in the first place. He'll kill someone yet.

JUDGE. Quite true. A case for the very severest probation.

MADGE. A rampaging lunatic, who swears he won't leave stick or stone standing. And the word is that you've given him the run of these lands. They say —
(*Coming downstage, she breaks off on seeing feathers from the torn cushion.*)

409

WADE. That is a lie.

MADGE. They say you protect him. . . . Feathers . . . honestly. You don't even sweep the floor.

(*She sets her drink down and begins to pick up wisps of feathers.*)

WADE. One more despicable slander.

MADGE. Well, it doesn't look swept.

WADE. I mean that I give shelter to criminals. If that – what's his name? Mongan? – if that blackguard dared to set foot within a mile of here I'd have him jailed.

(MONGAN *comes in, D.L., looking just as dangerous as before.* MADGE *is down on one knee. The* JUDGE *stares at* MONGAN, *whereas* WADE *goes on talking as if he did not exist.* MONGAN *sidles catlike towards the door behind the reredos.*)

WADE (*unhesitatingly*). I am beset by scurrility and innuendo. No one respects the law more than I do. I am the avowed enemy of wrongdoers, of men of violence, and when I encounter criminality in whatever shape, I do not flinch. Punishment – swift, unfaltering and dire – must be its fate. And yet backbiters and begrudgers tear my character to shreds.

(MONGAN, *scuttling across the room, must go around* MADGE, *who is still kneeling. She peers short-sightedly at his boots.*)

MADGE (*not looking up*). Shift your feet.

(MONGAN *darts around her.*)

Doesn't even polish his shoes.

WADE. Furthermore . . .

MRS WADE (*to* MONGAN). Hello . . . terribly glad you could come.

WADE. . . . I will not countenance or condone any show of force against that house or its disgusting occupants. Peaceful means must win the day.

(MONGAN *disappears, R., as* MADGE *gets to her feet.*)

MADGE. I'm glad to hear it.

NESSA (*off*). Oh, look. Here comes Mr Wade's valet.

(MONGAN *comes tearing back, his escape route blocked by the returning group, offstage.* WADE *at once grasps* MADGE *by the arms and looks fiercely into her eyes, turning her so that she has her back to* MONGAN.)

WADE. You do believe me . . .

MADGE. What are you doing?

WADE. In my sincerity and truthfulness . . .

MADGE. Get your hands off.

WADE. . . . when I say that I repudiate this man of death . . . that I cast him out. Out . . . *out.*

(MONGAN, *taking the hint, makes for the outer door.*)

MADGE (*freeing herself*). You must be mad. Is there gorilla blood in you?

WADE. Forgive me. Sometimes I overwhelm myself.

(MONGAN *has vanished behind the curtains, which billow for a moment. The slam of the outer door.*)

MADGE. Mauling me as if — What was that?

(*She sees that the* JUDGE *has risen from his seat and is pointing after* MONGAN.)

Pronnsias, are you sick?

JUDGE (*hoarsely*). Mongan.

MADGE. Who? What about Mongan?

WADE. I think he said Mangan.

MADGE. He said Mongan.

JUDGE. Just now when you were kneeling, he —

WADE. First it was Mongan, now it's Mangan. Two very different names, you know. (*Deliberately*) So which was it, Judge . . . Mongan or Mangan?

JUDGE (*a pause, then*). Urrghh.

WADE. Now we'll never know.

(*From a long way off there are two blasts on a police whistle.*)

MADGE. Did you hear that?

WADE. What?

MADGE. It was a whistle.

WADE. I suffer from asthma.

(*The* BISHOP *enters, R., using a crozier as a walking stick and followed by the rest of the tour group:* NESSA, ISEULT, SLEEHAUN *and* THERESE.)

BISHOP. Hello, we're back, I'm knackered.

WADE. Did we enjoy ourselves?

NESSA. It was an education.

BISHOP. Mrs Fitzackerly allowed me to appropriate St. Patrick's crozier. And I agree: it's genuine.

WADE. Splendid.

BISHOP. 'Made in Taiwan' . . . to deceive the gobshites.

ISEULT. There was that exquisite silver chalice, too, from the long ago before the strangers came and tried to teach us their ways. A lump came in my white throat. I thought: that workmanship . . . how many people of genius, how many true artists are there today?

SLEEHAUN. Nary a one.

ISEULT. Pardon me?

SLEEHAUN. You're right, there's none.
(*She regards him glacially.*)

WADE. With one lovely and luminous exception . . . (*indicating* ISEULT) would you not agree?

SLEEHAUN. Who's that?

ISEULT. You bold man, you take me up on every word. No, I won't have it. All I am is a country girl. You'll make me vain and spoil me.

WADE. I'll say no more.

ISEULT. . . . Even if 'tis true.

WADE (*to the group*). Well, now . . . our little tour isn't quite over yet. Is it, Mrs Fitz?

THERESE (*alert*). Isn't it?

ISEULT (*to herself: a new adjective*). Luminous.

WADE. Mrs Lawless has been chiding me in her bantering way on the lack of improvements. Not a penny spent, wasn't that it? Well, just before we go to our delicious repast, I'm sure she'll welcome the chance of being proved mistaken. (*Pointing R.*) You've seen the old; now let Mrs Fitzackerley show you the new. (*He points D.L.*)

BISHOP. Sod me, are we off again?

THERESE. Shall we all step through to the annexe?

BISHOP. Certainly. (*In mock exhaustion, to* NESSA) I'm in agony, hold me up.
(*He puts an arm around her waist as they start out.* SLEEHAUN *smiles indulgently and is about to follow with* ISEULT.)

WADE. Perhaps the dynamic Mr Sleehaun would consent to stay and bear me company. (*To* MADGE, *inviting her to accompany the others*) Dear lady . . .

MADGE. It won't change my mind. I'll oppose you, no matter what.

WADE. And I admire your integrity.

MADGE. Oh, yes?

WADE. I may have my faults – it's possible – but I'd sooner lose to an honest opponent that win to the applause of toadies. That is sincere.

MADGE (*uncertain*). Huh. (*To the* JUDGE) Well, I suppose we must take a look: shift yourself. (*Passing* SLEEHAUN) And I do know that gentleman's face.

412

WADE. Darkness returns . . . hurry back!

(*The* JUDGE *and* MADGE *are ushered out by* THERESE, *following the* BISHOP, NESSA *and* ISEULT. WADE *waits smiling until they have gone, D.L.*)

Potato-faced old ratbag, I'll get her, I'll get her. (*To* SLEEHAUN, *sharply*) *Does* she know you?

SLEEHAUN. Never, I swear it.

WADE (*half to himself*). She knows him.

(*He goes to the bar and tops up his drink.*)

SLEEHAUN. Sir, I wanted to say how honoured Nessa and I are to be here. Not just in Kill itself as your guests, although that too of course, but to be among the kind of people that . . . well, that a man who has any regard for his wife would like her to mix with.

WADE (*not attending*). Ah-ha.

SLEEHAUN. I mean, persons of quality like Miss Mullarkey and Judge Lawless. And the Father.

WADE. Who?

SLEEHAUN. Nessa's captivated by him.

WADE. Father! He's no more a priest than I am.

SLEEHAUN. He's what?

WADE. He was once, not any more. He likes to pretend.

SLEEHAUN. You mean he's — Oh, my God.

(*He grabs a cushion.*)

WADE. He maintains that when he's dressed as a priest he enjoys himself.

(SLEEHAUN, *about to disembowel the cushion, remembers that* NESSA *is with the* BISHOP.)

SLEEHAUN (*again*). Oh, my God. (*He starts out.*)

WADE. Where are you going?

SLEEHAUN. He's got an arm around my wife.

WADE. Come back here with that cushion. You can kneel to him later.

SLEEHAUN. Kneel?

WADE. He pretends he doesn't like it, but he loves it. Now come back here, I want you.

SLEEHAUN. But that —

WADE (*thunderously*). Do as you're told . . . now.

(SLEEHAUN *returns reluctantly. As he passes* MRS WADE, *she catches him by the sleeve.*)

MRS WADE. You must forget the other man.

SLEEHAUN. Ah?

MRS WADE. The one before you, her true love. Forgive her. What causes a woman's heart to wither and die, you see, is not the absence of tenderness, but the deep knowledge within her that she will never be shown it again. That is the worst.

SLEEHAUN. Very good. Yes.

(*She relinquishes her grip and returns to her thoughts.* SLEEHAUN, *unnerved, backs away. As he turns,* WADE *puts a glass of brandy in his hand.*)

WADE. Drink this.

SLEEHAUN. Actually, I'm on gin and —

WADE (*taking the cushion*). Sleehaun, I begin to have misgivings. I took you for a man of ice, of snakelike calm. You're behaving like a sex-mad duck on a hot-plate.

SLEEHAUN. Sorry. It's because . . . (*He falters.*)

WADE. Out with it. Drink your gin.

SLEEHAUN. Nessa and I are as devoted as two people can be. We're famous for it, never apart. I mean, read 'Business and Finance' . . . it says so. Tonight, I had a bit of an upset. I found out . . . (*All choked up*) Excuse me.

WADE. My shoulders are broad.

SLEEHAUN. Thanks. (*He clamps a hand on* WADE*'s shoulder.*)

WADE. Oh, God.

SLEEHAUN (*glancing at* MRS WADE). I was told there'd been a man in Nessa's life before she met me. It was a shock. I always thought, you see, that I was the first. She even swore it on the prayerbook . . . I made her. And now this.

WADE. Steady, man.

SLEEHAUN. I am; now I am. In her life, the only male person she ever mentioned was a boy who used to sit beside her at school. Who minds that? Children. I mean he left to enter the — (*The word 'priesthood' freezes on his lips. He emits a low moan of intense anguish.*)

WADE. Heart attack?

SLEEHAUN (*on the move*). I'll kill him.

WADE (*restraining him*). Will you be still?

SLEEHAUN. He's come back unfrocked.

WADE. Sleehaun . . .

SLEEHAUN. She always had a religious streak, now I know why.

WADE. I have need of you.

SLEEHAUN. She's out there kneeling to him, because – you said it yourself – he loves it, he loves it. (*Registering*) Pardon?

WADE. I am entrusting you with a commission on which depends the future of Kill. Your domestic gibberings can wait. For the next three minutes you will hang from these lips. Do you understand me?

(*Pause.* SLEEHAUN *is a man who will never close a door if it is avoidable.*)

SLEEHAUN. Well, I'm . . . fond of you, of course . . .

WADE. Sleehaun, I have had my eye on you, this eagle's eye. I like the cut of your jib. That's a geographical term, spelt g-i-b from the Rock of Gibraltar, meaning craglike. You are a developer. You have had the acumen to realise that whereas under our antiquated laws one requires permission to build, anyone can tear down without hindrance. Well done.

(*En passant, he pats* SLEEHAUN *on the shoulder.* SLEEHAUN *closes his eyes, puckers up and waits.*)

Your true renown, however, rests elsewhere. Across this lovely land, old women in chimney-corners speak of you in hushed reverence, tears in their rheumy eyes. You are a phenomenon. I salute you.

(SLEEHAUN *opens his eyes and discovers that* WADE *is indeed saluting him, Roman-style.*)

SLEEHAUN. Me?

WADE. What modesty. I salute the most prodigious, the most compulsive, the most dedicated groper of our time.

SLEEHAUN. Beg pardon?

WADE. If it is feminine and below the waist, your hand moves towards it as a ship to a haven, as a cuckoo to the nearest nest. Your thumbprint has embossed half the bottoms in the land, countless thighs bear your imprint, dry cleaners mention you in their prayers . . .

SLEEHAUN. Now wait —

WADE. In foreign climes they talk of you in whispers. Italians grow pale.

SLEEHAUN. It's a lie.

WADE. My boy, you could grope for the Olympics.

SLEEHAUN. Excuse me, but I do take exception. Because a man suffers the odd time from short-sightedness, people slander him.

WADE. You belittle yourself . . . you who have elevated mere lechery to an art form. Others fiddle, you give concerts. And what permutations. The Backhand Grope, the Underarm and the Freestyle: from butterfly touch to overflowing handful, you have beaten the world.

415

(*He grasps* SLEEHAUN'*s wrist and turns his hand, palm up.*)
Why, man, it's arse-shaped. And, as others before me have
tamed the forces of nature for mankind's benefit, I intend to
harness these powers of yours.

SLEEHAUN. You want a grope?

WADE. More, much more. (*Solemnly*) How would you like to be
the one who develops the alms house?

SLEEHAUN. You mean . . .

WADE. I mean, tear it down, brick by brick . . . level it. That is my
intention.

SLEEHAUN (*awed*). God in Heaven.

WADE. Well, then?

SLEEHAUN. I'd go down in history. You mean you'd give me the
job of —

WADE. I reward loyalty, Sleehaun. My promises are a household
word. Unfortunately . . .

SLEEHAUN. I'll do anything.

WADE. . . . to get the alms house I must first be re-established in
this one. And I have an enemy, a creature who connives at my
downfall. A female Judas who stands between my destiny and
yours. The woman Lawless.

SLEEHAUN. The judge's wife?

WADE. And you're going to get her.

SLEEHAUN. Get?

WADE. She's had her chance.

SLEEHAUN. Me? Get?

WADE. My hold upon her will come after yours. With the threat of
scandal, she'll be exactly where I want her.

SLEEHAUN. Excuse me, sorry, bit confused. When you say 'Get
Mrs Lawless', what you mean is —

WADE. Ravishment, Sleehaun.
(SLEEHAUN'*s knees buckle. If a character in a play could be
seen to turn ashen, he would.*)
Haven't you observed how that woman *throbs*? I know her.
Beneath that gruff and — what's a delicate word for it? —
repulsive exterior, she craves to be swept away on a tide of lust.
She dreams of brutish passion, of searing kisses, palpitating
loins.

SLEEHAUN. Mrs Lawless?

WADE. Would I lie to you? She wears her mask well, mind. That
faint hint of being unattainable . . .

SLEEHAUN. I noticed.

WADE. But underneath, a smouldering furnace, yearning to be stoked. (*Extending a hand*) Take my word for it and good luck.

SLEEHAUN (*ignoring the hand*). I think I know just the man, friend of mine. He'd do it, if we can only get him out of the asylum.

WADE. Do I detect reluctance?

SLEEHAUN. I can't, don't ask me.

WADE. I have a plan . . .

SLEEHAUN. Nobody can stoke her, she's gone out. It's like trying to demolish a round tower with a corkscrew.

WADE. I'll do the similes, Sleehaun.

SLEEHAUN. You don't understand. Three years ago there was a . . .

WADE (*stonily*). A what?

SLEEHAUN. . . . An evening out. I was sitting next to her at a dinner of the Georgian and Regency Demolition Society. I went down under the table to pick up my napkin, and accidentally —

WADE. Good God.

SLEEHAUN. She wanted to send for the police. I had to climb out a lavatory window . . . a pure mishap, and if she remembers where she saw me —

WADE. What a man. Already he's broken the first sod . . . how can we fail?

SLEEHAUN. We? Where does we come into it?

WADE. Have your forgotten the alms house? I'm not a corrupt man, Sleehaun: when I buy someone, I pay handsomely. And when I cannot buy, when this hand is bitten —

SLEEHAUN. I've heard.

WADE. . . . when an ingrate insults my generosity . . .

SLEEHAUN. Look, maybe I'll just feel her out during dinner. No, what I mean is —

WADE. After dinner? What dawdling is this? The time is now.

SLEEHAUN. I feel faint.

WADE. My plan is foolproof . . . stay upright. They'll be back here within seconds. Two minutes later, at my signal, Mrs Fitzackerly will slip away and go directly to the switch which controls the electricity. Kill will have one of its frequent blackouts.

SLEEHAUN. I have to sit down.

WADE. Bear with me. Darkness. Jocular cries of 'Where was Moses?' and other quips. After thirty seconds, the lights will come on again . . . time enough for you to have seized Mrs Lawless, stifled her cries of token protest and carried her off bodily to ecstacies undreamt of.

SLEEHAUN (*moaning: a new terror*). Nessa will be here.

WADE. 'Oh, goodness me, where are Mrs Lawless and Mr Sleehaun? Why, that considerate man must have taken her to see the antiquities of Kill . . . how kind.' Simple. And mark me, Sleehaun, when you both join us at dinner, I trust that her manner will be coy and her appetite poor.

SLEEHAUN. You're mad. In the nicest, sanest possible way, of course. It can't be done . . . not with her.

WADE. Too late.

(*He indicates the group returning, off.*)

My God, for your sake I hope she's not insatiable. Dear me, an accident?

(*This, as* THERESE *enters, followed by the* BISHOP *and the* JUDGE, *who are carrying an unconscious* NESSA. ISEULT *and* MADGE *bring up the rear.*)

THERESE. I'm afraid Mrs Sleehaun isn't quite herself.

SLEEHAUN. Nessa . . .

BISHOP. The poor lady has had what you might call a weakness.

SLEEHAUN (*savagely*). What did you do to her?

BISHOP. Me? Shag all.

JUDGE. I think, perhaps, on the sofa.

BISHOP. Right you are, lead on.

JUDGE. Or if we sat her in a chair . . . (*He stops*). Urrghh.

BISHOP (*as* NESSA *concertinas between them*). Hey up, man.

MADGE. On the sofa, Pronnsias . . . lay her flat.

THERESE (*to* SLEEHAUN). It's the tiniest indisposition. No cause for alarm.

(NESSA *is laid on the sofa.* SLEEHAUN *is hovering anxiously.*)

BISHOP. Ah, she's grand, tip-top. Maybe if we loosened something?

SLEEHAUN (*dangerously*). Watch it.

JUDGE. It was so unexpected.

ISEULT (*to* WADE). We were on our way back, happy as children, and as we were passing the door of the kitchen I made a weenchy remark about how exquisite the smell of the food was. She turned the eyes up in her head and was gone from us.

SLEEHAUN. Nessa, speak to me.

(NESSA *murmurs faintly.*)

A button? You've lost a button?

JUDGE. I think she said 'mutton'.

BISHOP. That's what it is: hunger. The poor whoor is famished.

(THERESE *has fetched a glass of water.*)

418

THERESE. Sip this, Mrs Sleehaun. Yes, I do think the sooner we eat the better.

(NESSA *moans.*)

BISHOP. Hang on, she's gone again.

MADGE (*to* WADE). That was a delightful tour of the crypt. Great improvements, I must say. Card tables and slot machines.

WADE. The nucleus of our new leisure centre.

ISEULT (*to the* BISHOP). Amn't I brazen, but would it help, do you think, if I played to her?

WADE. All proceeds to the Kill restoration fund, members of the board of trustees admitted half-price. Baccarat and Spin the Bottle, special odds to big spenders, watch out for announcement of Gala Opening. And next year —

MADGE. You're not going to be here next year.

WADE (*smiling*). True. Unless that great heart of yours unexpectedly softens.

(MADGE *snorts and goes over to* MRS WADE.)

MADGE. Mrs Wade, we've ignored you disgracefully. You'll be with us at dinner? You feel up to it?

WADE. Mr Sleehaun . . .

(SLEEHAUN*'s attention is focussed on* NESSA*, who has begun to sit up.*)

NESSA. I'm better now. I'm so ashamed, I dunno what came over me.

BISHOP. Sure it could happen to a layman.

SLEEHAUN (*ignoring him, to* NESSA). You're sure, now?

NESSA. I'm grand. Don't fuss, such an embarrassment.

WADE (*again*). Mr Sleehaun . . .

SLEEHAUN. Excuse me. (*To the* BISHOP) Touch her and I'll swing for you.

(*He crosses to* WADE. *En route, he must pass* MADGE, *who is now sitting next to* MRS WADE.)

MRS WADE. . . . I was telling a young man (*seeing* SLEEHAUN) . . . that one, about tenderness and how I'm afraid I've seen the last of it.

MADGE. Oh, I'm sure you're mist—

(*She sees that* SLEEHAUN *is smiling winningly at her.*)

SLEEHAUN. Hello . . . heartbreaker.

MADGE. Glassy-eyed drunk, it's disgusting. (*To* MRS WADE) What nonsense you talk. No more tenderness!

WADE. Sleehaun . . .

SLEEHAUN (*arriving*). I'm here.

419

WADE. Your time has come. Stiffen yourself.

SLEEHAUN. Pardon me?

WADE (*calling*). Mrs Fitzackerly . . .

SLEEHAUN. Look, I've had a think, and I —

WADE. I never think; thought is fatal. (*To* THERESE) Wouldn't you agree it's time we heard the dinner gong?

THERESE (*with meaning*). I'll attend to it directly.
(*She starts out, disappearing D.L.*)

SLEEHAUN. Wait . . . stop her. I can't do it, the wife is sick.

WADE. Picture of health.

NESSA (*to the* BISHOP). No, honestly, I feel great.

SLEEHAUN (*bitterly*). Thanks.

WADE. Remember, you have thirty seconds.

SLEEHAUN. It's impossible. I know her sort: she thinks she'll go straight to heaven because sex was purgatory. Besides, she hates me.

WADE. Who mentioned affection?

SLEEHAUN. Listen . . . on my knees —

WADE. Spare me the details. Don't bungle this, Sleehaun. The men who fail me are the accursed ones who dare not drink and drive. Think of our destiny, of Kill, of morality. On your mark . . .
(*He propels* SLEEHAUN *behind* MADGE.)
(*To the others*) And now, it wouldn't at all surprise me . . .

BISHOP. Don't say it. Food at last!

SLEEHAUN. God . . . save me.

MRS WADE (*to* MADGE, *a cry*). Tenderness! Tenderness!
(*The lights go out. Pitch darkness. A moment's silence.*)

BISHOP. Holy feck.

JUDGE. Madge, I've gone blind.

NESSA. What is it? What's happened?

ISEULT. O my God, I'm heartily sorry for having offended Thee . . .
(*There is the sound of a gasp, almost a cry, which is abruptly stifled, then a scuffling noise and a grunt from* SLEEHAUN. *A few crashes during the following.*)

WADE. Let us not panic. Our lighting system is temperamental, and if we could all be quite still for just a few seconds —

BISHOP. Who's banging around?
(*A groan from* SLEEHAUN.)

WADE. . . . then the over-ride system, which I myself invented, will automatically restore the current.

BISHOP. Ha-ha. Where was Moses, begod?

ISEULT. . . . I firmly resolve, by Thy holy grace, never more to of-
fend, and to amend my life —
(*A door slams.*)
. . . Amen.

NESSA. Tony? Tony, say something.

WADE. Any moment now. Five . . . four . . . three . . . two . . .
(*The lights come on.* GENERAL *jubilation.* WADE *has moved
downstage. Of* SLEEHAUN *there is no sign.*)

BISHOP. You clever bugger, you.

JUDGE. What a relief.

ISEULT. Sure he's a born genius.

NESSA (*rising*). But where's Tony?

WADE. Who?

NESSA. He's not here.

WADE. Why, neither is he? How very strange. And gracious me,
Mrs Lawless is gone also.

JUDGE. Madge?

MADGE. What do you mean, I'm gone? I'm here behind you.
(WADE *freezes. He moves to one side, looks and sees* MADGE.)

WADE. Ah. So you are. Indeed. Immovable.
(*He puts a finger to his brow, trying to fathom what went
wrong.*)

MADGE. The idea.

ISEULT. Excuse me. Heaven knows, 'tis not my place to be pass-
remarkable . . . but where is Mrs Wade?

WADE. Mrs . . . ?

ISEULT. Your wife.
(WADE *looks and sees that* MRS WADE's *chair is empty.*)

WADE (*wearily*). Oh, Christ.
(*From off-stage we hear the low reverberation of the dinner
gong.*)

BISHOP. *That*'s where they are!

NESSA. Where?

BISHOP. Oh, a cute pair. They couldn't wait for the gong, and
they're off stuffing themselves.

JUDGE. Of course. (*To* WADE) Should we go in?

WADE. Eh? Please . . . straight through. (*Attempting to rally*) By
all means . . . let us to our muttons.
(*At the last word,* NESSA *gives a faint cry and her legs
buckle.*)

BISHOP (*catching her*). Wait . . . she's off again.

421

MADGE. Oh, poor girl.

BISHOP. I tell you it's hunger. Get her feet, Judge, and we'll carry her in. Once she's put sitting in front of food, it'll bring her to.

JUDGE. Yes, yes . . . I have her.

BISHOP. Ladies, you go first. (*To the inert* NESSA) A bit of nourishment, and you'll be laughing.

(*They troop out, D.L., with the* JUDGE *and the* BISHOP *carrying* NESSA. WADE, *left alone, surveys the room, a man deeply wronged by the gods. Resigning himself to the fates, he is about to follow his guests when five notes come ponderously from the organ. He looks up, winces and totters out. The stage is empty. The same notes come again, but faster. Then again: an arpeggio.*)

CURTAIN

ACT TWO

Ninety minutes have passed. The guests are sitting around in various stages of repose or lack of it. There is a quivering high-pitched sound which we take a moment or so to identify as a musical saw in full whine. In the organ loft, ISEULT *is providing the after-dinner entertainment. She sings to her own accompaniment* (see lyrics on p. 457). *The song is a lament, and its poignancy causes* WADE *to weep unashamedly. The* BISHOP *listens gravely; the* JUDGE *has nodded off;* MADGE *sits stolidly.* SLEEHAUN *and* NESSA *are sitting side by side. Her vicissitudes have caused* NESSA *to be less than fully enthralled by the performance.* SLEEHAUN *yawns at one point; she nudges him. At another juncture, there is a laugh from* MRS WADE, *as if a pleasurable experience has suddenly come to mind.* THERESE *is not present. Liqueurs have been served.*

The recital ends. ISEULT *bows her head and assumes an attitude of prayer. Applause.* WADE *claps slowly with measured deliberation.*

BISHOP. Ah, excellent. Wouldn't you say, Judge?

JUDGE (*coming to*). Without a stain on her character.

NESSA. It was lovely.

WADE (*imperiously*). Miss Mullarkey, come down here.

ISEULT. Sure will I make it the even dozen?

WADE. Come here, I say.

(*Reluctantly,* ISEULT *comes down from the organ loft, carrying her saw.*)

WADE. My friends, we are creatures of the world, mistrusting and cynical, made hard of heart by men's dishonesty. But as you lie in bed tonight, remember this face and these tears.

(*He dislodges a tear with a fingertip and takes it on a brief tour of the company.*)

You see it, eh? Eh? Eh?

MADGE (*muttering*). Have it stuffed.

WADE. So sublime is that woman's artistry that not only am I

423

unashamed to weep, but I declare that any man who can withhold an honest tear is not a man at all, but a renegade and a blackguard.

(*He glares at* SLEEHAUN, *who is for a moment uncomprehending, then buries his face in his hands and emits a sob.* ISEULT *arrives at stage level.*)

Miss Mullarkey, forgive me for cutting short your recital. We are but mortals: a surfeit of perfection would be the end of us. Not only have we been charmed beyond words by your thrilling voice —

ISEULT (*to the room*). All I am is a vessel . . .

WADE. . . . and by your mastery of that superb instrument which is a symbol both of our musical genius and our love for honest toil — you have it in your hand, Miss Mullarkey — but we applaud your choice of song.

BISHOP. Hear, hear.

WADE. Consider the sentiments. A mother weeps — but joyfully — for her son, slain by the oppressor's bloody hand.

ISEULT (*mildly*). And may God wither it.

WADE. Amen. Ask in the village: the mothers of Kill are the jewels in our crown. Not for them the stony road of old age and, at the end of it, death, never knowing how their children will fare without them. Here the children go first. What anxiety is thus removed! How can a mother fail to rejoice, knowing that her son will not now grow up to become a disappointment, or get into rough company, or marry a strap of a creature who isn't a patch on herself? What happiness for a woman's declining years. (*A sob returns to his throat*). Forgive me. Miss Mullarkey, I pay homage.

(*He kisses her hand.* MRS WADE *is again moved to mirth.*)

NESSA (*to* SLEEHAUN). She's much more cheerful than she was earlier.

ISEULT. I wasn't at my best tonight.

WADE. You were glorious.

ISEULT. Yes, but it wasn't my best. You see, I usually fast before I perform: it adds a spiritual quality. And I ate so much of that delicious dinner . . . I can still taste it.

BISHOP. It's more than herself did. (*To* NESSA.) You never touched a pick.

NESSA (*mortified*). Oh, now.

WADE. Perhaps our poor efforts weren't to Mrs Sleehaun's liking.

NESSA. They were. It's only because . . .

424

SLEEHAUN (*desperately*). Nessa is expecting.

NESSA. Tony!

BISHOP (*joyfully*). Shag off.

SLEEHAUN. So she gets these weaknesses.

BISHOP. And who better entitled? Keep the home fires burning, what? Give it a good p— (*Amending*) Great stuff.

NESSA. Tony, honestly.

MADGE. I knew the second I laid eyes on her. The complexion.

WADE. Miss Mullarkey sings of motherhood, I speak of it, and Mrs Sleehaun puts us both to shame. My congratulations.

NESSA. But —

SLEEHAUN. Thanks very much.

WADE (*to* SLEEHAUN). How did you find her? With a guide dog?

SLEEHAUN. Pardon?

JUDGE. What joyful news in these dark times. Our own children are quite grown up, but they can't decide what they want to do. Extraordinary.

MADGE. Isn't it? Will this be your first, Mrs Sleehaun?

NESSA. Since the hysterectomy, yes.

(*This could be a conversation-stopper were it not that* ISEULT *is attempting to regain centre-stage.*)

ISEULT. And congratulations from me, too, although of course I speak from innocence.

MADGE. Since the hyster—

ISEULT. But no, no, it was not my best. When I get to heaven, God will say to me: 'I gave you a precious gift, Iseult, and you went and had your dinner first.' I was bold.

WADE. You'll play for us again, Miss Mullarkey.

ISEULT. Right, so.

(*She heads for the organ loft.*)

WADE (*retrieving her*). . . . in the happier days ahead. Perhaps . . . yes, I see it in my mind's eye. You, the incandescent star of a great charity concert —

ISEULT (*a bright hard smile*). Charity?

WADE. . . . and a display of fireworks to mark the triumphant unification of the alms house with Kill.

MADGE (*out of temper*). I think it's time we made a move.

WADE. So early? Ridiculous.

ISEULT. Tragic to relate, I never do charity recitals. The shy sort I am, if I wasn't paid I'd get to thinking that maybe I wasn't any good.

MADGE (*on her feet*). Pronnsias . . .

425

WADE (*a hint of panic*). I won't hear of it. Five more minutes.

MADGE (*with private meaning*). If we stayed a hundred years, it wouldn't help you. (*To the* JUDGE) You have a day ahead of you in court, and before bedtime we have to go through your verdicts.

WADE. A nightcap, I insist. (*To the* BISHOP) Your good self?

BISHOP (*stirring himself*). Jasus, it's all hours.

MADGE. Perhaps, seeing as our car is as good as wrecked, the Father might find room for us in his.

BISHOP. Room for a hundred.

SLEEHAUN. We had a great evening. It was —

BISHOP. Whoa, there. (*Taking the floor*) Before we say our separate farewells, allow me to claim the ancient privilege of my cloth.

SLEEHAUN (*to* NESSA). His cloth . . . the nerve.

BISHOP. We have been done by right royally.

JUDGE. Well said.

BISHOP. The legendary hospitality of Kill has been excelled. We have gloried in a meal, a banquet, which will linger on in memory.

(NESSA *sways gently*.)

We have had good talk and good companionship. And no minstrel of olden days ever sang more sweetly than did Miss Mullarkey. (*Waggishly*) Mind, when you do meet the Man Above, you'll have to learn a new instrument.

ISEULT. I hate the harp. 'Tis so common.

BISHOP. Most unforgettable, however, has been the benign presence of our fabled host. Wit, raconteur, philosopher and bon vivant . . . sportsman, philanthropist, visionary, preservationist, regular mass-goer and —

(THERESE *hurries in from D.L.*)

THERESE. Do please excuse me. There's been a —

WADE. One moment, Mrs Fitzackerly. (*To the* BISHOP) Please . . . don't go on.

BISHOP. . . . and above all, patriot and warrior of destiny.

MADGE (*muttering*). Next thing, he'll call him a man of peace.

BISHOP. Not to mention a man of peace. You have inspired us all by your dedication to an ideal. And when a certain property is ours once again, I need not tell you who will be honoured to celebrate the first mass in it.

WADE. Words fail me.

BISHOP. So there.

WADE. What can I possibly say?
   (*Overwhelmed, he drops on one knee and kisses the* BISHOP*'s ring.*)
SLEEHAUN (*nodding*). I knew it, queer as a coot.
THERESE. I apologise, but this really is most urgent. The police have asked that nobody leave here for the next half-hour.
ISEULT. The police?
MADGE. They've asked what?
THERESE. I'm assured there's no cause for alarm.
MADGE (*to* WADE). If this is another one of your tricks —
WADE. It is nothing of the sort. (*To* THERESE) Is it?
THERESE. The fact is, there's been another explosion at the alms house.
BISHOP. Holy shit.
MADGE. What did I tell you? Mort Mongan.
THERESE. It would appear so. They're searching the grounds, and they ask that everyone stay indoors as a precaution. It shouldn't take long.
WADE. Are you saying that the police came to this house?
THERESE. Of course not. They know that the law doesn't apply here . . . (*To the others*). Mr Wade has lifetime immunity. They approached me as I was putting the gift into Mr and Mrs Sleehaun's car.
SLEEHAUN. A gift?
NESSA. For us? Ah no, you sh—
WADE. It's a Kill tradition. We give all our guests cold cuts when they leave. And especially as Mrs Sleehaun had no
   (NESSA *teeters violently.*)
BISHOP. Watch her.
SLEEHAUN. Steady, love . . . sit down. She can't help it. It's the thought of muh . . . (*amending*) murder.
JUDGE. But was anyone killed?
THERESE. Thankfully not. However, one of the male occupants of the alms house was badly injured.
WADE (*deadpan*). Monstrous.
MADGE. I told you Mongan was a rampaging lunatic . . . but you'd never heard of him, he didn't exist. Now see what it's come to . . . a man as good as blown to bits.
BISHOP. What terrible times. Look here, if you think it seemly, let's say a short prayer for the poor fellow.
WADE. A good thought.
JUDGE. By all means.

(*Except for* MRS WADE, *they all bow their heads in prayer.*)

BISHOP (*crossing himself*). Thank you. And now we'll say a prayer for the man who was injured.

(MADGE *looks blankly at him. The others pray in silence, lips moving.*)

MRS WADE. I wasn't aware it caused deafness.

BISHOP. Amen. Now we're grand.

MADGE. People are no longer safe on the streets.

SLEEHAUN. It's not good enough.

JUDGE. As for the police and the so-called law courts, don't talk to me.

ISEULT. Excuse me, but who is this Mr Mongan?

BISHOP. An unfortunate.

JUDGE. You know him?

BISHOP. I know of him. He was a foundling, adopted by an unemployed man of the town. A sad case. His foster-father told the boy that he was of noble lineage, that his titles and estates had been usurped. He put the blame on . . . (*a look at* MRS WADE) on, forgive me, a certain family. His adopted mother taught him songs and stories of old injustices. She dinned it into him that forgiveness was a crime and vengeance a sacrament. His priest, an uneducated man, assured him that heaven was his birthright and Protestants were godless. At school, he was made to memorise a litany of the dead. They taught him that living was for weaklings and death was a badge of manhood. He never worked or sought employment. After all, if you believe yourself to be of noble birth . . . !

JUDGE. Remarkable.

ISEULT. Then how in the wide world did he go wrong?

BISHOP. Shagged if I know.

WADE. More liqueurs, anyone?

MADGE (*to* WADE). An hour ago, you said that if Mongan came within a mile of here you'd hand him over to the police. Well, now's your chance.

WADE. Is it? (*To the* BISHOP) A cognac?

MADGE. If he gets away, it'll be to come back another night and maybe take someone's life. We have four able-bodied men . . .

THERESE. The police advise us —

MADGE. Yes, and the more people who help them the sooner he'll be put where he belongs.

WADE. Delightful.

MADGE. What is?

WADE. The feminine mind. It soars from one conclusion to the next, never faltering, never wrong. And if one of us were to lay hands on Mongan, what of the risk?

BISHOP. Well, *I* daren't touch him. In a fit of madness he might hit me and damn his soul.

MADGE. Risk? There's four of you and one of him.

WADE. I mean, supposing he's innocent?

MADGE. Are you mad?

WADE. That explosion . . . how do we know it wasn't a gas leak or a back boiler?

MADGE. Oh, for —

WADE. Or a dastardly attempt on Mongan's own life? An infernal device which went off prematurely, injuring by a supreme irony none other than the perpetrator himself in his fiendish attempt to snuff out the existence of one of God's creatures. Why can't women ever hit upon the obvious?

(MADGE *turns from him, exasperated.*)

Mind, prove to me that he's guilty, and this hand will smite him to the dust.

MADGE. Pronnsias . . .

JUDGE. Listening, my pet.

WADE. Can I say fairer?

MADGE. Go out there and help the police.

JUDGE (*stockstill*). Yesss . . .

MADGE. Well, do it.

WADE. Judge, enlighten us. Do you choose to go outside, or would you prefer —

MADGE. Stop that. Pronnsias, I've given you a request.

JUDGE. I have considered the evidence . . .

MADGE. I said, get out there.

JUDGE. . . . and can find no precedent in law. A judge, my dear, cannot hunt down a criminal any more than the police can try one. I speak of different worlds. It is their function to bring wrongdoers to the bar of justice; the function of the courts is to release them.

MADGE. You wait. (*Thrusting a thumb at him*) Tomorrow, this gets arthritis. Father Bishop . . .

BISHOP. Ma'am, I would become an occasion of sacrilege. Otherwise —

MADGE. I see.

BISHOP. . . . I pledge that you would behold an arse invisible for dust.

MADGE (*not with much hope*). You, then . . . Mr Sleehaun?
(SLEEHAUN *behaves at though he is having an earnest conversation with* NESSA.)

SLEEHAUN. Let me go, don't forbid me . . . please, I'll be ashamed of my manhood. Nessa!

NESSA. What?

SLEEHAUN. That's it, remind me I have mouths to feed. How can I hold my head up? (*To* MADGE) It's no use . . . don't ask for reasons.

MADGE. My God. Men, you call yourselves.

WADE. Dear friend, how you agonise. See it our way: it's none of our business.

MADGE. People are being blown to —

WADE. And what people they are. Lovely people. (*To the* BISHOP) You, sir . . . if you walked among them, do you think they would fawn or cringe? What price a reverential orgasm?

BISHOP. No?

WADE. Those pagans?

BISHOP. I heard rumours.

WADE. Believe them. (*Turning to* ISEULT) As for music in their hearts . . .

ISEULT. Oh, don't.

WADE. There is none . . . not of your kind. They sing of kissing in haystacks, never of death and mothers. They play wind instruments.

ISEULT (*murmuring*). Bomb them, bomb them.

WADE. You, Judge . . . in Kill the law is a work of art. It exists for its own sake, perfection on a pedestal. (*He gestures off.*) There, they degrade the law by putting it to work like a farmhand. They demand that it be enforced.

JUDGE. Scandalous.

WADE (*to* SLEEHAUN). As for you, what do you think of businessmen who get up an hour earlier than you do, who hold you to bargains and work an hour later?

SLEEHAUN. That's dirty.

WADE. Isn't it? So what have these . . . Martians to do with us?

ISEULT. Bold people.

BISHOP. Rapscallions.

MADGE. Excuse me, but I was told that in your Father's house there were many mansions.

BISHOP. Millions of 'em. As a lay person, however, you may not be aware of a little-known encyclical by the late Pope Pius XII in which it is laid down that the non-Catholic ones are padlocked.

JUDGE. Good Lord.

BISHOP. Bloody sure He is.

ISEULT. And, if I could put in my prate again – I'm a horror – God will punish those people and burn them for their badness, and if we were to interfere with Him by helping them, He'd burn us as well.

WADE. Miss M., you're a theological delight. Friends, she has said it: let us cultivate our own garden –

MADGE. Ragweed and nettles.

WADE. The Judge will mark out our borders, the Father's prayers will keep the frost off, and the ladies will tend the –

ISEULT. . . . Roses.

WADE. Whatever. Time enough to –

(SLEEHAUN *coughs*.)

And Mr Sleehaun will supply the manure. Time enough to dig up other gardens when they're ours.

MADGE. You're the most irresp—

WADE. Always that tune of yours that bids us all dance to it. Are we not allowed to try a gavotte of our own? Why do you insist that we all hop and glide in step like . . . like ladies off to the cloakroom.

MADGE. Like what?

WADE. I mean, when one goes they all do.

MADGE. You *are* mad. I never heard such rubbish in my –

(NESSA *arises*.)

NESSA. Excuse me. I just want to –

THERESE. May I be of help?

(NESSA *shakes her head and goes out D.L.*)

MADGE. I don't know why I waste my time talking to you. If that's your idea of sense, then –

ISEULT. I'll just go with her.

MADGE. Miss Mull—

(ISEULT *follows* NESSA *out. The men watch, then look at* MADGE. *She twitches, bites her lip. A brief emotional and physical struggle, then she goes out with dignity, trying not to run.*)

WADE. A remarkable lady. Might I ask, Judge, how it was you came to –

(MRS WADE *rises, as if to follow the other ladies. The men look at her. She is distracted, as if by a recollection, laughs and sits again.*)

431

How came you to capture such a jewel?

JUDGE. Madge? It happened the year I took silk . . . Nineteen —
The date eludes me, but it was a leap year.

WADE. Really?

JUDGE. Yes. I recall I was appearing for an elderly couple who had
been robbed at gunpoint and beaten to a degree where one of
them was maimed for life. They were charged with incitement
by possession of valuables. An open and shut case: of course we
lost.

BISHOP (*sighing*). They will do it.

JUDGE. Madge was a great comfort to me. I can still hear her sweet
voice at the altar, saying: 'He does, he does.' Alas,
like the most perfect of women, she has her foibles. She cannot
bend.

WADE. Never?

JUDGE. Intransigent.

SLEEHAUN. Still, you had children.

JUDGE. Yes, we — (*He looks at* SLEEHAUN *in bemusement.*)

WADE. What you mean is: Mrs Lawless will never honour me with
her endorsement.

BISHOP. What's this?

THERESE. The Judge's wife is opposed . . . dare I say insanely and
pathologically . . .

JUDGE. That's fair.

THERESE. . . . to the renewal of my employer's lease here.

BISHOP. Feck off.

THERESE. And if he goes, the hope passes with him of regaining
the alms house in our lifetime. By speaking out, I know I face
instant dismissal: so be it. If this . . . great man is given a man-
date, the violence which at this moment rages will be done away
with. He offers us peace, material wealth undreamed of, a
cultural renaissance and improved weather. Deny him, and Kill
and its people face a new dark age. (*To* WADE.) Now punish
my insolence.

WADE. I'll overlook it because it's true.

BISHOP. I'm gravely disturbed. What can the lady possibly have
against you?

(WADE *takes him by the arm and walks him once around the
room, speaking swiftly and confidentially.*)

WADE. The Judge must never know. His wife is hopelessly
enamoured of me. With your Eminence's awareness of the
baser cravings of the lesser sex, he will appreciate how my

432

chaste rejection of her attentions has turned her ravening lust into an insane and unappeasable hunger for revenge. (*As they arrive back at the* JUDGE *and* SLEEHAUN) Not a word.

BISHOP. I knew there was a sensible explanation.

JUDGE (*to the* BISHOP). No doubt you have been apprised. Yes, my wife claims that our host's first duty should be to the well-being of Kill . . . that he should mend the roof, pay his debts and work honestly.

BISHOP (*sotto, to* WADE). He'll believe anything.

JUDGE. The question is, what is to be done?

BISHOP. You couldn't, I suppose, stretch a point and vote in spite of her?

JUDGE. Father, I would face a life sentence without remission. Obedience to Madge has been my northern star. To defy her now would be as unthinkable as . . . hah, as putting cyanide in her cocoa.

WADE. Ah.

BISHOP. Ha-ha. What are you thinking of?

WADE. All-night chemists.

(*They sit pensively.* SLEEHAUN *taps the* BISHOP.)

SLEEHAUN. Could I have a word with you?

BISHOP. Most certainly. Pardon us.

(*They move to one side.*)

SLEEHAUN. I didn't have a chance to talk to you over the dinner.

BISHOP. To be sure. It seemed to me that you were a trifle fatigued. Also, there was melancholy, as in one oppressed by a deep sorrow. Are you up shit creek, my son?

SLEEHAUN. Never you mind where I am. I know all about you.

BISHOP. Holy cow, unmasked again.

SLEEHAUN. Parish priest my elbow.

BISHOP. I was once.

SLEEHAUN. I heard. And now you want women to kneel to you.

BISHOP. Me? Not at all, it's optional. The older women are addicted to it. I no sooner walk into a room than they're on the floor. Last week, I had a ninety-year-old: great agility.

SLEEHAUN. Yecch.

BISHOP. Sure as long as they enjoy it. But the younger ones . . . times are on the move. Nowadays you're in luck if you get an oul' kiss. That gorgeous wife of yours . . .

SLEEHAUN. Careful . . .

BISHOP (*whose brandy glass has been tilting*). Thank you. She's an old-fashioned girl. A born kneeler.

SLEEHAUN (*in horror*). Nessa?

BISHOP. Mind, that's merely my impression. She restrained herself this evening because she didn't like to expose me.

SLEEHAUN. Because she —

BISHOP. In front of them. Still, I'll lay you odds she'll go down before the night's over.

SLEEHAUN. Listen.

BISHOP. I'm here.

SLEEHAUN. Do you see the green in my eye?

BISHOP. Stand in the light.

SLEEHAUN. I happen to have a model marriage, a Catholic marriage. And I know what a husband's duty is. It's to know all about lust and impure desires and pleasure, and to make sure his wife never does.

BISHOP. Full marks.

SLEEHAUN. I wish the pair of us were someplace else, but we're not. So all I'll say is that any rotten, perverted, unfrocked sod that comes out of the past and tampers with my Nessa is going to get this . . . (*He thrusts his clenched fist at the* BISHOP's *nose*) just for starters. Have you me?
(*He stalks upstage. The* BISHOP *muses for a moment, then crosses to rejoin* WADE *and the* JUDGE.)

WADE. What was that about?

BISHOP. We had a most pleasant chat. Then I lost track of him, but he seemed to want to burst somebody's snot.

WADE. Mrs Fitz, will you entertain Father Bishop and the Judge? I want a word with that young man.
(*He crosses to* SLEEHAUN.)
Sleehaun, you're going to pieces. Get a grip on yourself.

SLEEHAUN. I'm sorry I came here.

WADE. You're what?

SLEEHAUN. I hate this poxy place.

WADE. Don't add blasphemy to your other crimes.

SLEEHAUN. What crimes?

WADE. Have you forgotten? You let me down, Sleehaun, with a bang.

SLEEHAUN. I don't care. You and your promises. You swore black and blue I could demolish the alms house. Next, you told that woman saw-player she could give a concert in it. Then you invited that mockery of a priest to say Mass in it.

WADE. Well?

SLEEHAUN. Well, which?

WADE. We shall demolish it, and sing in it, and pray in it: I am all
things to all men. Sleehaun, you don't deserve this, but I'm going to give you a second chance.

SLEEHAUN. No!

WADE. Keep your voice down. (*To the others*) I've been asking
him if he can bear to go home.

SLEEHAUN. Yehmmm . . .

(*This, as* WADE *clamps a hand over his mouth.*)

WADE. Quiet. Fate has smiled upon us . . .

SLEEHAUN. Please don't give me a second chance.

WADE. A gummy smile, yes, but we have been granted, you and I,
a few precious minutes to get that woman where we want her.

SLEEHAUN. We? It's *we* again.

WADE. Sleehaun, you're looking at a disillusioned man. To
achieve my ends, I have lied, connived, falsified and slandered.
I have blackmailed and blackguarded. And for what? My
reward for this lovable scampery is to be distrusted. Well,
tonight the niceness is at an end. We are going to fix her.

SLEEHAUN. How?

WADE (*slowly*). I think I have it.

SLEEHAUN. Yes?

WADE. And it's foolproof. (*An arm around* SLEEHAUN) Supposing . . .

SLEEHAUN. Uh-huh?

WADE. . . . supposing we pretend that the electricity has failed.
Then . . .

SLEEHAUN. Where's the way out?

WADE (*holding him*). Wait. You, under cover of darkness, can —

SLEEHAUN. I don't need me coat, you can keep it.

WADE. Will you stop fidgeting! Where's your backbone?

SLEEHAUN. Here, and it still aches.

WADE. So this is my thanks. Et tu, Sleehaun!

SLEEHAUN. Look, can't you get her another way? Everyone has a
flaw in them . . . what makes her different? I mean, she must
have a weakness.

WADE. She does, she married him. What galls me is that a solution
stares me in the face. It's there . . . I can sense it. (*To heaven*)
Oh, God . . . you know me. You're aware of what I've ac-
complished. If you're not livid with jealousy . . . send me a sign!
(*A pause.*)
He hates me.

(*There are whistles off, much nearer than previously.*)

435

BISHOP. Whoors in heat, what's that?

JUDGE. The police . . . they — Look.

(*The beam of a flashlight sweeps across the stained-glass window from outside.*)

BISHOP. Mongan. They must be on to him.

WADE. They dare not enter this house. Did you bribe them, Mrs Fitz?

THERESE. Of course. I have a receipt.

WADE. Well, then.

(*The curtains billow as the main door is thrust open. MONGAN comes in, panting from exertion. He is carrying a smallish object in a brown paper bag.*)

This is a gross and unwarranted invasion of —

(*He breaks off, seeing who the intruder is. The others, except for MRS WADE, are numb with shock as MONGAN advances further into the room. As he looks from one to ther other, he snarls like a cornered animal. The BISHOP crosses himself.*)

SLEEHAUN. Oh, God . . . oh, Nessa.

JUDGE (*a whisper*). It's Mongan . . . what are we to do?

BISHOP (*ditto*). Say a prayer we're not bollixed.

SLEEHAUN (*aloud*). I think I'll just go and check if our car is all —

(*As he makes to move, MONGAN snatches up ISEULT's saw and hisses at him: a snake about to strike.*)

(*retreating*) On the other hand, who'd touch it?

(*MONGAN, now armed with the saw, turns his attention from SLEEHAUN to where the JUDGE and the BISHOP are standing in horror.*)

BISHOP. Why does he look at me? For shit's sake I'm a man of God.

(*As MONGAN moves towards him, THERESE intercepts.*)

THERESE (*suddenly, briskly*). Really, this is too bad. You know you're supposed to use the side entrance. (*To the others*) This is Crichton . . . Mr Wade's valet. It's been his night off.

WADE. Has it?

JUDGE. Your . . . valet?

WADE. Of course. (*To MONGAN, heartily*) So where have you been tonight —

THERESE. Crichton.

WADE (*almost overlapping*). . . . Crichton?

THERESE. Need we ask? Out dancing again, where else?

SLEEHAUN. Aaahh.

(*His knees buckle. WADE catches him by the elbow.*)

THERESE (*to* MONGAN). And now that you're here, you can make yourself useful. I'll relieve you of that . . . we've had quite enough music for the moment.

(*She attempts to take the saw.* MONGAN *resists.*)

Perhaps we'll allow you to play for us later. (*She gets the saw away from him*). Now you take the guests' glasses; I'll refill them and you can serve. You won't need that either.

(*She takes the paper bag away from him.* MONGAN *snarls and grabs for it.* THERESE *sets it down.*)

Thank you. Now first of all . . . Mr Sleehaun . . . (*She pushes* MONGAN *towards* SLEEHAUN) there. (*To the others*) Bear with him. It isn't his proper work, you see, and he's Union.

(*She dispatches* MONGAN *towards* SLEEHAUN. *The* BISHOP *and the* JUDGE *converse with determined matter-of-factness. During this,* SLEEHAUN *backs away.* MONGAN *follows, a claw-like hand outstretched for the glass. It becomes a pursuit.*)

BISHOP. Yes, the laity tell me that the servant problem is murder.

JUDGE. Is it not! My dear wife . . .

BISHOP (*attentive*). Ah?

JUDGE. . . . employed a woman with the most impeccable references to come in and clean for us. A treasure, so we thought. She stole the table mats.

BISHOP. No!

THERESE. Mr Sleehaun . . .

SLEEHAUN. Move it.

(*He brushes her aside in his flight. A growl from* MONGAN.)

JUDGE. Sadly I ask myself, who today is to be trusted?

BISHOP. At the risk of being cynical, shagging few. The blight of modern life is that dishonesty both in employment and society has come to be accepted as the norm.

(SLEEHAUN, *with* MONGAN *close behind, is not hanging about. Squeezing behind the* BISHOP'S *chair, he turns it so that the latter is facing* MONGAN *at point-blank range.*)

(*With a dazzling smile*) But of course there are many shining exceptions.

SLEEHAUN (*climbing over the* JUDGE'S *lap*). 'Scuse me.

(THERESE *has moved to cut off his retreat.*)

THERESE. Do allow me. (*She takes his glass and gives it to* MONGAN.) There. Now the others, Crichton.

WADE. For myself, Father, I have always impressed on the people of Kill, who look to me for moral guidance —

BISHOP (*to* MONGAN, *yielding his glass*). Aren't you very good! Isn't he? He is.

WADE. . . . that to abstain from crime is not enough. We must each of us be our own policeman.

JUDGE. I couldn't agree more. (*As* MONGAN *takes his glass*) Terribly kind of you.

WADE. Filching table mats . . . how disgusting. I say that if the fabric of our society is to survive, we must unhesitatingly point out the vandal, the assailant and the thief. Our voices must, heedless of the consequences to ourselves, ring out with a common cry of . . . 'Unclee-ean!'

BISHOP. Dear man, my exact words from the pulpit.

JUDGE. And mine from the bench.

BISHOP. For all the good it does.

JUDGE. Hopeless.

(MONGAN, *pausing uncertainly, has now come down to* MRS WADE, *who is holding an empty sherry glass. He takes it from her. She looks at him and at his blackened hands.*)

MRS WADE. Am I to have another sherry? How lovely. And what attractive gloves.

(*As* MONGAN *heads for* THERESE *and the bar,* NESSA *returns.*)

NESSA. Miss Mullarkey is right behind me, and Mrs Lawless is — (*Seeing* MONGAN) Oh.

WADE (*perhaps weakly*). That's my . . . ah, valet.

NESSA. I know.

WADE. You do?

NESSA (*waggling her fingers at* MONGAN). Ooo-ee!

THERESE. You were saying about Mrs Lawless?

NESSA. She says she'll be here in a minute.

WADE. Oh, good . . .

NESSA. Because there's only room enough in there for one at a — (*She trails off apologetically and resumes her accustomed seat.* SLEEHAUN *is immediately at her side.*)

SLEEHAUN. Nessa . . .

NESSA (*crossly*). Leave me alone. (*Brightly.*) Is there any news of the police managing to catch that man yet? . . . What's his name . . . Mort —

(*The following three speeches overlap each other by perhaps half, the* BISHOP *coming in last, as usual.*)

WADE. Not a sign, no. In my opinion, the cunning fellow has again given them the slip.

JUDGE. He's more than a match for them. I should say they'll never bring him to book.

BISHOP. He's miles away by this time, and more power to him. Sure what is he but a poor persecuted shagger.

SLEEHAUN. Nessa, we're never going to get out of here alive. That man is —

NESSA. I had to go to the ladies' because you upset me, telling them I was expecting.

SLEEHAUN. Well, you upset *me*.

NESSA. When?

SLEEHAUN (*indicating the* BISHOP). With him. Come to that, how do I know I'm the father?

NESSA. Tony!

SLEEHAUN. Ha-ha, I'm no idiot.

(ISEULT *returns from D.L.*)

WADE. Miss Mullarkey . . .

ISEULT (*modestly*). I came back.

WADE (*peering past her*). And all alone, bravo. Mrs Fitz, perhaps you'd be kind enough to step outside and see if the . . . ah, weather has cleared up.

THERESE (*taking his meaning*). Let's hope it has. Crichton, will you serve our guests?

(*She goes out by the main door.* MONGAN *comes down to the* JUDGE *and the* BISHOP *with two recharged brandy glasses.*)

ISEULT (*seeing him*). Why, who is this?

BISHOP
JUDGE } (*together*). Crichton the valet.

ISEULT. The valet? (*To* WADE) Ah, you nice nice man, you, may God reward you, and so He will, for giving work to poor tinkers.

(*She advances on* MONGAN, *addressing him in the tone one might reserve for a defective child.*)

You will never have heard of me, but I do sing a song called 'Weep, Weep for the Wandering Women'. (*Extending her hand*) All I am is Iseult Mullarkey.

(MONGAN *growls at her and backs off.*)

Ah . . . agus tá Gaelig agam-sa freisin. Tabhair dhom do lámh. (*Trans.: 'I speak Irish, too. Shake hands!'*)

(MONGAN *picks up the saw and waves it threateningly.*)

ISEULT (*pleased*). I will, I will . . . I'll play it for you later. (*Returning to the company*) I have no private life . . . none.

JUDGE. We were talking, Miss Mullarkey, about the prevalent wave of dishonesty.

BISHOP. Yes, for a poetic people, we seem to have absorbed the cynicism and hardness of the times. (*To* WADE.) Yourself would agree?

(WADE *is looking towards D.L. in fear of* MADGE*'s return.*)

WADE. What? (*Abstractedly.*) Yes, it's one of our treasures. (*Crooking a finger.*) Mr Sleehaun?

(SLEEHAUN *is staring at* MONGAN, *who is bearing down on him, a brandy in one hand, the saw in the other.*)

SLEEHAUN. Tony Sleehaun . . . great fan of yours . . . wife and four children.

NESSA. Don't tell him our business.

WADE. A private word . . .

NESSA. You're wanted.

(SLEEHAUN *takes the direct route, over the back of the sofa.* WADE *talks to him with some urgency.*)

ISEULT. I always wish we lived in the olden times of the heroes and warriors. When there was chivalry . . . is that the word? . . . and lovely ladies fair and noble deeds. And if you stole something they'd chop your hands off.

SLEEHAUN. What do you mean, lock her in the lavatory?

WADE (*walking him D.L.*). Just do it.

SLEEHAUN. But what if she —

WADE. *Get . . . out.*

(*He almost flings* SLEEHAUN *out, D.L.*)

(*Aloud*) At the far end, on the right. (*To the others*) Too shy to put his hand up . . . I can always tell.

(MONGAN, *finding himself with an unwanted brandy, gives it to* MRS WADE. *She takes hold of his sleeve.*)

MRS WADE. Gloves. When my mother was a girl, she and her friends wore gloves – and hats – to luncheon, did you know that? No, long before your time, of course: in the golden age when people had manners. Everyone runs nowadays. So difficult, I think, to move quickly and be polite. And they've become cross and bad-tempered . . . it's the result of at last getting what you wanted and then not liking it. (*Looking at her brandy*) I wanted sherry . . . I suppose a brandy will do.

(*She relinquishes her hold on* MONGAN. THERESE *returns by the main door.*)

WADE. Mrs Fitz.

THERESE. Happily the weather seems to have cleared up.

WADE. No clouds in sight?

THERESE. The storm has moved off towards the east.

WADE. Excellent. Look here, Crichton my man, I think we can now manage for ourselves.

(*There is a repeated crashing noise off L., as of a heavy body pitting itself against a door.*)

NESSA. Sacred Heart, what's that?

WADE. Distant thunder . . . the departing storm. (*To* MONGAN) So you may as well retire.

(SLEEHAUN *comes back at a run, braking sharply.*)

NESSA. Tony, was it you making that dreadful —

(*The noise is repeated.*)

You couldn't have. There it is again.

BISHOP (*to* WADE). Thunder . . . is that what you said it was?

WADE. Possibly not. The hedgehogs often come indoors when it rains. They're blind, you know . . . they trip over things.

(*A crash off, that has the suggestion of finality, and the clang of a heavy metal object hitting a stone floor.*)

Yes, there the little devils are. Come along then, Crichton, time for beddybyes. (*As* MONGAN *makes for the main door.*) No, no . . . the domestic quarters are *that* way.)

(*He pushes* MONGAN *towards the exit, R., and relieves him of the saw.*)

Just switch on my blanket and put the bible by the bed. Goodnight.

(*As* MONGAN *vanishes behind the reredos, there is a chorus of farewells.*)

BISHOP. God bless you, my son. Sleep tight.

ISEULT. Beir buaidh agus beannacht! (*Trans.: 'Victory and blessings!'*).

JUDGE. Goodnight, Crichton . . . so very kind.

NESSA. 'Bye-eee.

(WADE, *the* BISHOP *and the* JUDGE *breathe deeply with relief.*)

SLEEHAUN. I wouldn't have missed that. Now we know what gracious living is.

WADE. Thank you, we'd be lost without him. Well, now that we've —

JUDGE. Madge! What in the —

(*This, as* MADGE *returns from D.L. She is carrying St. Patrick's crozier: it is now bent almost double.*)

WADE. Our eclipse is over; the moon comes forth and sheds her —

(*His eye falls on the crozier*).

MRS WADE. Which one of you used this to lock me in the lavatory?

441

BISHOP. Oh, shite, the good crozier.

JUDGE. To lock you in the —

WADE (*murderously*). Sleehaun . . .

THERESE. Oh, how dreadful.

JUDGE. That priceless relic . . . who bent it?

MADGE. I did. Well, how was I to know what it was? Somebody wedged it between the washbasin and the door of the W.C.

WADE. Infamous.

JUDGE. Perhaps it could be straightened?

BISHOP. No, they're never the same again . . . I know.

MADGE. I intend to find out who barred that door. (*To* WADE) And if you turn out to be at the back of this . . .

WADE. That suggestion pollutes my ears. I say, woe betide the perpetrator of this outrage, this slur on our hospitality. He shall be hunted down . . .

SLEEHAUN. Maybe it was someone from the alms house.

WADE. What?

SLEEHAUN. I said, maybe it —

WADE. Oh, rare Sleehaun. That's it . . . the alms house. An act of unprovoked and barbaric aggression.

MADGE. Rubbish.

JUDGE. It could hardly have been one of us, Madge.

WADE. True. Nobody left this room.

BISHOP. Not a soul, I'll vouch for that.

ISEULT. But surely Mr —

NESSA. No, you're wrong. Nobody did.

WADE. So there.

NESSA. Except Tony.

(*The guests look at* SLEEHAUN, *who looks at* WADE, *who looks elsewhere.*)

ISEULT (*severely*). Bold man.

NESSA. Tony, you never.

MADGE. You . . . it was you.

SLEEHAUN (*feebly*). A little joke.

MADGE. A joke? You call locking up women in lavatories a . . . (*Commandingly*) Pronnsias!

JUDGE. Ah?

MADGE. Haven't you got a tongue?

NESSA. He doesn't do it at home.

JUDGE. Good, that's mitigation.

NESSA. I don't know what got into him.

JUDGE. Then perhaps Mr Sleehaun could enlighten us?

SLEEHAUN. I . . .

NESSA. Tell them.

SLEEHAUN. Mrs Lawless is such a nice, jolly sort of woman, I thought she'd laugh.

JUDGE. Remanded for a medical report.

MADGE (to WADE). And you. What have you to say?

(WADE *finds a welcome distraction. It is the paper bag forgotten by* MONGAN.)

WADE. Look . . . oh, goodness me, Crichton has left his package behind.

MADGE. Who's Crichton?

JUDGE
BISHOP } (*together*). Mr Wade's valet.

MADGE. Who?

WADE. It's probably a spot prize he won at the dance. I'll just see if I can —

(*He starts out, then stops as a thought occurs to him.*)

MADGE. That's it. Run away . . . off you go.

(WADE *gingerly holds the bag up to his ear. A stunned look comes on his face.*)

(*Pointing at* SLEEHAUN) I've had my eye on him all night, and I have doubts of his sanity. First, he made certain familiar remarks to me. Then he came in twenty minutes late to dinner and fell asleep. It was his snoring that roused Mrs Sleehaun from her faint. But that wasn't enough for him . . . no, now he locks me in the —

(WADE *unwillingly looks into the bag and as quickly away again.*)

WADE. Aaagh.

MADGE. Lovely, oh yes. Make light of it.

(WADE *reels, a hand to his forehead.*)

Look at him jeering. I will not be made a mock of.

BISHOP. Might I interpose a note of sanity. (*To* MADGE) At the risk of offering offence to your good self, while it is reprehensible to imprison a person in a shithouse, it is hardly a mortal sin. Let us not forget, however, that Mr Sleehaun has bent St. Patrick's crozier, a sacred artefact. Now that is not good enough . . . the 'Made in Taiwan' is illegible.

SLEEHAUN (to the company). It was dark, I didn't see . . . I'm sorry.

BISHOP (mollified). Arrah, boy, three Hail Marys.

MADGE. But the damage . . .

BISHOP. We'll blame it on Cromwell.

WADE. Mrs Fitz . . .

THERESE (*at his side*). Are you unwell?

WADE. Get them out of here. (*He indicates the bag*). Now.

THERESE. Why? You don't mean . . . ?

WADE. Loyal friend . . . no fuss, but with your usual innate dignity. Just get them —

THERESE. Jasus, gerrowa me way.

(*She goes tearing across the room and out, D.L.* WADE *watches her departure.*)

WADE (*sadly*). I had magnetism once.

BISHOP. Well, now that everything has been straightened out . . . (*a glance at the crozier*) *nearly* everything, I wonder if the all-clear has gone yet.

NESSA (*quietly*). I want to go home.

JUDGE. Has anyone the time? (*To* WADE) Sir?

WADE (*in shock*). Ah?

JUDGE (*displaying his wrist*). The . . . um.

WADE (*looking distractedly into the bag*). Eleven o'clock.

JUDGE. So late?

BISHOP. Nothing like it. It's only ten to.

WADE. Oh, yes?

BISHOP (*showing his watch*). Never a second out. You're fast . . . you've robbed us of ten minutes.

ISEULT. Oh, don't talk of time. I'll be thirty soon.

BISHOP. Get away.

WADE. Ten minutes? (*He looks into the bag*).

ISEULT. And twenty-nine even sooner.

WADE. It's *set* for eleven . . .

BISHOP. What is?

JUDGE. Perhaps one of us should take a prudent look outside?

WADE (*suddenly himself again*). That won't be necessary. Mrs Fitzackerly informs me that the police have abandoned their search. Despite their best efforts, the fugitive Mongan has gone to earth.

MADGE. More incompetence.

JUDGE. Lamentable.

BISHOP. . . . Give you the sick.

WADE. And so, with broken-hearted reluctance, I think it might be opportune if we made our farewells.

MADGE. For once we agree.

WADE. Alas, Mrs Fitzackerly has retired with a migraine. (*To*

444

MADGE, *winningly*) Dare I impose upon our guests to retrieve their own outdoor apparel?

MADGE. I'm staying here.

WADE. What?

MADGE. I'm going nowhere . . . that pup upset me. Pronnsias, you get the coats.

WADE. But —

(*He watches as she places her handbag – large in size – on an armchair or the sofa, then sits, wedging it behind her.*)

BISHOP. We can shift for ourselves, well able to. (*As he heads out, roguishly to* SLEEHAUN) And no jack-acting with the cloakroom door.

(SLEEHAUN *makes a lunge at him and is held back by* NESSA.)

NESSA. Will you stop. You've disgraced me all evening.

BISHOP (*allowing* ISEULT *to precede him*). Angels before saints.

ISEULT. Wicked, wicked.

NESSA (*to* SLEEHAUN). Come on, now.

WADE (*musically*). Mr Sleehaun . . .

SLEEHAUN. Oh, God pity me.

NESSA. Talk to the man and be good.

(*She follows the* JUDGE, ISEULT *and the* BISHOP *out.* MADGE *sits, rock-like.*)

WADE. I asked him to stay because I propose giving him the dressing-down of a lifetime.

MADGE. Huh.

WADE (*loudly, crossing*). Now see here, Sleehaun . . .

SLEEHAUN. Don't come near me.

WADE. I have good news. My faith in you is unimpaired . . .

SLEEHAUN. What's the good news?

WADE. Sleehaun, as your benefactor, do you think for one moment that I could allow you to leave here, despising yourself as a failure?

SLEEHAUN. Let me . . . I'll get over it.

WADE. Fortune's smile has widened. (*Proffering the bag*) Take this.

SLEEHAUN. What is it? (*Recoiling.*) It ticks.

WADE. It's a clock. What do you expect: hiccups?

SLEEHAUN. Nessa . . .

WADE. Heed me, Sleehaun. I have been dishonest. I have attempted to gain my ends by foul means. Henceforth, I mend my ways. I intend to embrace the time-honoured principle which has made our people what they are today. Bribery.

SLEEHAUN. I see. Well, if you could help with the overdraft . . .

445

WADE. Not you: her. You may not be aware that Mrs Lawless has one all-devouring passion. Horology.

SLEEHAUN. Good God.

WADE. She collects clocks, Sleehaun.

SLEEHAUN. As well?

WADE. Rare examples of a dying art . . . show her an antique timepiece and she slavers with greed. She guards her collection like a tigress its cubs.

SLEEHAUN. I'm not stealing any clock.

WADE. You are going to *give* her a clock. When she arrives home tonight and finds this priceless object in her handbag, her heart will melt.

SLEEHAUN. . . . In her handbag?

WADE. She will know that I have sacrificed my most cherished possession. How then can she say me nay?

SLEEHAUN. Hold on. You want me —

WADE. . . . To put it in her bag. An act of Christian kindness done by stealth.

SLEEHAUN. All I have is your word that what's in that bag —

WADE. It's a clock.

SLEEHAUN. For all I know, it could be a —

WADE. It's a clock.

SLEEHAUN. Well, it looks to me like the paper bag that fellow . . .

WADE. Crichton.

SLEEHAUN. . . . Crichton came in with.

WADE

SLEEHAUN } (*together*). It's a clock.

WADE. My dear man, if my honest word isn't good enough, look for yourself.

(*He gives the bag to* SLEEHAUN, *who accepts it suspiciously and prepares to look inside.*)

Only consider. If this . . . insane suspicion of yours were justified, if that bag did contain an object other than a clock . . . which would you prefer? That it remained in your possession, as it now is, or that it passes into hers?

(*He steps back to forestall the return of the bag.* SLEEHAUN *realises that he is now in possession.*)

SLEEHAUN. Where's her handbag?

WADE. Behind her.

SLEEHAUN. Oh, God.

WADE. Act boldly, Sleehaun . . . (*looking at his watch*) and swiftly. I rely on you.

(*He strides towards* MADGE.)

SLEEHAUN. Wait. Why am I always left holding the —
MADGE (*beadily*). Well?
WADE. Dear friend . . .
SLEEHAUN (*self-hypnotically*). It's a clock, it's a clock.
WADE. . . . I have berated Mr Sleehaun for his conduct. He now
begs you . . . (*He signals to* SLEEHAUN *to come behind where*
MADGE *is sitting*) to permit him to apologise humbly, profusely
and briefly.
SLEEHAUN (*arriving*). Mrs Lawless, I'm —
MADGE. Where is he?
WADE. Ashamed to look you in the eye.
(*He glares at* SLEEHAUN, *indicating that he should get to work.*
Throughout the following, SLEEHAUN *rolls up a sleeve*
and plunges an arm into the depths of the chair behind
MADGE. *The handbag is wedged fast and his efforts become*
increasingly physical. MRS WADE *looks on with interest.*)
SLEEHAUN. I'm very upset that you were upset. I don't know what
came over me. I'm inclined to believe that maybe I had a
blackout.
MADGE. Don't believe you.
SLEEHAUN. Well, it was pitch dark, so I can't be sure. And I've
had a lot of annoyances tonight . . . soul-searing relevations as
a result of which Nessa and I have had to put an end to all sham
and pretence between us and face the future uncertain that we
will survive, but with honesty and a new awareness.
(MADGE'*s face shows utter bewilderment.* SLEEHAUN, *intent*
on his task, becomes violent in his attempts to prise the
handbag loose. MADGE *is being lifted bodily out of her*
chair.)
SLEEHAUN. And what's more —
WADE (*worried*). Mr Sleehaun . . .
SLEEHAUN. I won prizes for good behaviour at school. I informed
on people for smoking . . . even the brothers.
(*He grunts from the strain.* MADGE *is hanging on to the arm of*
her chair.)
I'm a pillar of the business community, ask anyone, and I beg
your forgiveness for locking you in the lavatory, because I have
. . . (*another grunt*) only the greatest respect and would never
. . . insult a woman or —
MADGE. Oh! (*She springs to her feet, outraged*). He felt me.
WADE. He never.
SLEEHAUN. I never.

MADGE. I say he did. He dared . . . that reptile dared to put his hand on —
(*She gasps with the horror of a new and more dreadful revelation.*)
Oh, my God . . . that hand.

SLEEHAUN (*looking at his hand*). Pardon?

MADGE. Now I know where I've seen him before.

SLEEHAUN. It's a lie.

MADGE. I was uncertain about the face, but the hand . . . I'd know that feel anywhere. He molested me at a dinner . . . nine thirty-seven p.m., August the fifteenth three years ago, we had pork. (*Denunciatory*) He is the man who felt me!

SLEEHAUN. Please . . . shhh!

WADE. Well said. I exhort calmness.

MADGE. I tell you it's true. The police were sent for. He escaped. They put up roadblocks. What else do you need to know?

WADE. Well, if you had the right time . . .

MADGE. Time?
(*The* JUDGE *comes in from D.L. with his coat and* MADGE's.)
Pronnsias . . . (*She crosses to him.*) That is the man who tampered with me.

JUDGE. What? Do you mean at nine-thirty seven p.m. on August the —

MADGE. Yes!

JUDGE. We had pork.
(WADE, *seeing his chance, snatches the paper bag from* SLEEHAUN *and stuffs it into* MADGE's *handbag.*)

MADGE. The sex pervert who gave me nightmares for a month. I kept feeling that hand feeling me.

JUDGE. This is most disquieting.

MADGE. Send for the police, I want him arrested.

SLEEHAUN. No . . .

MADGE. Do it.

SLEEHAUN. I'll plead insanity.

JUDGE (*nodding*). Case dismissed.

WADE. My friends, please . . . (*Sotto to* SLEEHAUN *as he passes*) This is the tricky bit. Ma'am, your distress is a knife in my vitals. However, our primary concern is for all to get home safely . . . retribution can wait. You said, I think, that you were going in Father Bishop's car?
(MRS WADE, *on her way to the bar for a refill, gropes* SLEEHAUN.)

SLEEHAUN. Wah.

(*He looks at* MRS WADE, *who smiles back demurely.*)

WADE (*with sinister emphasis*). So I'll just have a word with his driver.

MADGE (*glaring at* SLEEHAUN). Ought to be locked up for life.

WADE. I said, I'll have a talk with his driver.

MADGE. Do. (*Then*) Why? What for?

(WADE *has taken money from his pocket. His intent is to arouse* MADGE*'s suspicions.*)

WADE (*blustering*). Why, to . . . make sure that he . . . ah, takes the right road . . . that you don't get lost on the bog or . . . accidentally left behind.

MADGE. What are you up to?

WADE. Nothing.

(*He guiltily puts the money away.*)

MADGE. What was that money for . . . to bribe him? Why should we get lost . . . or left behind?

WADE. No reason. I just thought —

MADGE. That you'd have a word with the driver. Well, you're not going to. *I'll* do the talking.

WADE (*feigned alarm*). You mustn't.

MADGE. Oh, mustn't I? You and your schemes. Haven't you realised yet that when I'm around you've met your match?

(*The* BISHOP *returns from D.L. dressed for the journey home.*)

Father Bishop, where's your car parked?

BISHOP. Beside the shagging stables.

MADGE. Thank you.

(*She takes her coat from the* JUDGE *and starts out.* WADE *notices that she has left her handbag behind.*)

WADE. And fear not. I shall take full responsibility for the safety of your —

SLEEHAUN. Clock.

WADE. . . . valuables. You may leave them in full faith.

(*As he intends,* MADGE *at once returns and snatches the handbag from him.*)

MADGE (*in triumph*). Hah!

WADE. Ah-hah?

(*Turning, she favours* SLEEHAUN *with a parting scowl.*)

SLEEHAUN. Ho-ho?

(*She goes out by the main door.*)

WADE. What an energetic lady.

449

JUDGE. Indeed, yes: she never stops. A regular bombshell.

WADE. Isn't she? Which reminds me . . . what time is it, Father, by that watch of yours which is never wrong?

BISHOP. Two minutes to the hour. And the ladies are back with us.

(*This, as* NESSA *and* ISEULT *return. The latter carries her cloak.* NESSA *has* SLEEHAUN's *overcoat.*)

(*Moving to assist*) Miss Mullarkey, allow me.

WADE. Two minutes. I am not a conceited man, Sleehaun, because if I were it would mean I was less than perfect. But you have tonight been privileged to witness a display of superior cunning, miraculous timing and heroic audacity.

SLEEHAUN. When was that, then?

WADE. At times like this, I wish I were an ordinary person so that I could look up to me.

ISEULT. But where is Mrs Lawless?

BISHOP. She's having a word with my driver.

JUDGE. No doubt she'll report to us in a moment.

NESSA (*to* SLEEHAUN). Were you a good boy and did you have a nice talk to him?

SLEEHAUN. Yeah. He gave the Judge's wife a present.

NESSA. Isn't he nice!

SLEEHAUN. I helped him slip it into her handbag.

WADE (*overhearing*). Sleehaun!

SLEEHAUN. I was just telling Nessa —

WADE. It's a clock.

SLEEHAUN (*to* NESSA). It's a clock.

NESSA. Gorgeous.

ISEULT. I'll put my saw away and then I'm ready.

WADE. Linger a moment. In Kill, we have a saying: 'It speaks poorly of the welcome when the guests depart before the stroke of eleven.' So humour me.

ISEULT. Poor welcome, indeed. You have us spoilt.

WADE. No, no: it is you who spoil *me*.

(*He walks among them, touching each one. In the case of the* BISHOP, *he twists his wrist for a glimpse of the time.*)

Could I have wished for worthier guests? Only in this land in all the world does the natural balance survive . . . for can there be a more perfect equality than saying one thing and doing another? But of all my visitors tonight, let me pay tribute to one . . .

ISEULT (*coyly*). Wicked man.

WADE. . . . . To Mr Sleehaun.

ISEULT (*not coyly*). Wicked.

SLEEHAUN. Me?

WADE. . . . A man who embodies all that is unique in our faith, our law, our culture and our commerce. For without him, where would the likes of me – supposing that they existed – be today?

BISHOP (*applauding*). Hear, effing hear.

NESSA. Tony, I'm proud of you.

WADE. Speech . . . thirty seconds.

(SLEEHAUN *has the floor. He grasps his lapels like an after-dinner speaker who is unaccustomed to terseness.*)

SLEEHAUN. Thank you. Uh . . . I am reminded of the story about this sailor who was cross-eyed and went to Hong Kong looking for a bit of stuff.

JUDGE. A bit of . . .?

BISHOP. I think I've heard it.

SLEEHAUN. And he met this Chinawoman who was mustard, and she was all on. Grand . . . except there was one thing wrong with her . . .

ISEULT. He's got it all backwards.

SLEEHAUN. Will you let me tell it? This Chinawoman —

(*The front door slams open.* MADGE *has returned, her mood no sunnier than at last sight.*)

JUDGE. Look who's here.

WADE. It's a mirage . . . ignore it.

SLEEHAUN. This Chinawoman had a great big —

MADGE. Who put this in my handbag?

(*With her upstage hand she displays a familiar-looking brown paper bag.* WADE *emits a cry of terror and moves behind* SLEEHAUN *who is now his shield.*)

And don't start that again.

JUDGE. In your handbag?

MADGE. Just now . . . I was talking to Father Bishop's driver. I was leaning into the car when something slid out of my bag. I rummaged around on the floor and I found this.

ISEULT. But what is it?

NESSA (*proudly*). Tony put it there.

MADGE (*to* SLEEHAUN). You did?

SLEEHAUN. Yes, me.

WADE (*into his ear*). It's not a clock.

SLEEHAUN. No, him.

MADGE. Well, we'll soon find out. I can't say I care much for the feel of it.

451

(*She is about to look into the bag.* WADE *makes to flee, but finds that* SLEEHAUN, *paralysed, is holding on to his sleeve cuffs.*)

WADE. Don't open that bag. Take it for a walk . . . get out, shoo. Sleehaun, let go of me.

MADGE. What's up with him?

WADE. Either let go or run with me. Never mind . . . I'll carry you.

(*He attempts to lift* SLEEHAUN, *who is maintaining his death-grip.*)

ISEULT. Mercy on us.

MADGE. The man's deranged.

BISHOP. I've seen that bag before. Crichton —

MADGE. Who?

BISHOP.

JUDGE (*together*). Mr Wade's valet.

WADE. What is he fed on? I can't lift him.

NESSA (*smiling*). Stop, the pair of you. (*To* MADGE) They're having a little joke. Show me.

WADE. Don't touch it.

SLEEHAUN. Nessa . . .

NESSA. Aren't they dreadful. It's a little present for you.

MADGE. For me?

NESSA. Yes, it's a —

WADE. No!

(NESSA *has taken the bag from* MADGE *and, still smiling, looks into it. A pause. Her eyes widen in horror. She screams, then screams again. She flings the bag from her in revulsion before fainting into the* BISHOP*'s arms.*)

BISHOP. Ah, shite . . . not again.

(NESSA *has thrown the bag to* SLEEHAUN. *He hands it to* WADE, *who hands it to* MRS WADE, *who happens to be passing. Her mind elsewhere, she hands it to the* JUDGE.)

JUDGE. Extraordinary conduct. Now what on earth . . . ?

(*He peers into the bag.*)

WADE. Careful . . . look out.

MADGE (*apprehensive*). Pronnsias, mind . . .

JUDGE. It's . . . going off.

(WADE *and* SLEEHAUN *cry out and duck.*)

Yes . . . cold cuts of mutton. Definitely off.

WADE.

SLEEHAUN (*together*). Mutton?

ISEULT. Honest to God.

452

MADGE. More tomfoolery.

ISEULT. Two dreadful men. (*A small, tight smile*) I'm sore from laughing.

BISHOP. Excuse me, but Mrs Sleehaun seems once again to be not herself.

JUDGE. Another little weakness? (*To* WADE) Do you mind?

(*He gives the paper bag to* WADE *to hold and assists the* BISHOP *to carry* NESSA. WADE *and* SLEEHAUN, *baffled, look into the bag, then at each other.*)

BISHOP. Ready?

JUDGE. All in order at my end. On the sofa, as usual?

MADGE. It isn't natural. She ought to see a doctor. (*Severely, to* SLEEHAUN) And much concerned about her you are.

WADE. Mutton . . .

SLEEHAUN. And he's right: it's going off.

(*There is an explosion outside. Everyone is shocked into stillness, except* WADE, *who crosses to* MADGE.)

WADE. You see, dear friend . . . Mrs Fitzackerly put souvenir cold cuts in Father Bishop's car and Mr Sleehaun's. But since your car was immobilised, I took the liberty of opening your hand-bag and —

MADGE. Will you never mind about your cold mutton. What was that?

JUDGE. The alms house, do you think?

BISHOP. Much nearer home, I'd say . . . this home.

ISEULT. Are we safe?

WADE. As houses, Miss Mullarkey.

MADGE. Now aren't you proud of your stewardship? Bombs going off in your own yard.

WADE. One *small* bomb . . . be fair.

MADGE. Fair? A house falling down from laziness, lands gone to jungle, murderers wandering at will, and all because you and your sort do nothing all day but spout words, coloured words like confetti at a wedding. And then you go to bed at night and pray to God you'll never get the alms house, because if you did you know the talking would have to stop. It's maddening.

BISHOP. Talking, ma'am . . . what talking? I shall preach in it.

ISEULT. And please God, I'll sing in it.

SLEEHAUN. And as for me, I'll —

WADE. Develop it.

SLEEHAUN. To the ground.

WADE. So where does talking come in?

(THERESE *enters from D.L. She is holding a cloth object from which smoke rises.*)

THERESE. The explosion . . .

WADE. No damage, Mrs Fitz?

THERESE. I'm afraid someone has blown up Father Bishop's car.

BISHOP. *What*?

THERESE. It's quite beyond repair, what there's left of it . . . and the driver is nowhere to be seen. All I could find was . . . his cap.

MADGE. You don't mean . . . ?

BISHOP. Oh, my God.

WADE. This will be avenged. I promise reprisals . . . we will not stand idly by.

ISEULT. Dreadful happenings.

BISHOP. Oh, my God, my God.

JUDGE. To be sure . . . there, there.

BISHOP. Blown to atoms.

JUDGE. I know.

BISHOP. It's the Cardinal's car. I borrowed it.

SLEEHAUN. Was it insured?

BISHOP. Don't be so thick, of course it wasn't insured. Who'd prosecute him?

THERESE. I'm afraid there's something else.

BISHOP (*glowering*). Feckin' eejit.

THERESE. Mongan isn't off the property as we thought. The alms house has been set on fire.

WADE. That settles it. Everyone must leave here now, before the police come. I'll not have my guests harassed or annoyed. Mr Sleehaun . . . yours seems to be the only car left intact. Can you manage?

SLEEHAUN. Suppose I'll have to.

WADE. If we're ready, then? I suggest you leave by the north gate . . . the flames from the alms house will show you the pot-holes.

MADGE. Pronnsias . . . out.

JUDGE. We'll take our leave. (*To the* BISHOP) Have you ever had the disagreeable feeling of having forgotten something?

BISHOP⎱ (*together*). Mrs Sleehaun . . .
JUDGE ⎰

(*They move to pick up the still inert* NESSA.)

BISHOP. Feet or shoulders, which?

JUDGE (*freezing*). Urrgh.

BISHOP. Take the feet.

454

(*They pick her up.*)

JUDGE. Yes, well, I think we have everything.

WADE. Just a moment.

(*He comes forward with the paper bag and lays it on* NESSA*'s bosom. She moans.*)

BISHOP. Oh, grand . . . she's coming round. (*To* WADE) Sir, my personal misfortune does not absolve me from the duties of a guest. Thank you . . . I enjoyed myself. It was blooming well great. (*Referring to the 'blooming'*) Excuse language.

WADE. Goodbye. (*Detaining* MADGE) Mrs Lawless . . . a moment.

JUDGE. Most pleasant.

(*He and the* BISHOP *go out carrying* NESSA *between them.*)

WADE. Miss Mullarkey, make haste. Have you your saw?

ISEULT. 'Twas exquisite.

WADE. Too kind.

ISEULT. And I know I haven't the right to ask it, for beneath my fame and stardom what am I but a simple person that God in His goodness allows to serve Him, but if I invited you to my next concert, would you come?

WADE. I shall with pleasure.

ISEULT (*a smile, retrieving her hand*). Book early.

(*She goes out.*)

MADGE. Well, what is it? What do you want?

WADE. Pardon me.

(*He crosses to* SLEEHAUN *and, during the following, walks him to the door.*)

SLEEHAUN. Anyway, there was this Chinawoman, and she had the most enormous —

WADE. Sleehaun, we shall go forward, you and I, as one. A word of advice. Always think of the distant future, my boy, never the present . . . because today becomes yesterday in no time, and who wants to live in the past?

(SLEEHAUN *stops, trying to unravel this.*)

Work it out in the car. And to show my faith in you, I intend to become godfather to the child your lovely wife is expecting.

SLEEHAUN. Pardon?

WADE. Godfather and benefactor. So what have you to say to that?

SLEEHAUN. The only thing is . . .

WADE. Yes?

SLEEHAUN (*finding a solution*). We'll adopt one tomorrow.

(*He goes out.*)

WADE. Excellent. Drive . . . (*he frowns, shrugs*) carefully.

MADGE. And now is it my turn?

WADE. Forgive me. I merely wanted to say in private and as a friend that you can rely on my complete discretion.

MADGE (*amused*). Your discretion? About what?

WADE. Where is your handbag?

MADGE. My . . . ? (*Remembering.*) I left it in Father Bishop's car. I thought then we'd be driving home with him.

WADE. To be sure.

MADGE. What has my handbag to do with —

WADE. Depend on me. I'll have what's left of it removed from the wreckage before the police come.

MADGE. The . . . police?

WADE. What's more, no one will dare as much as whisper that a lady as prominent and as untouched by scandal as yourself was the last – in fact, the only – person to go near that car all evening. You have my word.

(*Pause. She looks at him, appalled and aware that he has won.*)

MADGE. You . . . gurrier.

(*She goes out.*)

WADE. Safe journey!

(*He closes the door. He is all but rubbing his hands in triumphs when he sees that the forgotten MRS WADE is on her feet.*)

MRS WADE. You will forgive me if I retire. Do stay, if you wish: the servants will attend to you. I'm so sorry my husband couldn't be with us. An amusing man, but far from well. You can see quite through him to the wallpaper behind. Good night. I have an impression that I enjoyed myself.

(*She goes out around the lower end of the reredos.*)

WADE. Mrs Fitz.

THERESE. This is the guest list for tomorrow.

WADE. Good. I'll have the ashes of that alms house. Every scorched brick and charred floorboard . . . mine.

THERESE (*reading*). A diplomat, police commissioner and wife, newspaper editor, a sculptress and a teacher.

WADE. The same menu?

THERESE. Of course. I'll leave a note for the cook. Then will there be anything else?

WADE. Hopefully.

(THERESE *goes out, D.L.* WADE *is alone. Pause.*)

All clear!
(MORT MONGAN *comes from behind the upstage end of the reredos. He and* WADE *look at each other.*)
Son!
MONGAN. Dad!
(*They embrace.* WADE *goes to the record player, inserts a tape and briskly goes up to the organ loft.* MONGAN *pours himself a drink, then mounts the throne dais and sits, very much at home and at ease. There is organ music: 'A Nation Once Again.' As it swells to a climax* WADE *slowly sinks downward like the organist in a cinema, waving a hand at his audience.*)

(CURTAIN)

ISEULT'S SONG

They've put a rope around my neck
And told me I must die,
For that's the cowardly Saxon's aim,
To hang an Irish boy.
(ISEULT is the kind of singer who rhymes 'boy' with 'high')
And when you see my lifeless corpse,
Oh, mother, do not cry,
But think of me a rebel bold
And fill your heart with joy.

Although I've thrown a hundred bombs,
I've never told a lie,
And so I'm safe from them who'd scheme
My good name to destroy.

So as I mount the gallows steep,
From there to swing on high,
Oh, Mother, be both glad and proud,
And raise your glass and sing aloud,
For your son is in a martyr's shroud,
A perfect Irish boy.

457

BIBLIOGRAPHICAL CHECKLIST

Plays

The Poker Session, Evans Bros., London 1963
The Late Arrival of the Incoming Aircraft, Evans Bros., London, 1968
The Patrick Pearse Motel, Samuel French, London, 1972
The Au Pair Man, Samuel French, New York & London, 1974
Da, Proscenium Press, Newark, Delaware, with The Society of Irish Playwrights, Dublin, 1975; revised edition, Atheneum, New York & London, 1978; Acting edition Samuel French, London 1979, New York 1980
Summer, Samuel French, London 1979, New York 1982; Brophy Books, Dublin 1988
Da, A Life, Time Was, Penguin, Harmondsworth, Middx., 1981
Madigan's Lock, Samuel French
Mick and Mick, Samuel French, London, 1983
    Also contains *A Time of Wolves and Tigers*
Time Was, Samuel French, London
The Mask of Moriarty, Samuel French, London, 1986, & Brophy Books, Dublin, 1987
Pizzazz, Samuel French, London, 1986, containing *A View from the Obelisk, Roman Fever, Pizzazz*
A Life, Samuel French, London, 1980 and New York, 1982
Madigan's Lock and *Pizzazz*, Brophy Books, Dublin, 1987

Prose

Leonard's Last Book (essays), Egotist Press, Enniskerry, Co, Wicklow, 1978
Home Before Night (memoir), Andre Deutsch, London 1979; Penguin, Harmondsworth, Middlesex, 1981
Leonard's Year, Brophy Books, Dublin, 1985
Leonard's Log, Brophy Books, Dublin, 1987
Leonard's Log – Again, Brophy Books, Dublin, 1988
Out After Dark (memoir), Andre Deutsch, London, 1989; Penguin, Harmsworth, Middlesex, 1991
Parnell & the English Woman (novel), Andre Deutsch, London 1989
A Peculiar People

Dramatic Adaptations

Stephen D. Adapted from James Joyce's *A Portrait of the Artist as a Young Man* and *Stephen Hero*, Evans Bros., London and New York, 1965

Adaptation of Hugh Leonard's Work

Interlude by Tony Gray [based on the filmscript of the same name by Lee Langley and Hugh Leonard], Hodder & Stoughton, London, 1966

Unpublished Plays

The Italian Road, produced Dublin, 1954
The Big Birthday, produced Dublin, 1956
A Leap in the Dark, produced Dublin, 1957
A Walk on the Water, produced Dublin, 1960
The Quick and the Dead, produced Dublin, 1967
The Barracks, produced Dublin, 1969
Moving, produced Dublin, 1992

Unpublished Works – Adaptations of Others' Plays

The Passion of Peter McGinty, produced, Dublin, 1961
  (Based on Ibsen's *Peer Gynt*)
Dublin One, produced, Dublin, 1963
  (Adaptation of James Joyce's *Dubliners*)
The Family Way, produced, Dublin, 1964
  (Adaptation of Eugène Labiche's play *Célimare*)
The Saints Go Cycling In, produced, Dublin, 1965
  (Adaptation of Flann O'Brien's novel, *The Dalkey Archives*)
Some of My Best Friends are Husbands, produced, Dublin, 1976
  (Adaptation of play by Eugène Labiche)
Liam Liar, produced, Dublin, 1976
  (Adaptation of Keith Waterhouse and Willis Hall's play *Billy Liar*)

Television Plays

A Walk on the Water, Granada, 1960
A Kind of Kingdom, ABC, 1963
A Triple Irish, BBC, 1963

The Second Wall, BBC, 1964
Realm of Error, ABC, 1964
My One True Love, ABC, 1964
Second Childhood, ABC, 1964
Do You Play Requests?, AR, 1964
The View from the Obelisk, AR, 1964
I Loved You Last Summer, ABC, 1964
Great Big Blonde, ABC, 1965
Death in England, ABC, 1965
The Retreat, BBC, 1966
Silent Song, BBC, 1966
Love Life, ABC, 1967
A Time of Wolves and Tigers, BBC, 1967
No Such Thing as a Vampire, BBC, 1968
Satisfaction Guaranteed, BBC, c.1968
The Corpse Can't Play, BBC, 1968
Pandora, Granada, 1971
White Walls and Olive Green Carpets, Thames, 1971
Game for a Corpse, BBC, c.1971
The Virgins, Thames, 1972
The Dead, Granada, 1972
The Last Campaign, ATV, 1978
The Ring and the Rose, Thames, 1978
London Belongs to Me, Thames, 1979

Television Plays, unproduced (with dates of writing)

Kate Times Two, LW, c.1972
The Ghost of Christmas Present, BBC, 1972
The Truth Game, Thames, 1972

Television Adaptations of Stage Plays

A Leap in the Dark, Granada, 1960
Stephen D – first version, BBC, 1962
Stephen D – second version, BBC, 1966

Television Plays (series)

The Irish Boys (trilogy), ABC, 1962
Saki Stories (13 parts), Granada, 1962
The Liars (2 parts), Granada, 1962, 1963

Family Solicitor (3 episodes), 1963
Jezebel ex UK (1 episode), ABC, 1963
Triangle (1 of 3 plays), 1963
Maupassant Blackmail Series (2 series), Granada, 1964
The Hidden Truth (2 parts), A–R, 1964
Undermind (1 episode), ABC, 1964
Blackmail Series (1 episode), ABC, 1965
Public Eye (2 episodes), ABC, 1965
Sweets to the Sweet (2 parts), A–R, 1965
Insurrection (8 parts), RTE, 1966
Simenon (2 plays), BBC, 1966
The Informer (2 parts), A–R, 1966
Out of the Unknown (2 episodes), A–R, 1966, 1967
Conan Doyle Series (2 plays, 1 in 2 parts), BBC, 1968
The Assassin (in Jazz Age Series), BBC, 1968
A Man and His Mother-in-Law (in Detective Series), BBC, 1968
Talk of Angels (in Ronnie Barker Playhouse Series), A–R, 1969
Hunt the Peacock (in Detective Series, adaptations from H. R.
    Keating), BBC, 1969
Love Story (2 episodes), A–R, 1969
W. S. Maugham Series (2 stories), BBC, 1969, 1970
Me Mammy (3 series, 21 episodes, in Comedy Playhouse Series),
    BBC, 1969, 1970, 1971
The Sinners (1st Series, 9 parts), Granada, 1970–71
The Sinners (2nd Series, 9 parts), Granada, 1971–72
High Kampf (2 parts), BBC, 1971
Six Dates with Baker Series (2 parts), A–R, 1973
Tales from the Lazy Acre (7 episodes), A–R, 1973
Father Brown Series (? episodes), Thames, 1974
O'Neill, WGBH
Hunted Down, Thames, 1989
Parnell and the English Woman (4 episodes) Thames, 1991

Television Serials, based on others' work

Great Expectations (Charles Dickens, 10 parts), BBC, 1967
Wuthering Heights (Emily Bronte, 10 parts), BBC, 1967
Nicholas Nickleby (Charles Dickens, 13 parts), BBC, 1968
The Possessed (Fyodor Dostoevsky, 5 parts), BBC, 1969
Domby & Son (Charles Dickens, 13 parts), BBC, 1969
A Sentimental Education (Gustave Flaubert, 5 parts), BBC, 1970
The Moonstone (Wilkie Collins, 5 parts), BBC, 1970

461

Country Matters (H. E. Bates, 5 parts), ?BBC, 1972–73
Strumpet City (James Plunkett, 7 parts), RTE, 1979
The Little World of Don Camilo (Giovanni Guareschi, 13 parts), BBC, 1980
Good Behaviour (Mollie Keane, 3 parts), BBC, 1983
The Irish RM (Somerville & Ross), ?BBC, 1985, 1987

Television Sketches

The Diana Rigg Show (1 episode), BBC, 1977

Film Scripts

The Poker Session, 1967
Great Catherine, 1968
Interlude, 1968
Lord Dismiss Us, 1968
The Inheritance, 1968
The Scarperer, 1969
Whirligig, 1970
A Portrait of the Artist as a Young Man, 1970
Percy, 1971
Our Miss Fred, 1972
Rakes Progress, 1974
Herself Surprised, 1977
Widows' Peak, 1985
Da, 1988

IRISH DRAMA SELECTIONS
ISSN 0260–7962

1. SELECTED PLAYS OF LENNOX ROBINSON
   Chosen and introduced by Christopher Murray
   Contains *Patriots, The Whiteheaded Boy, Crabbed Youth and Age, The Big House, Drama at Inish, Church Street,* bibliographical checklist.

2. SELECTED PLAYS OF DENIS JOHNSTON
   Chosen and introduced by Joseph Ronsley
   Contains *The Old Lady Says 'No!', The Moon in the Yellow River, The Golden Cuckoo, The Dreaming Dust, The Scythe and the Sunset,* bibliographical checklist.

3. SELECTED PLAYS OF LADY GREGORY
   Chosen and introduced by Mary FitzGerald
   Contains *The Travelling Man, Spreading the News, Kincora, Hyacinth Halvey, The Doctor in Spite of Himself, The Gaol Gate, The Rising of the Moon, Dervorgilla, The Workhouse Ward, Grania, The Golden Apple, The Story Brought by Brigit, Dave,* Lady Gregory on playwriting and her plays, bibliographical checklist.

4. SELECTED PLAYS OF DION BOUCICAULT
   Chosen and introduced by Andrew Parkin
   Contains *London Assurance, The Corsican Brothers, The Octoroon, The Colleen Bawn, The Shaughraun, Robert Emmet,* bibliographical checklist.

5. SELECTED PLAYS OF ST. JOHN ERVINE
   Chosen and introduced by John Cronin
   Contains *Mixed Marriage, Jane Clegg, John Ferguson, Boyd's Shop, Friends and Relations,* prose extracts, bibliographical checklist.

6. SELECTED PLAYS OF BRIAN FRIEL
   Chosen and introduced by Seamus Deane
   Contains *Philadelphia, Here I Come, Translations, The Freedom of the City, Living Quarters, Faith Healer, Aristocrats,* bibliographical checklist.
   Only for sale in North America. Published by Faber & Faber in Great Britain.

7. **SELECTED PLAYS OF DOUGLAS HYDE**
   Chose and introduced by Janet Egleson Dunleavy and
   Gareth Dunleavy'
   Contains *The Twisting of the Rope, The Marriage, The Lost
   Saint, The Nativity, King James, The Bursting of the Bubble,
   The Tinker and the Sheeog, The Matchmaking, The School-
   master*, bibliographical checklist. This volume publishes the
   original Irish language texts with Lady Gregory's translations.

8. **SELECTED PLAYS OF GEORGE MOORE AND EDWARD
   MARTYN**
   Chosen and introduced by David B. Eakin and Michael Case
   Contains Moore's *The Strike at Arlingford, The Bending of
   the Bough, The Coming of Gabrielle, The Passing of the
   Essenes*; and Martyn's *The Heather Field, Maeve, The
   Tale of a Town, An Enchanted Sea*, Bibliographical Checklist.

9. **SELECTED PLAYS OF HUGH LEONARD**
   Chosen and introduced by S. F. Gallagher
   Contains *The Au Pair Man, The Patrick Pearse Motel,
   Da, Summer, A Life, Kill*, Bibliographical Checklist.

10. **SELECTED PLAYS OF T.C MURRAY**
    Chosen and introduced by Richard Allen Cave
    Contains *Autumn Fire, Sovereign Love, Maurice Harte,
    The Briery Gap, The Pipe in the Fields, Birthright,*
    Bibliographical Checklist.

11. **SELECTED PLAYS OF MICHAEL MACLIAMMOIR**
    Chosen and introduced by John Barrett
    Contains *Where Stars Walk, Ill Met by Moonlight, The
    Mountains Look Different, The Liar, Prelude in Kazbeck
    Street*, 'On Plays and Players', Bibliographical Checklist.